*American Science Fiction
Television Series of the 1950s*

American Science Fiction Television Series of the 1950s

Episode Guides and Casts and Credits for Twenty Shows

by PATRICK LUCANIO *and*
GARY COVILLE

McFarland & Company, Inc., Publishers
Jefferson, North Carolina, and London

British Library Cataloguing-in-Publication data are available

Library of Congress Cataloguing-in-Publication Data

Lucanio, Patrick.
　　American science fiction television series of the 1950s : episode
guides and casts and credits for twenty shows / by Patrick Lucanio and
Gary Coville.
　　　　p.　cm.
　　Includes bibliographical references and index.
　　ISBN 0-7864-0434-5 (library binding : 50# alkaline paper) ∞
　　1. Science fiction television programs—United States—Catalogs.
I. Coville, Gary, 1949–　　.　II. Title.
PN1992.8.S35L83　1998
016.79145'75'0973—dc21　　　　　　　　　　　　　　　　97-45051
　　　　　　　　　　　　　　　　　　　　　　　　　　　　　　　CIP

Manufactured in the United States of America

McFarland & Company, Inc., Publishers
　Box 611, Jefferson, North Carolina 28640

For I dipped into the future, far as human eye could see,
Saw the Vision of the world, and all the wonder that would be.
—Alfred, Lord Tennyson, *Locksley Hall*

Table of Contents

Preface

In the 1950s, science fiction on television was a perfect match of form to function—or rather, to fiction. Television in its infancy was seen as the nearest thing to an actual Buck Rogers gadget that technology had yet produced. Here was a mysterious box that delivered not only sounds, like radio, but also pictures of everything from wrestling matches to trips to outer space. With such fantastic devices right in their living rooms, Americans were ready to believe anything was possible through science and technology—which explains, at least in part, the preeminence of science fiction as popular entertainment during the 1950s.

Curiously, this symbiotic relationship between television and the fantastic elements of 1950s science fiction has been, for the most part, ignored by both media historians and science fiction devotees. Indeed, many works on science fiction television merely skim the fifties, noting the series and commenting vaguely on program content and production backgrounds. Specific information about the series is frequently lacking. Unfortunately, the writers of these texts often end up rehashing previously published works, frequently perpetuating errors to the point where inaccuracies are widely regarded as truth. For example, in reference to *Commando Cody, Sky Marshal of the Universe*, Alex McNeil in *Total Television* (4th edition, 1996) and Ed Naha in *The*

Science Fictionary: An A-Z Guide to the World of SF Authors, Films and TV Shows (1980) identified Cody's assistant, played by Aline Towne, as Joan Albright. Gary Grossman in *Saturday Morning TV* (1981) repeated the Albright surname, as did Harris Lentz III in *Science Fiction, Fantasy and Horror Film and Television Credits* (1983), Stuart Fischer in *Kids' TV: The First 25 Years* (1983), George Woolery in *Children's Television: The First 35 Years* (1985) and Vincent Terrace in *The Encyclopedia of Television* (1986) among other reference authors. But primary sources from the series show that Cody's assistant is Joan *Gilbert*—the same character, again played by Aline Towne, found in the serial *Radar Men from the Moon*.

Such flawed efforts do not necessarily suggest carelessness or fabrication. Most likely the authors made their best guesses based on the available information for these series, often dishearteningly scant. We want to emphasize that we make no pretext of having the absolute answers; like those before us, we have resorted to our best guesses when information proved unavailable.

As every historian understands, access to primary sources is the key to compiling a credible analysis of any subject. Television historians, for whom the programs themselves are the primary sources, face multiple disadvantages because of the lamentably ephemeral nature of 1950s television. Prior to the advent of videotape in 1956, television was more or less grounded in real time. While kinescope films were routinely made as a means of carrying programs to sections of the country not accessible by microwave relay or coaxial cable, the kinescopes (once shown) were habitually turned back to the Eastman Kodak Company at a salvage value of seven cents per pound. The result is a woefully inadequate visual record of the early days of television.

Worse still, in recent years a disturbing trend has corrupted the surviving sources to the point where they are no longer reliable artifacts of their era. This corruption is being effected—and history thus being rewritten—through a series of negligent or even willfully destructive acts. In some cases, technical processes like time compression and colorization have egregiously altered the original works. In other cases, the legal rights to programs have transferred to companies or individuals who place new production credits at the beginning and end of the programs, creating an illusion that the new owners somehow participated in the original creation. A recent instance is the Fox network reissue of Gerry Anderson's 1960s Supermarionation series *Thunderbirds*. Although beyond our range here since it is a 1960s offering, the woeful results of the reissue bear discussion as an example of how source material has been destroyed. First, the episodes were whittled to half-hour lengths from their original one-hour running time; essentially, they were compressed into special effects showcases. Second, new and faddish dialogue was added that changed the original characterizations of the series' protagonists, the Tracy family. Third, Barry Gray's famous Thunderbird march as well as his effective incidental score was replaced by rock music in an apparent attempt to provide a modern ambiance. The cumulative effect is the deplorable peeling away of the original character of the program. Today's audience receives a false version of the show's original intent.

Another danger to source material from the 1950s is the clumsy butchering of shows to make room for additional commercials. Many scenes have been excised entirely. The result, naturally, is often disjointed and incompre-

hensible storylines. A case in point is the very popular series *Adventures of Superman*, which, though a product of the 1950s, remains in syndication and is available for the home video market. But a definitive original *Superman* episode is an elusive quarry. For example, a 16mm print of the first-season episode "Crime Wave" contains an opening narration over a rapid-pace montage of criminal activity culled from previous episodes and stock footage; however, the current Warner Home Video release of this episode deletes the narration, slows the pace and replaces much of the original footage with longer scenes of the stock footage. Why were these changes made? The editing did not alter the narrative as such, but certainly it altered the pace of the opening. Perhaps Warner decided that the narration was quaint and had no value for today's audiences.

In another, more disturbing example, a broadcast print of the second-season episode "Panic in the Sky" eliminated an entire sequence between Clark Kent and a woman farmer that provides the first and quite effective impression of Superman's amnesia. In the scissored version of the episode, seen by thousands in a local broadcast market, Superman returns to Earth and then, as Clark Kent, steps into Kent's apartment; the audience has no hint of Superman's amnesia until Perry White speculates about Clark's condition. Apparently, to cram more commercials within the confines of a half-hour, plot development can be sacrificed and aesthetic integrity be damned.

Even when editors eliminate altogether supplementary material, some understanding of the programs' cultural effect is lost. Again, except for a few 16mm prints in the hands of collectors, the available episodes of the first-season *Adventures of Superman* eliminate the closing preview for the following week's episode. In those previews—spectacular montages obviously influenced by motion picture trailers—a commanding voice demands that we not "miss the next thrill-packed episode in the amazing *Adventures of Superman*," in which the viewer will find "action, adventure and mystery." Not a single preview survives in the Warner video releases, nor does one find the previews in episodes released for broadcast. Not even the "TV-land specialists" of cable station Nickelodeon's "Nick at Nite" preserve the artifact. For today's audiences, the significance of the series in its own era is sacrificed—but sacrificed for what? Additional commercial time? Or is the editing merely an effort to "update" by eliminating what the editors feel is, again, quaint and hence valueless today?

Compounding the problem, many of these television shows have fallen into the public domain. This in itself is not a bad thing for the historian; however, once in the public domain, these programs unfortunately fall prey to companies that release the shows in the cheapest possible manner. Often recorded at the inferior "extended play" (EP) speed, marred by frequent tracking problems and abysmal print quality, such video releases routinely turn off audiences from the whole concept of "Golden Age" television. Few of these releasing companies demonstrate any love for the programs themselves. Instead, like their big brothers noted above, they demonstrate a desire to scavenge carcasses for a few royalty-free dollars.

The purpose of *American Science Fiction Television Shows of the 1950s* is foremost to be a reference guide to the early days of TV science fiction. In defining "science fiction," we have been forced to make certain choices. First, such programs as *Inner Sanctum*, *Lights Out* and *Suspense*, which usually dealt with horror and the fantastic, occasionally featured science fiction narratives. But we assert that these series were primarily horror shows and do not belong in this work. Second, we have omitted "science fact" programs like Disney's *Man in Space* trilogy, the Bell Science Series (*Our Mr. Sun*, *The Strange Case of the Cosmic Rays*, and others) and *The Johns Hopkins Science Review*. Third, we have not covered science-fiction episodes from such anthology series as *Westinghouse Studio One*, *Kraft Television Theatre* and *Playhouse 90* because our research has been inconclusive at this point. We have located titles and little else; since these episodes were broadcast live, our hope for finding copies remains dismal.

So what do we mean by science fiction? At the risk of being simplistic, we mean narratives whose interests lie in the possibilities of modifying physical reality. What you will find here are fictions about space travel, time travel, scientific experimentation and scientific knowledge—that is, stories about the manipulation of the physical world rather than stories that attempt to plumb secrets of metaphysics or that shed light upon actual scientific endeavors.

We have chosen to include only those programs shown on American screens. The British series *H.G. Wells' Invisible Man* was broadcast in America in syndication and is therefore included; it is, however, the only British series covered in this book.

As far as possible, this book furnishes complete information about early science fiction television in the United States. In conducting our research, we viewed hundreds of hours of programming, evaluating episodes for characterization, substance, style, and historical and cultural influences, all the while recording cast and production credits from the programs and from available press material in an effort to be as reliable as possible for such an elusive art form.

Unfortunately, for the reasons explained above, we have not always been able to view the series chronicled in these pages. The amount of information we provide indicates exactly what source material has (or has not) been available. For instance, our coverage of *Adventures of Superman* includes detailed production history and background information because the facts are as readily available as the episodes themselves. On the other hand, production information on *The Man and the Challenge* is nearly nonexistent; during our lengthy research period, we were afforded only one single episode for viewing. Consequently, the entry on this series is embarrassingly terse.

Where brief summaries substitute for detailed episode guides, the reader can assume that either we were unable to view any episodes (e.g., there are apparently no surviving kinescopes of *The Atom Squad* and *Rod Brown of the Rocket Rangers*) or we viewed only a handful; in some instances, only titles and dates were available.

In the absence of actual episodes we have turned to the written word, primarily to newspaper television logs, newspaper reviews, and magazine pieces as well as various memoirs and reference works. All sources consulted are listed in the bibliography. We wish to draw particular attention, however, to the following, although it must be stated that we often found these works to be in disagreement among themselves (and moreover we have on occasion disputed some of their data ourselves): George W. Woolery's *Children's Television: The First Thirty-Five Years, 1946-1981, Part II: Live, Film and Tape Series* (Scarecrow, 1985); Harris M. Lentz's *Science Fiction, Horror & Fantasy Film and Television Credits, Volume 2: Film Index; Television Index* (McFarland, 1983); Tim Brooks and Earle Marsh's *The Complete Directory to Prime Time Network TV Shows, 1946-Present* (Ballantine, 1995); Alex McNeil's *Total Television: A Comprehensive Guide to Programming from 1948 to the Present* (Penguin, 1996); and Alan Morton's *The Complete Directory to Science Fiction, Fantasy and Horror Television Series* (1997).

A book of this nature is seldom the work of the authors alone; we are indebted to many people for aiding and abetting our efforts. Sharon Lind Williams and Ted Okuda, respectively the former and current editors of *Filmfax* magazine, have supported our examinations of early television science fiction over the years. (Portions of this book originally appeared in *Filmfax*, most notably the sections on *Science Fiction Theatre*, *Men into Space*, *Johnny Jupiter* and *Flash Gordon*.) Dale Ames, publisher and editor of the *Galaxy Patrol* newsletter, also energetically supported this project. Steve Holland, television's Flash Gordon, and Wright King, television's most familiar Ernest P. Duckweather, have contributed recollections. Jack Mathis, Barbara Lucanio, Steve Hahn and Denise Houser have all participated in their own special ways, and the list goes on: David P. Miller, Nell Williams, Paul Field and Morleen Getz-Rouse. Cinemacabre Video generously facilitated our research by providing a complete run of *Science Fiction Theatre* episodes.

It is now nearly half a century since *Captain Video* initiated the cycle of science fiction on television. Central to the storylines of *Captain Video* (and countless other science fiction programs) was the concept of time travel and a special respect for history. Today we find ourselves appreciating television's early science fiction heroes as objects of history themselves. If perusing this book awakens a few dormant recollections and a vague regret that the world has become poorer for the loss of the talent, creativity, energy and sheer fun that went into the production of these programs, then we will feel that we have successfully presented our most enjoyable subject. But let us emphasize that we make no excuses for our love for these programs. Moreover, we make no attempt to present them as works of art; nor, on the other hand, do we mock their low-budget qualities or simple narratives. Our goal is to allow the shows to speak for themselves, and to celebrate these creative accomplishments that were so much a part of the sense of wonder that permeated the American 1950s.

Introduction

The Conquest of Space in an Age of Wonder

I.

A segment of current American culture seems to take great pleasure in deriding the 1950s, a decade frequently described as an age of phobias and repression, of anti-intellectualism and inanity. On closer examination, however, there is less to the indictment than meets the eye and ear. Many critics fail to realize that although the 1950s provided fertile ground for demagogues such as Wisconsin's Joseph McCarthy, the same decade provided a tool for plowing him under, namely his exposure on national television as a charlatan hiding behind a certain five o'clock shadow. Moreover, while the simple homilies of programs such as *Donna Reed* and *Ozzie and Harriet* are deemed pabulum, the same cannot be said for the cultural cuisine offered by Alistair Cooke's *Omnibus* and the live dramas by remarkable writers like Paddy Chayefsky, Reginald Rose, Gore Vidal, Tad Mosel, Rod Serling and Horton Foote.

The defining characteristics of the 1950s were idealism and wonder. Americans believed in themselves, in their country, and in their ability to progress through moral resolve as well as through advancements in science and technology. There were good reasons for this optimistic self-confidence. Those who had lived through the Great Depression and World War II had seen financial despair replaced by a booming wartime economy, and a violent conflict brought to an Apocalyptic end by American science. Wonder over the atomic bomb induced a new determination to turn away from despair and toward a more secure and settled climate. As a collective culture, then, Americans of the 1950s believed in pursuing a future free from the evils that had pervaded the past (such as economic hardship and war) and were infecting the present in the shape of economic inflation and Stalinism. The United Nations was an effort to bring countries together to settle their differences before blood was shed; domestically, the presence of federal troops in Little Rock left no doubt as to America's new conviction that racism was an evil.

Moral citizenship, proudly taught in schools, would conquer most problems; and what moral citizenship couldn't conquer, science would. Of course, science had un-leashed the destructive force of the atom; but to assuage our fears of the bomb, we merely recast the destroyer into "Our Friend, the Atom," who was introduced in a January 23, 1957, episode of *Disneyland*. To further ease the anxiety, President Eisenhower quickly approved the "Atoms for Peace" program to demonstrate that science would usher in a world of harmony and peace, presumably sus-tained by atomic energy. Although these actions may seem dubious in hindsight, one can hardly fault their intention, which was to increase American support for scientific exper-imentation. To a certain extent the support was rewarded: Among other things, science allowed humans to triumph over the natural scourge of polio.

Although some saw science and technol-ogy as dehumanizing agents, the predominant attitude was one of fascination and wonder. This attitude was partially instilled in 1950s culture by television. Years before Neil Arm-strong took that giant leap for mankind on the surface of the moon, Americans began to be conditioned to accept such a fantastic feat with equanimity. After all, the Moon—and many planets, for that matter—had been conquered hundreds of times on television. In its infancy, television had the power to elicit a childlike sense of wonder. Because television was new and amazing—providing pictures and sounds just as events were actually happening—and because the cultural climate of the 1950s acknowledged the basic integrity of the pre-vailing religious, social, economic and politi-cal institutions, Americans were willing to take all that they saw and enjoyed on faith, includ-ing the various technological wares touted on television through the ubiquitous "word from our sponsor." Audiences came to believe in the fleeting, ghostlike figures of Captain Video, Tom Corbett, Rocky Jones, Captain Midnight, Buzz Corry, Rod Brown, Flash Gordon, Colonel Ed McCauley and the other heroes of space whose exploits for God and country were paraded across the small blue-gray tele-vision screens manufactured in the United States of America by DuMont, Sylvania and Philco.

As we have noted, television itself seemed

a remarkable piece of science fiction magic. The television set resembled some fantastic machine conjured up by the imaginations of those pounding away on Underwood type-writers for two cents a word and the promise of a byline in upcoming issues of magazines like *Amazing Stories*. It seemed only natural that worlds of wonder should be found inside the magical box. Thus it was easy to accept Buzz Corry and the crew of the Terra V exploring the surface of Mars looking for lost treasure, or Rocky Jones and the crew of the Orbit Jet risking their lives to prevent one of Cleolanta's mad schemes to enslave a plane-tary race. These situations seemed eminently believable coming from a machine that regu-larly delivered pictures of worlds we had not realized existed. To the typical inhabitant of Salem, Oregon, or Madison, Wisconsin, places like Hong Kong and Bucharest were as alien as Mars or Pluto. One had to read about these places or see them in movie travelogues inside theaters; one had to *make an effort* to learn. But with television in the home, the world sud-denly became commonplace—right in the liv-ing room. If Bucharest was becoming familiar, then why not Saturn or Uranus?

Against this backdrop, consider the liter-ature of science fiction, itself dependent upon and springing from a sense of wonder. In a way, the term "science fiction" is something of an oxymoron. "Science" is firmly rooted in fact, always searching for proof, while "fiction" is born of the vagaries of the human imagina-tion. Such a combination produces tales char-acterized by a form of schizophrenia; fact and fiction co-exist in an uneasy and seldom bal-anced alliance. For writers and critics of such fiction, the issue has always been how much emphasis to place on each of the competing elements. If a story emphasizes science, it becomes a factual marvel, eliciting a "what will they think of next" response. If a story empha-sizes fiction it becomes an escapist diversion eliciting a childlike "gee whiz" response. But because the promise of science throughout the 1950s was so pervasive and expectations so high, the mix of science and fiction on television was constantly being tested much like a scientific formula itself, and the various series spawned by that ongoing experimentation tell us much about the evolution of 1950s thought.

The decade began with the "gee whiz" response, inspired by juvenile science fiction that is best expressed as space opera (or what is derisively described as "cowboys and Indians in outer space") with its emphasis on escapism and adventure. Science, though present, is largely incidental to such programs. Actually it is hardly science at all but rather "scientism," or a veneer of science with spotty applications of jargon. In programs like *Captain Video*, *Space Patrol* and *Commando Cody*, *Sky Marshal of the Universe*, incredible gadgets with impressive designations (e.g., Captain Video's famous "opticon scillometer") substitute for actual science.

By mid-decade, however, the juvenile science fiction series were suddenly displaced by programs grounded in hard science. Raygun heroes were replaced by methodical yet nonetheless stalwart scientists concerned more with theory and effect than with derring-do. In programs like *Science Fiction Theatre*, *Men into Space* and *The Man and the Challenge*, the gadgets and theories were either already in existence or at least extrapolated from current knowledge. In these programs, television fulfilled a didactic function, making the case for actual science, not fiction. As a result, these programs laid the public relations groundwork for man's first real-life steps into outer space.

II.

At mid-decade, television was moving away from being mere entertainment; it was beginning to take itself seriously as an advocate of public policy. In the spring of 1954, by the expedient of pointing cameras at a Senate hearing, the infant medium crippled Senator Joseph McCarthy and proved him to be a bully and a liar. One could seriously argue that from that point, unconsciously at least, the television industry began to see itself as an emerging voice for social change. Certain changes began to take place in the medium. The completion of the coaxial cable and microwave relay system, which allowed the Army-

McCarthy Hearings to be beamed live to a fascinated public, extended television's physical and psychological reach. The emerging trend away from live to recorded programming, which accelerated after 1956 with the development of videotape, allowed for the archiving of television programs, and industry officials began to believe that the material they broadcast was worth preserving.

But television remained a live medium for most of the 1950s, and as such it spoke more directly, with greater spontaneity, and as a result, more believably than film. Performers sometimes fumbled their lines right in front of audiences—massive audiences. (Boris Karloff once described acting for live television as being in front of "eight million eavesdroppers, but you are alone in the world for half an hour.") Some scenes worked and some scenes did not. Indeed, early television had all the excitement of an opening night on the stage; and just as in the theater, audiences were apparently more interested in the story than anything else. The lack of color, the absence of fancy graphics, the dearth of lavish and expensive costumes apparently mattered not one whit to audiences. They remained simply fascinated with the miracle of television itself, enchanted with the "sense of wonder" stories this new technology was choosing to tell, be they high-end live dramas from *Westinghouse Studio One* or popular adventures from *The Secret Files of Captain Video*.

Against this background, perhaps it is easier to understand how some of the most popular series of the early 1950s could also be among the most inexpensive. The most impoverished of the competing commercial networks was the DuMont network, established by Allan B. DuMont and his DuMont Laboratories as a means of creating interest in the television sets and equipment he was manufacturing. DuMont did not possess either the talent or the money of major radio networks NBC, CBS and, to a lesser extent, ABC, which were then entering into the television fray. Nevertheless, because the DuMont network had the good fortune to come into prominence during an age of public faith in science and technology, it was able to compete successfully for several years (before being done in by its

The Dumont Network logo.

lack of resources) by offering content that had a distinct and lucrative appeal.

To compete with television's earliest sensation, *Texaco Star Theatre* with Milton Berle, DuMont offered Bishop Fulton J. Sheen, standing before a chalkboard and talking about the precepts of Christian faith. Millions of viewers tuned in. Star status and dazzling formal qualities never entered the contest. DuMont's single camera on Bishop Sheen and his chalkboard was enough for the millions who apparently preferred his message over the shenanigans of Uncle Miltie.

But head and shoulders above all of DuMont's programming was the phenomenally successful and influential *Captain Video and His Video Rangers*, DuMont's succinct science fiction program, which premiered June 27, 1949. Again, the series' formal qualities were limited to say the least (the prop budget was $25.00 a week), but the program represented a near-perfect match of theme and audience. Within five years after the end of

the Second World War, science and technology were revolutionizing the American lifestyle. New consumer goods resulting from that technology were flooding the market, with television sets at the fore. Within this milieu, *Captain Video and His Video Rangers* unexpectedly captured the popular imagination by extolling the value of technology itself. DuMont's vice-president, James Caddigan, lamely commented in *Time* (December 25, 1950) that *Captain Video* had an educational bent since it "sets up in a child's mind the idea of what electronics can do," although those electronics were outlandish even for 1950. Perhaps a more important attraction was the program's creation, in the guise of Captain Video, of a stalwart role model to whom impressionable youngsters by the millions swore their allegiance.

Captain Video was an archetypal hero modified in form to appeal to a new time and place. He was Odysseus, Hercules, Hector and Achilles, but the sword was supplanted by the ray gun. At the apex of his popularity, Captain Video possessed enough mythic quality to compel a considerable number of adults to take notice of his extraordinary influence. In fact, Captain Video in the person of actor Al Hodge was among the witnesses called to testify before a United States Senate committee investigating television violence in 1954. Hodge spoke passionately of Captain Video's commitment to moral authority and the supremacy of justice and fair play. Hodge assured the committee, as reported in *Newsweek* (November 1, 1954), that "we don't even use the word 'kill'" in the series, and that in lieu of capital punishment Captain Video's prisoners were always sent to "rehabilitation centers on the planet Ganymede." Moreover, Hodge, a Sunday School teacher, a radio actor noted for his role as the Green Hornet, and a man who genuinely believed in teaching by example, saw no conflict between his closely held convictions and the violence often called for in a *Captain Video* script. Hodge told the committee, "You have to have villains in a hero program or there's not any use for a hero," adding that violence for the sake of violence was always in "bad taste."

In fact, the space heroes of 1950s television adhered very much to the Captain Video model and perhaps even to Hodge's persona. Larger than life, they conscientiously served as spokespersons for morality; despite their individual qualities, they shared a sense of self-sacrifice for the good of the group. Like Al Hodge, these actors took their roles seriously; they found themselves trying to transform into the model citizens they had been hired to play before the cameras in order to assure Americans—particularly children—that moral behavior was not confined solely to the character appearing on the screen.

To publicly affirm their resolve, many of these heroes swore noble oaths, and they asked their followers to do the same. Oaths were certainly common throughout the 1950s, and they were generally administered and taken without self-conscious reserve or a sense of duress. Only when the terror of McCarthyism set in and loyalty oaths became a means of weeding out "disloyal" Americans did such pledges become matters of controversy. Until then,

oaths were looked upon as positive affirmations of ideals and values. Captain Video expected all his Rangers to take the Official Ranger Oath: "We, as official Video Rangers, hereby promise to abide by the Ranger Code and to support forever the cause of Freedom, Truth and Justice throughout the universe." Captain Midnight closed each of his adventures by reminding his viewers of the oath of the Secret Squadron, declaring, "Justice through strength and courage." The first episode of *Tom Corbett, Space Cadet* began with the young cadets taking the oath expected of all cadets at Space Academy; Tom and his crew swore to "safeguard the freedom of space and to uphold the cause of peace throughout the universe. To this end I dedicate my life." Perhaps the most elaborate of the oaths belonged to the Rocket Rangers. Commander Rod Brown required an elaborate oath designed to elicit a high degree of commitment from his troops—and could it have been coincidence that the particulars of the oath numbered ten?

1. I shall always chart my course according to the Constitution of the United States of America.
2. I shall never cross orbits with the rights and beliefs of others.
3. I shall blast at full space-speed to protect the weak and innocent.
4. I shall stay out of collision orbit with the laws of my state and community.
5. I shall cruise in parallel orbit with my parents and teachers.
6. I shall not roar my rockets unwisely, and shall be courteous at all times.
7. I shall keep my gyros steady and reactors burning by being industrious and thrifty.
8. I shall keep my scanner tuned to learning and remain coupled to my studies.
9. I shall keep my mind out of free-fall by being mentally alert.
10. I shall blast the meteors from the paths of other people by being kind and considerate.

Even in the beginning, television had a remarkable facility for mimicry, and the success of *Captain Video and His Video Rangers* sparked a series of imitators that would persist for the next ten years. The focus would shift along the way, moving audiences away from the fanciful tales of *Captain Video* to the sober experiments of *The Man and the Challenge*. Even so, "The Man," the single extraordinary figure always at the center of the story, would remain a moral and ethical paragon; he would be more than human though less than divine, always a figure of strength, courage and inestimable personal rectitude. Scratch the surface of any of these heroes, from Captain Midnight through Buzz Corry, Rocky Jones, and Superman to Colonel Ed McCauley, and for all of their perceived dissimilarities we would still find Captain Video; moreover, scratch the surface of Captain Video and we would be left with a peculiarly 1950s personality: a little self-righteous, maybe, but more than willing to sacrifice for a cause greater than individual expedience.

This propensity for personal responsibility was consistent with the approach taken by the writers and directors of science fiction television. Stories and characters reinforced a communal ideal rather than advocating an ego-driven political or social ethic. Captain Video, Captain Midnight and Tom Corbett were heroes who may have been too good to be true, who were short on flaws and beyond moral reproach, but whose values were seldom in question since they were the values that American institutions were expected to promulgate and buttress. These heroes believed in their culture as inherently superior and benevolent, and therefore it was their moral duty to function as advocates of those ideals. The opening signature to *Adventures of Superman* described the Man of Steel as fighting for "truth, justice and the American way." Just as American role models were expected to strive toward those goals, the nation's lesser mortals were trained from infancy to stretch themselves in the same direction. Each morning, hands over hearts, they pledged their allegiance to the nation's flag and to "one nation, under God, indivisible, with liberty and justice for all." The reality may have fallen short of the goal, but by defining an ideal to work towards, these children were setting an ambitious agenda for their generation.

III.

The science fiction genre spread across the four networks during the 1950s once *Captain Video* proved the viability of such storylines. The first to fall into network formation was *Tom Corbett, Space Cadet* in the autumn of 1950. The CBS series was based on a novel by science fiction writer Robert A. Heinlein, and perhaps because of Heinlein's celebrated name, scientific accuracy was necessary. Whereas the staff at work on *Captain Video* never seemed to worry about the scientific principles behind many of their inventions, the producers of *Tom Corbett* went to considerable lengths to mix legitimate science with entertaining and imaginative plots. Toward that end, writers reportedly consulted the Hayden Planetarium a dozen times a day in an effort to achieve precision in their scripts; moreover, the producers employed Willy Ley, one of the leading rocket experts of the day, as technical adviser. If Ley said a proposal was feasible, it could be incorporated into the script; if he turned thumbs down on an idea, the writers went back to their typewriters. One script handed to Ley, for example, read, "In ten years, three men had met death while patrolling the Mars-Jupiter comet watch." The rocket expert, after making pages of mathematical calculations based upon the laws of probability, required that the line be changed from "ten years" to "fourteen years." Ley's editorial control over *Tom Corbett* even extended to the physical aspects of the show, to the consternation of the actors involved. Live television was difficult enough, what with the demands for quick scene changes and costume changes, but whenever a *Tom Corbett* script called for radioactive substances Ley firmly insisted that the actors don their fifteen-pound space suits and lumber about on stage under the intense heat of the lights. The discomfort of those costume demands reportedly caused more than one disgruntled cast member to insist that he would "rather die of radioactivity."

Most of the other television science fiction in the first half of the decade, however, eschewed authenticity, preferring to present unencumbered plots with excitement usually winning out over science. Certainly that was the case with *Captain Video* and with *Space Patrol*, the long-running rival to *Tom Corbett*. In fact, in a television special titled *They Went to the Stars*, a nostalgic look at the early days of science fiction television produced some twenty years after the fact, Frankie Thomas (who starred as Tom Corbett) noted the chief differences between *Tom Corbett* and *Space Patrol*. Thomas told Ed Kemmer, who starred as Commander Buzz Corry in *Space Patrol*, that "our shows weren't as similar as I thought," noting that the science of *Space Patrol* "was sort of anything goes and ours was carefully tied to present-day research and serious projections of the future." Thomas added that "our stories were a bit different, too," concluding that "while *Space Patrol* concentrated on fantasy, mystery and plot, *Tom Corbett* placed its emphasis on characterization and personal conflict."

In *Space Patrol* and most other science fiction series, "science" was usually just a sprinkling of jargon into the various storylines. Audiences who preferred characterization and personal conflict could always watch the eminent anthology series *Westinghouse Studio One*, and youngsters interested in "real" science could always tune in *Mr. Wizard*, an educational series with Don Herbert patiently demonstrating a wide variety of scientific principles. Adults seeking science could also tune in *The Johns Hopkins Science Review*, which placed a weekly spotlight on the wonders of science.

But as the decade progressed, science fiction programming began to appear more respectable, if only because the programs began to follow, albeit indirectly, the path blazed by *Mr. Wizard* and *The Johns Hopkins Science Review*. In the real world, scientific endeavors were progressing at a rapid pace, and television brought pictures of science at work into the home. In particular, the photogenic rocket experiments were widely broadcast. The push was on to convince the adult population that the new technologies would place the moon and stars within reach, which left the space opera fantasies in rather eccentric positions. Although crucial to inspiring the sense of wonder that would pave the way for scientific missions to other worlds, children's programs

like *Captain Midnight*, *Flash Gordon* and *Rocky Jones* apparently had served their purpose and would soon give way to more scientifically sophisticated works.

These works, discussed below, were actually inspired by a series of magazine articles that ran at the same time as the space operas. In the early 1950s, *Colliers* published a series of richly illustrated and superbly written articles about the feasibility and necessity of exploring space. At first glance the articles might have appeared merely informative "high-brow" pieces, factual footnotes to the more adventurous space operas of television. But the public took a second look and discovered that the *Colliers* pieces soberly outlined the means by which man could take his first steps into outer space. Complemented by the striking illustrations of noted space artist Chesley Bonestell, the *Colliers* series, written by Willy Ley and fellow scientists like Heinz Haber and Wernher von Braun, attracted a widespread and appreciative public following.

At mid-decade, then, television began to lend its influence to this active, broad-based effort in the scientific community. Foremost among those who took special note of the articles was Walt Disney, who was coincidentally in search of material for his "Tomorrowland" segment of the *Disneyland* television series. Working in collaboration with Ley, Haber and von Braun, Disney produced a landmark series for his program beginning with "Man in Space," first broadcast on March 9, 1955, and followed by "Man and the Moon" and "Mars and Beyond" on December 12, 1955, and December 4, 1957, respectively. To distinguish these programs from science fiction, series supervisor Ward Kimball christened the series "science faction." But the programs were far from the perceived stodginess of similar science programs; the facts were there, but they were conveyed in a most entertaining way. Light-hearted animated segments illustrating, for example, weightlessness or gravity were bridged by on-camera commentaries by the scientists, whose expositions on the complexities of space travel were detailed yet readily accessible to the lay audience. The high point of the episodes, however, was the animated sequences illustrating space flight.

So popular was the trilogy that Ley, Haber and von Braun became celebrities. Disney, never one to miss a marketing opportunity, commissioned von Braun's designs for spaceships and space stations as model kits for kids. This pleased von Braun, since the more his ideas of conquering space remained in the public eye, the better the chance for the program to come to fruition. The stratagem worked; the space series caught the imagination of President Eisenhower, who requested that a print of "Man in Space" be sent to the Pentagon, where it was screened for two weeks by top officials. From there, serious speculation about space travel filtered down to all levels of government, eventually leading the way to increased government attention to a space program.

The popularity of the "Tomorrowland" programs on *Disneyland* in 1955 marked an abrupt turnabout for the treatment of science fiction on television. In that year, *Tom Corbett* and *Space Patrol* both folded, and *Commando Cody* and *Captain Z-RO* came and went with barely a flash on the television screen. Meanwhile, Ziv Television's *Science Fiction Theatre* proved a major contributor to the new attitude in science fiction programming. The syndicated series, produced by Ivan Tors and debuting in 1955, presented dramatizations based on current lines of scientific inquiry. Much of the series' strength lay in its believability, due partly to the plays themselves—which were so heavily steeped in realistic science that their authenticity seemed beyond refutation—and partly to the mature demeanor of the series' dapper and reassuring host, Truman Bradley. Each week Bradley, a former radio announcer, introduced the theme of the present drama by showing the audience "something interesting." This "something interesting" was a demonstration of a scientific principle on which the forthcoming drama was based. The result was a sense that the drama was not so much fiction as extrapolation. In effect, *Science Fiction Theatre* was able to bridge the gap between science and fiction with clever and interesting narratives about man's relationship to science and technology.

Although the Ziv organization possessed an uncanny ability to turn current headlines into popular television fare, it was not unfailingly prescient. In the case of the popular *Science Fiction Theatre*, production of the series ended too soon to capitalize on one of the most important and politically charged headlines of the decade: the successful launch of the Soviet Union's orbiting Sputnik I spacecraft on October 4, 1957. Although scientists and the reality-based television programs had been preparing the public for a first step into space, it took this event to jar the government into action. For Americans, the emotional shock of a Russian rather than a United States satellite orbiting the world was startling; it sounded very much like Dr. Pauli or Cleolanta or the Ruler threatening the world, but it wasn't fiction. The threat had to be answered, not by a space patrol or by a group of Rocket Rangers, but by practical science.

The Ziv organization almost immediately began planning two new science fiction series to take advantage of the changed political and scientific facts of life, series that would take their lead from one fundamental question: Was the human being physically and psychologically fit to make the effort at conquering space? No Captain Video or Commander Buzz Corry could meet this new challenge; it was a job that called for the descendants of Tom Corbett. The new programs were succinct character studies in which personal conflicts co-existed with problems posed by science. Ziv's *The Man and the Challenge*, also produced by Ivan Tors, premiered September 12, 1959, on NBC and followed the experiments of the rather obsessed Dr. Glenn Barton (George Nader), whose weekly assignments invariably centered around the need to test the extreme limits of man's physical and psychological capacities. But unlike heroic narratives of the past, the stories often shifted focus from Barton to one of his subjects; in fact, Barton was often treated as a secondary character who functioned as the catalyst for a story that probed the endurance of one of Barton's human subjects. Though duty, honor and courage would prevail by the end of the drama, the subject would nonetheless suffer doubt and anxiety before coming to a moral conclusion. If Barton's research was excessive, it was nonetheless necessary, since the "Race for Space" between America and

Soviet Russia demanded answers to difficult questions.

The second Ziv series was *Men into Space*, which debuted September 30, 1959, on CBS. This series offered a detailed forecast of life a few short years in the future when America and the Soviet Union would vie for a place in the heavens. The series focused on Col. Ed McCauley (William Lundigan), who, as field commander of a moon project, responded to all the emotional baggage humans carried in their conquest of space. Like Dr. Glenn Barton, McCauley was often on the sidelines as his very human astronauts dealt with career issues, family stress and professional duties. In responding to their needs, McCauley learned that no matter the accomplishment, people remain people; he was forced to deal not only with the scientific and technological demands of the lunar enterprise, but also with the darker side of human life. Even on the Moon, McCauley learned firsthand and quickly that wherever man goes, avarice and murder follow.

The "prestige dramas"—anthology series such as *Westinghouse Studio One*—tended to insure television's credibility with critics in the 1950s. Mindful of their reputation, such series at first shied away from science fiction because, one supposes, the genre was not held in the highest critical esteem. However, these respectable series did occasionally venture into science fiction, if only to exploit the public's interest in themes of human adaptability to scientific progress. The human response under conditions of stress and peril was a theme made to order for the anthology dramas, and as science fiction became an acceptable form of dramatic expression, the anthologies were quick to mine its intricacies. One of the first science fiction dramas on a prestigious anthology show was "It Might Happen Tomorrow," with Barry Nelson, presented on *Westinghouse Studio One* on January 24, 1955. The summary included in television listings suggests a character study: "The first man to fly beyond the fringe of the atmosphere into the realm of emptiness beyond—and what happens to him."

On August 18, 1957, *TV Playhouse* presented "The Dark Side of the Moon," dramatized by Arthur Sainer from a story by Sainer and Alexander Singer. This play highlighted the human issues so much a part of scientific concern during the second half of the decade. The story deals with a five-man crew selected for the first expedition to the moon, and Sainer's script scrutinizes, with a critical eye for detail, the personal lives of the men selected, and the psychological effect of their selection on their family relationships. In particular, the story focuses on Harry Baker (Biff McGuire), a geologist who is blissfully secure in his research position at Columbia University. Though stunned at his addition to the team, Baker accepts the challenge, despite bitter opposition from his wife (Kathleen Maguire). The conflict between husband and wife served as a metaphor for America's own internal conflict.

Science fiction made one of its more notable television appearances on *Desilu Playhouse* on November 24, 1958, when William Bendix and Martin Balsam starred in "The Time Element" by Rod Serling. Pete Jenson (Bendix) is a "part-time unsuccessful bookie" who, in a recurring dream, finds himself being pulled back into the past, specifically to Honolulu on December 6, 1941. Jenson is convinced that he is actually being shifted back and forth in time, but his psychiatrist (Balsam) provides rational explanations for Jenson's "dreams." The psychiatrist later spots Jenson's picture in a neighborhood bar, where he learns that Jenson actually died in the bombing of Pearl Harbor. Though this play stretched a science fiction element—time travel—to the level of fantasy, "The Time Element" provides further insight into the evolving nature of television science fiction during the 1950s because it was the genesis of Serling's later series *The Twilight Zone*.

Since the time of Lucian, science fiction has functioned as a milieu for satire, and nowhere was this satirical bent better illustrated in the 1950s than in Gore Vidal's "Visit to a Small Planet," originally broadcast on *Goodyear Television Playhouse* on May 8, 1955. As directed by Jack Smight, the play stabbed at human arrogance and self-indulgence, particularly as bolstered through science. Assuring the audience of humanity's gifts, one of the characters boldly states, "If there's any travel-

Clark Kent (George Reeves) as pitchman for Kellogg's Sugar Smacks in the second season of *Adventures of Superman.*

ing to be done in space, we'll do it first." But the sudden arrival of Kreton (Cyril Ritchard), the "visitor," disproves the notion of man's omnipotence, and Kreton's intellectual and technological superiority is terrifying to the deflated humans (even more so in the later film version, when Jerry Lewis played Kreton). Making matters worse, Kreton is afflicted with a quirky and erratic personality, and his desire to restage the Civil War to allow the South to prevail serves to humble not just those living in the 1950s, but audiences of any era.

IV.

It was no coincidence that so many space heroes of the 1950s wore uniforms, for each hero was a member of a military or paramilitary organization. Such a characterization is understandable, considering that the United States had just successfully concluded one conflict (World War II), was engaged in a ground war in Korea and was preparing to deal with Communism in Vietnam. The U.S. was also deeply engaged in a broader Cold War. On all fronts, the country was pinning expectations of victory on the effectiveness of the military services buttressed by new technologies that, it was hoped, would eventually put a stop to war.

In terms of symbolic value, the military organizations that the heroes belonged to mattered less than the uniforms themselves. The uniforms provided a certifiable identity by which audiences came to recognize the moral authority of the heroes. A uniform was less a sign of militarism than a sign of belonging. The uniforms worn by Captain Video, Captain Midnight, Buzz Corry and Commando Cody signified the communal resolve to co-exist in harmony.

This sense of community was also perpetuated by the experience of television itself. Rather than dividing, television was continuing a trend that radio had begun, bringing the masses together. This trend proved extremely lucrative for sponsors; through television their products became part of the national consciousness. In 1950s television, as in radio, a program was associated with a single sponsor, whose commercials conformed to the program content. Thus the sponsor became a part of the experience and, for better or worse, the audience came to accept both sponsor and program as a unified whole. Speak of Superman and one spoke of Kellogg's; speak of Powerhouse candy bars and one spoke of Captain Video; speak of Ovaltine and one spoke of Captain Midnight. To many this is commercialism of the most insidious kind, but the point is that the commercials' capacity to identify themselves with the shows reflected the ideal of unity that so pervaded the American 1950s.

A decade after Col. Ed McCauley conquered the moon on television came yet another man in a uniform, a retired naval commander named Neil Armstrong, who led a real-life expedition of men to the moon's surface. In so doing, he fulfilled a dream as old as the human race. Naturally, the same device that had foretold the event—the television set inside the living room—was there to show the dream coming true. In television terms, is there any significant difference between Col. McCauley setting foot on the moon and Neil Armstrong doing so? Not really. As far as television is concerned, both events blend into one, the fictional and the actual. But perhaps this blending is the source, at least in part, of television's great power to define a goal and help push for its attainment—a power amply demonstrated in the 1950s as events unfolded, on the small screen and in the larger world.

Adventures of Superman

Of all the programs covered in this book, *Adventures of Superman* remains the most commercially successful, the most enduring and perhaps the most endearing. No other series can compete; all 104 episodes have been in continuous circulation since the series' premiere in 1953. Moreover, no other series can claim as faithful a following as *Adventures of Superman*, a following that includes not just Internet fan clubs but two books, Gary Grossman's excellent *Superman: From Serial to Cereal* (Popular Library, 1976) and Michael Bifulco's episode guide *Superman on Television* (Bifulco Books, 1988). Definite reasons for the series' success remain elusive, but certainly the foresight by producers to film the final seasons in color assured for profitable reissues in the 1960s when color television became affordable. But success is seldom based solely on technical change, and in the case of *Adventures of Superman* much of its success is due to its own aesthetic élan. The series never attempted to be anything more than what it was, a highly entertaining melodrama rooted deeply in its comic book origins; in fact, its best feature is sheer escapism in the best tradition. Episodes featured clear and distinct crises which always led to satisfying conclusions; this is particularly true of the first two black and white seasons.

The series evolved from tense crime thrillers under producer Robert Maxwell to more comic book–inspired and didactic morality plays in the second season (and beyond) under producer Whitney Ellsworth. Many commentators on the series prefer the Maxwell episodes to any of those produced by Ellsworth. Maxwell clearly preferred suspenseful crime thrillers over anything else: "The Haunted Lighthouse" follows Superman's efforts to thwart a smuggling ring; in "The Monkey Mystery" Superman battles a spy ring; "The Mind Machine" follows a gangster's efforts to disrupt Senate crime hearings; "No Holds Barred" exposes racketeering in the wrestling game; "Czar of the Underworld" follows the accident-prone filming of a motion picture based on Clark Kent's exposé of mobster Luigi Dinelli; and "Crime Wave" follows Superman's efforts to capture 12 violent mobsters in Metropolis. Maxwell seldom balked at depicting violence. For example, in "Night of Terror," the cold-blooded murder of motel manager Mr. King, though not shown, is discussed, and Mrs. King, shown bleeding from facial wounds following a pistol-whipping, is nursed back to health by Lois. In "The Birthday Letter" callous villains remove the braces from a disabled little girl to keep her from going for help, and in "The Evil Three" a sadistic villain pushes a woman in a wheelchair down a ramp to what is apparently her doom. Such sequences are hardly what one would think of as children's entertainment (although in today's children's programming, such scenes would be conventional).

In general, most of the first season episodes are fast-paced and done in a style that clearly resembles B-movie thrillers rather than comic books; as Gary Grossman has noted, the preview at the end of each episode added to the B-movie quality by having the distinct flavor of movie "coming attractions" trailers.

A close examination of the series, in a strictly aesthetic sense, shows that the two black and white seasons are as similar as they are different. The second season, under Ellsworth, certainly tones down the violence and the heavy-handed thriller quality of the first season; of note here is that Lois Lane is recast from the venomous feminist who seems to genuinely dislike Clark Kent—perhaps due to Phyllis Coates' portrayal rather than to Maxwell's scripting—to a more reserved yet nonetheless independent Lois in the person of Noel Neill, who had played the part in two Columbia serials. But more important, the second-season criminals are depicted as moronic rather than sadistic, and this underscores Ellsworth's own didactic approach (especially for children). The audience may have sympathy for the crooks, but the audience will never have empathy for the crooks. This is certainly true when examining villains like Hank, Louie, and Joyce in "The Dog Who Knew Superman," and henchman Toots in "Jimmy Olsen, Boy Editor." Hank remains degenerate by literally hating dogs, but sophomoric Louie changes allegiances when he realizes that Hank is about to kill the dog in question. Joyce, the moll, remains pure, since Superman returns the dog to her care, knowing the dog will be loved. In "Jimmy Olsen, Boy Editor," Toots is simply a big lug without brains but with a heart, and our sympathies go out to him because he is a friendly yet misguided individual.

But despite the criticism leveled against these depictions of villains by many devotees and reviewers alike, such characterizations are actually few in the second season. For the most part, the villains are soft versions of Maxwell's villains. For instance, there is little sympathy for Luke Maynard in "The Big Squeeze," for Capt. McBain in "The Golden Vulture," for

Fairchild in "The Face and the Voice" or for Dr. Gregory Barnak in "Star of Fate." In each instance, the villain is cold-blooded, is inclined to murder, and possesses no redeeming value. The difference, then, between, say, Dr. Ort in Maxwell's "The Secret of Superman" and Dr. Barnak in Ellsworth's "Star of Fate" is that the violent tendencies in Ellsworth's villains have been assuaged, either by a sympathetic henchmen (e.g., Toots) or, in the case of Barnak, by softer plots. Dr. Ort drives the plot by seeking Superman's identity, but Barnak is secondary to the real conflict of "Star of Fate," which is to discover the antidote for a poison that has infected Lois; Barnak's mad pursuit to own the Star of Fate seems like an afterthought.

Ellsworth, who was National Comics' point man for the entire series, relied more on comic book inspiration than Maxwell, whose proclivity for crime thrillers seemed to spring more from pulp fiction than comic books of the 1950s. As a result, the fantastic underlies many of the episodes in Ellsworth's seasons, from crazy inventions like Mr. Kelso in "The Machine that Could Plot Crimes" and the incredibly powerful and accurate model airplanes in "Beware the Wrecker" (an episode with a comic book ring to it), to outright science fiction themes like a runaway asteroid in "Panic in the Sky," nuclear contamination in "Superman in Exile," Kryptonite bullets in "The Defeat of Superman" and powerful explosives in "The Whistling Bird."

Unfortunately, the color episodes (seasons three through six) are witless and rather simple tales of little consequence. For the color seasons, Ellsworth altered everything. For the special effects flying sequences he opted to film new sequences rather than refilm present sequences for color. Although always redundant, the flying sequences of the black and white episodes had some variety. In particular, the second season offered a dynamic Superman pitching, yawing and rolling in front of various backgrounds including the standard Metropolis skyline as well as flights across the Atlantic ("Star of Fate") and atmospheric flights through the Metropolis skyline at night ("The Boy Who Hated Superman" and "The Clown Who Cried"). Moreover, special sequences were filmed to meet the require-

Frame sequence of Jack Glass's photographic effects for Superman's flight to the asteroid in "Panic in the Sky."

ments of individual episodes, such as Superman's flight to the asteroid in "Panic in the Sky" and his flight through the thunderstorm in "Superman in Exile." But the color episodes offered little variety in 52 episodes; the same skyline footage was used for both day and night, supplemented by a closer shot on Superman with blurred clouds in the background. Nowhere is this more pronounced and aggravating than in "The Jolly Roger." Here, the script called for Superman to save an island by blocking incoming shells fired from a U.S. Navy battleship. To accomplish this, the repetitious flying sequence was printed left to right followed by the same sequence printed right to left; no bombs are seen exploding. What is quite evident, as so many have observed, is that the "S" on Superman's costume is backwards in the reversed shots.

The depictions of villains was also altered. Now the villains were stooge-like caricatures played more for comedy than intimidation; fre-

quent performers Herb Vigran, Ben Welden, Sid Tomack, Billy Nelson and George Chandler seemed to mock their previous villainous roles by overacting in silly plots in such episodes as "Mr. Zero," "Flight to the North" and "The Big Forget." The plots themselves became whimsical or sentimental rather than melodramatic; searching for the perfect lemon meringue pie drives the plot of "Flight to the North," and the sentiment expressed in "Joey," "The Prince Albert Coat," "The Stolen Elephant" and "Mr. Zero" borders on satire. In "Blackmail" and "Whatever Goes Up" the denouement makes it quite clear that we are not to take the episodes too seriously; the villains survive violent explosions, reappearing with their faces covered with soot and their clothing in shreds. They become slapstick figures, and presumably we are to laugh at their appearance and demeanor rather than revel in their own defeat.

Like so many television programs of the

era, the series had its origins in radio; Robert Maxwell and his wife Jessica had produced the final seasons of the radio series. Maxwell's penchant for crime thrillers was already apparent in the radio series, but the television series' origin also owes a lot to a series of animated films produced by Max Fleischer in the early 1940s. These 17 color short subjects featured the voice of radio's Superman (Clayton "Bud" Collyer), but seemed more like the Ellsworth programs than the Maxwell thrillers; using the fantastic, including incredible inventions and machines, the cartoons were not so much violent as action-oriented. Maxwell or Ellsworth, or both, borrowed the opening signature for their television series from Fleischer's cartoons. The narration in the films follows the basic radio opening with the axiomatic "faster than a speeding bullet, more powerful than a locomotive, able to leap tall buildings in a single bound"; visually, Fleischer places Superman standing with arms akimbo as the narrator explains Superman's brief history about being a strange visitor from another planet with extraordinary powers. At the appropriate point the Superman figure dissolves into Clark Kent before dissolving back to Superman with the announcer intoning the familiar closing line that states that Superman "fights a never-ending battle for truth and justice." For television, the phrase "and the American way" was added, which, since the 1960s, has offended many commentators by, as they charge, limiting Superman to an American ideal too often associated with patriotic as well as cultural imperialism.

In effect, Maxwell's pilot for the series was a feature-length film, *Superman and the Mole Men*, released in 1951 by Lippert Pictures. It was later edited into a two-part episode titled "The Unknown People." Maxwell wrote the script (using the pseudonym Richard Fielding) and Lee Sholem directed. George Reeves and Phyllis Coates were featured in their roles as Clark Kent/Superman and Lois Lane; the roles of Perry White and Jimmy Olsen from the comic books and radio programs would be added for the series along with an original character, Inspector William J. Henderson, an authority with the Metropolis police department.

It should also be noted that two serials, produced by Sam Katzman for Columbia Pictures, predated the series. Kirk Alyn and Noel Neill starred and Thomas Carr co-directed with Spencer G. Bennet the first serial, simply titled *Superman* (1948). Carr's later contribution to the television series cannot be overestimated; in fact, the best episodes belong to Carr and writer Jackson Gillis, who together knew exactly the kind of series they were making. Gillis's scripts are obviously inspired by comic books; his narratives flow quickly, leaving little room for realistic progression or character analysis. Critics censuring *Adventures of Superman* for lack of characterization or realism are not seeing the inherent value of the series; essentially, such critics are merely speaking a different language since one simply will not find realism or insight into characters or actions in the series. Rather, what one will find is clearly pronounced characters distinguished as "police officer" or "citizen" or "villain" or "innocent" who react to stimuli without much motivation. What drives the plot is incident, and Gillis understands this. His narratives grow from one fantastic element to another, cemented only by an interior logic that frequently has nothing to do with the real world of cause and effect. For example, no one really believes that a small model airplane controlled by apparently nothing, in "Beware the Wrecker," can carry enough explosive to destroy an entire cargo ship. But the model plane makes sense within the confines of that particular drama; the explosive is never explained nor is the power for flying the model aircraft explained since such explanations would get in the way of the story proper. What matters is that someone is sending specially armed model airplanes to wreak destruction upon Metropolis.

What Gillis writes, Carr visually enhances. He relies on long takes and frames his cast in postures similar to comic book panels. Carr frequently uses two-shots without cutting on dialogue because, for Carr, dialogue is present only to advance the narrative action. What matters for Carr is creating action and allowing that action to speak for itself, and nowhere is this more apparent than in the flying sequences of the second season. Grossman notes that it was Carr who devised the running take-offs, i.e., having Reeves run toward the camera, hit a small trampoline and then leap over the camera. Such a contrivance is most effective in Gillis's script for "Panic in the Sky," in which, according to Grossman, Carr angled the observatory fence toward the camera to give the impression of one mighty leap by the Man of Steel.

The second serial, Bennet's *Atom Man vs. Superman* (1950), again with Alyn and Neill, is the first Superman dramatization outside of radio to feature Lex Luthor, played here by Lyle Talbot. Not one of the 104 episodes of *Adventures of Superman* featured or even alluded to Lex Luthor, Superman's comic book nemesis.

Also, it should be noted that an episode titled "Stamp Day for Superman" was filmed but never broadcast since it was a promotional film for the U.S. Treasury Department. The episode, featuring Billy Nelson as villain Blinky and Tris Coffin as school principal Mr. Garwood, was distributed in 16mm to schools to advance the Savings Stamps program. Thomas Carr directed the 15-minute episode from a script by David Chantler. National Comics also distributed a comic book based on the episode.

The dates listed below have been culled from various sources, and though the series is credited as an ABC network series, some syndication may have taken place in West Coast markets since disparities exist between listed broadcast dates. Although the dates fluctuate, the order of episodes remained the same.

Technical Information

FORMAT. Filmed half-hour series recounting Superman's war on crime in the American city of Metropolis.

BROADCAST HISTORY. *Network:* ABC and syndication through Motion Pictures for Television, Inc., and later in reissue through Flamingo Films, with current syndication through Warner Brothers Television and Warner Home Video; Superman is also available from Columbia House Video Club. *Original Airdates:* February 9, 1953, to December 9, 1957. *Sponsor:* Kellogg's. *Seasons:* Six. *Total Episodes:* 104 (52 B/W and 52 color).

Signature

OPENING. The opening signature for this series has become as familiar as any on television. The exploding comet that reveals the title *Adventures of Superman* followed by the pistol shot, the racing locomotive, the skyscraper, Superman in flight and that majestic pose with the American flag in the background have become an American icon. Over these images, of course, is the excited babble of voices, trying to decide what's in the sky: Bird? Plane? We all know the answer—the "strange visitor from another planet," come to Earth to fight for "truth, justice and the American way." The chief announcer for the opening was Bill Kennedy; Charles Lyon introduced the show on behalf of Kellogg's.

Kennedy: Yes, it's Superman, strange visitor from another planet who came to Earth with powers and abilities far beyond those of mortal men. Superman, who can change the course of mighty rivers, bend steel in his bare hands. And who, disguised as Clark Kent, mild-mannered reporter for a great metropolitan newspaper, fights a never-ending battle for truth, justice and the American way.

COMMERCIAL BREAK. At the halfway point in each episode, the narrative would crossfade to an image of the Superman shield zooming toward the viewer with Charles Lyon telling us, "We'll return to the *Adventures of Superman* in just a moment."

CLOSING. In the first season, Maxwell ended each episode with a movie trailer-inspired preview of next week's program. Using the shield as background, the title "PREVIEW" was shown before dissolving to a series of scenes from the program. Bill Kennedy then would warn the audience not to miss Superman's next "thrill-packed" battle "against the forces of evil." At this point, the scene dissolved back to the shield and a series of titles accompanied Kennedy's finish: "There's action! Adventure! And mystery!" This image was followed by the image of the typical Superman stance, this time superimposed over bursting fireworks; Charles Lyon closed with a final plug for Kellogg's. After the first season, the preview was replaced by a more staid conclusion. Like its predecessor, the closing opened with a quick zoom through space accompanied by Kennedy's reminder, "Don't miss the next thrill-packed episode in the *Adventures of Superman.*" But no preview followed, just Lyon's familiar proclamation that the series was "presented by Kellogg's, the greatest name in cereals."

Production Staff

Production: National Periodicals Inc.; the following title appears in the closing credits, with Charles Lyon offering a voice-over in the final season only: "Superman is based on the ["original" added by Lyon] character appearing in *Action Comics* and *Superman* magazines." *Theme Music:* Leon Klatzkin.

SEASON 1. Produced at RKO-Pathé Studios in Culver City, 1951.

Producers	Robert J. Maxwell and Bernard Luber
Associate Producer	Barney A. Sarecky*
Directors of Photography	Clark Ramsey* and William Whitley
Art Direction	Ernst Fegté* and Ralph Berger
Film Editor	Al Joseph
Dialogue Director	Stephen Carr
Sound Engineer	Harry Smith
Sound Cutter	Barton Hayes
Assistant Directors	Arthur Hammond* and Nate Barrager
Makeup	Harry Thomas
Wardrobe	Izzy Berne
Casting Director	Harold Chiles
Special Effects	Danny Hayes and Thol Simonson
Properties	George Bahr

SEASON 2. Produced at California Studios, 1953.

Producer	Whitney Ellsworth
Production Coordinator	David S. Garber
Production Manager	Clem Beauchamp
Story Editor	Mort Weisinger
Director of Photography	Harold Stine
Film Editor	Harry Gerstad
Assistant Directors	Jack R. Berne, Robert Justman and Ivan Volkman
Sound Engineer	Jean L. Speak
Special Effects	Thol Simonson
Photographic Effects	Jack R. Glass
Re-recording	Ryder Sound Services Inc.

SEASON 3. Produced at California Studios, 1954.

Producer	Whitney Ellsworth
Production Manager	Clem Beauchamp
Story Editor	Mort Weisinger
Film Editor	Sam Waxman
Assistant Director	John Pommer
Sound Engineer	Jean L. Speak
Special Effects	Thol Simonson
Photographic Effects	Jack R. Glass
Re-recording	Ryder Sound Services, Inc.

SEASON 4. Produced at Chaplin Studios, 1955.

Producer	Whitney Ellsworth
Production Manager	Eddie Donohoe
Production Coordinator	David S. Garber
Story Editor	Mort Weisinger
Director of Photography	Joseph Biroc
Film Editor	Sam Waxman
Assistant Directors	Gene Anderson, Sr., and Grayson Rogers
Special Effects	Thol Simonson
Sound Engineer	Earl Snyder

SEASON 5. Produced at Ziv Studios, 1956.

Producer	Whitney Ellsworth
Production Manager	Eddie Donohoe
Director of Photography	Harold Wellman
Film Editor	Sam Waxman
Art Director	John Mansbridge
Set Decorator	Jerry Welch
Assistant Directors	Louis Germonprez and Dick Dixon
Special Effects	Thol Simonson
Sound Engineer	Robert Post
Re-recording	Ryder Sound Services Inc.

SEASON 6. Produced at Ziv Studios, 1957.

Production	Whitney Ellsworth
Production Manager	Ben Chapman
Director of Photography	Joseph Biroc
Film Editor	Sam Waxman
Art Director	Lou Croxton
Set Decorator	Glenn Thompson
Assistant Directors	Bob Barnes and Edward Haldeman
Special Effects	Thol Simonson
Makeup	Gus Norin
Sound Engineer	Herman Lewis
Assistant Cameraman	Howard Schwartz

Indicates credits from the feature Superman and the Mole Men, *broadcast in two parts as "The Unknown People."*

George Reeves and Noel Neill clowning around between takes of *Adventures of Superman*.

Regular Cast

Clark Kent/Superman   George Reeves
Lois Lane (Season One)   Phyllis Coates
Lois Lane (Remaining seasons)   Noel Neill
Jimmy Olsen   Jack Larson

Perry White   John Hamilton
Inspector William J. Henderson Robert Shayne
Occasional Appearances: *Uncle Oscar Quinn* (two episodes), Sterling Holloway; *Prof. Lucerne* (two episodes), Everett Glass; *Prof. Pepperwinkle* (five Episodes), Phillips Tead

Episode Guide

SEASON 1

Superman on Earth (February 9, 1953). The planet Krypton is experiencing strange upheavals, and scientist Jor-El believes that the planet is self-destructing. His warnings go unheeded, and in a desperate attempt to save his family he begins constructing a rocket that will take them to safety. His calculations go awry when the destruction begins sooner than he reasoned. He orders Lara to board the rocket with their infant son Kal-El, but Lara decides to stay with her husband. Together they agree to send Kal-El to safety, and just before Krypton explodes the rocket is launched toward the planet Earth. The rocket crashes, and the unharmed infant is found by Eben and Sara Kent, who raise the boy as their own, naming him Clark. The boy obviously has superior powers, and as he grows to manhood the Kents teach him that with his great powers he has a great responsibility to the world. Upon Eben's death, Clark leaves home with the blessing of his mother. Packing a costume she fashioned out of the blankets he was wrapped in when they found him, Clark heads for the city of Metropolis where he seeks employment as a newspaper reporter. Arriving at the offices of *The Daily Planet*, Clark finds the place in chaos as reporters flock to cover the dramatic story of a man dangling from the mooring line of an in-flight dirigible. Seeing an opportunity, Clark makes a deal with editor Perry White that if Clark can get an exclusive interview with the man, White will hire him as a reporter. Clark then changes into his costume and uses his ability to fly to rescue the man. Clark then changes back into his civilian clothes and corners the man for an exclusive interview. Back at *The Daily Planet*, White keeps his word and gives Clark a job, but what is now causing a stir is the story of the "strange man" who came out of the sky to rescue the man. Fellow reporter Lois Lane turns to Clark and demands answers to such questions as, "Just how did you get to this man long before anyone else did?" Clark answers, "Maybe I'm a superman, Miss Lane." *Director:* Thomas Carr. *Writer:* Richard Fielding (pseudonym for Robert Maxwell and Whitney Ellsworth).

Cast:

Jor-El	Robert Rockwell
Lara	Aline Towne
Rozan	Herbert Rawlinson
Gogan	Stuart Randall
Eben Kent	Tom Fadden
Sara Kent	Frances Morris
Rescued Man	Dabbs Greer
Miss Bachrach	Dani Nolan
Young Clark Kent	Joel Nestler

The Haunted Lighthouse (February 16, 1953). Clark Kent opens the episode with narration explaining that Jimmy Olsen traveled to Moose Island to visit his Aunt Louisa and cousin Chris, two relations he hadn't seen for some time. What started as a family reunion becomes a great mystery when Jimmy finds Chris to be aloof and bellicose and Aunt Louisa to be overly submissive to Chris's harsh demands. An eerie voice claiming to be drowning and crying for help haunts Jimmy's visits to the nearby abandoned lighthouse. Jimmy meets a sailor named Mack who mistakes Jimmy for Chris; when Jimmy mentions this to Chris and Aunt Louise, Chris accuses Jimmy of spying and warns him to stay away from the old lighthouse. Rumors in the village circulate that the lighthouse is haunted. One night Jimmy sees a light emanating from the lighthouse, and upon investigating finds a knife thrown at him by Chris and yet another warning to stay away from the place. When he returns to his bedroom, he finds a note purporting to be from Aunt Louisa entreating his help. Hopelessly confused and frightened, Jimmy makes an urgent call to Kent, who, as Superman, flies to the island. Kent discovers the secret: The lighthouse is a staging area for smugglers, and Chris and Aunt Louisa are members of the gang. Superman leads the Coast Guard to the smugglers. The real Aunt Louisa is found, informing Jimmy that the imposter is Mrs. Carmody and that Chris is actually *her* son; the real Chris is away serving in the United States Coast Guard. *Director:* Thomas Carr. *Writer:* Eugene Solow.

Cast:

Chris	Jimmy Ogg
Alice	Allene Roberts

Mrs. Carmody	Maude Prickett
Mack	William Challee
Aunt Louisa	Sarah Padden
Coast Guard Commander	Steve Carr

The Case of the Talkative Dummy (February 23, 1953). Lois and Clark take Jimmy to a vaudeville show for his birthday, and after a few moments of a Mr. Marco and Freddy, a ventriloquist act, the dummy seems to take on a voice all its own. So eerie is the effect that Marco becomes agitated and leaves the show. Intrigued, the reporters go backstage and meet with Marco. He says that Freddy has acted this way before, and that he believes it is a second ventriloquist in the audience disrupting the show. The next day, Perry White assigns the reporters a series of armored car robberies, and it soon becomes apparent that the robberies and the ventriloquist act are connected. Clark learns that a theater usher is actually conveying the schedules of the armored car via the "talkative dummy" to two thugs sitting in the audience. *Director:* Thomas Carr. *Writers:* Dennis Cooper and Lee Backman.

Cast:	*E.J. Davis*	Tristram Coffin
	Mr. Marco	Syd Saylor
	Harry Green	Pierre Watkin
	Usher	Robert Kent
	Safe Man	Phillip Pine
	Armored Car Guard	Steve Carr

The Mystery of the Broken Statue (March 2, 1953). The reporters investigate a series of incidents in which a dapper man named Paul Martin and his quisling enter curio shops and pay for the pleasure of breaking plaster statues. After seven shops are hit, Kent reasons that the men are after something hidden inside the statues, and this inspires Lois to start buying up plaster statues hoping that her purchases will lead to Martin. When it does, Martin kidnaps her. At Inspector Henderson's office, Clark unravels the mystery, showing that the various objects found inside the plaster statues lead to a rebus, PO97M, or Post Office 97 at the main post office. There, Martin is arrested by Henderson as Martin claims a ceramic pig. Once broken, the pig surrenders a celebrated gemstone ruby. *Director:* Thomas Carr. *Writer:* William C. Joyce.

Cast:	*Paul Martin*	Tristram Coffin
	Mr. Bonelli	Michael Vallon
	Ellie's Gift Shop Owner	Maurice Cass
	Mr. Edwards	Steve Carr
	Pete	Wade Crosby
	Dart	Joey Ray
	Police Officer	Phillip Pine

The Monkey Mystery (March 9, 1953). A Central European scientist named Moleska entrusts a locket containing a secret atomic formula to his daughter Maria. He tells her to give it to no one but the President of the United States so that his formula will be used only for the good of mankind. As the police arrive, Maria kisses her father farewell and makes her way to America, but spies are already on her trail. Their agent is an organ grinder named Tony who uses a monkey dressed in a Superman costume as a courier. Clark and Lois pause one afternoon to watch the monkey perform, and when Lois gives a donation she receives a message explaining that Maria arrives in Metropolis on a night train. She keeps this information to herself, but Tony soon realizes that the monkey exposed the spy ring. The ring takes action, but Superman saves Lois and Maria from enemy agents who would use the atomic formula to conquer the world. *Director:* Thomas Carr. *Writers:* Ben Peter Freeman and Doris Gilbert.

Cast:	*Maria Moleska*	Allene Roberts
	Tony	Michael Vallon
	Harold Crane	Harry Lewis
	Max	William Challee
	Doctor	Steve Carr

Night of Terror (March 16, 1953). At the Restwell Tourist Camp in the Blue Mountains near the Canadian border, Lois finds the unconscious body of hotel manager Mrs. King lying behind the counter, but before Lois can summon help she is taken captive by two thugs. Lois learns from Mrs. King that gangsters were using her camp as a hideout for criminals fleeing into Canada; the two thugs murdered Mrs. King's husband, and are now awaiting the arrival of a notorious killer named Baby Face Stevens. Lois manages to phone *The Daily Planet*, but finds that Clark is away. Jimmy takes it upon himself to rescue Lois, but before leaving for the Blue Mountains he leaves Clark a note. When Jimmy arrives at the camp, the gangsters mistake him for Baby Face Stevens, but when the real Stevens shows up Jimmy is exposed and their doom is apparently sealed. Meanwhile, Clark returns to his office where Miss Bachrach tells him that Jimmy left a note for him, but the note is missing. She tells Clark that the note said something about Lois being in trouble in some place with "well" in it. Clark calls Mr. Quinn of the tourist bureau and learns that there are three tourist camps with "well" in it. Clark changes into Superman and makes contact with two of the sites before finding Restwell just in time to save Lois, Jimmy and Mrs. King. *Director:* Lee Sholem. *Writer:* Ben Peter Freeman.

Cast: *Mrs. King*   Ann Doran
    Solly   Frank Richards
    Mitch   John Kellogg
    Miss Bachrach   Almira Sessions
    Oscar   Joel Friedkin
    Mr. Quinn   Steve Carr
    Baby Face Stevens   Richard Benedict

The Birthday Letter (March 23, 1953). Cathy Williams is a seven-year-old handicapped girl who writes a letter to Superman asking him to take her to the fair so that she can have fun like the rest of the children. The letter so touches Perry White that he assigns Lois to write a feature story on the girl. Later, a gangster named Cusak mistakenly phones Cathy, telling her the location of counterfeit printing plates before he is gunned down in the phone booth. Lois's story appears in *The Daily Planet*, and the intended receivers of the message, Marcel Duval and his wife Marie, reason that Cusak dialed a wrong number and that Cathy received the message. Duval orders his henchman, a big lug named Slugger, to impersonate Superman; he dons a shoddy costume and convinces Cathy that he is Superman, returning the girl to Duval's apartment. Superman then arrives at Cathy's apartment where he is met by Cathy's mother, who demands to know what Superman has done with her daughter. Rival newspapers pick up a story that Superman has kidnapped Cathy, and the public is outraged. At Duval's apartment, Slugger's emotions get the best of him and he decides

to help Cathy, but as Slugger attempts to return Cathy to her home, Duval enters and makes Slugger a prisoner. Cathy finally remembers the location, the Lambert Company, and Duval and Marie leave to find the plates but not before removing Cathy's braces so she will be unable to go for help. Clark and Lois learn the location of Duval's apartment and rescue Cathy and Slugger. Cathy tells them about the Lambert Company, and Clark dashes for an exit, proclaiming, "This is a job for Superman—I mean, I've got to find him!" The police surround the Lambert building and Superman appears, apprehending the Duvals. Back at her home, Cathy is visited by the *real* Superman, who takes her on a flight through Metropolis. *Director:* Lee Sholem. *Writer:* Dennis Cooper.

Cast: *Cathy Williams*   Isa Ashdown
    Slugger   John Doucette
    Mrs. Williams   Virginia Carroll
    Marcel Duval   Maurice Marsac
    Marie Duval   Nan Boardman
    Mr. Perkins   Jack Daly
    Cusack   Paul Marion

The Mind Machine (March 30, 1953). Senator Taylor is holding hearings on crime in Metropolis, targeting Lou Cranek and his mob. Desperate, Cranek and his henchmen invade the laboratory of Dr. Edward Stanton, kidnapping the inventor and stealing his amazing "hypnotherapy machine," a machine that allows a therapist to control a patient's thoughts. Stanton's assistant Hadley tells Clark Kent that Stanton and his invention were taken from the laboratory, and that Hadley is worried that in the wrong hands the machine would be deadly. At a Crime Committee hearing, syndicate accountant Carl Wagner suddenly refuses to testify against Cranek. Wagner leaves the chamber with Clark and Lois in hot pursuit. The irrational Wagner steals a woman's car, and when he wrecks it he seizes a school bus. Superman swings into action, ultimately stopping the bus and finding Wagner dead at the wheel. Hadley and Clark use Stanton's airplane to scour the mountains above Metropolis in the hope that the plane's radar will locate Stanton's machine. When the radar gets a fix on the machine, Clark learns that Lois is about to testify at the hearings; Clark slugs Hadley into unconsciousness, sets the auto-pilot, changes into Superman and then crashes his way into Cranek's mountain hideout. During Superman's scuffle with the crooks, Stanton destroys his machine, telling Superman that the machine's potential for abuse outweighs any good that can come from it. *Director:* Lee Sholem. *Writers:* Dennis Cooper and Lee Backman.

Cast:
Lou Cranek	Dan Seymour
Curly	Ben Welden
Dr. Edward Stanton	Griff Barnett
John Hadley	Steve Carr
Senator Taylor	James Seay
Carl Wagner	Frank Orth
Bus Driver	Lester Dorr

Rescue (April 6, 1953). Lois, assigned to research a story on mine safety in Carbide, Pennsylvania, follows mine inspector Sims on his rounds. Sims bars old-timer Pop Polgase from using his mine since Sims declares that the tunnels are unsafe. Pop, however, attempts to convince a local miner named Stan Hocker to help in the mine, but Stan realizes that the shafts are unstable and refuses to help, leaving Pop in the mine. Pop's careless swing of an ax strikes the rotten timbers, causing a cave-in. Stan sounds the alarm, bringing the miners and Sims to the site. The resourceful Lois dons miner's clothing, enters the mine and finds Pop trapped beneath a timber. Her effort to save him, however, goes awry, causing the tunnel to collapse. Crews hastily dig their way to the trapped couple, but just as they are about to break through, coal gas is detected and the operation is suspended. Clark Kent arrives, learns that Lois is trapped, becomes Superman and makes his way through the rubble to the nearly unconscious victims. At this point, light from a miner's helmet touches off the gas, but Superman is able to shield the victims from the blast. He then holds the timbers so that Lois and Pop can escape. *Director:* Thomas Carr. *Writer:* Monroe Manning.

Cast:
Pop Polgase	Housely Stevenson, Sr.
Inspector Sims	Fred Sherman
Stan Hocker	Ray Bennett
Lafe Reiser	Edmund Cobb
Harry Hansen	Milton Kibbee

The Secret of Superman (April 13, 1953). Clark Kent is awakened at one o'clock in the morning by a frantic call from Mrs. Olsen; she tells Clark that Jimmy hasn't come home and that she is gravely worried. Clark assuages her fears by telling her that Jimmy is probably on an assignment. Clark then calls the *Daily Planet* building, at which point the line goes dead. A man named Rausch has Jimmy under some kind of hypnotic spell, and he orders Jimmy to unload the private files on Superman. Once Rausch has collected the files, he makes his escape just as Superman arrives at the office. Changing into Clark Kent, he brings Jimmy back to consciousness, but Jimmy can remember nothing of the ordeal. Later, Perry White, dining at the News Club, is given a drug by a waiter; once Perry is under the influence of the drug, the waiter demands that he tell the secret of Superman's identity. Perry claims that he has no knowledge of Superman's identity. Just then the *real* waiter appears but collapses before he can warn Perry that the waiter is an imposter. Inspector Henderson, investigating the strange occurrences, discovers that Perry was drugged with a powerful truth serum used by enemy agents. Clark learns that he and Lois are next on the list of victims, and through deception he befriends Rausch, who leads him to the office of Dr. Ort, the mastermind behind the scheme. At police headquarters, Clark explains the ruse to Henderson, but when Jimmy phones and Lois cuts off Jimmy, Clark suspects trouble. Superman then flies to Ort's laboratory where he saves Lois and Jimmy from being murdered by Ort. During the struggle, Lois, under Ort's spell, identifies Superman as Clark Kent, but when the drug wears off and the police arrive, Lois can remember nothing, much to Superman's relief. *Director:* Thomas Carr. *Writer:* Wells Root.

Cast:
Dr. H.L. Ort	Peter Brocco
Rausch	Larry Blake
Mrs. Olsen	Helen Wallace
Herman	Joel Friedkin
Cook	Steve Carr

No Holds Barred (April 20, 1953). Brutish wrestler Bad Luck Brannigan uses a unique paralyzer grip to put seven opponents into the hospital. Because Brannigan's manager is the notorious Mortimer Murray, Perry White suspects trouble. White calls Clark into his office where Clark is introduced to national collegiate wrestling champion Wayne Winchester. White's plan is to have Wayne observe the night's bout between Brannigan and his opponent to see if Wayne can spot any kind of illegal activity. After watching the match, Wayne reports that the match looked more like attempted murder than a sporting event. Later, Wayne and Lois are ringside during the match between Brannigan and Adonis. When Adonis is defeated, Brannigan boasts that he is unbeatable, but Wayne charges the ring and challenges Brannigan to a "no holds barred" match, calling Brannigan and cheat and a phony. Clark then learns that Brannigan's skill comes from the "ancient secrets" of a Hindu named Swami Ramm; Ramm is being forced to train Brannigan in order to avoid deportation. Superman visits Ramm in Murray's holding cell, where Ramm confesses that it was not his intent to reveal the secrets to evil men like Murray. Superman assures Ramm that Murray is deceiving him, and that Superman will help Ramm escape if Ramm reveals the secrets to Superman. Ramm agrees, and Superman as Clark Kent conveys the secrets to Wayne. During the match, Wayne uses Ramm's secrets to void Brannigan's paralyzer grip, thereby defeating the otherwise inept wrestler. Knowing that Ramm has somehow betrayed him, Murray orders Ramm's murder, but Superman arrives in time to thwart their efforts. With Murray and his henchmen dispatched, Ramm agrees to use his powers to heal the injured wrestlers. *Director:* Lee Sholem. *Writer:* Peter Dixon.

Cast:

Wayne Winchester	Malcolm Mealy
Mortimer Murray	Herburt Vigran
Bad Luck Brannigan	Dick Reeves
Swami Ramm	Tito Renaldo
Sam Bleaker	Dick Elliott
Crusher	Henry Kulky

The Deserted Village (April 27, 1953). As fog swirls around a sign reading "Clifton by the Sea; Population 525," a gloved hand appears and scribbles out the 5 and 2, leaving just 5. A figure dressed in radioactive protective clothing now makes his way along one of the town's deserted streets. Clifton is Lois's hometown, and because her childhood friend Miss Taisy cannot be reached—nor can anyone else in Clifton—Lois and Clark decide to take the hour drive to Clifton to discover the reasons for the mysterious isolation. Arriving in Clifton, Lois and Clark find Miss Taisy aloof and seemingly uncaring. In addition, they are introduced to pharmacist Peter Godfrey and his son Alvin, who explain to Clark that the town is dying; the oyster beds have dried up, leaving unemployment. Clark also notices that nearly everyone left carries a gas mask. Lois wanders off to a cave where she is met by the man in the radioactive suit. He gasses Lois, knocking her unconscious. He is about to bury her when Superman comes to the rescue. The man turns out to be Alvin; the sinister plot was hatched by Peter Godfrey, who had discovered a new element called hydrozite in the surrounding caves. He used the radiation suit and poison gas to frighten the citizenry so that he could control the mining of the element. Miss Taisy and the others hoped to solve the problem on their own, but they are nonetheless thankful for the intervention of Superman. *Director:* Thomas Carr. *Writers:* Dick Hamilton and Ben Peter Freeman.

Cast:

Miss Taisy	Maude Prickett
Dr. Jessup	Fred E. Sherman
Peter Godfrey	Edmund Cobb
Alvin Godfrey	Malcolm Mealy
Miss Walton	Ann Tyrell

The Stolen Costume (May 4, 1953). A fleeing hoodlum named T-Ball finds refuge inside Clark Kent's apartment, where he accidentally trips the entrance to a secret closet and finds Superman's costumes. He takes a costume and flees into an alley but not before getting shot by a police officer. T-Ball makes his way to the apartment of a mobster named Ace where T-Ball dies before revealing the location of the apartment where he found the costume. But the costume itself excites Ace and his moll Connie; when Ace wants to know why Superman isn't wearing the costume, Connie reasons because "he wants to be the other guy." This leads them to trace T-Ball's activities in order to find the owner of the costume. Meanwhile, an anxious Clark Kent has called in an old friend, private detective Candy Meyers, for help in finding something that Clark cannot reveal. Later, Candy reports that the police found T-Ball's body in a vacant lot, but nothing of value was found on him. Clark orders Candy to remain in Clark's apartment while he visits the morgue to check on T-Ball himself. Connie finds Clark's apartment and believes Candy is Clark. She reports back to Ace, and together they decide to plant a bomb in Clark's apartment, believing that if he survives the blast he must be Superman. Clark returns to the apartment with Candy, and moments after Candy notices the closet door is open, Clark rushes in and saves Candy from the explosion. Ace then phones Clark, offering to barter for the costume. Clark agrees to a meeting and then forces Candy to leave the apartment. But Candy suspects trouble and decides to wait on the street near the apartment. Ace and Connie arrive and, still believing Candy to be Clark, they confront him. Candy agrees to accompany them back to their place. Clark follows Ace, Connie and their captive Candy back to Ace's apartment. Just as Ace is about to give Candy the ultimate test—fire point blank into Candy's heart—Clark breaks into the apartment and quickly knocks Candy cold. Ace and Connie now know that Clark is indeed Superman, and they offer a deal. But Clark tells them that he doesn't make deals with criminals. Ace threatens to expose Clark as Superman, but Clark says that they won't get the chance. Superman flies the couple to the frozen north where, high on a hill, he tells them that they will find warm shelter, and that he will supply their every need until he can figure out how to insure their silence. After Superman flies away, Ace leads Connie in an effort to escape the frozen hill; they both fall to their deaths. *Director:* Lee Sholem. *Writer:* Ben Peter Freeman.

Cast:

Ace	Dan Seymour
Connie	Veda Ann Borg
Candy Meyers	Frank Jenks
T-Ball	Norman Budd
Police Officer	Bob Williams

Mystery in Wax (May 11, 1953). Dr. John Hurley receives an invitation to a new unveiling at Madame Selena's wax museum in Metropolis.

Arriving at the festivities, he is joined by several prominent members of the community. Madame Selena enters and unveils her next morbid exhibit, saying that "it now becomes my unhappy duty to reveal to you the person who within the next six months will die!" The exhibit is revealed, and it is a wax sculpture of Hurley. Later, Hurley is found wandering aimlessly along a wharf where he casually jumps into the harbor, an apparent suicide. The next day, Perry White tells Clark and Lois that he knew Hurley, and that he is confident that Hurley was far from being a despondent fellow. Perry assigns Clark and Lois to investigate Madame Selena, believing that she is up to no good. At the museum, Lois and Clark seek an interview with Selena; while they wait for her to make an appearance they tour the "Hall of Death" exhibit where they find wax sculptures of recent suicide victims complete with tape-recorded ruminations on their deaths. Lois finds the whole thing morbid, and Selena prefers to speak with Clark. Selena explains that her predictions are the result of "hearing voices from another world." She also reports that her next prediction is imminent. Later, Clark, Lois and Perry attend Selena's unveiling, and this time the unveiling reveals a wax sculpture of Perry White. Perry is outraged and promises to expose Selena and eventually run her out of town. That night Perry is found wandering near the wharf, and eventually Inspector Henderson must report to Clark that Perry's shoes were found near where he jumped into the harbor. Lois returns to the wax museum where she overhears Selena telling her husband Andrew Dawn that there is room for additional exhibits in her private museum below. When the coast is clear, Lois takes the trap door to the underground hall where she finds all the "suicide victims" alive inside cells. Perry orders Lois to call Henderson, but Andrew uses chloroform to render Lois unconscious. Henderson and Clark are above in the museum, and Clark/Superman's X-ray vision reveals the underground prison. As Superman he descends into the underground prison to free the captives. Later, Perry explains that Andrew had impersonated the victims in order to make Selena's "predictions" come true. *Director:* Lee Sholem. *Writer:* Ben Peter Freeman.

Cast: *Madame Selena*   Myra McKinney
          Andrew Dawn   Lester Sharpe
          Dr. John Hurley   Steve Carr

Treasure of the Incas (May 18, 1953). On the streets of Metropolis, Prof. Laverra stops Lois and offers her $1000 if she will represent him inside an auction house where an Incan tapestry is about to be put up for bid. Seeing a story in his offer, she obliges and enters. A sinister, scar-faced fellow named Pedro Mendoza accosts Laverra at gunpoint; Mendoza forces Laverra into an alley where Laverra is promptly dispatched. When Lois returns from the auction carrying the tapestry, Mendoza introduces himself as a friend to Prof. Laverra, and says she should hand over the tapestry to Mendoza. Lois refuses and tells Mendoza that if Laverra wants the tapestry, he can find her at the *Daily Planet* building. Later, Lois shows the tapestry to Clark and points out that someone has cut out of the tapestry what appears to be a star. On a routine visit to the morgue, Clark discovers that the body of Laverra was found behind the auction house, and he calls Lois to identify the body. But before she can do so, she is met by Mendoza, who demands the tapestry. When she refuses, Mendoza knocks her unconscious and flees with the tapestry. Clark later tells Lois that Laverra was a professor at the University of Peru, and that she should let him handle the story from that point on. Undaunted, Lois makes reservations on a flight to Peru and convinces Perry to let her go; he agrees on the condition that she take Jimmy with her. Lois and Jimmy arrive in Peru where they learn from the police captain that an investigation is underway into the affair of Laverra. At the university they are met by Anselmo (Laverra's assistant), Dr. Questa and, to their great surprise, Clark. Questa explains that Laverra believed that the tapestry was the key to the location of a lost Incan treasure; moreover, Questa believes that the star missing from the tapestry is the clue that could lead to the treasure. That night, Anselmo enters the office and steals the tapestry, phoning Mendoza of his success. The next day, Clark suggests that they all travel to the Madira area where, after studying Incan folklore at the university, he believes the treasure may be

hidden. Anselmo volunteers to take Lois and Jimmy, and in the wilderness Anselmo deliberately strands the two reporters. Undaunted, Lois and Jimmy hike to the opening of a cave where they find Anselmo's car; as they enter, they are confronted by Mendoza and Anselmo, who chain the couple to the rock walls before igniting the fuse to a stick of dynamite. Just in time Superman crashes through the rock walls to hurl the dynamite at the fleeing villains. The explosion buries Mendoza and Anselmo, and Lois and Jimmy are released from their chains. The treasure is turned over to the authorities. *Director:* Thomas Carr. *Writer:* Howard Green.

Cast: *Pedro Mendoza*   Leonard Penn
          Prof. Laverra   Hal Gerard
          Police Captain   Martin Garralaga
          Dr. Questa   Juan Du Val
          Anselmo   Steve Carr
          Taxi Driver   Juan Rivero

Double Trouble (May 25, 1953). A ship docks in Metropolis harbor, and a health inspector named Fischer enters the cabin of Count Von Klaben. Fischer reveals his true identity by saying that he has been sent to accompany Von Klaben to a secret rendezvous where radioactive material stolen from U.S. Army bases in Germany will be exchanged. Von Klaben knocks Fischer unconscious, then disguises himself as a Frenchwoman before leaving the boat. Noticing the phony ambulance attendants, Von Klaben asks Jimmy to deliver a package to the attendants. When Jimmy takes the parcel to the two men, they shove him into the back of the ambulance and drive away, all before the horrified eyes of Lois. Jimmy is taken to the office of Dr. Albrecht, who opens the package to find it empty. Jimmy says he knows nothing about the package other than saying that a Frenchwoman asked him to deliver it to the ambulance attendants. Albrecht orders his henchmen to place Jimmy in a closet while Albrecht attempts to make sense of the apparent double cross. Albrecht later learns that Fischer was found dead in the cabin of Madame Charpentier; Albrecht is then certain that Von Klaben is masquerading as Madame Charpentier. Meanwhile, at police headquarters, Inspector Henderson tells Clark that Fischer was a German agent, and that male fingerprints were found all over the murder weapon. Clark reasons that a man is masquerading as a woman, and that this man is responsible for a major double cross in a smuggling operation. Retrieving the fingerprints from the police laboratory, Superman flies to Frankfurt, Germany, where Clark is met by Col. Redding of Army Intelligence. Redding tells Clark that there will be most likely a match, but before anything can be done Clark comes face to face with an orderly named Schumann who happens to be a dead ringer for Fischer. Major Lee then explains to Clark that a million dollars worth of radium is locked inside the safe. As they enter the safe to examine the radium, Schumann appears and locks them inside the safe. In the darkness, Clark is able to break the lock. Schumann makes his escape, but Superman returns to Metropolis where Clark returns to police headquarters. Henderson tells Clark that Madame Charpentier made her escape on a train, and Clark becomes Superman and intercepts the train. On board, Superman captures Von Klaben along with the stolen radium and returns Von Klaben and the radium to Metropolis. Meanwhile, Henderson and his officers have surrounded the office of Albrecht, who vows to fight to the death. Superman breaks down the door and holds Albrecht and his henchmen at bay. As Henderson enters, taking them into custody, Superman frees Jimmy from the closet. *Director:* Thomas Carr. *Writer:* Eugene Solow. **Cast:** *Fischer/Schumann*

	Howland Chamberlain
Dr. Albrecht	Rudolph Anders
Count Von Klaben/Madame Charpentier	
	Steve Carr
Fingerprint Man	Jimmy Dodd
Kreuger	John Baer

The Runaway Robot (June 1, 1953). Two petty crooks named Rocko and Mousie are holding up a jewelry store when they are interrupted by the arrival of a robot which tells them to "put up your hands, you're under arrest." The robot is so clumsy that Rocko and Mousie are able to flee, but the robot now goes out of control, dumping the loot onto the floor and then crushing the gems under its iron feet. As the robot makes for the store manager, a diminutive fellow named Horatio Hinkle enters and stops the robot. For his efforts at trying to stop the robbery, Horatio finds himself behind bars. Protesting, Horatio claims that he is a correspondent for *The Daily Planet,* which is affirmed by the arrival of Clark, Lois and Jimmy. Complicating matters is that the robot has now been stolen from the police department. Horatio warns Clark that Hero (the robot) would be a dangerous machine in the hands of evildoers. Meanwhile, Rocko and Mousie report to their boss, Chopper, that a mechanical man interrupted the jewel heist; Chopper ignores their excuses until another hood calls with the news that he has stolen the robot from police headquarters. Chopper also learns that the inventor is staying in Clark Kent's apartment. Chopper wants Horatio to reprogram Hero so that it will break into the vault at the Metropolis Trust Company, but when Horatio balks he and Hero are locked inside a closet. Horatio then uses the radio inside Hero's chest to call his assistant, Marvin, who in turn calls Clark. Lois intercepts the message and goes to Chopper's hideout. Lois is then taken captive by Chopper, and when Chopper threatens Lois, Horatio acquiesces. Hero is modified, and then sent to the trust company. While making its escape, Horatio programs Hero to pull fire alarms, bringing the fire department to the area. When Chopper sees what Horatio did, Mousie takes the controls, but the robot runs amok, making for Lois. Superman arrives, and Mousie directs Hero toward Superman. As the robot assaults Superman, the robot is pulled apart by the Man of Steel, falling into a pile of rubble. The stolen jewels are returned, and Chopper and his henchmen are jailed. *Director:* Thomas Carr. *Writer:* Dick Hamilton.

Cast:

Horatio Hinkle	Lucien Littlefield
Chopper	Russell Johnson
Rocko	Dan Seymour
Mousie	John Harmon
Marvin	Robert Easton
Police Officer	Herman Cantor

Drums of Death (June 8, 1953). Perry White's sister Kate and Jimmy Olsen are making a documentary film in Haiti, and recent footage screened in Perry's office shows a vicious voodoo witch doctor prowling the jungle. Perry is worried because he has not heard from Kate or Jimmy for over a week. Clark says that he will go to Haiti to find out what is going on, and Perry insists on going along. In Haiti, Clark and Perry are met by Barbarier, the local police official, who interprets the native drums beating in the background. William Johnson then introduces himself, offering to guide Clark and Perry into the jungles. Then Johnson sees a frame enlargement of the voodoo witch doctor and tells them that he wants nothing to do with the witch doctors of the area. Clark examines a bandanna Johnson left behind and ruminates on its significance. Clark then finds an eavesdropper named Masters, who agrees to guide them into the jungle. Later, Superman visits the jungle and, using his X-ray vision and super-hearing, he finds inside a cave Kate under the spell of the witch doctor; the witch doctor demands to know why Kate was taking pictures inside their sacred temple, but she has no answers. Later, Superman visits Kate, and he discovers that she is in some kind of hypnotic trance. She claims that the paper chains around her neck are actually iron chains, and she chants that she must obey Legbo, the witch doctor. Superman then finds Jimmy, who is only pretending to be under the spell. Superman tells Jimmy to continue the charade until Superman can tie everything together. The next day, Clark and Barbarier visit Dr. Jerrod to test the bandanna; meanwhile, Masters leads Perry into a trap at the temple. Legbo orders Masters to be locked up, and Perry is led to join Kate and Jimmy. Legbo places the trio inside a chamber whose walls begin closing in on them. Dr. Jerrod reports to Clark that the stain on the bandanna was nothing but cocoa butter, and Clark urgently leaves the office. As the walls are about to come together, crushing the prisoners, Superman bursts through the wall, saving them and stopping Legbo. Superman then notes that cocoa butter can be used to darken a man's skin, and at that point he takes a cloth and rubs away at Legbo's face, revealing Legbo to be Johnson. Perry says that Masters was also in on the plot to scare people away from the "temple" while Johnson and Masters searched for an ancient treasure. *Director:* Lee Sholem. *Writer:* Dick Hamilton.

Cast:

William Johnson/Legbo	Henry Corden
Masters	Leonard Mudie
Kate White	Mabel Albertson
Barbarier	Milton Wood
Dr. Jerrod	George Hamilton
Voodoo Drummer	Smoki Whitfield

The Evil Three (June 15, 1953). A vacationing Perry White and Jimmy Olsen stay at the Hotel Bayou, a once prominent but now broken-down hotel in the middle of nowhere. Perry and Jimmy encounter the three strange people living there: Macey Taylor, Col. Brand, and the wheelchair-bound Elsa. As Perry and Jimmy enter the hotel lobby, they are met by Macey, who warns them not to stay in the hotel because it is haunted by the ghost of Macey's uncle, George Taylor, but Perry remains adamant, preferring to stay the night so that they can fish the nearby stream in the morning. Perry smells a story, and so he returns to his car and uses the car phone to call Clark; Perry asks Clark to find everything he can on George Taylor. That night, Jimmy sees the ghost of Uncle George, but Perry tells him he's only dreaming. Later, Perry and Jimmy find a hidden doorway that leads to an earthen cellar. Despite Jimmy's protestations, Perry leads him down the ramp to the cellar where they find a skeleton; Perry believes that the skeleton is the remains of George Taylor. Just then Macey appears and knocks both Perry and Jimmy unconscious. Elsa remains at the top of the ramp, screaming maniacally how she wants no more killing, but Macey ignores her and then orders the Colonel to destroy Perry's car. Meanwhile, Clark is unable to call back to Perry, and this worries him so he turns into Superman and heads for the Hotel Bayou. Perry and Jimmy escape the cellar and return to their rooms where they begin to pack, but Elsa stops them with a shotgun, telling Perry and Jimmy that Macey murdered George in order to get George's buried loot. Macey and the Colonel, she continues, scare people away from the hotel so they can search for the location of Uncle George's buried money. Elsa then tells them that she'll lead them to the money if Perry and Jimmy will help her escape Macey. They agree, and with Elsa at the top of the ramp, and Perry and Jimmy back in the cellar digging where Elsa claims the treasure is buried, Macey pushes Elsa down the ramp before trapping Perry and Jimmy inside the cave. Superman arrives and saves Perry and Jimmy. The evil three are then taken into custody by the police. *Director:* Thomas Carr. *Writer:* Ben Peter Freeman.

Cast: *Macey Taylor*   Rhys Williams
       Col. Brand   Jonathan Hale
       Elsa   Cecil Elliott

The Riddle of the Chinese Jade (June 22, 1953). Harry Wong agrees to help small-time hood John Greer steal the priceless Kwan Yin jade from Chinatown philanthropist Lu Sung, who wants to donate the jade to the Metropolis museum. Wong's motive is simple: he wants cash so that he can marry Lu Sung's niece, Lilly. When Wong has second thoughts, Greer assures him that no one will be hurt, and that the jade statue will glean millions on the open market. Wong reluctantly agrees. Wong tells Greer that he can gain access to Lu Sung's residence via a tunnel beneath the street that links Wong's home with that of Lu Sung. An explosive is then planted inside Lu Sung's business. Meanwhile, in Lu Sung's apartment, Clark and Lois are interviewing Lu Sung and his niece about his philanthropy; suddenly, the bomb explodes and all but Lilly rush to the business below. Wong and Greer enter from behind the hidden door and take the statue, but when Lilly tries to stop them she is taken captive by Greer. Wong crosses the street to Lu Sung's business where he feigns no knowledge of how or why an explosion would rock Lu Sung's. The discussion is shattered by Lois's scream from upstairs; Clark, Wong, and Lu Sung rush to Lois's aid, and discover that the jade is missing along with Lilly. Clark then notices bamboo dust on Wong's shirt; Clark tells Inspector Henderson that the jade was packed in a box with bamboo dust. Back at Wong's apartment, Wong tries to convince Lilly that he took the jade in order to make a better life for the two of them. She rebukes Wong and he turns to Greer, demanding payment immediately. Greer balks, and a fight ensues with Wong knocked cold. Greer takes Wong and Lilly to the tunnel where he opens a water main, allowing the tunnel to fill with water. Greer then enters Lu Sung's apartment where he knocks Lu Sung unconscious and takes Lois hostage. Meanwhile, Superman uses his X-ray vision to find Wong and Lilly in the tunnel; surrounded by fascinated members of Chinatown, Superman tears up the street and rescues Wong and Lilly. Greer now appears from Lu Sung's, holding Lois hostage in an attempt to get away with the jade. Superman stops him. When Lu Sung refuses to file charges against Wong, Henderson looks the other way, leaving Lilly and Wong to be wed. *Director:* Thomas Carr. *Writer:* Richard Fielding.

Cast: *John Greer*   James Craven
       Harry Wong   Victor Sen Yung
       Lu Sung   Paul Burns
       Lilly   Gloria Saunders

The Human Bomb (June 29, 1953). A wealthy businessman named Conway wagers $100,000 that fellow businessman "Bet-a-Million" Butler cannot hold Superman at bay for 30 minutes. Butler takes the challenge, and arrives at the *Daily Planet* building as "Mr. Bomb." Lois scoffs at him, at which point he grabs and chains himself to her with handcuffs. Under his trenchcoat are several sticks of dynamite attached to a detonator. Jimmy rushes to Perry's office with the news just as Butler takes Lois out onto the ledge many stories above the streets of Metropolis. Butler tells Perry that he wants to see Superman, but when Clark hears of this he accuses Perry of staging a publicity stunt and angrily leaves the building. Superman then appears, landing on the ledge next to Butler. Superman takes the stick of dynamite given to Jimmy, and flies into the sky where it detonates. Convinced that Butler is on the level, Superman returns to hear Butler's demands. Butler says that he is earning a wager, that he has no plans to hurt anyone or to steal anything permanently. All Superman has to do is allow Butler's henchmen to rob a nearby museum. Superman agrees, but also states that he refuses to remain with Butler. Superman enters an office where he sits at a desk, casting a shadow on the wall. He then tells Jimmy to get a tape recorder. When Butler questions whether Superman is still in the office, Superman has Jimmy record his answer:

"No comment until the time limit is up." Perry then moves into the window to block Butler's view at which point Superman changes place with Police Inspector Hill, whose shadow is similar to that of Superman's. Butler asks another question, and Jimmy replays the response. With Superman's plan working, he flies to the museum and stops the robbery. Jimmy, however, gets the idea that Butler is a fake and tries to defeat him on the ledge, but Jimmy loses his footing and falls. Superman catches him, and during the commotion Inspector Hill and the other officers capture Butler. When Butler tells them that the whole thing was nothing more than a wager, Lois slaps him. *Director:* Lee Sholem. *Writer:* Richard Fielding.

Cast: *Bet-a-Million Butler*   Trevor Bardette
       Inspector Hill   Marshall Reed
       Conway   Dennis Moore
       Officer Riley   Ted Ryan
       Henchman   Lou Lubin
       Receptionist   Aline Towne

Czar of the Underworld (July 6, 1953). Clark Kent and Inspector Henderson are in Hollywood assisting in the production of a film based on Clark's gangland exposé of kingpin Luigi Dinelli. Like all mobsters, however, Dinelli plays rough. The first incident occurs on the eve of their departure for Hollywood; with Clark and Henderson in Clark's office, Dinelli phones and harangues Clark about the series of articles Clark wrote. Unknown to Clark, Dinelli's henchmen are in a nearby office building, their gunsights fixed on him. The assassination attempt fails, and Dinelli tries another plan. He sends a henchman named Ollie to masquerade as the studio chauffeur. Ollie picks up Clark and Henderson at the airport, but instead of taking them to the studio he takes them to an abandoned garage on the pretext of checking the tires. Ollie locks Clark and Henderson inside and tells an accomplice that Dinelli wants to take the two himself. In the dark garage, Superman knocks out the guard and frees Henderson. Further attempts are made on the production company, including the assassination of an actor. Clark states that he is going to spend the night at the studio to protect the production, hoping this will bring Dinelli and his mob into the open. But Superman himself visits Dinelli and takes him back to the studio where he confines the mobster to Clark's trailer. Superman then brings Henderson to the studio where they find a hose attached to the exhaust from a nearby car going into the trailer. Superman breaks in and rescues Dinelli. Superman then sees a man in the rigging above; he jumps to the rigging and captures him. The man turns out to be the studio guard, but further investigation reveals that the guard is actually Frank Dinelli, Luigi's brother. But before he can confess, Dinelli slays his brother. Dinelli is apprehended, but he claims that they have nothing on him. Superman sternly decrees that a murder charge will be filed against Dinelli for killing his own brother. *Director:* Thomas Carr. *Writer:* Eugene Solow.

Cast: *Luigi Dinelli*   Tony Caruso
       Ollie   Paul Fix
       Studio Guard/Frank Dinelli
             John Maxwell
       Postello   Roy Gordon
       Director   Steve Carr

Ghost Wolf (July 13, 1953). There's trouble at Lone Pine Timber Company, the primary supplier of newsprint for the *Daily Planet.* Timberjacks are quitting their jobs, scared off by reports of a mysterious lady and her "ghost wolf." When operations manager Sam Garvin reports the news to Perry White, Perry orders Garvin to hang on until he sends a team of reporters to look into the situation. Clark, Lois and Jimmy are sent to Lone Pine where, on the final leg of their journey, Clark notices that support struts of the Devil's Gorge trestle have been weakened. Clark quickly becomes Superman and flies to the gorge, where he supports the trestle as the train passes. Superman as Clark then returns to the train where he feigns ignorance about the threat. Later, the three reporters interrogate Garvin, who explains that rumors are circulating throughout the forest that a woman prowls the forest and changes into a werewolf. Clark scoffs at his remarks and announces that he intends to get to the bottom of the mystery. That night, the wolf visits Lois in her cabin, frightening her into near hysterics. Clark wishes to search for the wolf, but Lois insists on staying with Clark and Jimmy in the 112–bed bunk house. The next morning, Lois finds a golden earring in the woods, but before she can discern its meaning she is again visited by the wolf. Her screams bring Clark and Jimmy, and this time Clark orders Lois and Jimmy to stay put while he investigates. Lois, as usual, ignores Clark's advice; she and Jimmy pack clubs and go on their own to investigate. Soon they discover that the forest is burning, and Garvin sees through his binoculars timberjack Olivier starting the spot fires. As the fire spreads, Lois and Jimmy find themselves surrounded by the inferno, but Superman arrives in time to save them. Meanwhile, Garvin has cornered Olivier, and nearby is Babette DuLoque and her timber wolf. Garvin recognizes Babette as the daughter of the late founder of Lone Pine; Olivier orders Babette to send the wolf against Garvin, but she refuses. Superman appears and saves Garvin from Olivier. It is then revealed that Olivier had been poisoning Babette's mind with the lie that Garvin murdered her father to gain control of the company; Garvin says that her father died of natural causes and that Garvin has her inheritance safely locked away. Olivier's scheme was to marry Babette, thereby getting her inheritance. Meanwhile, the fire rages, threatening to destroy the entire forest and nearby towns. Superman flies the end of a telephone line through the clouds in the hope of attracting lightning that will eventually cause a downpour. His strategy works; the rains extinguish the fire. *Director:* Lee Sholem. *Writer:* Dick Hamilton.

Cast:

Sam Garvin	Stanley Andrews
Babette DuLoque	Jane Adams
Jacques Olivier	Lou Krugman
Railroad Conductor	Harold Goodwin

The Unknown People—Part One (July 20, 1953). Clark and Lois are taken by public relations officer John Craig to the Havenhurst experimental site of the National Oil Company, site of the deepest oil well in America, near the small town of Silsby. Pop Shannon, the company's guard, tells Craig that the drilling operation is being shut down. Surprised, Craig leads Clark and Lois to Bill Corrigan, project manager, who says that upon his

recommendation the site is being mothballed. That night at the Silsby hotel, Clark and Lois decide to take another look around the site. At the site, the cap to the well is opened and out pop two humanoid creatures of small stature. When Clark and Lois arrive, they find Pop Shannon dead; Lois believes that the old man died of heart failure, but when Clark leaves to look around, the two creatures appear before Lois. Upon hearing Lois's scream, Clark returns to hear Lois tell of what she had just seen. Later, Corrigan reveals to Clark that the reason drilling stopped was because the drill broke through into empty space, indicating that maybe the earth is hollow. Corrigan adds that he found microcosmic organisms on the drill bit, and he thinks there may be a civilization at the center of the earth. Clark believes that members of the civilization may be wandering the streets of Silsby. As Clark and Corrigan start to leave, Clark notices that Pop's oranges are glowing in the dark. Clark reasons that the creatures handled the oranges and that they may be radioactive and hence dangerous to the community. Meanwhile, the two creatures are befriended by a little girl who plays ball with them. At the Silsby hotel, Luke Benson is leading a mob that wants to expel the creatures, but Clark demands that the authorities take charge. At the girl's house, her mother enters the bedroom and screams at the sight of the little creatures. The scream brings Benson's mob to the house, where they are met by Superman. He tells the mob that the girl is unharmed. Benson is not assuaged and challenges Superman, who takes Benson's shotgun and twists it into worthless metal. Superman says that it is men like Benson "who make it difficult for people to understand one another." Undaunted, Benson orders his men to get their dogs and chase the creatures to the river. Superman orders Corrigan to take the little girl to the hospital for decontamination, then flies to the nearby dam where he finds Benson's mob holding the two creatures at bay. At this point, the narrator speaks: "Hunted by men and dogs! Trapped on the high parapet of the dam! These strange little creatures from the dark center of the earth are now at the mercy of Luke Benson and his mob! What will happen? Stand by for a preview of Part Two of 'The Unknown People' in the *Adventures of Superman*."

The Unknown People—Part Two (July 27, 1953). Superman warns Benson not to harm the creatures. Benson fires point-blank at Superman and realizes it cannot injure Superman. A member of the mob fires his rifle at the one of the creatures. Hit, the creature falls from the dam, but Superman catches him and takes him to the hospital and safety. The second creature flees to a mining shack for shelter, but Benson and his mob set the shack ablaze. Convinced that they have destroyed the creature, the mob makes its way back to town. But the creature has escaped through the floorboards and makes his way back to the well. Meanwhile, Superman has convinced Dr. Reed, the physician in attendance, to ignore the superintendent's admonitions about the creature; Dr. Reed then treats the little man. Craig and Corrigan arrive and tell Superman that the mob is on its way to the hospital. Losing patience, Superman once again confronts Benson and his mob; he warns them that no one is allowed into the hospital. When someone fires a shot that nearly hits Lois, Superman loses all patience and forcibly collects all the guns. Meanwhile, two creatures led by the victim carry a ray gun into the upper world and make their way toward the hospital. When the victim spies Benson, they open fire. Superman steps in the way and saves Benson's life. Superman carries the injured creature to the well where the others take him back to the center of the earth. A few moments later and the well is destroyed, apparently by the creatures themselves. *Director:* Lee Sholem. *Writer:* Richard Fielding.

Cast:

Bill Corrigan	Walter Reed
Luke Benson	Jeff Corey
John Craig	Ray Walker
Sheriff	Stanley Andrews
Pop Shannon	J. Farrell MacDonald
Hospital Superintendent	Frank Reicher
Weber	Hal K. Dawson
Little Girl	Beverly Washburn
Mother	Margia Dean
Jeff Reagan	Byron Foulger
Creatures	Billy Curtis, Jack Banbury, Jerry Marvin, Tony Baris

Crime Wave (August 3, 1953). Metropolis is at the mercy of a crime wave. In Perry White's office, the Citizens Committee is meeting to brainstorm ways to check the violence. Perry introduces Metropolis's "number one citizen," Superman, who vows to clean up the city. Walter Canby, representing the committee for clean government, promises his full cooperation. Superman acknowledges that Nick Marone and Big Ed Bullock are among the local crime kingpins, but the identity of Mr. Big remains a mystery. At Mr. Big's hideout, Marone and Bullock are worried that Superman is going to win the war on crime, but Mr. Big, who is always in shadow, assuages their fears with plans of his own to control Superman. Mr. Big first orders the mob to "pour it on"; and this leads to Marone's and Bullock's arrest; but since the police cannot charge them with any crimes, they are released. Marone and Bullock regroup at Mr. Big's hideout, where Mr. Big outlines his plan; he'll send his moll Sally all over town getting all the information she can on Superman, including who his closest friends are, where he appears and so on. Sally later returns with movie footage of Clark Kent entering an alley and Superman emerging. Sally then calls Clark and tells him that Mr. Big is ready to turn himself in only if Superman will meet him at a hideout on Dover's Cliff near Willow Falls. Clark tells Perry to hold the latest edition because Clark will have the scoop of the century by announcing the identity of Mr. Big. Superman flies to the hideout where he is met by the Professor, who demands that Superman enter the room. Superman obliges, and then the doors slam shut, trapping Superman. As Superman tries to break through the doors, the Professor starts a machine that sends lightning bolts against Superman. Superman struggles and then collapses; it appears that Mr. Big has defeated Superman. At this moment, Mr. Big enters; he turns out to be Walter Canby. Superman then swings into action and captures the whole lot. Back at Perry's office, Perry tells his pressmen to run the edition, disappointed in Clark's failure. But just then Superman arrives with Walter Canby in tow, saving Metropolis from Mr. Big's reign of terror. *Note:* See discussion of text in introduction. *Director:* Thomas Carr. *Writer:* Ben Peter Freeman.

Cast: *Walter Canby*   John Eldredge
    Nick Marone   Phil Van Zandt
    Big Ed Bullock   Al Eben
    The Professor   Joseph Mell
    Sally   Barbara Fuller
    Tony   Bobby Barber

Season 2

Five Minutes to Doom (September 14, 1953). Joe Winters, a county building inspector and family man found guilty of murder, is not an ordinary thug, which intrigues *The Daily Planet*. As a result, he is offered $10,000 if he will tell his story to the *Planet*. Knowing that his family will need the money, Winters agrees. He tells Clark and Lois how he suspected a contractor named Wayne of using substandard steel in building an overpass. Winters says that he had many encounters with Baker, the project manager, until Baker attacked him in the supervisor's office at the construction site. During the scuffle, someone shot Baker and then dropped Winters' gun into the office. Winters was arrested and convicted of Baker's murder, but Winters believes that Wayne had Baker killed to keep Winters from exposing Wayne's scam. Clark offers him hope, saying that the *Planet* will look into the affairs of Wayne. Unknown to Clark and Lois, however, is that their conversation with Winters is overheard by a prison informant who calls Wayne and tells him what the reporters are up to. Wayne immediately dispatches a thug with a bomb to intercept the reporters. While driving back to Metropolis, Clark and Lois pick up a hitchhiker. He places his lunchbox in the back seat, and when he reaches his destination he leaves the lunchbox in the car; Lois immediately wonders why he would do this, and so she takes the wheel while Clark takes the box and leaps from the moving automobile, rolling down a hillside as the bomb explodes. Lois returns, but since the bomb has blown away most of Clark's clothing, leaving his Superman costume exposed, he asks her to throw him his trenchcoat. Lois then states that she has never seen anyone act so courageous, and Clark replies, "You mean it's something you'd expect Superman to do?" Lois sheepishly agrees, and Clark replies, "Lois, sometimes I think you

underestimate me." (This exchange between Clark and the *new* Lois Lane, now played by Noel Neill, sets the stage for the new relationship between the two characters in the remaining episodes; a relationship that is softer than the often spiteful resentment by Lois toward Clark in the first season). Clark and Jimmy inspect the scene of the murder and determine that someone could have shot Baker just as Winters described. Meanwhile, Lois compiles all the data on the site, noting that someone could have made millions off the project by substituting substandard material. She goes to Wayne's office where his secretary offers to show her his files, but Wayne stops her and then throws Lois out. Jimmy, disguised as a vacuum cleaner salesman, gains entry to Wayne's office and appropriates the papers. With proof now in their possession, Winters should be able to get a new trial; however, the phone lines are dead so Clark is unable to make contact with the governor. Superman takes over, flying to the governor's mansion where the governor signs the reprieve. As the clock spells doom for Winters, already strapped to the chair, Superman crashes through the prison wall and saves Winters. *Director:* Thomas Carr. *Writer:* Monroe Manning.

Cast: *Joe Winters*   Dabbs Greer
    Warden   Sam Flint
    Wayne   Lewis Russell
    Baker   Dale Van Sickel
    Turk   John Kellogg
    Miss Cooper   Jean Willes
    Mrs. Winters   Lois Hall
    Governor   William E. Green

The Big Squeeze (September 21, 1953). Clark Kent arrives at the office of Mr. Foster, head of Metropolis Furriers Inc., to present Foster's good-natured employee, Dan Grayson, with the *Daily Planet* Citizen-of-the-Year award. Foster assures Clark that no man deserves the award more than Dan, a pillar of the community. Meanwhile, Dan gets a phone call from Luke Maynard, an old acquaintance, who sarcastically congratulates Dan. Intimidated by the call, Dan forgetfully locks himself inside the vault, triggering the alarm. Foster and Clark rush to his aid, but Dan says only that he accidentally accomplished what he had always feared: locking himself in with the time lock on and the poisonous gases leaking into the vault to preserve the furs. When Foster laments that they'll need "a Jimmy Valentine," Clark replies, "Maybe I can get one." Clark then excuses himself and turns into Superman, who flies through the window and removes the vault door, freeing Dan. Dan returns home where he is met by his wife, Peg. Just as he relates the incident to her, the doorbell rings and Dan is confronted by Luke. Luke tells Dan all about Luke's blackmail business; Luke tells Dan he will remain silent about Dan's sordid past as long as the money keeps flowing in. Dan' young son Tim has overheard the conversation, and despondently refuses to speak with his father as Dan tries to explain the circumstances. Meanwhile, at *The Daily Planet*, Perry White orders Clark, Lois and Jimmy to gather background material on Dan. Dan meets a second time with Luke, agreeing to pay him hush money, but Luke demands that Dan steal furs for him. As Dan contemplates Luke's extortion, Clark, Lois and Jimmy arrive to tell Dan the story has hit the papers. Everyone is jubilant except Dan, who tells them to find another man. The next day, Tim visits Clark and tells Clark about what he overheard. Clark departs for Metropolis Furs where he confronts Dan. Dan explains to Clark that when he was a youth he stole a car as a prank and was sentenced to three years, and that Luke Maynard is blackmailing him. Clark tells Dan that perhaps Superman can help. But Luke steals the furs and casts blame on Dan. Perry White is furious over Clark's choice for Citizen-of-the-Year, and Clark is obviously angered at Maynard's audacity. Meanwhile, Dan has secreted himself in the back of Maynard's getaway car. Dan confronts Luke, but Luke gets the best of him, holding him prisoner. Jimmy, who had been trailing them, calls Clark and reports Luke's whereabouts. Luke keeps Dan captive in a lead-lined mountain cave that thwarts Superman's X-ray vision, but Luke's nervous habit of cracking walnuts arouses Superman's super-hearing, and in a moment Superman crashes through the cave wall, saving Dan and capturing Luke. Later, Clark gives Dan the award, making it clear that people who make a mistake should always get

a second chance. *Director:* Thomas Carr. *Writer:* David Chantler.

Cast:

Dan Grayson	Hugh Beaumont
Luke Maynard	John Kellogg
Peg Grayson	Aline Towne
Tim Grayson	Bradley Mora
Mr. Foster	Harry Cheshire
Al	Ted Ryan
Police Officer	Reed Howes

The Man Who Could Read Minds (September 28, 1953). While Inspector Henderson directs a citywide dragnet in an effort to capture a notorious burglar known as the Phantom, Jimmy and Lois scour the streets for the burglar on their own. By chance, Lois spots a hooded figure running across a lawn. Jimmy gives chase and eventually tackles the man, but the burglar breaks away and flees to his car. Jimmy picks up an object left by the man and then he and Lois give chase in their car. The burglars fire at Jimmy and Lois, and the shots bring Clark, Perry and Henderson to the scene. Clark orders Perry to stop the car, then jumps out while Perry continues. Clark becomes Superman and rejoins the pursuit. The Phantom fires once more, hitting Lois's tire, causing her to lose control and head for a precipice, but Superman stops the car just in time. Perry arrives, and Jimmy shows them what he found: a toy top, a giveaway item from the Tip Top cafe in Metropolis. Later, a cafe parking valet named Monk, who is the Phantom *sans* mask, parks a luxury car, and before exiting jots down the address of the wealthy owners. Inside the club, the audience is entertained by Swami Amada and his assistant Lora. Lora wanders among the audience members, borrowing personal items and asking the swami to identify the items she holds. (Lora is secretly speaking into a tiny transmitter, giving the swami the correct answers.) Before retrieving the personal items, Lora makes wax molds of household keys. With Monk's knowledge of the locations and the fact that the owners are away from home, the perfect burglary is set in motion. Lois and Jimmy make the connection between the club and their burglaries, and Jimmy decides to masquerade as a foreign dignitary out on the town. When Swami Amada takes the bait, Jimmy and Lois sneak back to the hotel room and await the Phantom. When he shows they get the drop on him, but their plans are foiled when Swami Amada and Lora arrive and get the drop on Lois and Jimmy. The swami orders them out onto the ledge, but Superman arrives and takes Swami Amada and his gang into custody. *Director:* Thomas Carr. *Writer:* Roy Hamilton.

Cast:
Swami Amada	Lawrence Dobkin
Lora	Veola Vonn
Monk	Richard Karlan
Duke	Tom Bernard
Sergeant Healey	Russell Custer

Jet Ace (October 5, 1953). Perry White's nephew Chris is testing a new U.S. Air Force fighter jet at a local air base. Gen. Summers is joined by Perry, Clark, Lois and Jimmy for Chris's final test; suddenly, Chris begins to lose consciousness and the fighter is in trouble. Clark feigns being upset by the impending crash and leaves the room. He then changes into Superman and rescues Chris and the fighter. Back at Summers's office, they all rejoice at Chris's survival, but reporter Steve Martin, from a competing newspaper, is rebuffed by Chris; an angry Martin denounces the Air Force for playing favorites with *The Daily Planet*. Chris returns to his mountain cabin for rest and relaxation. Fearing that someone may be after the plans to the fighter plane, Chris hides the plans in the barrel of his shotgun. Just then two thugs, Frenchy and Nate, kidnap Chris. Perry is alerted to Chris's disappearance by helicopter pilot Tim Mallory, and assigns Clark and Jimmy to investigate. They find Chris's cabin empty, but a short time later they are visited by Frenchy and Nate, who begin searching the cabin for the hidden plans. Finding nothing, Frenchy and Nate exit. Clark tells Jimmy to remain at the cabin, and Clark leaves for the back country where he changes to Superman. Superman stops the thugs' car, and Frenchy explains that he and Nate are under orders from an unknown mastermind. Back at the cabin, the masked mastermind attempts to coerce Chris into revealing the location of the plans; Chris is able to remove his captor's mask, exposing Martin as the master spy. At that moment, Mallory returns to the cabin, and Chris is

forced to expel him, but before Mallory leaves Chris reminds Mallory to make sure that Perry receives the letter he sent him. Mallory agrees, but is puzzled by Chris's statement because he doesn't remember taking any letter from Chris. This is all a ruse to make Martin believe that Perry has the plans. Martin falls for it, ties Chris up and sets the cabin aflame. Mallory meets with Perry and tells him that Chris is back at the cabin, at which point Clark exits, becomes Superman and arrives in time to save Chris. Clark tells Perry to report that Chris died in the fire. In Summers's office, all are gathered for a second test of the fighter when Chris's voice comes across the speaker. Martin is unnerved, and when Chris appears, he flees. Chris gives chase and catches Martin in another office where the spy is knocked cold. *Director:* Thomas Carr. *Writer:* David Chantler.

Cast:
Chris White	Lane Bradford
Steve Martin	Larry J. Blake
Gen. Summers	Selmer Jackson
Tim Mallory	Jim Hayward
Frenchy	Richard Reeves
Nate	Ric Roman

Shot in the Dark (October 12, 1953). After Perry White scolds Clark for missing a major scoop—Superman's rescue of ten people from a burning building—Clark is visited by an elderly lady named Harriet Hooper, who constantly pleas for help from Superman. Her references to Clark as Superman intrigue Jimmy; Harriet displays a photograph of Clark changing into Superman in an alley. Now shocked, Clark says that there must be some kind of explanation for this picture. Harriet leads Clark and Jimmy to her young nephew Alan, an avid amateur photographer. Jimmy queries Alan about the photograph, and Alan explains that he took it with an infrared flash in an alley behind the *Daily Planet* building. Clark adamantly disavows the photograph, explaining that it had to be a double exposure, combining Clark and Superman onto a single negative. Clark smells smoke and finds a trash can aflame in Alan's darkroom. Clark extinguishes the fire, and Alan explains that a man has offered large sums of cash for a photograph Alan took of a man near a bouquet of tulips, prompting him to wonder if that same man might have entered the studio. Alan notices that the Superman negative is missing. Clark secures the photograph of the man and the tulips so he can check against records at police headquarters. Returning to his office, Clark is confronted by the man, who demands the photograph. Jimmy snatches the photo away from the man; the man gives chase with Clark following, and both are joined by Lois in the pursuit. Jimmy then hops aboard a subway train, and Clark overhears the man phoning his henchmen to derail the train. As Superman, he crashes through the tunnel and short-circuits the rails, causing the train to slow to a stop. Jimmy and Clark show the photograph to Inspector Henderson, who claims that the man in the photograph is Burt Burnside, a confidence man who reportedly died in a traffic accident a few years back. Clark plants a story that says that the photograph the mobsters want will be aboard a mail truck in the morning, and sure enough Burnside's henchmen stop and rob the truck. Unknown to them, however, the driver is actually Superman, who feigns death while the henchmen cart off the mail sacks. At their hideout, Burnside and his henchmen discover that the mail sacks are full of shredded copies of *The Daily Planet*. Just then Superman crashes through the doors, apprehending the henchmen and holding Burnside at bay. Burnside offers Superman a deal: If Superman flies him to safety, he'll destroy the photograph of Clark changing into Superman. Superman, however, makes no deals with crooks; spying the photograph in the safe, Superman surreptitiously uses his heat vision to destroy the photograph. Superman tells Burnside he'll have to deal with the police, and flies away. When Henderson, Clark and Jimmy arrive, Burnside opens the safe, but the photograph is burned. Angered, Burnside removes a derringer from his shoe and fires point blank at Clark to prove that Clark is Superman. Clark, uninjured, removes a silver dollar from his breast pocket, saying that his lucky dollar deflected the bullet. Burnside is led away, and Henderson laughs at the idea that Clark could be Superman. *Director:* George Blair. *Writer:* David Chantler.

Cast:

Burt Burnside	John Eldredge
Alan	Billy Gray
Slugger	Frank Richards
Bill	Alan Lee

The Defeat of Superman (October 19, 1953). Mobster Happy King turns to scientist Meldini for a method of eliminating Superman. Meldini believes that a native element of Superman's home planet, though harmless to him there, might be dangerous to him here on Earth. To prove his point, King sends henchman Ruffles with a machine gun filled with bullets made from various elements to a warehouse. There, Ruffles sets up the machine gun timed to a motion picture camera so that each frame represents a bullet fired at Superman. King then phones in a false report, sending Superman to the warehouse where he is struck by a spray of bullets from the machine gun. At one point, Superman grabs his shoulder. Ruffles retrieves the camera and the film is processed, and upon projection Meldini discovers that the element of interest is kryptonite. King then has Lois and Jimmy kidnapped, bringing Superman to a basement in an old building. Superman arrives, but Lois and Jimmy warn him that their captives have kryptonite. Jimmy brings the small sample closer to Superman, who suddenly drops to the floor. At Superman's suggestion, Jimmy rams the kryptonite into a lead pipe, and Superman revives. Superman decides that the best place for the element is at the bottom of the ocean, and so he hurls the pipe across the sky toward the ocean. King, Ruffles and Meldini, escaping in a car, are distracted by the furious sound of the flying container, causing Ruffles to lose control and plunge off a coastal cliff. *Director:* Thomas Carr. *Writer:* Jackson Gillis.

Cast:

Happy King	Peter Mamakos
Meldini	Maurice Cass
Ruffles	Sid Tomack

Superman in Exile (October 26, 1953). The nuclear stockpile at an experimental station called Project X malfunctions, and there will be a catastrophe if the reactor is not controlled by removing critical rods. Adams, the director of the station, summons Superman, who enters the radioactive chamber and shuts down the threatening reactor. Unfortunately, Superman's endeavor has left him dangerously radioactive. After chastising the scientists for dabbling in things that could harm people, Superman exiles himself to a cabin atop Blue Peak. The contamination is so high that Superman emits a glow in the dark; dejected and now introspective, he seems doomed to a life of isolation. With Superman in exile, crime begins to run rampant in Metropolis; a jewel thief named Ferdinand unleashes his two cronies, Regan and Skinny, upon Metropolis jewelry stores. The citizens of Metropolis are anxious; the police department is abused and overworked; and reporters at *The Daily Planet* wonder about the whereabouts of Clark Kent. When Lois stumbles upon Ferdinand's plans, she is kidnapped. When Superman hears of this, he decides to test the theory of the atomic scientists that may reverse the contamination effect. Superman leaps off the peak and flies into an electrical storm where countless bolts of lightning strike him; the massive electrical charge neutralizes the radioactivity. With Lois's life in peril, Superman appears, startling the incredulous Ferdinand, who is apprehended. With the crime wave averted, Clark Kent returns to his office where Lois points out that Superman and Clark are never around at the same time. Clark feigns innocence, and Lois replies, "You and Superman, I still wonder." *Director:* Thomas Carr. *Writer:* Jackson Gillis.

Cast:

Ferdinand	Leon Askin
Adams	Joe Forte
Allen	Robert S. Carson
Regan	Phil Van Zandt
Skinny	John Harmon
Fred	Don Dillaway
Sheriff	Gregg Barton

A Ghost for Scotland Yard (November 2, 1953). While on a trip to England, Clark and Jimmy find themselves in the midst of a media circus: A famed magician named Brockhurst, killed five years ago in a traffic accident, is expected to reappear this very night. Clark receives word from Perry White that Perry's British friend Sir Arthur McCready is somehow involved in this unusual situation. Clark and Jimmy travel to Sir Arthur's estate, where they are met by Sir Arthur's wife Mabel and their maid, Betty. Mabel tells them that Sir Arthur is neurotic over the whole mess, and that he drove away to seek Brockhurst. Clark sneaks away and changes into Superman. Meanwhile, Sir Arthur in his Rolls Royce hears Brockhurst's voice, taunting Sir Arthur for seemingly causing Brockhurst's death. As he drives nervously along the cliff-side road, Sir Arthur suddenly sees a monstrous image of Brockhurst's face in the clouds. The image is so paralyzing that Sir Arthur faints at the wheel. Superman arrives in time to keep the car from plunging off the cliff and returns Sir Arthur to his estate. Inspector Farrington of Scotland Yard, arriving to investigate the case, receives a threatening telephone call from Brockhurst. Meanwhile, Superman returns to the coast where he finds a strip of 35mm motion picture film; he examines it and discovers that it features the face of Brockhurst. Superman reasons that this strip of film must have been projected onto the clouds to create the ghost effect. Back at the estate, Jimmy finds a *live* Brockhurst holed up in the carriage house; the mad Brockhurst proclaims that he is fulfilling his master illusion—to return from the dead, and then reveals his plan of revenge against Sir Arthur. Brockhurst ties up Jimmy, plants a bomb inside the carriage house and flees in Sir Arthur's car. Superman returns, finds the bomb and hurls it into the sky where the explosion causes Brockhurst to lose control and plunge down a cliff. On their way home, Clark and Jimmy stop by a newsstand where the vendor offers a comic book featuring the latest adventures of Superman. *Director:* George Blair. *Writer:* Jackson Gillis.

Cast:

Brockhurst	Leonard Mudie
Sir Arthur McCready	Colin Campbell
Mabel McCready	Norma Varden
Inspector Farrington	Patrick Aherne
Betty	Evelyn Halpern
Newsstand Vendor	Clyde Cook

The Dog Who Knew Superman (November 11, 1953). Clark Kent comes upon an incident near a well and parks his car to investigate. He overhears a woman named Joyce chastising her companion Hank for allowing a dog named Corky to fall into the well. Clark changes into Superman and makes his way underground to rescue the dog. Joyce and Hank go on their way but not before Corky finds a glove dropped by Clark. Later, at their home, Louie, playing with a yo-yo, is awaiting their return when Joyce and Hank enter, still arguing about Corky. When Hank unleashes Corky, the dog makes a getaway through the open door. Hank says he will find the dog even if he has to place an advertisement in every newspaper. Corky makes a beeline for Clark's office. When Lois and Jimmy enter, Clark orders the dog out, but before Corky exits he takes the second glove with him. On his way to put an advertisement in *The Daily Planet*, Hank runs into Corky leaving the building, sees that he has the second glove and reasons that Corky knows the secret identity of Superman. Corky escapes Hank's grip and runs away. Hank returns to the apartment and orders Louie to spread the word all over town that a $5,000 reward is offered for the return of Corky. Louie decides that the best way to spread the word is to phone Clark and ask him to write a story about the missing dog. Clark asks Louie to come to the office, but just then Corky returns. Clark orders Jimmy to hide the dog so he can meet with Louie. Jimmy takes the dog, but outside the *Daily Planet* building Louie recognizes Corky in Jimmy's arms. Louie calls Hank, and Hank orders Louie to kidnap Jimmy. Jimmy refuses to answer any questions, so Hank puts Jimmy on a lie detector machine. The machine tells Hank that Corky is locked away in a kennel. When Louie wants to know why Hank wants Corky so much, Hank explains that Corky will lead them to Superman. Tangling with Superman is not what Louie wants, so he turns the dog over to the dog catcher, and then phones Clark telling him what Hank is up to. Clark then changes to Superman and rescues Corky from the dog catcher. Corky returns with Clark to his office where Clark tells Lois to keep the dog in the office until he finds out what is going on. Lois cares for Corky until Jimmy barges in and tells her that he had been kidnapped over the dog. Lois and Jimmy decide to turn over Corky to his rightful owners. They take Corky back to Hank's apartment, but when Lois demands a

story Hank throws her out. When Hank takes Corky out for a walk, Corky sees Clark and begins barking. Clark quickly ducks into an alley. Hank follows Corky into the alley where Hank is confronted by Superman. Superman picks up the diminutive man and hangs him on a burglar alarm, which brings the police. Back at the office, Clark has a touching discussion with Corky, saying that he cannot keep a dog around as long as he keeps his secret identity. Corky seems to understand. Clark tells Corky to go back to Joyce because she loves him, and tells Corky not to worry about Hank anymore because Hank is behind bars for kidnapping Jimmy. The dog exits, and Lois enters. Surprised to see Clark so morose, she quips, "You look like you've just lost your best friend." Clark very seriously replies, "Maybe I have, Lois, maybe I have." *Director:* Thomas Carr. *Writer:* David Chantler.

Cast: *Hank*   Ben Welden
     Joyce   Dona Drake
     Louie   Billy Nelson
     Dog Catcher   John Daly
     Man at Well   Lester Dorr

The Face and the Voice (November 16, 1953). When a petty crook named Scratchy bumps into Jimmy outside Perry White's office, Scratchy tells Jimmy that he is there to repair Perry's shoes. Scratchy then breaks into Perry's office and steals a phonograph recording of a July 4 speech delivered by Superman. Scratchy returns to the apartment of a master criminal named Fairchild just in time to see a plastic surgeon remove the bandages from the face of an ex-pugilist named Boulder. Beneath the bandages is the exact image of Superman. Fairchild then summons a voice teacher named Hamlet, who uses the record to teach Boulder to imitate the diction and speech delivery of Superman. That evening, Boulder-as-Superman enters a grocery store and demands that the clerk empty the cash register. Startled, the clerk obliges but nonetheless asks for a receipt. Boulder merely exits, cash in hand. The next day, competing newspapers blare headlines that read that Superman is a Super-crook. Clark argues that the clerk must have made up the story in order to hide his own embezzlement of the cash. Jimmy notes that the clerk never did see Superman fly away, then adds that an amount equal to the stolen cash was donated to a Metropolis charity—something that Superman would do. Later, Boulder enters a jewelry store and walks off with a studded necklace. The guard follows Boulder into an alley where he fires at him, hitting Boulder but doing no damage because Boulder is wearing a bulletproof vest. Waiting in the alley is Scratchy, who takes a picture of Boulder escaping. When they return to Fairchild's apartment, Boulder wants out because the danger level is too high. Fairchild, however, reveals to Boulder his ultimate plan. Fairchild explains that the real Superman is most likely in a state of frenzy, wondering whether he is going crazy. With Superman skeptical of his own identity, Fairchild and his gang will hijack an armored car filled with gold bullion worth $2 million. Fairchild's assessment of Superman is correct; after Jimmy shows Clark a photograph taken of Superman reportedly by an eyewitness, Clark decides to visit his friend Tom, a psychiatrist. When Jimmy goes off to interview the eyewitness, he recognizes him as Scratchy and soon finds himself a captive. Meanwhile, Boulder-as-Superman enters Perry's office; Boulder orders Perry to turn the jewels over to a charity. Perry tells Boulder-as-Superman that the citizens are getting angry at Superman's "Robin Hood behavior," but Boulder sternly warns Perry to consider the consequences should Superman ever turn angry against Metropolis. When Clark arrives, Perry tells him about the visit, and Clark replies, "That does it!" He exits the office and makes his way to the storage room where he becomes Superman. Superman flies directly to police headquarters where he tries to convince Inspector Henderson that someone is impersonating Superman, but Henderson, fearing that Superman has gone over the edge, disregards the claim. Just then, however, Henderson receives a phone call telling him that Superman is robbing an armored car. At the Metropolis Bank, Henderson is interviewing Hamlet, who claims that he saw Superman pick up the armored car and carry it away. But when Superman appears, Hamlet faints, and Superman tells Henderson that Hamlet is nothing but a stooge. Superman then flies in pursuit of

the armored car. In the country, meanwhile, Fairchild has placed Jimmy inside the back of a panel truck, awaiting the arrival of Boulder in the armored car. When Boulder arrives, they transport the bullion from the armored car to the truck. Once finished, Boulder takes a position in the back of the truck, and as Fairchild is preparing to drive away Superman descends upon him. Fairchild believes that Superman is Boulder and orders him back into the truck. When Superman refuses to take orders, Fairchild reveals his true colors by telling Boulder that the jig is up; Fairchild removes his pistol and fires, thinking that he is murdering Boulder. But the bullets bounce off, and Fairchild realizes that it takes more than a face and a voice to be Superman. The ricochet bullets ignite the gas tank on the truck, but Superman uses his super breath to extinguish the flames. Superman pulls open the doors and releases Jimmy as Boulder makes for a getaway. Superman stops him, and the crooks are taken into custody. *Director:* George Blair. *Writer:* Jackson Gillis.

Cast:

Boulder	George Reeves
Fairchild	Carleton G. Young
Scratchy	George Chandler
Plastic Surgeon	I. Stanford Jolley
Hamlet	Percy Helton
Grocery Clerk	William Newell
Store Guard	Nolan Leary
Radio Announcer	Sam Balter

The Man in the Lead Mask (November 23, 1953). Master criminal Marty Mitchell dons a lead mask—lead so even Superman cannot see his true identity—and walks into the Metropolis Post Office where he steals his wanted poster. He reveals enough information about himself that postal workers and customers believe the man in the lead mask is indeed Marty Mitchell. Inspector Henderson processes the fingerprints, but amazingly they do not match Mitchell's. This is all a demonstration by Mitchell to his fellow gangsters because he insists that, with the aid of a plastic surgeon known only as Doc, Mitchell has not only changed his appearance but his fingerprints as well. Because of this, Mitchell insists that he is a free man. Again to prove his point, he dines at a local diner where Clark is also dining, and Clark suspects the man as being Marty Mitchell. Clark uses a ruse to get the man to pass a glass of water, and later Clark returns to the *Daily Planet* where Perry White dusts for fingerprints on the glass. Perry concludes that the prints do not belong to Marty Mitchell. Meanwhile, a crook named Morell dons the lead mask and breaks into a safe in order to pay for his operation, but Superman intercepts his getaway. At police headquarters, Clark borrows the lead mask, and as Superman he follows the getaway car's tracks to Mitchell's country hideout. Donning the mask and a trenchcoat, Superman enters, and Mitchell—thinking he's Morell—orders him to accompany him on another safe job, this time at the *Daily Planet*. Superman reveals his identity, but when the mask is removed from Mitchell it is the *real* Mitchell; the lead mask was a ploy to hide the fact that two different men were masquerading as Mitchell. Superman then returns to the hideout and routs the gangsters. The scheme, fashioned by Mitchell and his henchman Canfield, was to dupe their fellow gangsters into believing that their identities and fingerprints could be altered—for a fee. *Director:* George Blair. *Writers:* Leroy H. Zehren and Roy Hamilton.

Cast:

Canfield/Mitchell	Frank Scannell
Doc	John Crawford
Scott	Louis Jean Heydt
Morell	Paul Bryar
Foley	John Merton
Marty Mitchell	Joey Ray
Waitress	Lyn Thomas
Radio Announcer	Sam Balter

Panic in the Sky (November 30, 1953). The citizens of Metropolis are in a state of fear as they gaze skyward toward a huge, threatening orb burning in the sky. At the observatory, Prof. Roberts tells Superman that the asteroid has changed course and is "coming straight toward us!" Against Roberts' warnings, Superman leaps into space and heads for a direct collision course with the asteroid. There is a great explosion, and the citizens cheer. However, Superman returns to earth in a daze; the impact with the asteroid has given Superman amnesia. Dazed and confused, he is able to change into Clark, and a woman gives him a lift into the city. He returns to his apartment where he is met by Jimmy, who tells him that Perry has been searching for him. But Clark yet remains dazed, ignoring much of what Jimmy says. Jimmy exits to pick up coffee and sandwiches, but returns and hears glass breaking. Running into the bathroom, he finds Clark unconscious on the floor surrounded by shards of glass from the shower door. Perry and Lois arrive, and Clark awakens and demands to know who they are. Lois realizes that Clark has amnesia. Later, Jimmy and Lois lead Clark around the building, hoping the familiar surroundings will jog his memory. Perry White reports that Superman's impact with the asteroid did not destroy but only sidetracked it, and that it is still a peril to the earth. As the asteroid again threatens Metropolis, Clark finds his costumes in the secret closet. When Jimmy arrives, Clark asks Jimmy if Superman's costume gives him his power, and Jimmy replies that only Superman can do super things. Clark escorts Jimmy out of the apartment, saying that somebody's got to do something, and then dons the costume. Still wearing his glasses, Clark sits in his chair and strikes the end table, causing it to collapse. He suddenly remembers his identity and springs out the window. At the observatory, Roberts holds an atomic detonation device that once exploded would destroy the asteroid, but he laments that only Superman can take it to the asteroid. All seems lost when Jimmy spots Superman descending toward the observatory. Superman takes the device and wishes everyone good-bye, but Roberts inspires hope by saying that the asteroid has cooled, and that "the elements that nearly destroyed you have been altered in the cooling process." Superman takes the atomic device to the asteroid and detonates it. The asteroid is destroyed. *Director:* Thomas Carr. *Writer:* Jackson Gillis.

Cast:

Prof. Roberts	Jonathan Hale
Woman	Jane Frazee
Roberts' Assistant	Clark Howat
Shop Owner	Thomas Moore

The Machine that Could Plot Crimes (December 7, 1953). Uncle Oscar Quinn, an eccentric scientist, has developed a super computer he dubs "Mr. Kelso." The constant noise generated by the computer irritates Uncle Oscar's neighbor, a two-bit thug named Larry McCoy, who finally barges into Uncle Oscar's laboratory. When Uncle Oscar explains what Mr. Kelso can do, McCoy asks him a "hypothetical" question: how to pull off a perfect robbery. Uncle Oscar feeds the information into Mr. Kelso, which responds through its ticker tape mechanism. McCoy stuffs it into his pocket as Uncle Oscar remarks that it is a good thing that no one there is a crook. McCoy then contacts his pal Nosey, and as a test they follow Mr. Kelso's instructions to the letter, eventually pulling off the perfect robbery of the Metropolis Bank. Inspector Henderson describes the crime as pure luck; everything that allowed them to get away, he says, was pure coincidence. Clark decides to investigate on his own. More perfect crimes are committed, and even Superman is stymied by all the "coincidences." Clark, Lois and Jimmy follow a lead that eventually brings them to Uncle Oscar and Mr. Kelso, but McCoy captures them and uses Kelso to plot one final master crime. With Uncle Oscar, Lois and Jimmy trapped in the laboratory, Clark finds himself bound and gagged in the back of McCoy's panel truck. Clark breaks his bonds and slugs McCoy before changing into Superman and breaking through the side of the truck. Superman flies to the laboratory and rescues Uncle Oscar, Lois and Jimmy, but Uncle Oscar stops Superman from pursuing the gang. Uncle Oscar explains that Mr. Kelso figured out that McCoy was using it for evil purposes, and that Mr. Kelso has made amends. McCoy and Nosey are caught by police after going the wrong way on a one-way street. All alone with Mr. Kelso, Uncle Oscar asks the computer for the identity of Superman, but Mr. Kelso answers, "Wouldn't you like to know." *Director:* Thomas Carr. *Writer:* Jackson Gillis.

Cast:
Uncle Oscar Quinn	Sterling Holloway
Larry McCoy	Billy Nelson
Nosey	Ben Welden
Pinky	Stan Jarman
Bank Teller	Sherry Moreland
Police Officer	Russell Custer
Radio Announcer	Sam Balter

Jungle Devil (December 14, 1953). Perry White assigns Clark and Lois to join a search for a man-and-wife expedition in a South American jungle. Aboard a chartered flight, pilot Bill Hurd offers Clark and Lois refreshments, which ultimately brings out a starving stowaway, Jimmy. As the plane flies near the last known location of the explorers, Clark orders everyone to a station where they are to keep a watchful eye out for any sign of the explorers. Clark takes the cargo hold at the rear of the plane where he quickly changes into Superman and takes a closer look. Finding what he needs, he returns to the plane at which point the engines begin to stall. Clark directs Bill to a landing location, and while Bill tends to the plane the others depart for the jungle. Soon they are surrounded by natives who take them to their camp where they find the explorers Dr. Harper, his wife Gloria and their guide Alberto. The reporters learn that someone must die for the sacrilege committed against their idol; Gloria explains that she removed the diamond from the idol to examine it when she dropped it into a deep pool of quicksand. Clark then takes a pith helmet and fills it with several white pebbles and one black pebbles; he says that whoever draws the black pebble will become the sacrifice. Using his X-ray vision, Clark reaches for the black pebble. Jimmy prepares to fight to the death for Clark, but he is held back by the others. The natives take Clark to the sacrificial pole where they tie him, but after the witch doctor ceremonially creates a massive billow of smoke, Clark has been replaced by Superman. Just then the "jungle devil," a gorilla, wanders into the camp and Superman's invulnerability causes the gorilla to retreat in fear. Seeing his power, the natives free Superman, but he changes back into Clark before reaching the others. Clark asks if anyone has tried to retrieve the diamond from the pool, and Gloria responds that it is too deep. Clark, however, has devised a plan. He takes a lump of coal, and using his super strength crushes it into a diamond before reaching into the pool and removing the diamond. The diamond is replaced, and all is well. Lois comments that they got out of trouble for once without the aid of Superman. *Director:* Thomas Carr. *Writer:* Peter Dixon.

Cast:

Dr. Harper	Damian O'Flynn
Gloria Harper	Doris Singleton
Alberto	Nacho Galindo
Bill Hurd	James Seay
Henchman	Paul Burke
Henchman	Joseph Vitale
Customer	Ralph Sanford
High School Boy	Edward Reider
High School Girl	Ruta Kilmonis

My Friend Superman (December 21, 1953). Tony's coffee shop near the *Daily Planet* building is the meeting spot for the reporters. The garrulous Tony proudly claims to be a personal friend of Superman's, and he has a twisted rifle mounted on the wall to prove it. Unknown to Tony's customers, a gangster named Spud and his henchmen are shaking him down, demanding protection money. Clark learns about this and talks Tony into testifying against the gangsters, but Spud informs Tony that should he ever talk, Lois will be found dead. Since she is away on business, Tony believes that the gangsters have her. Tony confides in Clark that he fears that Superman won't be around to help him, but when no one is looking Clark bends the rifle back to normal. Tony sees this, and Clark says that Superman must be around somewhere, protecting Tony. Tony then devises a plan to capture the gangsters; he bugs their booth, recording their conversations on a tape recorder in the back room. But when two high school students enter and play the jukebox, the sound is drowned out. Meanwhile, Perry tells Clark that Lois hasn't checked in, and now Clark begins to worry. As Superman paces in Clark's apartment, he gets a phone call. Jimmy, thinking he is talking to Clark, tells Superman that Tony has a recording of the gangsters but that it is hard to decipher because of the background noise. Superman wants to hear it anyway, and with his super hearing he reduces the background noise, hearing that the gangsters are glad that Lois is gone because it keeps Superman distracted. Back at the coffee shop, Lois appears, frightening the gangsters. Superman arrives and holds the gangsters at bay while Tony and the customers hurl cream pies at them. Later, Tony discovers that the rifle is once again bent, and his customers believe that he really does know Superman. *Director:* Thomas Carr. *Writer:* David Chantler.

Cast:

Tony	Tito Vuolo
Elaine	Yvette Dugay
Spud	Terry Frost

The Clown Who Cried (December 28, 1953). When *The Daily Planet* sponsors a telethon to raise half a million dollars for the Children's Camp Fun, Clark and Lois make a visit to the circus where they invite Rollo the Clown to appear on the program. Rollo's former partner, Crackers the Clown, has been asking Rollo for money, and when Rollo asks Crackers to join him in an act Crackers agrees just before he knocks Rollo cold. Crackers will now take the place of Rollo and abscond with the charity money. Jimmy, seeking Lois and Clark, wanders into Rollo's tent where he is met by Crackers-as-Rollo. But when Jimmy finds Rollo's body, Crackers ushers him to the tent of Hercules. Crackers-as-Rollo offers Hercules $100 if the strong man will keep Jimmy tied up until the end of the telethon, and Hercules agrees because he needs a new costume. Later, Clark, using his X-ray vision, finds Jimmy inside the tent, and so changing to Superman he enters the tent to be confronted by Hercules. After they spar in a one-way test of strength, Superman frees Jimmy, then exits. Outside the tent, Jimmy runs into Clark, telling Clark that he found Rollo unconscious in the tent. Crackers overhears the remark and stuffs Rollo in a trunk while he places himself in Rollo's former position. When Jimmy and Clark arrive, Crackers identifies himself as Rollo, saying that Crackers slugged him and got away with some cash, but says that the telethon must go on. At the telethon, with Clark as master of ceremonies, money continues flowing in, but what people really want to see is an appearance by Superman. Clark becomes Superman and makes his appearance on the telethon. Later, Rollo goes into his act. Because of Superman and Rollo, the accountant Tim reports, contributions are soaring. When Crackers-as-Rollo finishes his act, he pulls a gun and demands the money. Everyone believes it is a joke, but it becomes all too evident that the clown is serious. Clark reasons that Rollo isn't Rollo but Crackers.

Meanwhile, the real Rollo has escaped and made his way to the studio, where he confronts an escaping Crackers. Rollo gives chase across the rooftops, and when the two grapple, one pushes the other before losing his own footing. They both fall, and Superman catches just one. Crackers, lying on the street dying, asks Superman how he knew which one to catch, and Superman replies that Rollo wouldn't have pushed anyone off a precipice, not even Crackers. The real Rollo then entertains on the telethon. *Director:* George Blair. *Writer:* David Chantler.

Cast:

Rollo	William Wayne
Crackers	Peter Brocco
Hercules	Mickey Simpson
Tim	Charles Williams
Security Guard	George Douglas
Magician	Harry Mendoza

The Boy Who Hated Superman (January 4, 1954). In Metropolis Juvenile Court, Judge Allen turns the guardianship of young Frankie, nephew to notorious gangster Duke Dillon, over to Clark Kent, who believes that he can reform Frankie. Frankie, however, wants nothing to do with Clark or Superman, because both are responsible for putting his uncle behind bars. When Duke finds out that Clark wants Frankie to stay with him, Duke orders Frankie to move in at once so Frankie can find Clark's files on Duke's operation. That night, Frankie appears at Clark's apartment where he is welcomed with warm arms by Clark and Jimmy. Frankie tells Clark that he would like to be a reporter, and Clark agrees to take Frankie to work with him. Later, Frankie makes a visit to a debonair mobster known as the Fixer. Frankie wants the Fixer to arrange an escape for Duke, but Duke demands more money than what Frankie has. Frankie agrees to the higher price, and the next day he discovers how he can get it. When Lois walks into Clark's office and demands a voucher to purchase television sets for a children's charity, Clark signs it and off she goes. Frankie inquires about the system, and when Clark isn't looking he takes a voucher slip. That night, Frankie breaks into Clark's desk and removes the files on Duke; Frankie then calls the Fixer and orders him to pick up the files.

Clark returns to his apartment, where he finds Jimmy asleep and Frankie feigning; as he prepares for bed, Clark uses his X-ray vision to see Frankie get out of bed and drop the files onto the street below. Clark changes into Superman and follows the courier to Fixer's apartment. Fixer's henchman Babe arrives with the files just as Superman breaks through the window. Fixer hurls the files into the fireplace, but Superman's super breath extinguishes the flames. The next day, Clark and Perry White are grumbling about Jimmy's hoodlum-like manner that he is picking up from Frankie. Jimmy explains that he was trying to gain Frankie's confidence. When Frankie overhears Jimmy's confession, he angrily tries to exit but Jimmy stops him. Following Frankie to the street, Jimmy tells him that they are friends and he plans to stick by Frankie. Suddenly, Babe appears and drives Frankie and Jimmy to an alley where he demands the money Frankie owes Fixer. Frankie says that he doesn't have it and that it is to be used by Fixer to break Duke out of prison. Babe laughs, saying that Frankie was used by Duke, that Duke had no plans to take Frankie with him to South America. When Frankie defends Duke, Babe asks him to check out the airline tickets, and Frankie discovers that there is only one. Jimmy slugs Babe, and both Jimmy and Frankie subdue him. Returning to Clark's apartment, Frankie and Jimmy find a birthday party waiting for Frankie; Frankie is stunned because he never had a birthday party before. After he blows out the candle, he admits that his wish is that something that was supposed to happen tonight won't happen. With that, Clark sneaks into the bedroom and becomes Superman. Superman flies to an alley where a manhole cover is opening, but Superman stomps on it and then drags a car so that the tire keeps the manhole cover shut. At the party, Frankie confesses that he feels wonderful, and that he no longer hates Superman. *Director:* George Blair. *Writer:* David Chantler.

Cast:

Frankie	Tyler McDuff
Fixer	Leonard Penn
Babe	Richard Reeves
Duke	Roy Barcroft
Judge Allen	Charles Meredith

Semi-Private Eye (January 11, 1954). Private investigator Homer Garrity is rescued by Superman in the nick of time when a thug pushes over a chimney, spilling bricks all over the street. Later, Lois and Jimmy visit Garrity at his office; Lois wants Garrity to follow Clark for reasons she wishes not to divulge. Garrity says that he will help once he has finished a blackmail case. Jimmy becomes enamored of the private eye life, something that Garrity says is far from glamorous, and wishes to see all the equipment and gadgets Garrity uses in his trade. Garrity obliges, even showing Jimmy a secret room with the two-way mirror. When Garrity joins Lois in the office, Jimmy witnesses two thugs enter and kidnap Garrity and Lois. When they exit, Jimmy leaves the room and decides to become a private eye, pursuing Lois and Garrity on his own. Acting on a lead, Jimmy enters a pool hall and, acting like a jerk, gives a Hollywood-style performance as a gumshoe. He quizzes a little man known as Fingers about the whereabouts of Homer Garrity, and when Fingers exits Jimmy follows him. He strikes paydirt when he overhears Fingers make a call to ringleader Cappy Leonard. Jimmy then breaks in to take Fingers, but instead he ends up handcuffing himself to the bed. At Leonard's hideout, Leonard demands the blackmail evidence, but Garrity refuses to cooperate. Jimmy finally breaks free and makes his way to the hideout. When he arrives, he goes into his tough guy act only to be sent plunging through a trap door to a basement cell, where he joins Garrity and Lois. Learning of the kidnapping, Superman pressures a hood to reveal the location of the hideout. Garrity still refuses to cooperate, and so Leonard fills the cell with poison gas. Superman arrives and, using his super breath, inhales the gas. When Leonard and his gang try to escape, Garrity and Jimmy use judo to stop them. *Director:* George Blair. *Writer:* David Chantler.

Cast:

Homer Garrity	Elisha Cook, Jr.
Cappy Leonard	Richard Benedict
Fingers	Paul Fix
Noodles	Douglas Henderson
Morrie	Alfred Linder

Perry White's Scoop (January 18, 1954). A man wearing a deep sea diving outfit is gunned down in broad daylight in front of the *Daily Planet* building. Lying on the operating table, he mutters one word, "Quincy," before he dies. Perry writes in his paper that the victim "made startling and important disclosures" to the editor before dying. Jimmy questions the wording, but Perry responds that the crooks have no idea what the victim said, and that this should bring them out into the open. Perry then orders Jimmy to follow him because he's going to show Jimmy just how a good reporter works. Perry and Jimmy then rent a diving suit. Unknown to them is that two separate crime rings are following them. One ring, led by an exotic woman named Maria, wants to follow Perry and Jimmy to see if they will lead them to the secret, and the other ring, led by a debonair crook named Lynch, decide that Perry knows too much. As Perry prepares to wear the suit, Clark bends the helmet so it won't fit; Clark then volunteers to have the helmet fixed. Instead, Superman dons the suit, and when he appears on the street a car passes and fires at the man in the suit. The suit is removed, and Superman emerges and gives chase. The gunman says that he was hired by unknown people to gun down the man in the diving suit. Perry, Jimmy and Clark come to the conclusion that "Quincy" must be a telephone exchange, and that the diving suit is used for finding something hidden in water. They may have the location when they discover that a health club has a Quincy exchange. Clark and Perry, donning sweat suits, join the club where they are shown around by a brute named Bingham. Once inside, they discover a drained swimming pool and a huge tank atop the building for filling the pool. Their reconnaissance, however, is discovered by Bingham and his boss, Lynch, who lock Perry and Clark in steam cabinets. With the steam filling the room, Perry falls unconscious at which point Clark breaks through the cabinet and rescues Perry. Clark and Perry then send Jimmy into the tank where he finds nothing but a goldfish; attached to the goldfish is a cryptic message that Clark believes represents a boxcar number. Perry sends Clark back to the office to file the story while Perry and

Jimmy locate the car. What they find is a shipment of rolled paper, but the mystery is solved when Lynch, Bingham, Maria and her accomplice Max arrive and hold them at gunpoint. Lynch explains that the paper possesses special silk threads for printing counterfeit money. After Lynch and his gang transport the paper, Lynch turns against Maria and Max, ordering them to join Perry and Jimmy inside the boxcar as Bingham sets it afire. Clark and Lois arrive, and Clark sends Lois to get help while Clark changes into Superman. Using his super breath, Superman extinguishes the fire and then captures the crooks. A sheepish Perry White then asks Superman not to tell Clark that he needed Superman's help; Superman promises. *Director:* George Blair. *Writer:* Roy Hamilton.

Cast: *Lynch* — Steve Pendleton
Max — Jan Arvan
Maria — Bibs Borman
Bingham — Robert J. Wilke
Diver — Tom Monroe

Beware the Wrecker (January 25, 1954). The transportation industry in Metropolis is being terrorized by a saboteur who calls himself "The Wrecker." Before each disaster, the Wrecker phones Perry White demanding that the city pay $100,000 or face disaster. Inspector Henderson calls a meeting of the transportation directors to Perry White's office to review the situation, and a number of the directors wish to pay the blackmail. Suddenly, the Wrecker phones and demands to speak to Mr. Crane, head of the steamship lines. With Henderson and the others listening on the extension, the Wrecker demands money or a liner set to dock at Pier 19 will be destroyed. Henderson convinces Crane not to acquiesce, and he promises the police in force; moreover, Perry will use *The Daily Planet* to alert Superman. Later, they all gather at Pier 19, awaiting the arrival of the ship. Clark sneaks away and changes into Superman. Superman waits on the dock when his super hearing picks up a distinct sound. He leaps into the air and follows the sound, locating a model airplane filled with high explosives. Back at Perry's office, the group is pondering Superman's discovery when the Wrecker phones and promises to destroy several targets at once if his demands are not met. At the drop site, a package filled with blank paper is left upon a tree stump; with police hiding all around, the Wrecker will have a rough time retrieving the money. Hours pass, and all believe that the Wrecker got wise; when they return to get the package, they discover it gone. Clark, using his X-ray vision, notices that the tree stump is hollow. The Wrecker merely used the sewer system to retrieve the money. Clark then takes Lois and Jimmy to a carnival on a hunch. Clark directs their attention to the sounds, which turn out to be the identical background sounds heard in the Wrecker's calls. They split up, and Lois and Jimmy find a small house at the edge of the carnival. Inside they find several model airplanes like the one Superman caught. When a man named Hatch enters, carrying the blackmail package, they subdue him. But when they bring Clark back to the house, they find Hatch dead. Superman then calls a meeting of the directors and Henderson at Perry White's office. Superman explains that he will unmask the Wrecker, and when a model airplane flies into the office — controlled by radio by Jimmy — steamship director Crane runs for the door. Superman names Crane as the Wrecker and identifies his motive as greed, wishing to collect on the inflated insurance coverage of his liners. *Director:* George Blair. *Writer:* Royal Cole.

Cast: *Mr. Crane* — William Forrest
Airline Official — Pierre Watkin
Railroad Official — Tom Powers
Emile Hatch — Denver Pyle
Carnival Barker — Renny McEvoy

The Golden Vulture (February 1, 1954). On board the *Golden Vulture*, anchored off Metropolis, the sadistic Captain McBain severely chastises Scurvy the steward. Later, the steward scribbles a message, puts it into a bottle and hurls it into the harbor. While fishing, Jimmy finds the bottle and reads the note. Jimmy takes the note to his friends at *The Daily Planet* but unfortunately the writing has been smeared by the sea water. They are able to make out the name of the ship, however, and so Clark, Lois and Jimmy decide to investigate. With Clark distracted, Lois and Jimmy take a shuttle to the ship where they are welcomed aboard by Captain McBain. The first mate, Bennett, feigns an accident and breaks Jimmy's camera. In the captain's quarters, McBain shows them treasure items recently recovered from a cruise to the Caribbean. Scurvy enters with refreshments, but he is caught passing Jimmy a note. McBain now imprisons Lois and Jimmy along with Scurvy. Meanwhile, on the dock, Clark encounters a dock hand preparing to load cargo for the *Golden Vulture*. Using his X-ray vision, Clark learns that the crates are full of jewelry; Clark then hides behind a few crates and becomes Superman. He leaps into the air and flies to the ship where he changes back to Clark Kent. Clark finds Scurvy in the brig, and Scurvy explains that McBain takes stolen jewelry and fashions them into what McBain calls recovered treasures; he then sells the items to museums and collectors as the real thing. Dock hand Sanders arrives with the bogus cargo, and Clark uses his finger as a gun to order Sanders around the ship. Bennett finds Clark and strikes him to no avail. Clark puts up a fight before Jimmy and Lois block his attempt to turn into Superman. McBain then orders Clark to walk the plank; with Lois and Jimmy aghast, Clark plunges into the sea at sword point. A moment later, however, Superman descends from the sky and rounds up the modern-day pirates. Lois frantically entreats Superman to rescue Clark, Superman dives into the deep, and after a few moments Clark surfaces. Lois then wonders about Clark and Superman, but her musings are silenced when Clark pulls her into the drink. *Director:* Thomas Carr. *Writer:* Jackson Gillis.

Cast:
Captain McBain	Peter Whitney
Scurvy	Vic Perrin
Bennett	Robert Bice
Sanders	Murray Alper
Dock Hand	Wes Hudman
Sailor	Saul Gorss
Sailor	Carl Saxe
Sailor	Dan Turner

Jimmy Olsen, Boy Editor (February 8, 1954). Perry White is suffering from nightmares and insomnia; in particular, he dreams of Jimmy Olsen as editor, ordering about Perry as office boy. His dream comes true when he arrives at the office the following morning. There he finds a custodian replacing his nameplate with that of James J. Olsen, Editor. Thundering "Great Caesar's Ghost," Perry soon learns that today is the day that the youth of Metropolis run the city, a program heartily endorsed by Perry. Jimmy's first decision involves replating the front page; Jimmy places a major article that claims *The Daily Planet* has the goods on notorious bank robber Legs Lemmy. Lemmy, who is waiting for the statute of limitations to run out on bank robbery, is plenty interested in the story, and so he and his two henchmen make an unexpected call on Jimmy and Lois, holding them hostage inside Perry's office. Because earlier Clark had clicked on the intercom, Clark and Perry are able to hear everything that goes on in Perry's office. Legs decides to hold them all hostage until midnight when the statute of limitations runs out. Lois manages to take the machine gun away from one of the henchmen, she fires it until the gun is empty, and then tells Jimmy that time is up and that they should go. But Legs stops them; he removes his revolver and holds them at bay. With the police surrounding the building, Clark gets an idea; he runs into the store room and changes into Superman. He flies to Mercy General Hospital where he is given a can of anesthesia. He returns to the *Daily Planet* building and sends the fumes through the air ducts to Perry's office. Gradually, the inhabitants fall asleep. Clark and Perry then enter and take Lois and Jimmy to the window for fresh air. The police chief and mayor enter, and Perry is surprised to see that both the police chief and mayor are young men. *Director:* Thomas Carr. *Writer:* David Chantler.

Cast:
Legs Lemmy	Herb Vigran
Toots	Dick Rich
Henchman	Keith Richards
Doctor	Anthony Hughes
Boy Mayor	Ronald Hargrove
Boy Police Chief	Bob Crosson
Custodian	Jack Pepper

Lady in Black (February 15, 1954). Clark is working late at the office, but his work is interrupted by a phone call from Jimmy, who is staying in old Mrs. Jones' apartment while Jimmy's mother is away visiting relatives. Jimmy claims he is hearing noises and seeing things. When Clark hears that Jimmy has eaten junk food and that he is in the middle of a mystery novel titled *The Lady in Black*, he dismisses it all as Jimmy's imagination. Jimmy paces in the apartment, keeping an eye on a modern painting that seems to change its shape. When loud noises are heard, he opens the door to find Mr. Frank seated in his apartment with the door open. Mr. Frank tells him that the noise is just the old steam pipes, but he agrees to check the cellar. When Mr. Frank doesn't return, Jimmy goes to the cellar where he is knocked unconscious. Clark calls back, and when there is no answer Clark changes into Superman and flies to the apartment. There Superman finds Jimmy reclining on the couch with Mr. Frank tending Jimmy's head wound. Mr. Frank explains that Jimmy must have knocked his head on one of the low beams in the cellar. The next morning, on his way to work, Jimmy is confronted by a man with a large scar; the man tells him not to tell anyone that he was asking about the address. Jimmy moves to the bus stop where is confronted by a man wearing thick glasses talking to a woman in a black veil. The woman inquires about the address, and then becomes highly irritated when Jimmy tells her about the man with the scar. She pushes Jimmy back into the house, and pleads with Jimmy to protect her; she then hands over her bags and exits. As Jimmy follows her, a bag breaks open, spilling hundreds of dollars on the floor. Jimmy opens the door to follow her, only to be met by a dagger sticking in the door. Scared out of his wits, Jimmy rushes back to the apartment and phones Clark, but the phone goes dead. Jimmy runs back to the hall where he finds the money gone but Mr. Frank lying dead on the floor. Superman arrives, but there is no evidence of what Jimmy reports. Mr. Frank is well and alive, sitting inside his apartment; there is no money, no "Scarface" and no lady in black. When Mrs. Frank returns with groceries, she removes a toy dagger from her bag, telling them what the neighborhood kids had left on the door. An irritated Superman scolds Jimmy and then flies away. Inside the Frank apart-

ment, however, the plan is unveiled. The Franks and their henchmen, Joe and Glasses, are using the basement to break into an art gallery where they plan to steal prized paintings. Destroying Jimmy's credibility is one way to keep Superman away. That night, Jimmy hears the noises again and calls Clark; this time, Clark's super hearing picks up the voices of the henchmen in the background. Suddenly, the lady in black enters Jimmy's room. Superman arrives at the art gallery where he greets the two thugs. Fleeing from the basement, Frank turns and empties his pistol at Superman before he trips and knocks himself out. Superman enters Jimmy's apartment and uses his super breath to blow away the veil, revealing the lady in black to be Mrs. Frank. Superman explains the Franks' plan to Jimmy. *Director:* Thomas Carr. *Writer:* Jackson Gillis.

Cast: *Mr. Frank*   Frank Ferguson
         Mrs. Frank   Virginia Christine
         Joe   John Doucette
         Glasses   Rudolph Anders
         Police Officer   Mike Ragan

Star of Fate (February 22, 1954). An Egyptian named Ahmed gathers the reporters to witness the auction of a parcel wrapped in lead foil. Ahmed explains that the highest bidder will be one of two old friends of his late employer: Dr. Gregory Barnak, an Egyptologist, and Mr. Whitlock, owner of a curio shop in Metropolis. Both believe the parcel contains a valuable artifact, but Whitlock is also convinced that the artifact carries with it an ancient curse. Clark decides to check up on the two. After he leaves, Lois notices that Barnak has a gun pointed at Whitlock's back, which forces Whitlock to suspend bidding. Barnak is awarded the parcel. In the corridor, Whitlock pleads with Barnak not to open the box because of the ancient curse, but Barnak just scoffs at him and exits with his secretary Alma. At Barnak's home, he unwraps the parcel and finds a time-worn box; Alma wants to open it, but Barnak cautions against it until he knows more about the curse. Barnak leaves to conduct research, and Alma takes it upon herself to open the box. She smiles at what she sees just before she collapses unconscious onto the floor. Later, Lois and Jimmy arrive at Barnak's home to interview him but instead find the unconscious Alma. As they tend to her, Barnak returns and discovers that the box is missing; he reasons that Whitlock has taken it. At the curio shop, Whitlock examines ancient writings while his assistant, March, examines the box. Whitlock warns against opening the box, but March disregards him. In a moment, March lies unconscious on the floor. Barnak arrives and forces Whitlock to close the shop just as Clark and Lois arrive; with Barnak once again holding Whitlock at bay, Whitlock refuses to admit Clark and Lois. Instead, Whitlock takes a hand puppet of Superman and gives Clark and Lois a little show in which the puppet rescues other puppets. Satisfied that Whitlock is just eccentric, Clark and Lois proceed down the street. Meanwhile, Barnak ties up Whitlock and then takes the box. Before leaving he places a bottle of nitroglycerin upon a ledge near the opening of a cuckoo clock. At the hour the door will open for the bird to sing the time, pushing the bottle of nitroglycerin off and thereby causing an explosion. Suddenly, Clark realizes what Whitlock was doing with the puppets; he changes into Superman and makes it in time to save Whitlock from the hour of doom. Whitlock informs Superman that Barnak got away with only an imitation of the box; Whitlock possesses the real box. At Mercy Hospital, Dr. Wilson reports that the victims are in a state of suspended animation, and that death is imminent if an antidote cannot be found. Lois balks at the talk of superstition, and she walks over to the box and opens it. She finds the large sapphire inside the box, but before she can say anything she collapses into Clark's arms. Clark opens the box and finds a spring mechanism that launches a tiny needle filled with poison into the person's finger. Clark removes the sapphire, and beneath it is an ancient document that Whitlock translates. He says that the only antidote is the pyramid plant that grows at the base of the great pyramids in Egypt. Dr. Wilson says that the victims will die before a plant could be imported. Superman flies to Egypt where he finds the pyramid plant, and then returns to Metropolis where he delivers the plant to Dr. Wilson. Meanwhile, Jimmy has followed Barnak back to Barnak's home; there, Jimmy confronts him

but gets himself subdued by Barnak in the process. Barnak places Jimmy inside a sarcophagus, and to silence Jimmy empties his revolver into the sarcophagus. The lid is pushed open, however, and Superman emerges. Barnak is captured and the riddle of the "star of fate" is solved. *Director:* Thomas Carr. *Writers:* Roy Hamilton and Leroy H. Zehren.

Cast:

Dr. Gregory Barnak	Lawrence Ryle
Mr. Whitlock	Paul Burns
Alma	Jeanne Dean
Dr. Wilson	Arthur Space
Ahmed	Ted Hecht
March	Tony De Mario

The Whistling Bird (March 1, 1954). Clark and Jimmy are asked by Nancy Quinn, Uncle Oscar's niece (see "The Machine that Could Plot Crimes," above), to watch a demonstration of her uncle's new discovery, a hydro-molecular experiment that resulted in flavored postage stamps. At the laboratory, Uncle Oscar explains how he taught his pet parakeet Schuyler the final part of his formula for security reasons since he has been the victim of a recent burglary in which data was stolen. Uncle Oscar introduces his postage stamps that come in six delicious flavors and asks that Clark be the first to try one. But when Clark uses his fist to secure the stamp, it explodes. Clark reasons that Uncle Oscar's experiment has produced the mightiest chemical explosive ever devised. Later, when examining a photograph Jimmy took of Clark and Uncle Oscar, Clark discovers two faces peeking through an upper window. The National Security Commission is notified since Clark believes that there may be foreign spies on the trail of Uncle Oscar's invention. At the city park, Uncle Oscar and Schuyler are rethinking their formula when a beautiful woman named Dorothy stops by for a chat. Clark arrives and recognizes the woman as the one in the photograph; he takes Uncle Oscar aside, informing him that she might be a spy and that he should be wary of all strangers. Realizing that Schuyler was left with the woman, they return to the park bench to find the woman gone but Schuyler yet in his cage. Relieved, Uncle Oscar returns to the laboratory where he is met by Nancy and Jimmy, but at a crucial moment Uncle Oscar realizes that the woman must have substituted another bird. Uncle Oscar places an immediate phone call to Clark, but the woman and two accomplices enter the laboratory, forcing Uncle Oscar to hang up on Clark. Jimmy warns the intruders that Clark will contact Superman, but Speck (the master spy) is sure that Uncle Oscar will help them outwit Superman. Superman arrives at the laboratory but finds only Lois. After they exit, a wall panel opens and the spies and their captives exit. The foreign scientist congratulates Uncle Oscar on his lead-lined room for conducting nuclear experiments. Uncle Oscar is then forced to produce more of his formula, and after he does Speck orders Uncle Oscar, Nancy and Jimmy back into the hidden room. The spies then exit with the formula and Schuyler. Jimmy notices the sprinkler system above, and with a match he sets off the sprinkler which in turn sets off the fire alarm. With water filling the room, Uncle Oscar tells Jimmy that it was a fine attempt, but no one knows that the room exists. Back at the office, a report of the fire comes in; when Lois and the security agent leave, Clark changes into Superman and flies to the laboratory. The firefighters say it was a false alarm, but Superman's super hearing picks up the sound of the water running in the hidden room. He then breaks through the ceiling of the room and rescues the captives. Uncle Oscar then remembers his error in the formula, saying that it wasn't the force that ignited the explosion but that time makes the formula unstable. They rush into the laboratory where they find the formula bubbling, ready to ignite. Superman drinks the formula, containing the explosion within his stomach. At that point, Schuyler returns, repeating the word "Eldorado." Jimmy reasons that it must be the ghost town north of Metropolis. Superman leaps into the air and flies to Eldorado where he finds the spies and their formula. Seeing the flask bubbling, Superman orders the spies out of the building just in time to escape the explosion. The spies are rounded up, and Uncle Oscar returns to more experimentation. *Director:* Thomas Carr. *Writer:* David Chantler.

Cast: Uncle Oscar Quinn   Sterling Holloway
    Nancy Quinn   Allene Roberts

Speck	Joseph Vitale
Dorothy	Toni Carroll
Foreign Scientist	Otto Waldis
Security Agent	Marshall Reed

Around the World with Superman (March 8, 1954). *The Daily Planet* has sponsored a contest in which children write letters explaining why they want to see the world. Clark and Lois visit the winner, Elaine Carson, at her apartment and discover that Elaine is actually an adult and therefore disqualified from the contest. This doesn't bother Elaine because she claims that she didn't enter the contest and that she doesn't want anything to do with the reporters. She orders them out of her apartment, and they exit. After Elaine leaves, the reporters return to the apartment and find a young girl named Ann. When they tell Ann that Elaine won the contest, she is overjoyed. But Clark and Lois soon learn that Ann wrote the letter so that her mother could enjoy the world tour; moreover, they soon discover that Ann is blind. Further conversation reveals that Ann doesn't believe in Superman, and that she is adamant about having her mother win the contest. Suddenly Elaine returns and she orders the reporters out. Jimmy enters and snaps a picture, and this causes Elaine to threaten to call the police and to sue the newspaper. Back at the *Daily Planet* building, a furious Perry White orders Lois and Jimmy to do something about the mess—or else. Clark visits Dr. Anderson and learns that Ann's blindness was caused in a traffic accident. The car was being driven by her father, and ever since the accident there has been animosity between the mother and the father, and very little security for Ann. Clark wonders if her blindness is the result of, say, a tiny shard of glass implanted in her eye. Dr. Anderson says that it is a possibility, but it would need the best X-ray machine to detect any. Clark suggests that he knows where he can get one. Later, Clark and Lois return to the apartment, and Lois remains in the lobby awaiting for Elaine's return while Clark revisits Ann. Clark removes his glasses and enters the apartment where he presents himself as Superman. Ann says that he sounds an awful lot like Clark Kent, but Superman assures her that he is Superman.

Superman then stares into her eyes. Meanwhile, Elaine returns, fleeing from her husband's lawyer. Lois intercepts her, and together they have a talk, and Lois learns that ever since the accident she has wrongly blamed her husband Jim for causing Ann's blindness. Elaine wants to reconcile but she is afraid it is too late since Jim has retained an attorney. Lois and Elaine return to the apartment where they find Ann with Superman. Ann is jubilant because Superman has found the particle of glass impacting her optic nerve, and Superman explains that he will guide Dr. Anderson in surgery to remove it. The operation is a success, and Superman takes Ann on a world tour, promising her that on their return he will have a big surprise for her. Returning to Metropolis, Ann is delivered safe and sound to Perry's office, where her reconciled parents are waiting. *Director:* Thomas Carr. *Writer:* Jackson Gillis.

Cast: *Ann Carson*   Judy Ann Nugent
           Elaine Carson   Kay Morley
           Dr. Anderson   Raymond Greenleaf
           Attorney   Patrick Aherne
           Jim Carson   James Brown
           Radio Operator   Max Wagner

SEASON 3

Through the Time Barrier (September 13, 1954). Gangster Turk Jackson turns over a new leaf and decides to surrender to the police. After he signs a confession in Clark's office, Turk, Clark, Lois, Jimmy and Perry make their way to the elevator where they are met by Prof. Twiddle. He wants Clark to witness a demonstration of his new time machine, but Clark tells him that there is no time now. Turk, however, wants to see the demonstration since his stretch in prison will prevent him from being amused. Prof. Twiddle starts his machine, and in a moment the group finds itself in 50,000 B.C. Clark immediately senses the seriousness of the situation and he orders Twiddle to return them to the 20th century at once, but Twiddle admits that he hasn't quite mastered the return effect yet. Turk pulls out his pistol and makes it clear to everyone that he is now in charge. To secure his position, he demands the time machine from Twiddle. Twiddle notes

that all he needs is a particle of Coborium-X, a metal that can be found only in a meteorite. Superman obliges, but Turk refuses to turn over the machine. But a cave woman offers the time travelers what Turk believes are uncut diamonds. Turk then returns the machine so that he can return to modern Metropolis and live off the wealth of the diamonds. They all return, but Prof. Twiddle reports that the diamonds aren't diamonds at all but quartz crystal. *Director:* Harry Gerstad. *Writer:* David Chantler.

Cast: *Prof. Twiddle*   Sterling Holloway
           Turk Jackson   Jim Hyland
           Cave Woman   Florence Lake
           Cave Man   Ed Hinton

The Talking Clue (September 20, 1954). Inspector Henderson is trying to get the goods on a mobster named Claude James so he can finally capture James's boss, Muscles McGurk. In Henderson's office, Clark is introduced to Ray Henderson, the inspector's son, whose hobby is tape recording. Ray plays back for Clark the sound of bullets bouncing off Superman's chest, a recording he says he got while waiting in a police squad car. Ray next turns on his machine to capture the sound of the police teletype. An officer enters with James, and Henderson opens the safe to get the file on James; James notices that Ray is recording the tumblers in the combination. When James is released on bond he goes directly to McGurk with the news. Later, with Jimmy and Lois interviewing Ray about his unusual hobby, McGurk enters and pays Ray $100 for a recording. Later, after a series of clean burglaries, Henderson confesses to Clark that Henderson dictated a report on the city's entire burglar alarm system, and Clark reasons that Ray is an informant after Lois saw Ray sell a tape to none other than McGurk. Henderson is disappointed in his son. When McGurk kidnaps Ray, Henderson assumes that his son has runaway and joined the mob. But Ray cleverly leaves behind a series of tape-recorded aural clues. Superman figures out that an echo followed by the sound of a cannon means Echo Canyon, so he flies there, frees Ray and captures McGurk and his gang. Clark then explains to Henderson that McGurk did not get the alarm system report from a tape recording but from the tumblers recorded earlier; McGurk merely returned to the office and opened the safe, read the report and then replaced it. *Director:* Harry Gerstad. *Writer:* David Chantler.

Cast: *Ray Henderson*   Richard Shakleton
     Muscles McGurk   Billy Nelson
     Claude James   Julian Upton
     Police Officer   Brick Sullivan

The Lucky Cat (September 27, 1954). Clark and Jimmy investigate members of an anti-superstition club who are being threatened by a mysterious figure. Evidence indicates that the culprit is the group's superstitious landlord, Mr. Botts. The threats become real when member Charles King finds his business, King Chemical Company, ablaze until Superman extinguishes the blaze. At a meeting of the club, Clark's X-ray vision spies poison being painted on a black cat's claws, and this gives Clark the idea to flush out the villain. At the meeting, Clark uses the cat to ferret out the villain, King himself. Clark explains that King set fire to his own company, made the threats against the other members and attempted to poison Bill Green, the club's president, all with the idea that everyone would blame poor old superstitious Botts. *Director:* Harry Gerstad. *Writer:* Jackson Gillis.

Cast: *Mr. Botts*   Harry Tyler
     Bill Green   Charles Watts
     Charles King   Ted Stanhope
     Mr. Fredericks   Carl Hubbard
     Police Officer   John Phillips

Superman Week (October 4, 1954). As Metropolis prepares for its annual Superman Week, seven days of festivities honoring the city's number one citizen, thug Si Horton and his associate Matthew Tipps scheme to find some kryptonite. The evil duo kidnap Jimmy and, after feeding him a milkshake laced with truth serum, discover that kryptonite can be found in Metropolis Harbor (see "The Defeat of Superman"). They locate the kryptonite and stuff it inside a bust of Superman sculptured by a Metropolis artist. The ruse is discovered in time, but Superman faces a greater challenge when Clark Kent is supposed to interview Superman. Much to skeptical Lois's surprise, Clark is seen interviewing Superman on television, but we later learn that Superman merely dressed the bust in Clark's clothing, pre-recorded questions, and played them back for the interview. *Director:* Harry Gerstad. *Writer:* Peggy Chantler.

Cast: *Si Horton*   Herb Vigran
     Matthew Tipps   Paul Burke
     Woman Artist   Tamar Cooper
     Van De Glass   Jack George
     Bank Guard   Buddy Mason

Great Caesar's Ghost (October 11, 1954). Perry White is the key witness in the Morley trial, but as the trial approaches it appears that he is working too hard since he begins to act strangely. Unable to sleep, he calls Clark in the middle of the night, then he forgets why he called. A delivery man brings coffee, but Perry doesn't remember ordering it. Next he hears ticking coming from his desk and worries that a bomb might have been planted. He summons Superman, who finds no bomb. Superman tells Perry that he is under stress worrying about his testimony. The next day, Perry scolds Clark for not having the office wall heater moved as Perry ordered. Perry leaves the office but returns moments later and sees Clark lifting the heater and bending the pipes as if they were made out of rubber; this proves to be the last straw for Perry and he collapses onto a chair, recognizing that he needs a rest. At a country home, Perry utters his signature line "Great Caesar's Ghost," and suddenly there he is, Julius Caesar himself. Perry's butler Jarvis spreads the word that Perry's sanity is in question, and this bothers Henderson. But Superman discovers that Jarvis is part of the Morley gang, and that the gang has been orchestrating the incidents that account for Perry's strange behavior. The gang is rounded up, and Perry returns to his usual grumbling but lovable self. *Director:* Harry Gerstad. *Writer:* Jackson Gillis.

Cast: *Ghost of Julius Caesar*   Trevor Bardette
     Jarvis   Olaf Hytten
     Delivery Man   Jim Hayward

Test of a Warrior (October 18, 1954). John Tall Star visits Perry White in his office, asking about Perry's ability to contact the "great white bird" (Superman). Tall Star explains that his people are backward and in desperate need of progress. Tall Star's friend Red Hawk is college-educated like himself, and Red Hawk's aging father, Great Horse, is next in line as chief. Tall Star reasons that if Great Horse becomes chief, the title will eventually pass to Red Hawk, at which time Red Hawk will lead the tribe to progress. But the problem is that Great Horse is too old to pass the "test of a warrior," a grueling ritual that Tall Star believes is rigged by the Okatee medicine man, who wishes to control the tribe for his own purposes. Tall Star seeks Superman's help in assuring that Great Horse will succeed. At the Indian camp, Lois and Jimmy discover that Okatee has created an impossible ordeal for the aging chief, but in the nick of time Superman arrives and thwarts the plans of the medicine man. Great Horse is named chief, and the medicine man is shamed into banishment. *Director:* George Blair. *Writer:* Leroy H. Zehren.

Cast: *Great Horse*   Francis J. McDonald
Okatee, the Medicine Man
                             Ralph Moody
Red Hawk   John Tall Tree
John Tall Star   George J. Lewis
Okatee's Brave   Lane Bradford

Olsen's Millions (October 25, 1954). Jimmy is assigned to interview the eccentric Miss Peabody, a dowager who possesses hundreds of cats. When Jimmy accidentally locks one of the cats in her safe, he makes an urgent call to Clark for Superman's help. Superman arrives and removes the safe door, releasing the cat. When Miss Peabody sees what *Jimmy* has done, she insists on giving Jimmy $1 million. Jimmy then quits his job and decides to live the life of an independent playboy—of sorts. Meanwhile, a crook named Big George and his henchman, a big lug named Stacey Tracy, plan to bilk the young millionaire by sending a third partner, Herbert, to serve as Jimmy's butler. Herbert earns Jimmy's trust when Herbert throws out Stacey Tracy, who was masquerading as a figurative as well as literal gold digger. Jimmy and Lois then receive a note from Herbert saying that Superman wants

Jimmy to take his millions to a cabin in Pinehurst. Instead of finding Superman, they meet Big George, Stacey and the traitor Herbert. Jimmy burns his cash to send up a smoke signal which catches Superman's attention. Big George and his gang are apprehended, and Jimmy returns to *The Daily Planet* to beg Perry for his cub reporter's job. *Director:* George Blair. *Writer:* David Chantler.

Cast: *Big George*   George E. Stone
Stacey Tracy   Richard Reeves
Herbert   Leonard Carey
Delivery Boy   Tyler McDuff

Clark Kent, Outlaw (November 1, 1954). Inspector Henderson and the police have two thugs under siege, Foster and Curtis. Clark and Perry watch the gun battle; when Perry's attention is diverted, Clark slips away and becomes Superman. The police volley tear gas into the building, and with Curtis keeping the police busy, Foster sneaks out and plants some stolen money inside the glove box of Clark's car. The two crooks are finally apprehended, and Foster identifies Clark as a member of the mob. To prove it, Foster tells the police to look inside the glove box. Clark loses his job at *The Daily Planet* and spends some time in jail as a result of the phony evidence. He is then offered a job with the mob, and he accepts. The mob's true plan is revealed when Thomas Wingate, the owner of a swank jewelry store, is taken prisoner but made to believe that he is inside a hospital room under the protection of a government agent named Stoddard. Trusting the agent, Wingate reveals that priceless diamonds are inside a safe in his home. Foster and Curtis force Clark to get the diamonds, and to assure Clark's loyalty they have Jimmy and Lois kidnapped. Superman enters, and rather than commit a burglary, he flies to South America and borrows diamonds from a mine there. Clark returns with the diamonds, but Stoddard still isn't sure about Clark's loyalty; he orders Clark to kill Lois and Jimmy. Clark returns to the *Daily Planet* building where Lois and Jimmy are held captive, and he sets a chair afire in an office where Lois and Jimmy are trapped. Stoddard, however, has also captured Perry, and since Perry believes Stoddard is a government agent, he explains that Clark has infiltrated the mob to get the number one man (who happens to be Stoddard). Stoddard and his gang make an exit, but Superman captures them. Henderson, Lois and Jimmy arrive, and Clark explains that the chair he set on fire wouldn't burn for long because it was fireproof. *Director:* George Blair. *Writer:* Leroy H. Zehren.

Cast:

Stoddard	Tris Coffin
Foster	John Doucette
Curtis	Sid Tomack
Thomas Wingate	George Eldredge
Bennett	Patrick O'Moore
Secretary	Lyn Thomas

The Magic Necklace (November 8, 1954). A rumor spread by Prof. Jody about the ability of an ancient necklace to protect the wearer from harm intrigues mobster Jake Morrell, who breaks into the Metropolis Museum and attempts to steal the necklace. Lois and Jimmy are at the museum on an assignment; Lois tells Morrell that the necklace is still with the Jody expedition in Tibet. Morrell and his henchmen kidnap the two reporters and take off for Tibet. Clark learns that Lois's wallet was found on a runway at Metropolis Airport, and Inspector Henderson reports that Morrell's private aircraft left that night. Clark becomes Superman and flies to Tibet. Inside Jody's tent, Jody explains to a news correspondent how the necklace works; just as he is about to prove its amazing power, Clark walks in. Jody then places the necklace around Clark. When Morrell and his gang enter, Jody's assistant Akbar drops a gun and it goes off, striking Clark. Even Jody believes the necklace is magic at this point. When Jody refuses Morrell's offer, Jody takes the necklace and the money and makes a retreat; before he exits, however, he keeps the others restrained in mountain passages. Clark manages to become Superman, breaks through the mountainside and apprehends the mobsters. Prof. Jody explains that he made up the story so he could get funding for his archaeological expeditions. *Director:* George Blair. *Writer:* Jackson Gillis.

Cast:

Jake Morrell	Lawrence Ryle
Lazy	Frank Jenks
Clicker	John Harmon
Prof. Jody	Leonard Mudie
Akbar	Paul Fierro
News Correspondent	Ted Hecht
Airport Dispatcher	Cliff Ferre

The Bully of Dry Gulch (November 15, 1954). On a road trip, Lois and Jimmy stop at Dry Gulch, a quaint Western-style town complete with gunslingers, saloons and cowboys. Lois and Jimmy hear gunshots and enter the saloon, where they find an old prospector named Sagebrush "dancing" to bullets fired into the floor by gunslinger Gunner Flinch. No one protests the shooting except Jimmy and Lois, and for their trouble Jimmy is locked up in jail and Lois becomes the object of Gunner's affections. Lois manages to call Clark, and no sooner does she hang up the phone than Superman appears in Jimmy's cell, releasing him. Gunner then apparently shoots Pedro in cold blood, but Clark sees through the whole plot; as Superman he learns that both Pedro and Sagebrush are unwilling shills for bully Gunner so that Gunner can maintain his power over the town. With Superman's help, Pedro and Sagebrush put an end to Gunner's tyranny by forcing him to back down, the destiny of all bullies. *Director:* George Blair. *Writer:* David Chantler.

Cast:

Gunner Flinch	Myron Healey
Sagebrush	Raymond Hatton
Pedro	Martin Garralaga
Bartender	Eddie Baker

Flight to the North (November 22, 1954). A tall rube from the town of Skunk Hollow, Sylvester J. Superman arrives in Metropolis with his pet mule Lily Belle. When he signs the register at the hotel, the manager questions his identity and Sylvester assures him that he is the real Superman. Meanwhile, crook Leftover Louie Lyman is paroled and goes directly to Clark's office where he berates Clark for writing all those nasty things about him; Clark assures him that he won't write any additional articles if Louie stays clean. Louie returns to his apartment where he and his henchman Buckets argue about who makes the best lemon pies, Louie's old neighborhood girl Marge or Buckets' great aunt Tilly. They decide to make a bet. Sylvester reads in the paper that a woman named Marge needs Superman's help, and so Sylvester and Lily Belle meet Marge. She questions Sylvester's identity until he bends a steel bar. Her request is for Superman to take a freshly-baked pie to her boyfriend, Steve Emmett, an airman stationed in Alaska. Sylvester agrees and makes for Alaska with the pie. Meanwhile, Louie arrives and she tells him that she won't make a pie for anyone but her boyfriend, and so Louie makes for Alaska as well. Sylvester and Lily Belle deliver the pie to a bewildered Steve, who believes he is going stir crazy; moments later, Louie arrives and at gunpoint steals the pie, leaving Sylvester, Lily Belle and Steve captives of a vicious snow storm. Superman arrives, learns that Louie's plane was downed in the snowstorm and rescues Louie. Superman also takes Sylvester and Lily Belle back to Metropolis with Steve remaining at the base believing that he is crazy. Back in Metropolis, Buckets returns and tells Louie that his Aunt Tilly won't even talk to him. Sylvester, Lily Belle, and Clark visit Louie and Buckets, and learn that they both have decided to go straight. Sylvester and Lily Belle tell Clark that they have had enough of the big city, and are returning to Skunk Hollow. *Director:* George Blair. *Writer:* David Chantler.

Cast: *Sylvester J. Superman* Chuck Connors
      Leftover Louie Lyman   Ben Welden
      Buckets   Ralph Sanford
      Steve Emmett   Richard Garland
      Marge   Marjorie Owens
      Hotel Manager   George Chandler

The Seven Souvenirs (November 29, 1954). Superman captures a gang of crooks by bending a steel bar around them. When Inspector Henderson and Jimmy arrive to make the arrest and document it for *The Daily Planet*, Jimmy decides that he wants the bent bar as a souvenir, but the bar cannot be found. Later, when Jimmy finds it in a curio shop, the proprietor, Mr. Willie, tells him that it sells for $25 and that he has other Superman souvenirs for sale. Jimmy buys the bar and a brick, and reports to Clark and Lois. Lois then shows them a bent dagger she bought from the store. Suddenly, Mr. Jasper, owner of the Jasper Engineering Company, bleeding from an attack by a scar-faced man, falls into the office

seeking help. When they return to Jasper's office, they find nothing missing but a Superman souvenir, a bent dagger just like the one Lois owns. Clark visits the shop and asks Willie for a souvenir, and Willie offers him a dagger bent against Superman's chest by a foreign agent. Willie goes to the back room and Clark uses his X-ray vision to see Mr. Willie place a dagger in a vise and bend it. Clark enters and scolds Willie for faking souvenirs, warning that Superman wouldn't like it. Willie says he just sold one of the daggers to a woman, and Clark gives pursuit. He finds the woman a victim of an automobile accident, and so he becomes Superman and rescues her. She tells Superman that a scar-faced man was hiding in the back seat and demanded her knife. Clark then decides to make himself a victim to get at the bottom of the crimes, and before long he is clubbed by the scar-faced man and a henchman and taken captive. Once the dagger is in their possession, Clark is thrown from the car. They then make their way to a country house where their employer pays them for the daggers. Scarface and his henchman exit, but Superman intercepts them and holds them for Inspector Henderson. Lois, Jimmy and Henderson join Superman at the country home, which belongs to Mr. Jasper. Jasper says he has no knowledge of the two men, that he is just a collector of Superman memorabilia. Superman uses his X-ray vision to check out the daggers and realizes that his X-ray vision just converted the special alloy Jasper used into a million dollars worth of radium. The whole thing was a ruse to get Superman's X-ray vision to make the transformation. *Director:* George Blair. *Writer:* Jackson Gillis.

Cast: *Mr. Willie*   Phillips Tead
      Mr. Jasper   Arthur Space
      Scarface   Rick Vallin
      Louie   Steve Calvert
      Woman   Louise Lewis

King for a Day (December 6, 1954). When the King of Burgonia was assassinated years ago, his son, Prince Gregor, was smuggled into the United States. The teenage Gregor now prepares to return to Burgonia to return the country to democracy. Perry White assigns Jimmy the task of interviewing the young prince, and to make sure Jimmy doesn't get into trouble he sends Clark along. Jimmy and Gregor hit it off well, but Clark's X-ray vision catches a glimpse of a hidden bomb in the prince's apartment; he becomes Superman and saves Jimmy and the prince from instant death. In gratitude, Gregor gives Jimmy the royal ring so that Jimmy may hand it over to Superman. Gregor and his loyalists then leave for Burgonia, and Jimmy and Clark follow. Two spies, Miral and Rigor, believe Jimmy is Gregor when they see the ring on Jimmy's finger. With Clark away, the spies insist on escorting Jimmy to the palace; there, Jimmy is introduced to Baroness D'Amour, Gregor's intended bride, and Prime Minister Valance. Further attempts are made on Jimmy's life, but they are all thwarted when Clark arrives. In private, Clark tells Jimmy to continue the charade since Col. Gubeck of the loyalists will have time to sneak in the real Prince Gregor. Meanwhile, the country's dictator, Markel, orders Valance and his men to accuse Jimmy-as-Gregor of treason and execute him by firing squad. Jimmy is apprehended and placed in the line of fire, but Superman arrives and deflects the bullets. The real Prince Gregor and Col. Gubeck take Markel and his cohorts into custody. Jimmy then hands over the ring to Superman, preferring Metropolis and *The Daily Planet* to Burgonia. *Director:* George Blair. *Writer:* Dwight V. Babcock.

Cast: *Markel* — Peter Mamakos
Prime Minister Valance — Leon Askin
Prince Gregor — Chet Marshall
Baroness D'Amour — Carolyn Scott
Miral — Philip Van Zandt
Rigor — Jan Arvan
Col. Gubeck — Steven Bekassy

SEASON 4

Joey (September 12, 1955). Perry White's old friend Peter Thomas is about to lose his horse ranch and his prized race horse Joey. Perry decides to buy the race horse as an investment for *The Daily Planet* with proceeds going to charity. At the racetrack, however, the reporters find that Joey is far from a competitor, and Perry believes it is because the horse is homesick for his mistress, Thomas's grand-daughter Alice. Perry suggests that Lois and Jimmy bring Alice to the racetrack so she and Joey can be reunited. Unknown to the reporters, racetrack crooks Luke Palmer and his associate Sully have overheard the conversation, and since they have bet heavily on Rover Girl, they decide to visit Alice as well. When Lois and Jimmy arrive at the horse ranch, Sully meets them with a shotgun and orders them off the land, claiming Pete sold the property. Lois and Jimmy report back to Perry, who suspects foul play. Superman makes a visit to the ranch and flies Alice back to Metropolis. Joey retains his fortitude, and the race is on. But Luke and Sully have planted an electronic device under the saddle of Rover Girl which causes electric shock to excite the horse; Rover Girl wins the race, but Superman discovers the ploy and exposes the crooks. Luke and Sully are arrested and Perry returns Joey to its rightful owner, Alice. *Director:* Harry Gerstad. *Writer:* David Chantler.

Cast: *Alice* — Janine Perreau
Peter Thomas — Tom London
Luke Palmer — Mauritz Hugo
Sully — Billy Nelson
Track Announcer — Willard Bill Kennedy
Henchman — Jay Lawrence

The Unlucky Number (September 19, 1955). Vic's Lunch Room is sponsoring a contest in which the prize is a $15,000 home to the patron who guesses the number of beans inside a large jar. Clark gets suspicious when he sees notorious con artist Slippery Elm inside the diner, and he uses his super vision to count the beans. He then gives the number to a little old lady named Mrs. Exbrook. When the beans are counted by Mr. Kelley, Slipper Elm's guess comes within three of the exact count, but Mrs. Exbrook's guess is exact. Slippery and his associate Boots smell a rat, and they suspect their courier, Dexter Brown. Later, Dexter returns to his apartment which happens to be a room inside Mrs. Exbrook's home; as he stops to speak with Mrs. Exbrook's grandson Bobby, Slippery's gang drives by and sprays the house with bullets. Dexter is unhurt, and Bobby suspects that Dexter is Superman. Dexter is actually wearing a bulletproof vest, but he allows Bobby to think he's Superman. Meanwhile,

Perry has assigned Clark and Lois to investigate the increase in lotteries and games in Metropolis, and Lois buys a lottery ticket from a newsstand operator only to learn that she bought the rigged ticket. This angers Dexter, and so he tells the "collector" that he is leaving the organization and starting his own. But he must first get the ticket from Lois. When Dexter returns home, he discovers that Bobby has followed him all over town, and that Bobby now believes that Superman is a crook. Dexter explains that Superman uses the lotteries and games to finance his adventures, and Bobby accepts the explanation. Later, Dexter kidnaps Lois and returns her to his apartment, but when Boots and his gang of thugs enter, Dexter hides in the closet. Bobby tries to cover for Dexter, but Boots and his thugs spray the closet with bullets. The door opens and out comes Superman, who apprehends the thugs. Dexter then comes out and reveals the truth to Bobby; Dexter also swears to Superman and Bobby that he is changing his life, and that once he has served his time in prison he will be an honest and valuable citizen to Metropolis. *Director:* Harry Gerstad. *Writer:* David Chantler.

Cast:

Bobby Exbrook	Henry Blair
Dexter Brown	John Beradino
Mrs. Exbrook	Elizabeth Patterson
Slippery Elm	Russell Conklin
Boots	Jack Littlefield
The Collector	Alfred Linder
Mr. Kelley	Alan Reynolds
Newsstand Owner	Tony De Mario

The Big Freeze (September 26, 1955). A Metropolis politician named Buckley, who has known ties to mobsters, is challenging incumbent Wilson for the job of mayor. To insure Buckley's victory, mobster Duke Taylor sends an army of thugs to every poll in the city, and to control Superman he acquires the services of an eccentric scientist named Dr. Watts. Taylor then sends his stooge, Little Jack, with notes to Clark, Lois and Jimmy requesting their presence at the laboratory of Dr. Watts. When Clark arrives, Taylor informs him that Lois and Jimmy are held captive inside a lead-lined room, and that if Superman fails to show up at two o'clock a bomb will go off, killing Lois and Jimmy. Clark exits, and in a moment Superman crashes through the wall and rips off the lead door. As he enters the room the trap is snapped, and Superman's body temperature is reduced to minus 2000 degrees. He emerges as a frosted figure, described by Little Jack as a "snowman." The frozen Superman has no super powers. Superman changes into Clark and sneaks into Lois's office where he applies her makeup to his face and hands. Perry arrives and says that it appears Taylor's thugs are succeeding in intimidating the voters. Meanwhile, Dr. Watts is double-crossed by Taylor, and so he visits *The Daily Planet* where he wishes to redeem himself by showing Superman how he can reverse the effects of the "big freeze." Watts tells Clark to tell Superman that if Superman receives a blast of extreme heat, it may cure or kill him. Clark says he will deliver the message. Superman arrives at the Metropolis Iron Works where the guard allows him to enter the blast furnace. In a moment, a revitalized Superman appears and hurries to a polling site where he allows a voter to knock unconscious a surprised Little Jack. Perry then reports that voter turnout has increased and that the trend is reversing, that Buckley, Taylor and their crooks are on the way out. *Director:* Harry Gerstad. *Writer:* David Chantler.

Cast:

Duke Taylor	George E. Stone
Little Jack	Richard Reeves
Dr. Watts	Rolfe Sedan
Guard	Eddie Baker
Man at Polls	John Phillips

Peril by Sea (October 3, 1955). Clark Kent is editor *pro tem* of *The Daily Planet* while Perry is off at a secret laboratory near the ocean perfecting a method by which a new form of uranium called U-183 can be distilled from sea water. At Clark's invitation, Lois and Jimmy join him for a visit with Perry, and Jimmy is amazed at Perry's scientific ability. Later, Jimmy writes an article about Perry's success, and the publicity puts the experiment at risk. Clark orders Jimmy to go to the laboratory and tell Perry in person what he has done. Meanwhile, two smugglers named Ace and Barney, who happen to own their own full-size submarine, read about Perry's experiment and decide that Perry's U-183 is precisely the material they need to improve their smuggling business. When Lois and Jimmy reach the laboratory, Ace and Barney force the reporters to introduce them as scientists. Lois and Jimmy manage to convince the government guards, and the four of them enter Perry's laboratory where Ace and Barney take the formula and the U-183. Lois, Perry and Jimmy are locked in a walk-in safe, and Ace and Barney escape in their submarine. When Clark can't reach Perry by phone, he suspects trouble; he changes into Superman and flies to the laboratory, where he intercepts a torpedo fired by Ace heading for the laboratory. Ace looks through the periscope and finds a closeup of Superman, ordering them to surrender. Superman then releases the prisoners. *Director:* Harry Gerstad. *Writer:* David Chantler.

Cast: *Ace Miller*   Claude Akins
    Barney   Julian Upton
    Government Agent   Ed Penny

Topsy Turvy (October 10, 1955). A flagpole sitter cries out for help, claiming that he is upside down and falling. Superman arrives and rescues the man, believing the flagpole sitter has been out in the sun too long. Later, as Clark writes the story, eccentric scientist Prof. Pepperwinkle arrives with his latest invention, an anti-magneto gravitational register. With Clark, Lois and Jimmy looking on, Pepperwinkle activates the machine and suddenly the room appears to turn upside down. Just then, a carnival con man named Carny enters, and when he finds himself upside down he screams "Hey Rube" and makes a hasty exit. The professor reactivates the machine and the place is right side up. Later, Carny tells his associate, a big brute named Yoyo, about the machine, and how it would make for a good bank robbery tool. Carny and Yoyo then visit the professor and convince him that they wish to use the machine for carnival amusements. When Lois and Jimmy enter, however, they recognize what Carny is up to, and persuade Pepperwinkle to stop the demonstration. Yoyo threatens Lois's life, and Pepperwinkle is forced to activate the machine. Carny pulls off the bank robbery, using the machine to confuse his pursuers. When Clark hears about the circumstances of the robbery, he knows exactly where to go. As the professor activates the machine, Superman enters and apprehends Carny and Yoyo. *Director:* Harry Gerstad. *Writer:* David Chantler.

Cast: *Prof. Pepperwinkle*   Phillips Tead
    Carny   Ben Welden
    Yoyo   Mickey Simpson
    Flagpole Sitter   Charles Williams

Jimmy the Kid (October 17, 1955). When Clark Kent begins gathering evidence against J. W. Gridley, a crooked businessman, Gridley employs the services of a killer named Kid Collins. Collins just happens to be a double for Jimmy Olsen; Gridley's plan is to kidnap Jimmy and replace him with Collins. Gridley succeeds in kidnapping Jimmy, and Collins succeeds in masquerading as Jimmy. But Collins is caught breaking into Clark's files by Lois; he kidnaps her at gunpoint and keeps her tied up in Clark's office. Meanwhile, when Collins' girlfriend Macey finds Jimmy tied up in Gridley's office, she believes that Jimmy is Collins and sets him free. Collins enters Clark's apartment and trashes it looking for the Gridley file, and then by accident discovers the secret closet and the Superman costume. Collins returns to Clark's office with the costume and tries again to break open the cabinet. Lois, fascinated by the costume, unwittingly remarks that Perry has a key to the cabinet. Collins and Lois visit Perry at which point Jimmy enters, but Jimmy is knocked unconscious by Collins. Collins gets the key and meets up with Gridley and his thugs, but before any damage can be done Superman arrives and apprehends the criminals. Lois demands to know why Clark has Superman's costume, and he replies that Superman lent it to him so he could write a detailed description of the costume for an article on Superman. *Director:* Phil Ford. *Writer:* Leroy H. Zehren.

Cast: *Kid Collins*   Jack Larson
    J. W. Gridley   Damian O'Flynn
    Macey   Diana Darrin
    Mrs. Cooper   Florence Ravenal
    Henchman   Rick Vallin
    Henchman   Steve Conte

The Girl Who Hired Superman (October 24, 1955). An heiress named Mara Van

Cleaver seeks to place an advertisement in *The Daily Planet* to hire Superman. When Clark overhears this, he tells her that Superman is not for hire. But she replies that her wealthy family is entertaining a dignitary from South Argonia and that she will donate $10,000 to a charity if Superman will meet the diplomat. That night at the Van Cleaver manor, Superman makes his appearance and begins entertaining Orresto el Centro from South Argonia. With Superman handling the security, Centro's bodyguard, Casper, is dismissed. Unbeknownst to Superman, Centro and Mara's guardian Jonas Rockwell are planning to smuggle stolen engraving plates to South Argonia. The feat is done by loading the plates into Jimmy's camera; Centro asks Superman to fly the photographic plates to South Argonia as a goodwill gesture, and he obliges. Upon returning to the office, Jimmy realizes that something is wrong with his camera, and so he and Lois return to the manor. They are taken captive by Rockwell and locked in a lead-lined bomb shelter as Jonas and his gang prepare for a trip to South Argonia. Clark arrives, however, and warns Rockwell that the police are coming to question him; Clark and Mara are then taken to join Lois and Jimmy. Trapped in the bomb shelter, Clark is unable to effect a Superman rescue. A thunderstorm brews outside, and Clark (unseen by the others) uses his body to conduct electricity from the lightning to charge the batteries in a radio. The radio is then used to summon help. Mara apologizes, but Clark assures her that Superman knew she was only a dupe in the plan. Later, Clark finds Mara working for *The Daily Planet*, and she explains that Jonas squandered her inheritance. When Clark offers to return the $10,000, she refuses, saying that her rich lifestyle was a detriment to her well-being. *Director:* Phil Ford. *Writer:* David Chantler.

Cast: *Mara Van Cleaver*   Gloria Talbott
      Jonas Rockwell   John Eldredge
      Orresto el Centro   Maurice Marsac
      Casper   George Khoury
      Milly   Lyn Guild

The Wedding of Superman (October 31, 1955). Another crime wave has struck Metropolis, and Inspector Henderson and Mr. Fara-

day, the public defender, are discussing it with Perry. When Lois wants to get in on the meeting, Perry assigns her the advice-to-the-lovelorn column. Lois reluctantly accepts the job, but as she is poring over the letters she receives a bouquet of flowers from Superman. The card indicates that Superman needs to ask her an important question. She is perplexed by the gesture but agrees to meet with Superman. Later, she receives a call from Sometimes Mabel, a nefarious maid of the underworld, who tells Lois that she can identify the number one man behind the crime wave. Lois meets Mabel at Poole's Jewelry store where Lois learns that Faraday is the ringleader. Lois is then kidnapped by Faraday's gang. Clark has followed Lois, and when he sees what has happened he changes into Superman and rescues her from a dynamite detonation. Next, assassins fire at Lois from a moving car, but Superman lets them escape. Instead, he takes a diamond from a display case and places it on Lois's finger; Superman then requests her hand in marriage. The news spreads, with headlines blaring that Superman will wed reporter. Faraday then decides to marry Lois himself so she won't be able to testify against him in court. Faraday's henchman masquerades as a fashion consultant and asks Superman to fly to Switzerland for edelweiss for Lois's wedding gown. With Superman in the Alps, Faraday orders a wedding between Lois and himself, but Superman returns before the wedding can be performed. Superman then explains to Lois that Clark Kent cannot be the best man because Clark and Superman are one and the same. The wedding commences in Perry's office, but unknown to the party is that the cake carries a bomb. As it ticks away, an alarm clock goes off and Lois awakens from what turns out to have been a dream. *Director:* Phil Ford. *Writer:* Jackson Gillis.

Cast: *Mr. Faraday*   Milton Frome
      Sometimes Mabel   Julie Bennett
      Mr. Poole   Doyle Brooks
      Henchman   John Cliff
      Lorraine   Dolores Fuller
      Justice of the Peace Nolan Leary

Dagger Island (November 7, 1955). Perry White, acting as executor for the estate of

James Craymore, reads the will of the late millionaire to Craymore's three nephews: Mickey, a taxi driver; Jeff, a college professor; and Paul, a playboy. The will states that Craymore's millions are in diamonds, and that the heirs must assemble on Dagger Island in the Caribbean where they will follow a series of clues that will eventually lead one of them to a treasure chest full of the gems. Clark and Lois will serve as impartial judges who will supervise the treasure hunt; Perry entrusts the envelope with the clues to Lois. Later, someone applies chloroform to Lois and absconds with the envelope, but Perry assures everyone that the envelope contained empty sheets; the real one is locked in the safe. What is now apparent, however, is that one of the nephews is a desperate individual. On the island they are met with a fourth relative, a reprobate named Jonathan Scag who fancies himself a pirate. The adventurers now discover that someone has poisoned the water supply, but Superman uses his incredible strength to open a spring. From the clues it is apparent that the treasure is buried under a palm tree, but the island is riddled with palm trees. Mickey later claims that he found the diamonds, but he refuses to show anyone his booty and runs off by himself. Jimmy gives chase, and later finds a masked man holding Mickey at bay. When Mickey admits that he has no diamonds, the masked man chases Jimmy and ties him up in an old boat house. The masked man then starts dropping old cannon balls at Jimmy in the hope that he will reveal the location of the treasure. From a distance, however, Superman uses his X-ray vision to heat the balls and burn the masked villain. Jimmy is freed, and at the white palm at the center of the island, Paul suggests that the treasure is hidden in a coconut. When he climbs the tree and snatches the coconut the diamonds are revealed. Old man Scag is then exposed as the living Jonathan Craymore, and he admits that he used the treasure hunt just to see what kind of nephews he had. Paul says that he will share the treasure, and Jeff is exposed as the villain when Clark points out the blisters on his hands. *Director:* Phil Ford. *Writer:* Robert Leslie Bellam.

Cast: Jonathan Scag				Raymond Hatton
		Mickey Craymore			Dean Cromer
		Paul Craymore			Ray Montgomery
		Jeff Craymore			Myron Healey

Blackmail (November 14, 1955). A criminal gang has just robbed an armored car of half a million dollars, and Superman chases a thug named Bates and apprehends him with $13,000 in cash. Bates is sent to jail, but Inspector Henderson tells Clark that the money Bates had on him was not from the armored car robbery. Clark and Henderson figure that Bates was just a decoy, and Clark suggests that they release Bates and trail him. Bates then makes contact with ringleader Arnold Woodman, but Arnold tells him that he was paid to stay in jail. When Bates replies that Henderson let him go, Arnold realizes that Henderson has put a trail on Bates. Arnold uses Henderson's ploy to blackmail the inspector; Arnold's henchman Eddie Perkins visits Henderson, plants $20,000 and then tells the inspector that Eddie will sing about how Henderson released Bates after taking $20,000 from the gang. Henderson is caught, but Clark vows to help him out. Eddie overhears Clark, and reports to Arnold that Clark might bring Superman into the picture, but Arnold says he possesses a new weapon that can destroy Superman. Lois and Jimmy then find a note on Clark's desk saying that Bates is ready to give himself up if Clark will meet him at the hideout where Superman found him. Lois and Jimmy decide to scoop Clark, but they soon find themselves captives of Eddie. Lois and Jimmy manage to escape and report to Henderson, and he reluctantly agrees to arrest Eddie, even though the arrest will cost him his job. Eddie tells the police commissioner about Henderson's alleged acceptance of the bribe, saying that he will show the commissioner that Henderson stashed the money in a locker. But Clark finds the key hidden in the police squad car and removes the money. When Eddie finds the money gone, he believes that Arnold has double-crossed him and so he tells all. Superman arrives to arrest Arnold, but Arnold takes the new weapon and fires it at Superman. When the smoke clears, Arnold stands helpless and dazed, his face black with soot and his clothes torn and ragged. *Director:* Harry

Gerstad. *Writers:* Oliver Drake and David Chantler.

Cast: Arnold Woodman   Herb Vigran
      Eddie Perkins   Sid Tomack
      Bates   George Chandler
      Police Commissioner   Selmer Jackson

The Deadly Rock (November 21, 1955). Gary Allen, Clark's friend, arrives at Metropolis Airport where he attempts to make a phone call to Clark at the *Daily Planet* building. A little man places his valise next to Gary, causing Gary to collapse. Clark changes into Superman and flies to the airport where, as Clark, he finds Jimmy tending to Gary. Gary says that he has never fainted before, but Clark thinks his weakness may have something to do with Gary's plane wreck in Africa several years ago when Superman destroyed the great asteroid threatening the earth (see "Panic in the Sky"). Gary returns to the baggage claim when he stumbles again; this time Clark also feels the effect. Jimmy assists Gary while Clark fends for himself. Later, a doctor reports that Gary has been exposed to some kind of radiation, and Clark and Gary both believe that it is related to the plane wreck since the plane was showered by particles of the asteroid. Clark reports that the valise belonged to a man named Van Wick who arrived from Africa, and Jimmy believes the valise contained kryptonite. Meanwhile, Van Wick reports to gangster Big Tom Rufus, explaining that the valise contains kryptonite and that it will destroy Superman. Rufus agrees to pay Van Wick $8 million if Van Wick can destroy Superman, and so Van Wick and Big Tom's henchman, the Snorkel, take the valise to the *Daily Planet* building where once again Gary is threatened by the rays. Believing Gary to be Superman, the Snorkel and Van Wick return him to Big Tom's where they fire three bullets at him. The bullets have no effect, and so they are convinced that Gary is Superman. Jimmy tells Lois that a cabbie reported taking Van Wick to the home of Big Tom Rufus, and that Jimmy believes Van Wick has particles of kryptonite. Lois and Jimmy make their way to Big Tom's where they are captured. Superman arrives, but sensing kryptonite he can do nothing but observe. Big Tom then sets a bomb to explode

and makes his getaway. Superman finds a flame thrower at the house, and he tells Jimmy to throw the kryptonite into the fireplace. Superman then burns the kryptonite into ashes, breaks into the room and disables the bomb. Big Tom and his gang are captured, and Gary explains that the kryptonite must have made him impervious to bullets since there is no other explanation for why the bullets failed to harm him. *Director:* Harry Gerstad. *Writer:* Jackson Gillis.

Cast: Gary Allen   Robert Lowery
      Prof. Van Wick   Steven Geray
      Big Tom Rufus   Robert Foulk
      The Duchess   Lyn Thomas
      The Snorkel   Ric Roman
      Henchman   Sid Melton
      Doctor   Vincent G. Perry
      Airport Baggage Clerk   Jim Hayward

The Phantom Ring (November 28, 1955). Clark is investigating a series of robberies attributed to the Phantom when he receives a package containing a carrier pigeon and a note requesting that Clark meet with the crime ring to discuss the robberies; the note is signed, "The Spectre." Clark sends the pigeon and then changes into Superman to follow the bird. Meanwhile, in an isolated shack in the country, the Spectre and his gang are discussing their schemes when radar picks up both the pigeon and Superman. The Spectre throws a switch and he and his three henchmen, Rosey, Luke, and Joe, vanish into thin air; a lead-lined panel hides the radar, and Superman breaks in to find an empty shack. Later, Clark and Henderson discuss the robberies, and Henderson remarks that he thinks the gang is invisible. Meanwhile, Luke stands outside the Apex Jewelry Company when he suddenly becomes invisible; he opens the door, walks to a display case, and then walks out with a tray full of valuables. When the clerk explains what happened, both Clark and Henderson accept that the gang is invisible. Luke reports back that Clark is on to them, and so the Spectre orders his death. Luke kidnaps Lois and Jimmy, and the Spectre sends another message to Clark. Clark agrees to meet with the gang, this time by boarding a chartered airplane. While in flight, the gang materializes, and the

Spectre reports that he wanted Clark to join them but since he double-crossed them by sending Superman he is now to be eliminated. Clark is knocked unconscious and then thrown from the airplane. Meanwhile, Luke is waiting at the Metropolis bank when Superman arrives and takes him into custody. Knowing that each gang member carries a special coin that makes him invisible, Superman takes it from Luke and returns invisible to the hideout where he captures the gang and frees Lois and Jimmy. Clark later explains that he was sure glad Superman was there to catch him when the gang threw him out of the airplane. *Director:* Phil Ford. *Writer:* David Chantler.

Cast:
The Spectre	Peter Brocco
Rosey	Paul Burke
Joe	Lane Bradford
Luke	Henry Rowland
Al	Ed Hinton
Jewelry Store Clerk	George Brand

The Jolly Roger (December 5, 1955). Perry White assigns Clark, Lois and Jimmy a story on a small tropical island now called Island Abel that will be demolished by naval firepower. The reporters arrive on the island via seaplane and begin scouting when they are suddenly captured by a band of buccaneers led by Captain Blood. Apparently there have been pirates on the island for a couple of centuries. The reporters also find two castaways, Riffles and Tyler, who immediately make plans to steal the seaplane and gain their freedom. When Captain Blood comments about buried treasure, the two castaways side with Blood and help him imprison Clark, Lois and Jimmy. Lois protests, urgently telling Blood and his gang that the navy is about to shell the island, but such a threat only increases Blood's resolve to protect his island. He orders his crew to prepare an ancient cannon for defense. Clark slips away and changes into Superman, and Superman flies to the navy commander and requests that the assault be canceled. The commander cannot alter his orders without further proof, and so Superman returns to the island and has Jimmy photograph the pirates. Superman uses his super vision to develop the negatives to show the commander, but Superman is too late; the shelling commences, and Superman

takes to the sky to repel the falling projectiles. Seeing that the warheads are exploding in midair, the commander orders the shelling stopped. Clark then stops Riffles and Tyler from stealing the airplane. He later learns that in all the commotion the treasure chest fell into quicksand where it will remain buried. Back at the *Daily Planet* building, Perry dismisses as mere fantasy their story about living buccaneers on the island. *Director:* Phil Ford. *Writer:* David Chantler.

Cast:
Riffles	Ray Montgomery
Tyler	Dean Cromer
Capt. Blood	Leonard Mudie
Capt. Mudd	Myron Healey
Capt. Thud	Eric Snowden
Lt. Shultz	Patrick Aherne
Admiral	Pierre Watkin
First Mate	Chet Marshall
Woman	Jean Lewis

SEASON 5

Peril in Paris (September 10, 1956). While in Paris, Clark and Jimmy are met by Inspector Lonier who delivers a note to Clark from Anna Constantine, an actress who lives behind the Iron Curtain. The note requests that Superman meet with her to discuss an important matter about political freedom. Clark changes into Superman and flies to a Paris theater where he meets with Anna and Gregor, an old family friend. Anna asks that Superman fly the Constantine jewels to Paris, where they will be converted into cash that can be used to free her people from the Communists. Superman agrees, but he warns them that there will be trouble if they aren't on the level. Later, Superman returns, but as he is about to receive the jewels, two policemen enter and arrest Anna and Gregor as diamond smugglers; the officers also threaten Superman with arrest since they consider him an accomplice. Superman returns to Paris and, as Clark, demands to meet with Anna and Gregor, but Inspector Lonier replies that they are not in custody. Lonier and Clark believe that the police officers were phony. Lonier suggests that they make contact with an ex-smuggler named Jacques Ducray; the phony officers may want to deal with Ducray in fencing the jewels. Clark then sets up a plan in which Jimmy will pass as an American mobster in search of valuable jewels. The mobsters find Jimmy and take him back to their hideout. When Clark enters Ducray's store, he is met by an individual who claims that Ducray no longer owns the store. Meanwhile, at the hideout, Jimmy is doing his best to masquerade as an American mobster when the true ringleader, Gregor, comes forth to deal with Jimmy. Jimmy eventually falters, and Gregor orders Jimmy, Anna, and Ducray into a pit below the hideout. But Superman arrives, rescues the victims and captures the smugglers. *Director:* George Blair. *Writers:* Robert Drake and David Chantler.

Cast: | | |
|---|---|
| *Inspector Lonier* | Robert Shayne |
| *Anna Constantine* | Lilyan Chauvin |
| *Gregor* | Peter Mamakos |
| *Pierre LuMont* | Albert Carrier |
| *Raoul Durrant* | Charles LaTorre |
| *Jacques Ducray* | Franz Roehn |

Tin Hero (September 17, 1956). Mild-mannered bookkeeper Frank Smullins accidentally runs into a fleeing bank robber, capturing him unwittingly with a cat's cradle. Jimmy captures the whole thing on film. Jimmy then takes Frank to see Perry White, and Frank explains that he seems to have knack for being at places where news is breaking. Perry offers Frank a job, and Frank accepts it even though he claims that he is no reporter. Later, Frank and Clark are watching the bank where they see the bank president's pocket being picked by Fingers Danny. Frank gives chase, but when Fingers brandishes a gun Frank faints and Clark apprehends Fingers. The paper, however, plays it up that Frank caught another dangerous criminal. Later, Frank gets even more publicity when he comes across a bank robber named Marty walking out with cash from the vault. Frank orders him to surrender, but Marty pulls a gun and, again, Frank faints. Marty closes Frank inside the vault, but Superman releases him and forces Marty to flee without his booty. Meanwhile, Big Jack, the criminal ringleader, orders Frank's demise, but the crooks are afraid to carry out the plan because Frank seems to be guarded by Superman. Big Jack then orders the kidnapping of Frank's girlfriend Celia. The gangsters call *The Daily Planet* with the news,

but Jimmy intercepts the message and makes for Celia's home where Jimmy is bound and gagged and left next to Celia. Frank learns that Celia has been captured, so he makes like a hero and races to Celia's home with Lois in tow. Big Jack orders that the gas be turned on to eliminate Celia and Jimmy, but Superman enters and turns off the gas and then knocks Big Jack and Marty unconscious; Superman then props them up as if they are sitting on the couch. He tells Jimmy and Celia that he cannot release them at this time, and then he jumps out the window. In a moment, Frank breaks through the door, races to the couch and strikes the two criminals with swift punches. Frank releases Celia and Jimmy, and Lois enters to find Frank in the middle of another heroic capture. Back at the office, Frank resigns, saying that his former employer has offered him a promotion with a high salary. *Director:* George Blair. *Writer:* Wilton Schiller.

Cast: | | |
|---|---|
| *Frank Smullins* | Carl Ritchie |
| *Big Jack* | Jack Lomas |
| *Marty* | Frank Richards |
| *Celia Adams* | Paula Houston |
| *Fingers Danny* | Sam Finn |

Money to Burn (September 24, 1956). A spectacular fire is gutting the *Daily Planet* warehouse. While Lois and Jimmy watch, Perry confides that a large payroll was deposited that very day in the warehouse vault. As the fire grows in intensity, the reporters are befriended by Slim and his wisecracking partner, two men who take a lunch wagon called the Fireman's Friend to fires as a courtesy to the firefighters. When all seems lost, Superman arrives and extinguishes the fire, but the next day, Perry reports that the payroll is missing and that he is under suspicion for fraud. Perry decides to investigate on his own, and before interviewing the fire marshal he finds the Fireman's Friend parked outside an apartment building. Perry snoops inside the truck and finds an asbestos suit, but he is caught and taken to the warehouse where he is imprisoned inside the vault. Lois later reports to Clark that Perry hasn't returned, and so Clark visits the fire marshal and learns that Perry never made it to the fire station. That night there is another spectacular fire on the Metropolis waterfront, and the Fireman's Friend is serving coffee to the firemen. Superman breaks into the fire where he finds a man inside the asbestos suit. The man offers a deal to Superman; if Superman lets him go free, he'll reveal the whereabouts of Perry White. Superman reluctantly agrees, and the man replies that Perry is in the safest surroundings possible. Later, Clark interviews Slim and his partner, and they tell him that the last time they saw Perry, they served him coffee at the warehouse fire. Clark returns to the office, reporting what he found, and Jimmy replies that Perry never drinks coffee. That fact, coupled with the partner's incessant wisecracking, leads Superman to the "safest surroundings possible," the vault at the warehouse where he frees Perry. Perry reveals the location of the Fireman's Friend, and the two crooks are captured. *Director:* Harry Gerstad. *Writer:* David Chantler.

Cast: *Slim*   Mauritz Hugo
       Slim's Partner   Dale Van Sickel
       Fire Marshal   Richard Emory

The Town That Wasn't (October 1, 1956). While on vacation, Jimmy is stopped by a traffic officer near the town of Ackport. The officer forces Jimmy into court where he is assessed an unreasonable fine, leaving Jimmy virtually penniless. Jimmy returns to Metropolis and begins to write a story about speed traps, but Perry lectures him about using *The Daily Planet* for personal grudges. Perry then assigns Jimmy to work with Clark on a story about recent truck hijackings. Meanwhile, Lois is following the known route of a missing truck, and it leads to the town of Ackport. There Lois is arrested for impersonating a reporter. When she fails to report, Clark, Jimmy and Inspector Henderson give chase. Soon, Jimmy recognizes the location of Ackport, but the town isn't there. Clark realizes what is happening, and so he and Jimmy follow the road further until they are pulled over by another traffic officer. The three of them are hauled off to the courthouse where Henderson reveals himself as a police officer. At this point, the phony cops draw their guns and lead the trio to jail where they find Lois; the gang then exits to hijack an armored car. Clark manages to escape from jail, change into Superman and capture the crooks. *Director:* Harry Gerstad. *Writer:* Wilton Schiller.

Cast: *Judge*   Dick Elliott
       Police Officer #1   Charles Gray
       Police Officer #2   Terry Frost
       Truck Driver   Philip Barnes
       Waiter   Jack V. Littlefield
       Driver   Frank Connor
       Mr. Harris   Michael Garrett

The Tomb of Zaharan (October 8, 1956). Perry assigns Clark, Lois and Jimmy to interview two dignitaries, Abdul Ben Bey and Ali Zing, from Beldad. Perry believes that the men are surviving members of an ancient cult named Zaharan. In order to get their attention, Perry has Lois wear an ancient scarab necklace he borrowed from an archaeologist friend. At the airport, two thugs steal the necklace, but Superman thwarts their plan and they are taken into custody. Later, Clark returns the necklace to Lois, and the two dignitaries recognize the necklace as belonging to the queen of Zaharan. Convinced that Lois is the reincarnated queen of their cult, Abdul Ben Bey and Ali Zing invite Lois and Jimmy to Beldad. Once in Beldad, Lois and Jimmy are kidnapped and taken to a tomb where they are dressed in the ancient raiments of Zaharan. Abdul Ben Bey and Ali Zing then seal the tomb, and the poisonous gases rising from a pit threaten the lives of Lois and Jimmy. Meanwhile, in Metropolis, Clark and Perry receive a dispatch purportedly from Lois, but when Clark notes that she did not end the dispatch with the journalistic "-30-" he smells trouble. Superman flies to Beldad where, as Clark Kent, he learns the location of the tomb of Zaharan from the prefect of police. Superman then flies to the tomb, moves the giant stone and rescues Lois and Jimmy. Abdul Ben Bey and Ali Zing return to the tomb and, seeing the stone move, believe that the ancient prophecy of rebirth has been fulfilled. *Director:* George Blair. *Writer:* David Chantler.

Cast: *Abdul Ben Bey*   Ted Hecht
       Ali Zing   Jack Reitzen
       Prefect of Police   George Khoury
       First Thug   Jack Kruschen
       Second Thug   Gabriel Mooradian

The Man Who Made Dreams Come True
(October 15, 1956). Lois is interested in investigating the Dreamer, a spiritualist who claims he can help people control their dreams, but Perry assigns her to interview the superstitious King Leo of Sartania instead. Clark, meanwhile, is visited by the Dreamer, who requests that Superman pay a charitable visit to a young woman named Nancy Boyd, whose shyness makes her an unpopular figure. Clark changes into Superman and flies to the restaurant where he meets Nancy, but he soon learns that Nancy is not shy or unpopular; he does learn that she has visited the Dreamer and that he foretold Superman's visit. Clark convinces Lois to visit the Dreamer, but when she arrives she finds King Leo there; the Dreamer, fearing exposure, captures Lois so he can effect his plan of bilking millions out of the king. The king's bodyguard, Bronsky, worries about the king and convinces Clark that something terrible is about to happen. Superman then intervenes, first saving King Leo from electrocution and then from an automobile wreck. King Leo tells Superman that the Dreamer ordered him to do these acts because, the Dreamer said, to seek immortality the king must first tempt death. Superman exposes the Dreamer and sets King Leo free from his superstitious prison. *Director:* George Blair. *Writer:* David Chantler.
Cast: *King Leo of Sartania*   Cyril Delevanti
Rutherford Jones, the Dreamer

	Keith Richards
Ruby	Sandy Harrison
Bronsky	John Banner
Nancy Boyd	Laurie Mitchell
Mike Thompson	Hal Hoover

Disappearing Lois (October 22, 1956). Notorious bank robber Lank Garrett has been paroled, and the million dollars he stole has never been recovered. Perry offers an extra month's salary to the reporter who gets an exclusive interview with Garrett. Lois joins with Jimmy in a plan to scoop Clark; she schemes to make it appear that she has disappeared. When Clark stops at her apartment he finds someone else living there; when he questions the landlady and the custodian they say they have never heard of Lois Lane. Meanwhile, Lois and Jimmy disguise themselves as

cleaning people and gain entry to Garrett's apartment. When Jimmy accidentally reveals their true identities, Garrett admires their cunning and promises to let them have an interview. Later, Superman appears at Garrett's apartment and finds the stolen money stashed beneath the floorboards. Unknown to Superman, Lois and Jimmy have watched him locate the money. When he exits, Lois and Jimmy retrieve the money, but they are caught by Garrett. He orders his henchman, a bungler named Lefty, to escort them to Garrett's cave hideout. Lois manages to convince Lefty to break his ties with Garrett and become a self-made crook; Lefty then makes Lois his moll and Jimmy his henchman. Clark and Inspector Henderson return to Garrett's apartment, but the money is gone. Garrett berates Henderson, and then accuses Clark of seeking revenge against him. Later, Clark and Henderson return to Lois's apartment where they find Lefty; they get the drop on Lefty, but Garrett arrives and gets the drop on them all. In the commotion, Clark gets shot, and Lois, Jimmy, Lefty and Henderson are taken to Garrett's cave where he plans to bury them alive in a cave-in. Superman, however, arrives and saves them from instant death, and then captures Garrett and Lefty. Lois and Jimmy return to the office and present Perry with an exclusive story on Garrett's plan. *Director:* Harry Gerstad. *Writers:* David and Peggy Chantler.
Cast: *Lank Garrett*   Milton Frome
Lefty   Ben Welden
Sarah Green   Yvonne White

Close Shave (October 29, 1956). While waiting for a haircut at Tony's Barber Shop, Jimmy overhears Tony using the power of suggestion to reform criminal Rick Sable. So effective is Tony's technique that Sable nearly calls the police to report that a jewelry store is about to robbed. When Jimmy reports what he heard to Clark, Clark finds the story absurd and yet he worries about Lois because she is on her way to the jewelry store Jimmy described. Superman flies to the jewelry store and finds the robbers using Lois as a hostage; Superman uses his super vision to melt their guns, and then takes them all into custody. Jimmy meets with Tony and together they arrange a meeting with Sable, and as they make their way to Sable's home Lois appears. At the home, Sable's henchmen Trigger and Mickey take them all captive. Tony induces sleep for the two henchmen, and as they slumber Sable enters and unties Tony and his friends. Just then the henchmen awake, and Sable tells them that he is going straight and he pleads with them to do the same. Mickey rejects Sable's plea and pronounces himself the new leader of the organization. Sable agrees to a deal, however; they set a time bomb, and the one who stays in the room the longest will emerge as the leader of the group. Trigger runs out first, followed by Sable, leaving Mickey, who runs away, leaving Tony, Lois and Jimmy in the room with the bomb. Sable returns to free his friends but he discovers that the bomb is beyond the point of return. Superman, however, crashes through the wall and shields everyone from the blast. Sable explains that he left early so he could return to save the captives. Trigger and Mickey return to see how brave Sable was, and they become convinced that it is time to repudiate their criminal ways. Tony promises them all a job in his barber shop when they have paid their debt to society. *Director:* Harry Gerstad. *Teleplay:* Benjamin B. Crocker. *Story:* Steven Post.

Cast:

Tony Gambini	Richard Benedict
Rick Sable	Rick Vallin
Mickey Bragg	Jack V. Littlefield
Trigger Nelson	John Ferry
Harry Fix	Don Diamond
Lefty Hook	Harry Fleer

The Phony Alibi (November 5, 1956). Clark receives a tip from Inspector Henderson that the Ed Crowley gang just robbed a Metropolis jewelry store and that Schultzy Garfield is driving the getaway car. Clark changes into Superman, catches Schultzy and retrieves the jewelry. Meanwhile, Lois receives a visit from Prof. Pepperwinkle, who informs her that he has perfected a machine that can dematerialize human beings and send them through the telephone lines. Later, Clippy Jones, a member of the Crowley gang, returns to his apartment at the professor's home, and while inquiring about supper the professor shares his machine's ability. To humor the professor,

Clippy says he has a friend named Moe in Kansas City and that he wouldn't mind making a surprise visit. The professor fires up his machine and suddenly Clippy is gone; at Moe's place in Kansas City, the phone rings and then suddenly Clippy appears in a puff of smoke. Clippy informs Crowley that the professor has the perfect alibi for each member of the gang. Clippy robs the Fifth Street Bank, but in a flash he finds himself in San Francisco. Later, Crowley henchman Benny is recognized in a robbery, but he is also seen in Chicago. Henderson is at his wits' end. Lois and Jimmy visit the professor only to be met by Crowley and his gang. Realizing that Lois and Jimmy know their secret, the men suddenly dispatch the two reporters to the Yukon. Clark follows a lead and finds himself at the professor's home. He learns that the robberies always occur when the professor is taking his nap; he learns from the phone company that the last call made from the professor's home was to the Yukon. Superman then follows the phone lines and rescues Lois and Jimmy. Henderson rounds up the Crowley gang, and Prof. Pepperwinkle destroys his machine because he can no longer afford the long distance charges. *Director:* George Blair. *Writer:* Peggy Chantler.

Cast:

Prof. Pepperwinkle	Phillips Tead
Ed Crowley	John Cliff
Clippy Jones	William Challee
The Brain	Frank Kreig
Old Moe	Harry Arnie

The Prince Albert Coat (November 19, 1956). Floods have been ravaging the hills near Metropolis, and a plea is sent for assistance for the homeless. Young Bobby finds a bundle of what he believes are old, discarded clothes and offers them to the Flood Relief Committee. Two unsavory characters named Cueball and Mike retrieve the clothes for the committee. Later, Bobby's grandfather, Mr. Jackson, discovers the clothing missing; Bobby explains what he did, and Mr. Jackson laments that his life savings were sewn inside the lining of the old Prince Albert coat. Bobby and Mr. Jackson head to the Metropolis Community Relief agency where they tell their story to Mrs. Craig; she promises to locate the coat. Bobby makes his way to the *Daily Planet* building where he asks Lois and Jimmy for Superman's help. Lois writes a human interest story which alerts Cueball and Mike to their precious cargo. Remembering where they delivered the clothing, the two crooks return to Levee City to retrieve the coat. Meanwhile, Mr. McCoy, of the Levee City relief agency, gives the coat to down-and-out vaudevillian Mortimer Vanderlip. Lois, Jimmy and Bobby learn that Vanderlip has the coat and that he is on his way to Ivesville; overhearing the conversation, Cueball and Mike offer to drive the group to Ivesville. The crooks take Lois, Jimmy and Bobby to an isolated roadhouse where they are tied up. Meanwhile, Clark has learned that Cueball and Mike are criminals, and so Superman takes over. Arriving in Levee City, Superman prevents the dam from bursting, and then rescues Lois, Jimmy and Bobby after hearing Bobby blowing on a dog whistle. Superman then apprehends Cueball and Mike, retrieves the coat from Vanderlip, and returns to the Jackson home. When Grandfather Jackson removes the money from the coat, it is Confederate money—worthless paper. All seems lost until Thomas Summerfield, a bank officer, arrives at the Jackson home with some good news. After reading about Grandfather Jackson in *The Daily Planet*, Summerfield delivers Jackson a large check as interest on a deposit of gold left by Jackson's father many years before. *Director:* Harry Gerstad. *Writer:* Leroy H. Zehren.

Cast:
Bobby Jackson	Stephen Wooten
Grandfather Jackson	Raymond Hatton
Cueball	Phil Arnold
Mike	Daniel White
Mrs. Craig	Claire Dubrey
Mortimer Vanderlip	Frank Fenton
Mr. McCoy	Ken Christy
Thomas Summerfield	Jack Finch

The Stolen Elephant (November 19, 1956). Superman learns that Suzie, the star elephant of the Haley Circus, has been kidnapped, and this draws the ire of Superman since he promised the underprivileged children of Metropolis that Suzie would perform at a special picnic. Meanwhile, at a farm outside of Metropolis, young Johnny Wilson finds an elephant inside the barn and believes it is a birthday present from his mother. She is surprised to find the elephant, but she hasn't the heart to deny Johnny his present since the family is poor. Later, Mr. Haley reports to Clark that he has received a ransom note demanding $10,000 for the return of Suzie. Haley decides to pay the ransom rather than contact the police. Back at the barn, the elephant's kidnappers, Butcher and Spike, arrive to reclaim the elephant, but seeing that Johnny has found Suzie the two hoodlums claim that they are from the circus and are ready to retrieve the elephant. When Johnny doubts them, Butcher presents Johnny with a document which convinces the boy that they are official. Johnny later reads about the stolen elephant in *The Daily Planet* and immediately calls Clark. Superman arrives at the farm and Johnny tells him about the document, including a special number he memorized. Superman orders Johnny and Mrs. Wilson to meet Mr. Haley at the circus. Superman later arrives at the circus and is met by Jimmy, who tells him that a model airplane will take the ransom money to the kidnappers. Superman launches the airplane and then immediately gives chase. The airplane, however, was only a ruse to get Superman out of the way; Butcher and Spike appear and collect the money. Butcher and Spike are caught by the police after Superman realizes that the "special number" on the document was Butcher's car registration number. Bobby gets a job with the circus, and the underprivileged children get a performance from Suzie. *Director:* Harry Gerstad. *Writer:* David Chantler.

Cast:
Johnny Wilson	Gregory Moffet
Mrs. Wilson	Eve McVeigh
Mr. Haley	Thomas Jackson
Butcher	Gregg Martell
Spike	I. Stanford Jolley

Mr. Zero (November 26, 1956). An unidentified flying object is spotted over a desert near Metropolis, and the U.S. Air Force seeks Superman's help. Later, inside Clark's office, Jimmy is confronted by a little green man from Mars who says, "Take me to your leader." When Clark enters, the little man introduces himself as "Zero, zero, zero minus one" and explains that his fellow Martians have exiled him to Earth because he is too short; he says that all Martians are exactly four-feet-two inches tall, but Mr. Zero is only four-feet-one and three-quarter inches tall. When Lois enters, Mr. Zero turns and points, paralyzing her. Clark and Jimmy learn that Mr. Zero has the ability to immobilize people merely by pointing at them. Unsure of what to do with Mr. Zero, they take him to a store to buy him a change of clothes. By accident, Mr. Zero paralyzes Georgie Gleap, a two-bit crook, but Georgie forgives him only because Mr. Zero will be an invaluable tool in robbing banks. Gleap befriends Mr. Zero and convinces him that the employees at Lois's bank are evil. Fearing that Lois is in trouble, Mr. Zero enters the bank and freezes the employees and the bank guards. Gleap and his henchman Slouchy abscond with the money, and Mr. Zero returns to the *Daily Planet* building. There he realizes that he was duped by Gleap and Slouchy. Mr. Zero returns to Gleap's hideout, but he is captured. Superman arrives, and Mr. Zero uses his finger to paralyze the crooks. On Mars, the Martian Ruler sees that Mr. Zero has aided the great Superman, and so the Ruler requests that "Zero, zero, zero minus one" return to Mars immediately for induction into the Martian hall of fame. *Director:* Harry Gerstad. *Writer:* Peggy Chantler.

Cast:
Mr. Zero	Billy Curtis
Georgie Gleap	Herb Vigran
Slouchy McGoo	George Barrows
Store Clerk	Leon Altin
Martian Ruler	George Spotts

Whatever Goes Up (December 3, 1956). Jimmy Olsen has turned to chemistry as a pastime, and while experimenting in his basement laboratory he accidentally sprays a chemical extract all over the pants of a passing pedestrian named Gannis. Gannis descends to the laboratory where he is about to even the score with Jimmy when Superman makes an appearance, scaring away Gannis. When Superman hears how Jimmy created a new rubber ball, he urgently nabs the ball, saving Jimmy from an explosion. Superman then orders Jimmy to quit fooling around with chemistry, but Jimmy makes one last effort at creating something really newsworthy. His success is exhibited in Perry White's office, where the editor is amazed to see his paperweight floating in air. A boastful Jimmy explains that he has created an anti-gravity serum, and Perry orders Jimmy to turn it over to the military authorities. Major Osborne is contacted, and he asks Jimmy to continue his experiments. Jimmy and Lois return to Jimmy's laboratory where he admits to Lois that he can't remember how he made the formula; he tells her that he was trying to make a new chocolate cake mix and somehow ended up with anti-gravity serum. Gannis returns and demands at gunpoint the serum and its formula. But once again Superman arrives in time, chasing Gannis away. Later, Major Osborne tells Clark and Perry that government scientists have learned that once Jimmy's formula is mixed with water it becomes unstable and will explode; efforts to make contact with Jimmy fail, so Clark sneaks away to become Superman. Superman arrives at the laboratory where, once again, Gannis has Lois and Jimmy at bay. Gannis is about to be captured by Superman when Superman notices that Jimmy's serum has been mixed with boiling coffee. An explosion follows; Jimmy and Lois are protected by Superman while Gannis stands in a corner with his suit in shreds. Gannis is arrested, and Jimmy, seeing his laboratory asunder, decides to turn science back over to the scientists. *Director:* Harry Gerstad. *Writer:* Wilton Schiller.

Cast:
Gannis	Milton Frome
Major Osborne	Tris Coffin

SEASON 6

The Last Knight (September 16, 1957). Lois and Jimmy are covering the King Arthur and Knighthood exhibit at the Metropolis Museum when Jimmy finds a cufflink near a suit of armor. Later, at closing, the suit of armor becomes ambulatory and makes for a display case full of jewelry. The burglar alarm is tripped, bringing the security guard and Inspector Henderson. Lois and Jimmy are questioned, and one of the jewels is found on Jimmy. He says he has no idea how it got there, and then points out that the suit of armor is missing. Superman arrives and convinces Henderson that the jewel is fake, and that the real jewel is still in the display case. Meanwhile, at an old country castle, three men dressed in medieval attire hold a meeting of the Society for the Preservation of Knights and Dragons. The museum armor is worn by a man who calls himself Sir Arthur, and because of his success in removing the armor from the museum he is elected leader of the group of eccentrics. Arthur then explains that he lost a cufflink and that he believes it is in Jimmy's possession. Fearing exposure, the knights kidnap Jimmy and Lois, but Jimmy explains that he lost the cufflink. Sir Arthur then sends Sir Henry to Clark's apartment to search for the cufflink, but Sir Henry is caught by Henderson; Clark, smelling a story, claims that Sir Henry is a friend, and so Henderson lets him go. Sir Henry then explains that he is actually Oliver Smith, a retired businessman who enjoys playing knight. He also tells Clark that each member of the group has purchased negotiable bonds to fund their organization. Clark realizes that the last member of the group will be an incredibly wealthy individual. Clark convinces Smith to give up his eccentric hobby, and then borrows the suit of armor in order to expose the con man. Superman dons the armor and flies to the castle where he passes himself off as Sir Henry, but Sir Arthur sees through the ruse and sends Sir Henry and the others to the dungeon where he tries to kill them with poison gas. Superman removes the armor and saves them all. Sir Arthur is captured, and the remaining knights vow to return to normal lives. Jimmy then remembers that he placed the cufflink on his cuff for safe keeping. *Director:* Thomas Carr. *Writer:* David Chantler.

Cast:

Sir Arthur	Marshall Bradford
Sir Henry	Jason Johnson
Sir Lancelot	Pierre Watkin
Sir Gwaine	Paul Power
Security Guard	Thomas Dillon
Squire	Ollie O'Toole
First Policeman	Ronald Foster
Second Policeman	Morgan Windbiehl

The Magic Secret (September 23, 1957). Perry demonstrates to Jimmy the power of magic by levitating Lois. This piques Jimmy's interest in magic, and he decides to become a professional magician. Meanwhile, on a coun-

try road, Superman has stopped a getaway car and apprehended the two thugs, Kramer and Burns, who work for criminal mastermind D.W. Griswald. Superman discovers that Griswald himself had been directing the thugs' getaway by radio; Superman takes the walkie-talkie and warns Griswald that he will be next, and then uses his X-ray vision to destroy Griswald's transmitter. An angry Griswald vows to destroy Superman, and he seems to find the method when Prof. Von Bruner enters with a plan to destroy Superman. Von Bruner explains that kryptonite can kill Superman, and that he has dug a concrete walled pit 60 feet deep in the hills of Metropolis. Two miles away is a giant radar dish that collects rays from cosmic kryptonite and redirects them to the pit. Griswald reasons that if he kidnaps Jimmy, Superman will come to the rescue at which point he can trap him and kill him with the kryptonite rays. Knowing that Jimmy is interested in magic, Griswald offers magic lessons as an enticement; Jimmy shows up with Lois in tow and is captured by Griswald and his thugs. Griswald calls Clark, saying that he knows where Lois and Jimmy are hidden. Superman flies to the pit where he is about to rescue Jimmy and Clark when Von Bruner aims the kryptonite rays at the pit. The rays cripple Superman; Von Bruner activates the walls so they begin closing in on the victims. With the rays turned off, Superman gains enough strength to levitate Lois so she can block the walls. The gambit works. Superman captures Von Bruner and Griswald and then destroys the machinery. *Director:* Phil Ford. *Writers:* Robert Leslie Bellem and Whitney Ellsworth.

Cast:

D.W. Griswald	Freeman Lusk
Prof. Von Bruner	George Selk
Eddie Vogel	Buddy Lewis
Kramer	Jack Reynolds
Burns	Kenneth Alton

Divide and Conquer (September 30, 1957). Perry, Clark and Lois are in a Latin American republic where they hope to establish a *Daily Planet* bureau now that President Bateo has been freely elected. But revolutionaries, led by Vice-President Oberon and henchman Philippe Gonzalez, have planted a bomb inside the president's office. Clark, using Superman's super hearing, detects the tick of the bomb and uses an excuse to get everyone out of the room. He then becomes Superman and returns to save Bateo from the explosion. In moments, Oberon, Gonzalez and the reporters return to hear Bateo order Superman into prison until an investigation is complete. Superman agrees to be jailed even though he knows there will be further attempts on Bateo's life. In jail, Superman meets an old friend, Prof. Lucerne, who explains that if Superman can use his super concentration he may be able to divide in two. But Lucerne warns Superman that his strength will be halved in the process. After Lucerne exits, Superman concentrates until he splits in two. One Superman remains in prison and the other exits for Clark's apartment. The weakness is apparent as Superman is barely able to break through the bars and fly. At Clark's apartment, he is so weak that Perry and Lois believe he suffered injuries in the explosion. Perry orders Clark to remain at his hotel room while Perry and Lois join President Bateo in a tour of the rich mineral mines that drive the republic's economy. With Superman in prison, Oberon and Gonzalez dynamite the mine, leaving Bateo and the reporters trapped. After Oberon assumes office, he visits the prison to inform Superman that the citizens blame the Man of Steel for Bateo's death. Superman cannot break the bars due to his weakened condition; Oberon then believes that the stories of Superman are merely legend, and so he orders Superman released so the mob can kill him. But Superman gains enough strength to fly away, and he makes his way to the mine where the other Superman has found the trapped victims. The two Superman halves unite, and the one and only Superman plows through the mountain to rescue Bateo, Perry and Lois. Back at the presidential palace, Oberon is flaunting his power when Superman and Bateo enter. Bateo carries the detonator used to cause the mine explosion, and he reports that the fingerprints of Oberon and Gonzalez are all over the box; the two traitors are arrested. The tunnel created by Superman to rescue Bateo has allowed for easier and greater mining, meaning more wealth for the people. *Director:* Phil Ford. *Writers:* Robert Leslie Bellem and Whitney Ellsworth.

Cast: *President Bateo* — Donald Lawton
Vice-President Oberon — Robert Tafur
Philippe Gonzalez — Jack Reitsen
Prison Guard — Jack V. Littlefield
Prof. Lucerne — Everett Glass

The Mysterious Cube (October 7, 1957). Mobster Paul Barton is believed to be hiding inside a giant cube where he will wait out the statute of limitations on the various crimes he has committed. Barton's brother Steve and Barton's crony Jody explain to Clark and Inspector Henderson that the cube is impenetrable and that its scientist-creator is no longer living. Later, Superman makes a visit, but even he is unable to break through the mysterious substance that forms the cube. Superman then calls on his scientist friend Prof. Lucerne, who explains that if Superman can vibrate his molecules faster than the molecules of the cube he may be able to pass through the cube. But Lucerne warns Superman that it could be very dangerous, that should his concentration be diverted Superman could find himself trapped inside the walls of the cube. Superman decides to take the risk and enter the cube, but as he makes his way toward the center he overhears Steve telling his brother via radio that Lois and Jimmy have been kidnapped as insurance against Superman. Superman exits the cube and rescues Lois and Jimmy. When Superman learns that Barton's clock inside the cube is linked electronically to the atomic clock at the naval observatory, he flies to the observatory and requests that the commander change the time. The time is altered, and Barton exits the cube five minutes too soon; Henderson puts the cuffs on him. *Director:* George Blair. *Writers:* Robert Leslie Bellem and Whitney Ellsworth.

Cast: *Prof. Lucerne* — Everett Glass
Steve Barton — Keith Richards
Jody Malone — Ben Welden
Paul Barton — Bruce Wendell
Navy Commander — John Ayres
Acetylene Operator — Joel Riordin

The Atomic Captive (October 14, 1957). Dr. Latislav, a nuclear scientist working on atomic projects for the United States, has gone into hiding since being contaminated with radiation. He is found by Igor and Nicoli, foreign agents who demand his return to his native country in exchange for the lives of his two sisters. Latislav rejects their offer. Just as the two agents threaten force, Superman appears and saves him. Superman requests that Latislav work with him in rousting a spy ring, and Latislav agrees. Superman teaches him a whistling frequency that he can use whenever he needs Superman's help. Later, Clark, Lois and Jimmy are on hand to witness an atomic test in the Nevada desert; Lois and Jimmy, unaware of Latislav's contamination, sneak off to his nearby home for an interview. But Lois and Jimmy stumble upon X-29 and X-249, two spies who have been sent to kidnap Latislav. Lois and Jimmy manage to rescue Latislav, but in the escape they detour toward the detonation area where they run out of gas. Latislav then whistles, and the frequency is heard by Clark back at the bunker near the site. Clark pleads with Gen. Burrell to stop the detonation, but it is too late. Clark exits the bunker and turns into Superman. The bomb is detonated, but Superman uses his super power to turn the explosion back into itself. He then finds Latislav, Lois and Jimmy safe but nonetheless contaminated with radiation. Superman uses his super power to discharge the radiation, freeing not only Lois and Jimmy but Latislav as well. Back at the *Daily Planet* building, Dr. Latislav finds his two sisters waiting for him, thanks to Superman. *Director:* George Blair. *Writers:* Robert Leslie Bellem and Whitney Ellsworth.

Cast:

Dr. Latislav	Raskin Ben-Ari
X-29	Elaine Riley
X-249	Jan Arvan
General Burrell	Walter Reed
Nicoli	George Khoury
Igor	Mark Sheeler

The Superman Silver Mine (October 21, 1957). Mr. Pebble arranges a meeting with Superman at Perry White's office so Pebble can turn over a tract of his land for a summer camp for the children of Metropolis. In addition, he deeds over what he calls "the Superman Silver Mine" to pay for the camp. Superman accepts the gift, and all seems well until

Inspector Henderson reports that Mr. Pebble is a dead ringer for a small-time hood named Dan Dobey; Henderson adds that Dobey was severely injured in a car accident years before, resulting in a metal plate implanted in his head. The resemblance has not gone unnoticed by Dobey himself, who, with his henchman Boris, visits Pebble and kidnaps him. Dobey then sports a false mustache and assumes Pebble's identity. Fearing that Pebble may be Dobey, Lois and Jimmy visit the hotel room where they are met by Dobey-as-Pebble. Things seem in order until Dobey loses his false mustache; Lois and Jimmy are then kidnapped and taken to an old cave in the hills of Metropolis where they are imprisoned with Mr. Pebble. Clark pays a visit to Pebble's room where he uses his X-ray vision to see Dobey's metal plate. Clark reports back to Henderson before following Dobey and Boris to the cave. There, Clark becomes Superman and rescues Lois, Jimmy and Pebble. Dobey tries to escape, but Superman picks up an iron pipe and, using his X-ray vision, charges it with magnetism. Superman aims the giant magnet at Dobey's metal plate, and the crook is finally captured. Mr. Pebble then states that the location of the Superman Silver Mine is the land that they are all standing on. *Director:* George Blair. *Writer:* Peggy Chantler.

Cast:

Mr. Pebble	Dabbs Greer
Dan Dobey	Dabbs Greer
Boris	Charles Maxwell

The Big Forget (October 28, 1957). Prof. Pepperwinkle makes a visit to Lois Lane's office where he offers Lois his latest invention, a spray can of anti-memory vapor. One whiff, he says, and the victim will forget everything that has happened within the past several minutes. Lois tells the professor that she will borrow it for a week and report back to him. Later, Jimmy takes the vapor and decides to investigate the machinations of notorious crook Mugsy Maple and his stooge, Knuckles Nelson. Disguised as a hearing-impaired window washer, he enters Mugsy's apartment and eavesdrops on their plans to rob a bank, but Jimmy unwittingly gives himself away. Hoping the professor's vapor works, he tries to spray Maple with it but instead sprays himself. Suddenly, Jimmy can't remember a thing. Mugsy then tries the vapor on Knuckles and sees that it works. He sends Jimmy on his way and tells Knuckles they now have the perfect weapon. Jimmy reports back that he lost the professor's vapor; when a report comes in about a robbery in which witnesses can't recall a thing, all suspicion is directed toward Mugsy. Perry, Lois and Jimmy return to Mugsy's apartment where they are taken prisoner and driven to Mugsy's mountain hideout. Henderson and Superman arrive at the apartment, and Superman reasons that the private phone inside Mugsy's desk must be a direct link to the hideout. He orders Henderson to continue counting into the phone while Superman follows the telephone lines to the hideout. Superman changes into Clark Kent and walks into the hideout, and Mugsy sends Clark and the group to the basement. Mugsy releases cyanide gas, but he and Knuckles realize that they, too, are prisoners since Clark had locked the door. With the gas filling the room, Clark has no choice but to reveal himself as Superman; he uses his super breath to clear the room, and asks an amazed Jimmy to help him break open the iron door. Superman then takes Prof. Pepperwinkle's anti-memory vapor and, saying that he hopes it works, sprays the room. Back at Perry's office, no one can remember exactly what happened and Professor Pepperwinkle laments that he can't remember the formula for his anti-memory vapor. *Director:* George Blair. *Writer:* David Chantler.

Cast: *Prof. Pepperwinkle*   Phillips Tead
      Mugsy Maple   Herb Vigran
      Knuckles Nelson   Billy Nelson

The Gentle Monster (November 4, 1957). A desperate gangster known as the Duke makes threats against *The Daily Planet* for a series of articles exposing his operation. To effect his revenge he has employed a crooked scientist to devise a radio-transmitted balloon capable of delivering a bomb to the *Planet* building. Meanwhile, a report comes in to *The Daily Planet* that a weird man is prowling a neighborhood, and so Lois and Jimmy give chase and find themselves at the home of Prof. Pepperwinkle. The weird man is Pepperwinkle's robot Mr. MacTavish, who is described by the professor as harmless. The robot answers only to Pepperwinkle's voice, but for demonstration purposes he shows Lois and Jimmy a special microphone that converts anyone's voice to the professor's. Superman arrives and is introduced to Mr. MacTavish, but Superman suddenly becomes weak and needs help in exiting the house. It turns out that Prof. Pepperwinkle has used small amounts of kryptonite as the robot's power source. Witnessing the incident is Blade, the Duke's henchman, who quickly reports to the Duke; the Duke and Blade then steal Mr. MacTavish and for insurance purposes kidnap Lois. Superman and Pepperwinkle use a Geiger counter to locate Mr. MacTavish at a warehouse. Superman enters to stop the scientist from launching the incendiary balloon, but the kryptonite from Mr. MacTavish causes Superman to stumble and fall helpless. The balloon is launched, but Pepperwinkle is able to discharge the robot. Superman regains his strength and pursues the balloon. Once he catches it, he uses the radio control to return the balloon back to the Duke and Blade. The criminals confess their crimes and release Lois, and in exchange Superman deactivates the bomb. Back at Pepperwinkle's home, Clark, Lois and Jimmy are served a meal by Mr. MacTavish, now powered by ordinary electricity. *Director:* Howard Bretherton. *Writer:* David Chantler.

Cast: *Prof. Pepperwinkle*   Phillips Tead
      The Duke   John Vivyan
      Blade   Ben Welden
      Scientist   Orville Sherman
      Mr. MacTavish   Wilkie DeMartel

Superman's Wife (November 11, 1957). Another crime wave has descended upon Metropolis, and Inspector Henderson and the reporters are desperately trying to find the ringleader known as Mr. X. To provoke Mr. X, a plan is devised in which Superman will take a bride, thereby setting up a mortal target to threaten Superman's well-being. His bride is Sgt. Helen O'Hara of the Metropolis Police department, and no sooner has the announcement been made than Mr. X kidnaps Mrs. Superman. Meanwhile, for insurance, Mr. X has imperiled Clark, Perry and Jimmy by trapping them inside a bathysphere at the bottom of Metropolis

Harbor. Back in Metropolis, Mrs. Superman is bound to a bridge where Mr. X will dynamite a passing armored car. When Perry and Jimmy pass out, Clark breaks a hole in the bathysphere and pulls the thing to the surface where he frees Perry and Jimmy. He then changes into Superman, flies to the bridge, detours the armored car and frees Mrs. Superman before rounding up Mr. X and his gang. Much to Lois's relief, the wedding of Superman was actually a hoax, but Sgt. O'Hara says she wishes it had happened. *Director:* Lew Landers. *Writers:* Robert Leslie Bellem and Whitney Ellsworth.

Cast: *Sgt. Helen O'Hara*   Joi Lansing
Mr. X   John Eldredge
Dugan   John Bennes
Blinkie   Harry Arnie
Duke Barlow   Wayne Heffley

Three in One (November 18, 1957). Tex Dawson, owner of a circus, tells Perry White that because of financial problems he is closing down. Two of Dawson's top acts, Pallini the Human Fly and Harmon the Great, an escape artist, are crooks who devise a plan to blame a series of robberies on Superman. The first phase of their plan is for Pallini to scale a 17-story building and drop a rope for Harmon to enter an office and open a safe. Pallini gets away, but Harmon is stopped by Superman. Harmon tells Inspector Henderson that he acted according to Superman's wishes, that Superman flew Harmon to the seventeenth floor and demanded that he break into the safe. Later, Harmon picks the jail lock and escapes back to the circus where he joins Pallini. They convince Atlas the strong man to join them in a new venture they call a detective agency. Their first job is to rescue money from potential robbers from a safe, and so Atlas is requested to bend bars on an iron door so would-be robbers will think the money is already gone. At police headquarters, the report comes in that a robbery is in progress, and so Superman flies to the site where he finds the bars bent and the money gone. Henderson arrives and seeing the evidence believes that Superman is the robber. Superman is taken into custody. Pallini and Harmon convince Atlas that Superman is a crook, and with

Superman behind bars Pallini and Harmon are free to continue their crime wave. In jail, Superman asks Lois to plant a story reporting that the ball atop the flagpole at the new Chapman Building is made of pure gold. Pallini and Harmon take the bait; they convince Atlas that Superman stole the gold from orphans, and that it is their job to return it. Jimmy finds Harmon for an exclusive interview about closing the circus, but Harmon locks Jimmy inside an old trunk. Harmon orders Atlas to dump the trunk into a tank of water. With Jimmy missing, Superman reasons that Pallini and Harmon are the actual culprits, and so Henderson allows Superman to escape. Superman flies to the circus where he rescues Jimmy, then flies to the Chapman Building where he convinces Atlas that Pallini and Harmon are crooks. Together, Atlas and Superman capture the two crooks. Later, at Perry's office, Dawson says that he'll still have to close the circus because he lost his two star performers, but Clark volunteers the services of Superman until two new star attractions from Europe arrive. *Director:* Lew Landers. *Writers:* Wilton Schiller and Whitney Ellsworth.

Cast: *Harmon the Great*   Sid Tomack
Pallini the Human Fly   Rick Vallin
Atlas   Buddy Baer
Tex Dawson   Craig Duncan

The Brainy Burro (November 25, 1957). Clark, Lois and Jimmy are in Mexico on assignment where they watch a poor Mexican lad named Pepe and his burro named Carmelita perform a mind-reading act. People ask questions of the burro and she stamps out the answers with her hoof. In the audience are two American thugs named Tiger and Albert, and following Carmelita's demonstration they offer Pepe 200 pesos for Carmelita's services. Pepe agrees, and the two thugs take Pepe and Carmelita to a bank where they find the bank's president, Señor Lucke, tied to a chair. Pepe refuses to cooperate in the obvious bank robbery, but Tiger threatens to kill Carmelita if she doesn't read Lucke's mind and stomp out the combination to the vault. Pepe reluctantly agrees, the vault is opened, the money is stolen and Pepe and Carmelita are set free with the warning that should Pepe report the incident, Tiger will prove that Pepe was an accomplice. A dejected Pepe and his burro leave for the hills. The next day Police Inspector Tomeo visits the American reporters to question them about the robbery, but when Clark, using his X-ray vision, spots a bag loaded with money hidden under his bed, he quickly leaves the room and becomes Superman; Lois and Jimmy, however, are taken to jail. Later, Superman visits Inspector Tomeo, and Tomeo reports that Clark Kent is wanted for questioning. Meanwhile, Pepe and Carmelita visit Lois and Jimmy in jail, and Pepe admits to participating in the robbery. Carmelita then removes the bars, and Lois and Jimmy flee the jail. But Lois, Jimmy and Pepe are taken captive by Tiger and Albert, who whisk them off to the hills where the captives are tied to a rock near a flame-spouting gas line. Tomeo and Superman find Carmelita near the jail, and Superman is able to use Carmelita's ability to conclude that Tiger and Albert have taken Lois, Jimmy and Pepe. Superman flies to the location, extinguishes the threatening flame and captures Tiger and Albert. *Director:* George Reeves. *Writer:* David Chantler.

Cast: *Pepe*   Mark Cavell
Tiger   Mauritz Hugo
Albert   Ken Mayer
Inspector Tomeo   Natividad Vacio
Señor Lucke   Edward LeVeque
Waiter   Sid Cassell

The Perils of Superman (December 2, 1957). A man in a lead mask enters the *Daily Planet* building, makes his way to Perry's office and warns Perry, Lois and Jimmy that Superman will pay for breaking up the man's criminal activity by helplessly watching his friends die. As Clark enters, Perry warns the man that he will never get away with such a plan because Superman will see right through the mask, but the man replies that the mask is made of lead, that it is locked onto his head, and that he has ten other gang members walking the streets of Metropolis dressed exactly as he is. As the man exits, Clark follows and finds on the street outside the *Daily Planet* building numerous men in lead masks walking among the citizens. Perry and Lois leave on an assignment when

the man in the lead mask forces them to drive into the country where they are taken to a hideout and find a second masked man. Perry admonishes the criminals for being stupid, telling them that he even knows how to get to the hideout; the man asks him to repeat the directions, secretly recording the directions into a tape recorder. The man then calls Jimmy back at *The Daily Planet* and plays the recording; Jimmy believes it is Perry giving him orders to meet Perry at the hideout. Back at police headquarters, Clark and Henderson realize that Perry, Lois and Jimmy are now captives of the man in the lead mask. Clark offers himself as bait with the idea that Henderson and the police will be nearby. Clark enters his office where he is met by the masked man, but rather than going out to the street, Clark is taken to the roof where a helicopter whisks him away. Clark is taken an old factory where he is suspended above a vat of acid; the masked man reveals that his plan of revenge is based on old movie serials. The man reports that Perry is tied to a log at an old mill where he will be cut in half by a buzz saw; Lois is tied to railroad tracks; and Jimmy is riding a crooked mountain road where eventually acid will burn through the brakes and the steering column. The criminals then watch as Clark is lowered into the acid; they exit for the hideout, and in their absence Superman emerges from the vat. He flies off to the saw mill where he saves Perry by destroying the buzz saw. Superman then finds Lois and saves her from an approaching train. Next, he flies off toward the mountain road and rescues Jimmy. Later, in Perry's office, Henderson explains that Superman used his X-ray vision to find the key that would unlock the masks, hence finding the mastermind. *Director:* George Reeves. *Writers:* Robert Leslie Bellem and Whitney Ellsworth.

Cast: *The Man in the Lead Mask* Michael Fox
His Henchman   Steve Mitchell
Ethel   Yvonne White

All That Glitters (December 9, 1957). Prof. Pepperwinkle has invented a gold-making machine, and John Salem, the Secretary of the Treasury, and Delbert Carter, the President of the World Bank, request that he not develop or patent the machine because it would ruin the world economy. The professor agrees, telling Perry White and the others that he will never release the secret. Later, Lois and Jimmy are dining with the professor when Jimmy inadvertently talks about the machine; nearby are two criminals, Nick Mitchell and Elbows Logan, who immediately take an interest in the professor. Mitchell and Elbows arrive at the professor's laboratory and demand a few gold bars from the professor in exchange for the lives of Lois and Jimmy. The professor obliges but says that it will take some time; the crooks exit, and the professor shows Lois and Jimmy his automatic crook stopper, a device that releases overhead sandbags onto the crooks' heads. The device works when one of the sandbags hits Jimmy, knocking him cold. He awakens and tells Prof. Pepperwinkle that it will take more than sandbags to stop the crooks, but again the professor shows no concern because he has a second invention. He explains that he found a sample of kryptonite in his backyard, and when he analyzed he discovered that kryptonite is charged with both positive and negative particles; the negative particles are what weakens Superman but the positive particles are what gives Superman his super powers. He then shows Lois and Jimmy his new machine that separates the particles into edible capsules. Lois and Jimmy then take the positive capsule, and in a moment Jimmy is able to bend an iron bar; Lois then takes the bar and bends it back into its original shape. Jimmy runs to a wall and crashes through it, and then the two of them leap into the air and

fly through the skyline of Metropolis. The super Lois and Jimmy learn from a bank manager that the culprits are holed up in a warehouse, and so they fly to the location where they use their X-ray vision to find them inside a room. Lois and Jimmy break through the wall, take several bullets fired at them and then capture the two crooks. With immense pride they return to the professor's laboratory where he mistakenly activates the automatic crime stopper, hitting Jimmy once again. Jimmy awakens and realizes that it was all a dream just as the crooks return to get their gold bars from the professor. With no recourse, Prof. Pepperwinkle activates his machine. The crooks watch closely as he drops numerous ingredients including scrap iron, apple cider and a bar of platinum. The latter shocks the crooks, and Pepperwinkle explains that it takes $10,000 worth of platinum to make one gold bar worth $5000. This angers the crooks and they tie up Lois, Jimmy and the professor and leave them with a stick of dynamite. Superman arrives and throws the dynamite into the professor's gold-making machine; the explosion is contained but the machine is destroyed. *Director:* George Reeves. *Writers:* Robert Leslie Bellem and Whitney Ellsworth.

Cast:

Prof. Pepperwinkle	Phillips Tead
Nick Mitchell	Len Hendry
Elbows Logan	Jack V. Littlefield
Mr. Golby	Dick Elliott
Miss Dunn	Myrna Fahey
John Salem	George Eldredge
Delbert Carter	Paul Cavanagh

Atom Squad

Broadcast live each weekday afternoon out of NBC's Philadelphia studios, *Atom Squad* was an unabashed Cold War polemic steeped in a science fiction milieu. Although the series ran for only six months, the Cold War themes it explored were relevant for decades. Assigned to protect America's atomic secrets from her foreign adversaries, the Atom Squad reflected the genuine concerns of the 1950s.

Atom Squad premiered at a time when American soldiers were dying in a police action in Korea, when a number of America's atomic secrets had already been appropriated by Russia and when atomic spies like Klaus Fuchs, Julius and Ethel Rosenberg and Alger Hiss were monopolizing the daily headlines alongside politicians who were themselves capitalizing on a rising sense of hysteria.

When *Atom Squad* premiered on Monday, July 6, 1953, its first five-part serial, "The Man Who Stopped the Moon," introduced Steve Elliott (Robert Courtleigh), top investigator for the Atom Squad, and his partner, Dave Fielding (Bob Hastings). Operating out of the stereotypical scientific laboratory of the 1950s, this one secreted in New York City, their first on-camera assignment was to retrieve the purloined Neutrino Gun, a device able to stop the moon in its orbit. Of course, Elliott and Fielding track down the ex—Nazis responsible for the theft and prevent the gun from causing a global catastrophe. A steady stream of fantastic adventures followed on a more or less weekly schedule. Each adventure demonstrated, on one hand, the vulnerability of America to the ruthlessness of her enemies, but it also proved the physical and moral superiority of America as her representatives triumphed week after week. In "The Ship That Sailed to Nowhere," the Squad faced a Russian alliance with an American turncoat who had invented an underwater magnet which could be used to disrupt America's vital shipping. In yet another adventure, "The Scheme to Flood America," the Atom Squad confronted an effort to manipulate the weather and literally enlist nature against the United States.

Technical Information

FORMAT: Live 15-minute, five-times-a-week serial featuring the Cold War adventures of the Atom Squad charged with keeping America's atomic secrets out of the hands of foreign enemies.

BROADCAST HISTORY: *Network:* NBC. *Original Airdates:* July 6, 1953 to January 22, 1954. *Seasons:* 1. *Total Episodes:* 142 black-and-white.

Production Staff

Producer: Adrian Samish. *Head Writer:* Paul Monash.

Regular Cast

Steve Elliott   Robert Courtleigh
Dave Fielding   Bob Hastings
The Chief   Bram Nossem

Episode Guide

No episode guide available for this series.

Buck Rogers

Of the science fiction series discussed in this volume the most elusive is *Buck Rogers*. A short-lived series at the dawn of television, the show was broadcast live between April 15, 1950, and January 30, 1951. No kinescopes of the series are known to have survived. Of the 36 episodes aired, only three titles have been unearthed by researcher Alan Morton: "The Space Monster" (June 3, 1950), featuring the last appearance of Kem Dibbs in the role of Buck, "Slaves of the Mind Pirate" (June 10, 1950), featuring the first appearance of Robert Pastene in the title role, and "The Scarlet Crescent" (August 19, 1950).

For unknown reasons, Kem Dibbs left the series after only eight appearances. Although brief, his stint as Buck Rogers did lead to a long career in television and films including appearances on *Studio One*, *Playhouse 90* and *Hallmark Hall of Fame* as well as in films, among them *The Ten Commandments* (1956) and *Fate Is the Hunter* (1964).

TV's original *Buck Rogers* seems to have stayed within the framework originally established by writer Philip Francis Nowlan in his serialized novel, *Armageddon 2419 AD*, which first appeared in the August 1928 issue of *Amazing Stories*. Young Rogers took a job as a surveyor and was engaged in examining an abandoned mine on the outskirts of Pittsburgh, more than a little intrigued by the pungent atmosphere and glowing rock he discovered

within the mine. A sudden cave-in traps Rogers, but he is miraculously rescued by another, much later shifting of rock. When Dibbs, as Buck Rogers, stumbles out of the cave, he discovers an entirely new world. It is 500 years later; the strange gasses inside the mine put Buck in a state of suspended animation for half a millennium. Rogers meets Lt. Wilma Deering (Lou Prentis), Dr. Huer (Harry Southern) and Black Barney Wade (Harry Kingston). The capitol of the world is now the city of Niagara and mankind is engaged in a series of skirmishes with nefarious extraterrestrial forces. Buck quickly throws in his lot with his new friends.

The commercial success of DuMont's *Captain Video* appears to have prompted ABC to try a live science fiction show of its own, although ABC seems to have undermined its own efforts. Like *Captain Video* and several of the other early science fiction entries, the budget for *Buck Rogers* was minuscule. The dominant set was reportedly an archetypal laboratory secreted behind Niagara Falls. Much more damaging, however, was the replacement of the title character after only eight episodes. Dibbs's replacement Robert Pastene made only five appearances as Rogers and then the show seems to have gone on summer hiatus for almost two months, a situation which undercut efforts to build an audience. The 23 episodes which followed were unable to sufficiently redeem the series, and ABC seems to have made the decision to cut its losses and concentrate on other more promising entries in the science fiction field including *Space Patrol* and *Tom Corbett, Space Cadet*.

Allen Ducovny, producer of *Tom Corbett, Space Cadet*, suggested to an interviewer why he felt *Buck Rogers* failed as a series:

> One of the big troubles that this kind of program finds itself facing is that in the last few years youngsters have become pretty well aware of what science can do and what it can't do, so they're fairly critical on technical grounds of electronic razzle-dazzle in stories. *Buck Rogers* went in heavy for disintegrator-ray guns and mad scientists. Kids will accept only so much of that nowadays.

Ducovny's assessment of *Buck Rogers'* failure may or may not have been accurate; nonetheless, it is important to note that Ducovny's own show, *Tom Corbett, Space Cadet*, avoided those perceived pitfalls and prospered until the mid-1950s.

Technical Information

FORMAT: Live half-hour series recounting the familiar story of 20th century Buck Rogers, who awakens from a state of suspended animation in the 25th century.

BROADCAST HISTORY: *Network:* ABC. *Original Airdates:* April 15, 1950, to January 30, 1951. *Sponsor:* Peter Paul Candy bars. *Seasons:* 2. *Total episodes:* 36 black-and-white.

Production Staff

Producers: Joseph Cates and Babette Henry. *Director:* Babette Henry. *Writer:* Gene Wyckoff

Regular Cast

Buck Rogers   Kem Dibbs (4-15-50 to 6-3-50)
            Robert Pastene (6-10-50 to 1-30-51)
Lt. Wilma Deering   Lou Prentis
Dr. Huer   Harry Southern
Black Barney Wade   Harry Kingston
                              also Sanford Bickart

Episode Guide

No episode guide available for this series.

Captain Midnight

In one format or another, *Captain Midnight* had long been a part of America preadolescent culture. A popular radio show beginning in the late 1930s and running through the 1940s, the adventure serial also saw incarnations in comic books, various hardback print editions and a rousing 15-part Columbia serial before eventually stepping into the television limelight.

One of the great aural motifs of dramatic radio was of a church bell solemnly tolling midnight, the roar of a tiny plane triumphantly emerging from behind heavy clouds and the exuberant voice of announcer Pierre Andre calling listeners to another adventure of *Captain Midnight*. It seemed hard to imagine that the television version would be able to devise an equally memorable opening; however, the television edition of *Captain Midnight* succeeded in creating one of the most identifiable opening signatures of the 1950s. A word-for-word rendering was almost a required childhood catechism. Each episode would open with a high view of Captain Midnight's imposing headquarters, which resembled a combination laboratory and observatory. This was the central command post from which Captain Midnight and his closest confederates directed the far-flung operations of the Secret Squadron. The voice of the uncredited announcer would rise majestically above the stirring military-like music playing in the

background, revealing that we are looking at the mountaintop headquarters of CAPTAIN MIDNIGHT! Details as to Captain Midnight's background and origins were always kept vague and mysterious whether for radio or television. The Captain was described as a "war hero," but the wars seemed to change with the telling and retelling of the legend. The legend of Captain Midnight—real name, Red Albright—was born in the creative minds of two radio writers, Robert Burtt and Wilfred Moore, at a time when pioneering aviation was one of the consuming passions of our culture and the names of flyers like Charles Lindbergh, Wiley Post, Amelia Earhart and Lincoln Beachey were on the lips of millions of children and adults alike.

Burtt and Moore, like most of the rest of the country, were fascinated with the romance of flight, an era which had been inaugurated by the Wright Brothers a mere 30 years before. The writers previously created the juvenile aviation series *The Air Adventures of Jimmie Allen* in 1933. They would go on to create a similar series, *Hop Harrigan*, in 1942; in 1946, they would develop and write the successful *Sky King* series which would also eventually transfer to television. In 1938, however, Burtt and Moore would unveil on the radio airwaves their most successful creation, and one of the most listened-to adventure serials of all time, *Captain Midnight*. When television superseded

Opening signature of *Captain Midnight*, prominently featuring the sponsor, Ovaltine.

radio in the early 1950s as the dominant form of home entertainment, *Captain Midnight* would reappear, in altered form, as a leader in the Cold War resistance to totalitarianism.

The origin of Captain Midnight's name and life's mission was never revealed on the TV series. For something of an explanation, media historians must return to the radio series, where it was originally explained that at a low point in World War I a lone aviator, Red Albright, was handed a near-impossible task upon which would hinge the success or failure of the entire Allied cause. The daring flyer returned from successfully carrying out his mission precisely on the stroke of midnight and his exuberant commanding officer dubbed the young hero "Captain Midnight." After the war, Captain Midnight continued to fly hazardous missions as a private citizen, defending his country from an assortment of dangers.

In its first couple of seasons, the radio program was a regional series confined to broadcast stations in the Midwest and spon-sored by Skelly Oil. Captain Midnight's crime-fighting organization was originally known as the Flight Patrol. A sense of the history of Midnight's original organization may be gleaned from a message of greeting issued from Flight Patrol headquarters in the spring of 1940 to new and returning members of the Flight Patrol which tied membership to unfolding critical events overseas:

> Once again, it's the Spring of 1940—all of Europe is in flames and war clouds are gathering over the Pacific. Conscious of the growing danger in the world, Captain Midnight has called together a band of loyal friends to form the Captain Midnight 1940 Flight Patrol—a organization dedicated to the protection of democracy and the rules of fair play around the globe ... Rumors abound at club headquarters that government authorities are presently at work creating a new "super secret" organization which will combine elements of the Flight Patrol with certain official intelligence efforts. If this exciting development should

take place, all Flight Patrol members will become immediately eligible to join in the front ranks of the new group.

Both the radio and television versions of *Captain Midnight* led youngsters to believe that their participation was a vital contribution to the security of the country. By the fall of 1940, all rights to *Captain Midnight* had been obtained by the Wander Company, makers of the chocolate breakfast drink Ovaltine. *Captain Midnight* became a nationwide daily serial and his patriotic organization changed from the Flight Patrol to the Secret Squadron. During the 1940s, under Ovaltine's stewardship, *Captain Midnight* became one of the most generous dispensers of radio premiums on the airwaves. The most important of these giveaways were the yearly decoder badges which allowed Secret Squadron members to keep abreast of the latest important messages from headquarters. This interactive ploy was hugely popular with listeners and highly beneficial for the Wander Company, which required a proof of purchase from a can of Ovaltine in exchange for a decoder. The practice of issuing decoders would continue on television.

Captain Midnight exited the airwaves in December 1949. The postwar years had become something of an anticlimax for the serial heroes who had carried young listeners through the war. No villains loomed large enough to override the emotional letdown which seemed to be settling in after the war.

In an attempt to translate the former radio popularity of *Captain Midnight* to video, Ovaltine unveiled a new Captain Midnight to television in the fall of 1953 when *Captain Midnight's Adventure Theatre* began to air in selected video markets. This new series was reminiscent of the radio presentation insofar as its opening signature was concerned: a clock tolled the midnight hour and an echoing voice intoned, "C-A-P-T-A-I-N M-I-D-N-I-G-H-T." Next, the camera focused upon a young aviator sitting in the cockpit of a jet plane; discovering the audience, the pilot introduced himself: "This is Captain Midnight. I'll be on the ground in just 30 seconds with this week's exciting adventure, so stay tuned." After an Ovaltine commercial, Captain Midnight returned to the screen, but instead of offering

an original *Captain Midnight* adventure, the Captain merely introduced a movie serial chapter. Ovaltine must have soon realized that if Captain Midnight was to retain any credibility with the emerging television generation, storylines more substantive than a collection of movie serials would be required.

Before too much time elapsed, *Captain Midnight's Adventure Theatre* disappeared and was replaced in September 1954 with the revamped *Captain Midnight*, a weekly half-hour adventure series alternately sponsored by Ovaltine and Kix cereal. Filmed by Screen Gems, each episode of this new series had the distinction of offering distinct versions. The series was filmed first as *Captain Midnight*. Then, to provide for syndication under the auspices of a sponsor other than Ovaltine (who owned all rights to the Captain Midnight character), a second version was struck. The name Jet Jackson was dubbed over all references to Captain Midnight. In this way, two versions of each episode were prepared and eventually broadcast around the country.

Richard Webb played Captain Midnight and, of course, Jet Jackson. Sid Melton took the role of the Captain's faithful friend and mechanic, Ichabod Mudd. Olan Soule was assigned the newly created role of Aristotle Jones, "Tut," for short, an ingenious scientist working with Captain Midnight at the latter's mountaintop headquarters.

In the early 1950s, as *Captain Midnight* was making its way to television, the new medium was still appropriating many of the time-tested techniques of radio. Many of the juvenile video programs were still financially able to make premium offers to entice viewers. Ovaltine offered bright red plastic drinking cups and shakeup mugs for proofs of purchase of their product. Emblazoned with decals depicting a stylized Captain Midnight in helmet and gobbles, the plastic vessels featured such messages as "Ovaltine—the heart of a hearty breakfast" and "The Secret Squadron Way; drink Ovaltine every day." As part of their series responsibilities, Webb, Melton and Soule were instructed by the Wander Company to promote Ovaltine and the latest premium offer, whether it was a red Ovaltine mug, a plastic "Plane Puzzle" decoder or a

Richard Webb as Captain Midnight.

cloth patch which members of the Secret Squadron could wear proudly on their clothing. Youngsters proudly wearing their membership emblems were a fairly common sight in the mid–1950s.

Captain Midnight was updated over the years to reflect changing times. When the series began on radio, the Captain had been a hero of the First World War. Political and historical events soon plunged Midnight and his radio series into the thick of World War II each weekday afternoon. By the time of the television series, Captain Midnight had been redefined as a hero of the Korean War, and one was left to assume that his name now referred to some stroke-of-midnight heroics deriving from this latter conflict.

Captain Midnight was introduced to the television audience in an episode called "Murder by Radiation." At the beginning of the episode, viewers gleaned fragments of the story which connected Captain Midnight, Ikky and Tut to each other and to the Secret Squadron:

TUT: You were my friend when nobody else even knew I was alive. We were an odd combination: the campus hero and the greasy grind.

MIDNIGHT: You taught me all I know about science; I could never teach you anything about football.

IKKY: Gosh! Nobody could ever teach me anything.

MIDNIGHT: Ikky, if you weren't the best flight engineer in 70 states, I'd never made it back from that last recon run in Korea.

"Murder by Radiation," not unlike the majority of the entries in the *Captain Midnight* series, was constructed on a theme of competitive Cold War politics. A new radioactive element—Ormondium—had been stolen and it was up to Captain Midnight to retrieve it before it could be used by America's enemies.

One of the strengths of "Murder by Radiation" as a representative touchstone of the series is the introduction and heavy reliance on the Secret Squadron, the Captain's worldwide network of vigilant assistants (reminiscent of Sherlock Holmes' Baker Street Irregulars). Secret Squadron members were equipped with pocket locators which allowed them to remain in contact with headquarters, official membership cards, decoder pins, code books, signet rings and other items.

Captain Midnight actively recruited Secret Squadron members from his viewing audience. Joining the Secret Squadron was relatively simple, though living up to its high ideals of "justice through strength and courage" could be somewhat more difficult. To join merely required prospective members to submit the inner wax seal from a jar of Ovaltine to Captain Midnight, Box P, Chicago 77, Illinois. In a few weeks, a complete membership kit would be delivered; the only thing missing was the pocket locator, which was never included as part of the officially sanctioned membership package. How those Secret Squadron members featured on TV came into possession of their pocket locators was never explained, to the consternation of many young viewers.

The *Captain Midnight* series was skillfully packaged and presented, designed to capture and hold an audience of pre-adolescent patriots. The formula included exciting episode titles (promising more than could possibly be delivered), program content loaded with plenty of action and scientific gadgets, and inexpensive membership in the Secret Squadron complete with the previously mentioned membership cards, decoders and manuals. One of the most impressive devices was the Captain's TV telephone, "the visaphone." The visaphone allowed Captain Midnight to actually see who was calling. On more than one occasion this device permitted Midnight the luxury of knowing that the caller was being less than truthful.

To guarantee that viewers returned the following week, Captain Midnight, before final sign-off, offered a short teaser which made next week's show seem irresistible:

CAPTAIN MIDNIGHT: Attention all Secret Squadron members and fighters for justice everywhere! A friend of mine discovered the location of a satellite moon close enough to Earth to be used as a military space station, but before he could reveal his discovery to our government he was murdered. Our next mission is to find his murderer and the secret of the lost moon. We'll rendezvous here at headquarters. This is Captain Midnight signing off with the code of the Secret Squadron—justice through strength and courage. Out!

Or consider the promise presented at the close of "The Mark of Death" when Captain Midnight—using the age-old device of a teaser, coupled with the not-so-subtle appeal of a pulp magazine—outlined the following week's adventure:

CAPTAIN MIDNIGHT: Attention all Secret Squadron members! The Arctic Circle is the object of our next mission. There in the frozen North we'll meet the deadly challenge of enemy agents who are trying to sabotage our radar defenses—fight our way across the frozen tundra—face snowblindness and death as tons of snow and ice come crashing down on us in a thundering avalanche. We'll rendezvous here at headquarters, as usual. This is Captain Midnight signing off with the code of the Secret Squadron—justice through strength and courage. Out!

Captain Midnight never flew to the moon or the outer planets like Captain Video, Tom Corbett or Flash Gordon. He was restricted to the airspace of earth, usually piloting his private jet "The Silver Dart." The closest he ever came to leaving Earth orbit was in the adventures "The Lost Moon" and "The Human Bullet." Nor did he travel back and forth in time like Captain Z-RO. Nonetheless, *Captain Midnight* was heavily steeped in scientific technology. Secret Squadron headquarters routinely witnessed the development and testing of exotic formulae and inventions. Indicative of the 1950s paramilitary scientist, science for the sake of science was sublimated to the greater good and science for the sake of the survival of the state was the overarching theme. Given the dangerous political situations unfolding throughout the 1950s, such an outlook was easily explicable.

Some historians and social critics have suggested in recent years that television, and most notably series like *Captain Midnight*, somehow contributed to a communal passivity in which viewers were conditioned to accept unquestioningly Cold War decisions of their leaders, which in turn led to the mistakes of Vietnam. After Ovaltine withdrew its sponsorship, the series was rerun under the *Jet Jackson, the Flying Commando* title and constituted a familiar feature on television well into the 1960s, when the Captain Midnight/Jet Jackson style of Cold War militarism seemed at odds with the political philosophy of a large segment of the same American youth who had once proudly served in the Secret Squadron.

Technical Information

FORMAT. Filmed half-hour series recounting the heroic Cold War exploits of Captain Midnight and his "Secret Squadron."

BROADCAST HISTORY. *Network:* CBS. In syndication, the series was reissued as *Jet Jackson, the Flying Commando* and was distributed by Telescreen Advertising. *Original Airdates:* September 4, 1954, to January 21, 1956. *Sponsors:* Ovaltine (Ovaltine Food Products Co., a division of the Wander Company) and Kix Cereal (General Mills). *Seasons:* 2. *Total Episodes:* 39 black-and-white.

Signature

OPENING. The scene opens with an aerial view of Midnight's mountain observatory; a pounding military music backs up the announcer's words.

ANNOUNCER: On a mountaintop, high above a large city, stands the headquarters of a man devoted to the cause of freedom and justice ... a war hero who has never stopped fighting against his country's enemies ... a private citizen who is dedicating his life to the struggle against evil men everywhere ... *Captain Midnight*!

CLOSING. CAPTAIN MIDNIGHT: This is Captain Midnight signing off with the code of the Secret Squadron—"Justice through strength and courage." Out!

Production Staff

Production: Screen Gems, Inc. *Theme Music:* Don Ferris. *Producer:* George Bilson. *Director:* D. Ross Lederman. *Production Executive:* Fred Briskin.

Directors of Photography	Henry Freulich,
	Benjamin H. Kline, Ray Cory
Assistant Director	Irving Moore
Art Direction	Robert Peterson
Film Editor	Robert B. Hoover
Special Effects	Oscar Dallons, Paul Dallons,
	Franz Dallons
Set Decorators	Milton Stumph, Frank Tuttle
Assistant to Producer	Harold Greene
The Silver Dart	
	courtesy Douglas Aircraft, U.S. Navy

Regular Cast

Captain Midnight	Richard Webb
Ichabod Mudd (Ikky)	Sid Melton
Aristotle Jones (Tut)	Olan Soule

Episode Guide

SEASON 1

Murder by Radiation (September 4, 1954). Tut and the Secret Squadron experiment with Ormondium, the most powerful radioactive element in existence. When a sizable fragment of Ormondium is stolen by foreign agents plotting against the U.S., it becomes imperative to develop a defense against the deadly substance. *Writer:* Dane Slade.

Cast:
Jimmy Roberts	Tommy Ivo
Dr. Ormond	Wheaton Chambers
Loutrell	Peter Brocco
Marlowe	Harry Lauter
	also Henry Rowland

Electronic Killer (September 11, 1954). Captain Midnight is invited by old friend Dereck Strange to view the test of a new guided missile, the Nike. When Strange misses the test, Midnight and Ikky go to Strange's apartment and learn that he has been kidnapped. Enemy agents use drugs on Strange in an effort to procure his knowledge of the Nike missile. After gaining the information, the enemy agents place the unconscious Strange aboard a drone plane about to be destroyed as part of an Air Force test. Only Midnight's last-minute intervention saves Strange's life and captures the enemy agents. *Writer:* Dane Slade.

Cast:
Dereck Strange	Robert Bice
Gen. Howard	Charles Evans
Percy	William Tannen
Bart	Don Harvey
Fred	Mike Ragan

Deadly Diamonds (September 18, 1954). Captain Midnight and the Secret Squadron track down a dangerous band of diamond smugglers operating on both sides of the Mexican border. The assignment is made easier with the help of one of Tut's inventions, an Omni Counter, which reacts to precious gems and metals. *Writer:* Wallace Bosco. *Story:* William Lively.

Cast:
Jimmy Sawyer	Gary Gray
George Maynard	John Hamilton
Hank Rogers	Ed Hinton
Brady	John Cason
Snyder	Zon Murray
Sheriff	I. Stanford Jolley

The Lost Moon (September 25, 1954). The discovery of a "lost moon" closely orbiting the earth brings about the death of an amateur astronomer. Captain Midnight and enemy agents contend for the astronomer's secret, with both sides aware that whichever power reaches the platform in space first will control the earth. *Writer:* Dane Slade.

Cast:
Lt. Olson	Robert Anderson
Ling	Victor Sen Yung
Paul Ellwood	John Phillips
Woh	Eddie Lee
Sergeant	Brian O'Hara

Death Below Zero (October 2, 1954). Captain Midnight investigates the poisoning of a small dog belonging to a member of the Secret Squadron. The investigation leads to the solution of a bank robbery, but not before Captain Midnight almost meets his doom imprisoned in a cold storage locker. *Writer:* Wells Root. *Story:* Malcolm Stuart Boylan.

Cast: *Jefferson Bishop*   David Colmans
       John Sawyer   Kenneth MacDonald
       Shook   Henry Rowland
       Krause   Harry Lauter
       Fenton   Bob Woodward

Operation Failure (October 9, 1954). Captain Midnight travels behind the Iron Curtain to the small country of Balkavia. His assignment is to rescue Zabor, the country's foremost resistance fighter and symbol of freedom. Midnight succeeds in his mission but at the final moment Zabor elects to remain in his own country and continue leading the struggle for democracy.
Cast: *Zabor*   John Mylong

Trapped Behind Bars (October 16, 1954). Captain Midnight and Ikky go undercover behind prison bars to learn the secret of a series of prison riots. Yet another riot results in Captain Midnight and Ikky escaping along with a band of hardened prisoners. The Secret Squadron team learns that the riots have been part of an elaborate foreign plot against America. *Writer:* George Bricker. *Story:* Milton M. Raison.
Cast: *Rocky Billings*   Don C. Harvey
       Pete   Lennie Bremen
       Mr. Terhume Charles Postal
       Hargo   Mel Welles
       The Warden   Gene Roth
       Jones   Edward Foster

Counterfeit Millions (October 23, 1954). When counterfeit bills begin to flood the United States, Captain Midnight discovers a trucking company is being used as a means of distribution. *Writer:* Malcolm Stuart Boylan.
Cast: John Damler
              Paul McGuire
              Byron Foulger
              Robert Crosson

The Walking Ghost (October 30, 1954). A frantic squadron member requests Captain Midnight's help in exorcising a murderous ghost. Midnight, Ikky and Tut set up an electronic perimeter around the Southern mansion "haunted" by the ghost and catch a foreign agent plotting to use the site as a rendezvous point. *Writer:* Wallace Bosco.

Cast: *Martha Stanhope*   Sally Fraser
       Incana   Belle Mitchell
       Uncle Cyrus   William Fawcett

Secret of the Jungle (November 6, 1954). Captain Midnight and Ikky pay a surprise visit to Tut, who is in Africa collecting rare plant and soil samples. Hoping for a peaceful vacation, the Secret Squadron instead encounters the mystery of a stolen idol, a plot to foment native unrest, and a rich uranium deposit. *Writer:* Wells Root.
Cast: *Chuck*   René Beard
       Goranov   John Banner

Sabotage Under the Sea (November 13, 1954). Captain Midnight travels to the bottom of the ocean in search of an experimental missile that has mysteriously disappeared. An enemy submarine is detected hiding in an underwater cavern. *Writer:* George Bricker
Cast: *Steve Darby*   John Pickard
       Kroll   Philip Van Zandt

Isle of Mystery (November 20, 1954). When the queen of the small island of Luana abruptly withdraws her permission for the U.S. to conduct vital atomic tests on her territory, Captain Midnight and Ikky are commissioned to discover the reason why.
Cast: *Queen of Luana*   Nina Monsour
       also Zon Murray, David Garcia

The Curse of the Pharaohs (November 27, 1954). Summoned to Egypt by the daughter of an eminent archaeologist, Captain Midnight investigates the archaeologist's mysterious disappearance and the curse of the pharaohs. *Writer:* George Bricker.
Cast: *Eve Gamble*   Sheila Ryan
       Prof. Gamble George Eldredge
       Vornholt   Otto Reichow
       Naji   Naji
       Haseem   Frank Lackteen

The Deserters (December 4, 1954). Captain Midnight takes time from his busy schedule to assist a group of Secret Squadron members who have been evicted from their club house by a commercial developer. In the process, Midnight uncovers a bank robbery. *Writers:*

hcl-#13

7   CONTINUED:

                                  IKKY
                 Sure. It's like this: They
                 fire off the rocket -- BANG!
                 ... It flies through the air --
                 WHOOSH! ... It hits the water
                 -- SPLASH! ... It sinks to the
                 bottom -- BUBBLE, BUBBLE, BUBBLE!
                 ... Along comes a great, big
                 whale - GOBBLE, GOBBLE, GOBBLE!
                 See? ...

        He looks to them confidently for confirmation.

8   THREE SHOT MIDNIGHT TUT STEVE
        Looking at Ikky askance.

9   REVERSE SHOT IKKY
        His confidence somewhat shaken:

                                  IKKY
                 No?

10   GROUP SHOT FAVORING MIDNIGHT

                                MIDNIGHT
                     (dryly)
                 No.
                     (to Steve)
                 When do they fire the next rocket?

                                 STEVE
                 Tomorrow morning.
                     (gloomily)
                 And by tomorrow night, if I don't
                 recover it, they'll be firing me.

                                MIDNIGHT
                     (thoughtfully)
                 You know -- I'd like to take a
                 stab at recovering that rocket
                 myself, if you have no objection.

                                 STEVE
                     (heartily)
                 None at all. In fact, it'd be a
                 relief to have somebody else con-
                 firm what's been happening.

Malcolm Stuart Boylan and Wells Root. *Story:* Malcolm Stuart Boylan.

Cast:
Hi Foley	Stuffy Singer
Low Foley	Butch Bernard
James Van Dirk	Kem Dibbs
Rice	Harry Lauter
Schnoble	Henry Rowland
Davis	Rusty Westcoatt

The Electrified Man (December 11, 1954). An eminent scientist, a refugee from behind the Iron Curtain, requests that Secret Squadron headquarters be put at his disposal while he perfects his new process. The scientist is working on a countermeasure against the dreaded RD (Radioactive Dust) bomb. The process requires that the scientist be subjected to greater and greater doses of electrical energy. When the scientist exceeds tolerable limits of electricity, he becomes a walking death. *Writer:* Dane Slade.

Cast:
Prof. Berglund	Ian Keith
Lisa	Regina Gleason
Roselli	Norman Willis
Morton	Edward Foster

The Young Criminal (December 18, 1954). In an effort to help combat the rising tide of juvenile delinquency, Captain Midnight sponsors a gym as a means of keeping at-risk youth off the streets. One of the youngsters, Tommy Venters, is impressed with the lifestyle of a poolroom owner.

Cast:
	Jack Diamond
	Dick Rich

The Deadly Project (December 25, 1954). The Secret Squadron laboratory is placed at the disposal of a famous scientist working to develop a new heat-resistant metal urgently needed by the Air Force. However, the research is repeatedly stymied by a vindictive scientist who has developed a sonic gun and holds a deep-seated animosity for the scientist. *Writer:* Wallace Bosco. *Story:* Dick Morgan.

Cast:
Dr. Morgan	Pierre Watkin
Henderson	Philip Van Zandt
Dr. Vronik	Franz Roehn
Ditmars	Baynes Barron

Touchdown Terror (January 1, 1955). Gamblers try to bribe a star quarterback to throw an important game. Desperately in need of money to finance an operation for his sister, the young player is tempted but ultimately refuses to participate in the scheme. In retaliation, both the quarterback and Captain Midnight are kidnapped.

Cast:
	Terry Frost
	Mark Andrews
	Karen Green
	Maudie Prickett
	Greg Barton
	Joseph Hamilton

Top Secret Weapon (January 8, 1955). A young boy, a refugee from behind the Iron Curtain, seeks out Captain Midnight for asylum. What the Captain does not know is that the boy has been programmed to spy on a top secret weapon being developed at Midnight's mountaintop laboratory. Acting under hypnosis, the boy sabotages the weapon. At the last moment the youngster is able to fight off the effects of his hypnosis and provide Midnight with the information necessary to save Secret Squadron headquarters and to defeat the foreign agents behind the plot. *Writer:* Wells Root.

Cast:
Stefan	Aurelio Galli
Mr. Hoffner	Jack George
Mrs. Hoffner	Greta Granstedt
Grock	Aaron Saxon
	also Gregory Gay

The Human Bomb (January 15, 1955). A munitions genius is released from jail and immediately plots his revenge against Midnight and the law enforcement officials responsible for his conviction. *Writer:* Wallace Bosco.

Cast:
Volmer	Dick Rich
Judge Jonathan Bell	Gayne Whitman
Linden	Jarl Victor
Grantz	John Force
Billy Griffiths	Robert Lyden

The Mark of Death (January 22, 1955). Captain Midnight travels to India to deliver a

Opposite: A page from George Bricker's script for "Sabotage Under the Sea" shows a typical Ikky response to a problem.

goodwill message at the invitation of Bengra Tassi, the organizer of an important Asian Conference. Arriving in India, Midnight and Ikky are greeted with the news that Tassi has been kidnapped by a fiend known only as "The Executioner." Midnight must rescue Tassi before the Asian Conference can be subverted by enemies of democracy. *Writer:* Wells Root. *Story:* Tom Kilpatrick.

Cast:
Bengra Tassi	Ted Hecht
Ram Das	David Colmans
Kalyan Singh	Bobker Ben Ali
Landru	Peter Brocco
Knife Seller	Paul Marion

Arctic Avalanche (January 29, 1955). Returning from a mission to the North Pole, Captain Midnight and Ikky are persuaded to fly a sick Eskimo to a medical facility. When they reach the Eskimo's remote cabin, they are taken hostage by foreign agents. *Writer:* Wells Root.

Cast:
Zarka	Marc Krah
Sutoc	Philip Ahn
Gorba	Lane Nakano
Kindu	Tetsu Komai

Mystery of the Forest (February 5, 1955). Captain Midnight and Ikky travel to the Pacific Northwest timber country to investigate one of the largest non-nuclear explosions in history. Posing as lumberjacks, they uncover a compound which when added to wood creates a cheap and powerful explosive. Unless Midnight can defeat the men behind the development of this new weapon, the balance of world power may be altered. *Writer:* Milton M. Raison

Cast:
Gaynor	Don C. Harvey
Harris	Terry Frost
Prof. Harlow	Art Gilmore
	also Daniel de Jonghe

The Invisible Terror (February 12, 1955). A germ warfare attack is planned against the eastern United States by one of America's Cold War enemies. Midnight is called upon to recover a missing formula which would protect the country against the "Victory Virus." *Writer:* Wells Root.

Cast:
Dr. Hamilton	George Eldredge
Gorley	Jarl Victor
Raughlin	Bert Le Baron
Mannlicher	Mel Welles
Mrs. Radnor	Greta Granstedt

Saboteurs of the Sky (February 19, 1955). Midnight investigates the kidnapping of a Secret Squadron member and her father, a famous weather scientist who has developed the ability to conjure up hurricanes. *Writer:* Dane Slade.

Cast:
Sally Jensen	Frances Karath
Mr. Jensen	Vernon Rich
Salesman	Dick Grant
Fleck	George D. Barrows
Lorenz	Harold Dyrenforth
Neighbor	Dick Elliott

Peril from the Arctic (February 26, 1955). On a mission to Alaska, Midnight and Ikky respond to a Mayday message. After making a forced landing in a remote part of the North, they trek to a cabin which houses a renegade scientist experimenting with an anti-magnetic force which is intended to form the nucleus of a military attack against the United States. *Writer:* Dane Slade. *Story:* Roy Hamilton.

Cast:
Dr. Morelli	Mel Welles
Portman	Marshall Reed
Bass	Paul Marion
Major	Tyler McVey

SEASON 2

The Secret Room (October 29, 1955). Captain Midnight and the Secret Squadron expose a phony seance racket preying upon a wealthy society woman, the wife of famous physicist Prof. Woodman. The professor has invented a device to harness the rays of the sun, and the seance racket proves to be an elaborate scheme to obtain the Professor's invention. *Writer:* Wallace Bosco.

Cast:
Mrs. Woodman	Arlene Harris
Swami Yogora	Baynes Barron
Prof. Woodman	Hal Taggart
Bill Worth	Erik Paige
Hendricks	Chester Hayes

Mission to Mexico (November 5, 1955). Midnight and Ikky head to Mexico to track down an enemy radio station. The last intercepted message made reference to shipments of fissionable materials. The success or failure of the Secret Squadron may determine the fate of the entire Western hemisphere. *Writer:* Wallace Bosco. *Story:* Malcolm Stuart Boylan.

Cast:
Davis	John W. Truax
Hobson	Tyler McVey
Nicko	Alan Wells
Bandito	Ben Frommer
Commandante	Edward Colmans
Alvarez	Alfred Ward

The Frozen Man (November 12, 1955). A famous scientist, who has been developing a new metal which may be the key to space travel, is kidnapped. Captain Midnight locates the scientist in a state of frozen animation in the middle of a desert. In order to save the scientist's life, Captain Midnight must survive a nuclear test at ground zero. *Writers:* Roy Erwin and Wallace Bosco.

Cast:
Gen. Tetley	William Remick
Zorac	Jack Tesler
Volney	Lennie Bremen
Mrs. Harper	Mary Adams
Dr. Harper	Pat O'Hara

Doctors of Doom (November 19, 1955). The report of a "giant" roaming a small Maryland town draws the Secret Squadron into the investigation. The inquiry leads to a sanitarium where the only resident is a nuclear scientist who has been turned into a "scientific slave" for the benefit of a ruthless foreign power. *Writer:* Wells Root.

Cast:
Gladys Murphy	Frances Karath
Bluchner	Buddy Baer
Roush	Harold Dyrenforth
Prof. Edwin Genner	Jack George
Dr. Bowers	Harry Cody

Sunken Sapphires (November 25, 1955). Captain Midnight and Ikky assist a young woman and her brother in recovering a long-lost cache of family jewels with the aid of Tut's invaluable Omni Counter. Once the jewels are recovered, Midnight and Ikky must battle thugs to retain possession of the precious treasure. *Writer:* Anthony O. Scott.

Cast:
Helen Orloff	Donna Drew
Billy Orloff	Dickie Bellis
Gaston	Frank Richards
Lars Ekberg	Hank Patterson
Police Lieutenant	Henry Rowland

Master Criminal (December 3, 1955). The plans to a new jet engine under development at Secret Squadron headquarters attract one of the nation's top criminals. Pretending to surrender himself to Captain Midnight, the criminal gains access to the Captain's laboratory and the plans for the new jet engine.

Cast: Baynes Barron

Secret of Superstition Mountain (December 10, 1955). Prospecting in Arizona for a substitute for uranium, Midnight and Ikky stumble on a hidden treasure. Ghostly apparitions and other forces seem intent on robbing Midnight and Ikky of their discovery. *Writer:* Anthony O. Scott.

Cast:
Frank Adams	John Pickard
Bob Hansen	George Berkeley
Clem	William Fawcett
Indian Charlie	Charles Stevens

The Mountain of Fire (December 17, 1955). Captain Midnight and Ikky assist a group of scientists trying to develop a process for converting volcanic heat into electricity. When a long-dormant volcano springs to life, disrupting the research, sabotage is suspected. *Writers:* Robert Leslie Bellem and Ted Thomas.

Cast:
Frank White	Ralph Gamble
Carlos Perez	Alex Montoya
Pepito	Orlando Rodriguez
Jose	Paul Fierro

The Jungle Pit (December 24, 1955). Midnight and Ikky help a Japanese youngster locate his missing father—a Japanese soldier hiding on a Pacific Island, convinced that World War II has not ended. *Writer:* Anthony O. Scott.

Cast:
Jerry	Dominique De Leon
Kisano	Kazuo Togo
Van Ronk	John Banner
Tamba	Marvin Lindsay

Flight into the Unknown (December 31, 1955). After a prominent banker disappears with $500,000 of his bank's assets, Captain Midnight and Ikky trace the man to a small Pacific island where he is recovering from emotional exhaustion. The unwelcome arrival on the island of three greedy thugs complicates Midnight's efforts to help the distraught banker clear his name and return to his family. *Writers:* Wallace Bosco and Malcolm Stuart Boylan. *Story:* Malcolm Stuart Boylan.

Cast:

Walter Kurt	John Beradino
John Cabot Kingsley	Paul Keast
Mrs. Kingsley	Lorna Thayer
Mary Kingsley	Shelley Fabares

The Runaway Suitcase (January 7, 1956). A police officer is accused of taking a suitcase full of stolen money and forced to resign from the police force. He turns to Captain Midnight to help clear his name.

Cast:

Fred Connors	Gregg Barton
Tom Blake	Jimmy Karath
Detective Swan	Tom McKee

Million Dollar Diamond (January 14, 1956). Young Jimmy Gibson tells Captain Midnight about the strange and abusive behavior of his father, a gem expert preparing to cut a fabulous million dollar diamond. With the aid of Tut's new invention, a miniature television camera and transmitter, Midnight learns that Jimmy's father has been kidnapped and a double put in his place. The plan is to abscond with the diamond when it is delivered for cutting. Midnight arranges for the release of Jimmy's real father and the apprehension of the criminals behind the proposed theft. *Writer:* Robert Leslie Belem.

Cast:

Jimmy Gibson	Butch Bernard
Mrs. Drexel	Linda Damson
Mr. Gibson	Tom Glenway
Fake Gibson	Lee Garrets
Pedro	Bobber Ben Ali
Arturo	Manuel Paris

The Human Bullet (January 21, 1956). Captain Midnight agrees to test a revolutionary new rocket sled after the vehicle's first pilot is killed in its 800 m.p.h. test run. Midnight uncovers a sabotage plot to discredit the inventor and the invention.

Captain Video
and His Video Rangers

Almost half a century after its introduction as TV's first space opera, it is hard for many people to comprehend the widespread influence *Captain Video* had on the original television generation. Everything about *Captain Video and His Video Rangers* was cheap and primitive. And that observation is not made out of condescension or as a putdown, but rather as an admission of respect for what the series was able to accomplish during its life span. Television itself was a primitive but emerging medium on June 27, 1949, when *Captain Video* premiered over the DuMont Network. As critic Tom Shales observed, "The special effects were pretty tacky, but when you're a kid you don't require much to prick your imagination."

Like many of television's most successful innovations, *Captain Video* came about almost by accident. Jim Caddigan, DuMont's program director, encountered an airing of *Captain Marvel* and suggested to some of the assembled staff at DuMont that they should try their hand at creating a science fictional Captain something-or-other. Somebody came up with "Captain Video." From there the idea was turned over to writer Larry Menkin who recalls, "I came up with a structure—Sherlock Holmes and Dr. Moriarty." Holmes, of course,

was Captain Video and Moriarty was the Captain's arch nemesis, Dr. Pauli.

It was almost as simple as that. Of course, a cast still had to be selected and for the role of Captain Video a 34-year-old Broadway and radio actor named Richard Coogan was appointed. As the Captain's youthful assistant, "The Video Ranger," 15-year-old Don Hastings was picked. The role of Dr. Pauli, the evil scientific genius and guiding force behind the Asteroidal Society, fell initially to Bram Nossen. Directing *Captain Video* at the outset was Charles Polachek and writing many of the early plots was M.C. Brock.

Contrary to generally held belief, Captain Video was earthbound for the first several months of the series. In fact, most of the action took place at Video Rangers Headquarters, a place described by TV critic Jack Gould as "a room equipped with flashing bulbs, microphones, panels, dials, telephones, etc. By comparison, the central office of AT&T is just for beginners." Reportedly, only after ABC unveiled plans to serve up a new version of *Buck Rogers* did *Captain Video* manage to make it into outer space, and even then only after series star Richard Coogan went public with his dissatisfaction. "It's about time we got into the interplanetary stuff. I don't want to become

Opening signature of *Captain Video and His Video Rangers*, which consisted of a painted backdrop with superimposed letters.

stagnant in the role." *Buck Rogers* would last only a few months but the series could at least take credit for launching *Captain Video* out of Earth orbit.

It is a fair surmise, given the parsimonious nature of the DuMont Network, that *Captain Video* avoided rocketing off into space for as long as it did because of financial considerations. Quite simply, space travel was going to cost more production dollars. Only the threat that came from a competing network intent on cutting into *Captain Video*'s lucrative market seems to have convinced DuMont to allow the change in direction.

It is worth spending a little time looking at the interplay of cost-cutting measures and creative responses which resulted in an undisputed television legend. The first note of significance is the lack of extant recordings of the *Captain Video* series. Although researcher Alan Morton has made a "best estimate" of 1537 aired episodes, only four or five have resurfaced to date. As Morton points out, *Cap-*

tain Video kinescopes and, in fact, all of the other kinescopes in the old DuMont archives were destroyed at the end of the 1950s to glean a handful of dollars from the silver content of the films and to save storage costs for so many thousands of unprofitable films deemed worthless. In essence, *Captain Video* died as the series had lived—a pawn of the bean counters.

In spite of, or because of, an addiction to frugality, *Captain Video and His Video Rangers* tapped an emotional response from a huge audience during the first half of the '50s. One story told is that Adlai Stevenson was approached to make an important speech which would coincidentally conflict with one of Captain Video's nightly appearances. Stevenson emphatically turned down the request. "Seven o'clock on a weekday? No sir, not opposite *Captain Video*."

Certainly *Captain Video*'s influence on the popular culture was enormous. The DuMont Network, which was formed in large measure as a means of creating a market for DuMont television receivers, was more than satisfied with the success of the series, one of only a handful of true hits DuMont ever had to its credit.

The most popular programs of the day—*Captain Video* among them—were literally redefining family behavior and relationships. Coogan observed the change from the perspective of someone intimately involved in creating the social change. During his tenure as Captain Video, Coogan reported:

> The fathers in my neighborhood used to take their children to a nearby bar and grill to see *Captain Video*, whenever they had time. The owner would stop serving any drinks that half-hour and what happened then? A lot of families got television sets just so father wouldn't miss the Captain's latest adventure in Electronicland.

And the television sets sold by *Captain Video*? DuMont sets, of course! In fact, *Captain Video* sold a great many items beyond DuMont television receivers. The program sold lots of Power House candy bars as well as Skippy Peanut Butter and Post Cereal; all were prominent sponsors. At a time when the influence of radio was still keenly felt by the television industry, *Captain Video* frequently indulged in one of the longtime practices of radio, the premium giveaway. The array of premium offers included a "Flying Saucer Ring," a "Secret Seal Brass Ring," cast photos, membership cards in the Video Rangers, secret decoders, "Electronic Video Goggles," a "Secret Ray Gun," a rocket ship key chain and a series of 12 plastic space men. This made for a somewhat strange dichotomy: a munificent advertising income and a production budget of Lilliputian proportions.

The cast of *Captain Video* had to settle for rewards other than monetary. In an interview years later, Don Hastings recalled that he and other members of the cast actually made more from guest appearances at supermarket openings and county fairs than from the show itself. When Richard Coogan left the role in December 1950, it was speculated that the decision was at least in part dictated by a refusal to cut the cast in for a percentage of the lucrative licensing dollars accruing from the sale of Captain Video merchandise.

It required a great deal of physical and emotional stamina to survive the heavy demands of live television. *Captain Video* in its five-times-a-week serial format and tight budgets was hard on actors. Coogan left the role and concentrated his energies on the Broadway stage; Bram Nossen, the evil Dr. Pauli, left the show in June 1950 after he reportedly broke down under the pressure and asked to be replaced. The series would also go through an array of writers and directors. In fact, young Don Hastings, the Video Ranger, probably demonstrated the most staying power—appearing from day one through to the ringing down of the final curtain some six years later.

When Bram Nossen bowed out as Dr. Pauli, program executives hurriedly scouted around for a replacement and came up with Hal Conklin, who would serve in the role as needed until 1954 when he relinquished the part to Stephen Elliott.

To replace Richard Coogan, the decision was made to offer the role to veteran radio actor Al Hodge. Hodge had appeared in roles on such programs as *The Romance of Helen Trent*, *Ma Perkins* and *Bobby Benson and the B-Bar-B Riders*. He was also an early director on *The Lone Ranger* and most notably had held the lead on radio's *Green Hornet* from 1936 to 1943. Hodge seemed a perfect fit for yet another superhero part. Interestingly, when Hal Conklin replaced Bram Nossen, it was explained in the script that the perfidious Dr. Pauli had undergone plastic surgery in an effort to outwit Captain Video. However, six months later, when Al Hodge replaced Coogan, no plausible explanation was offered.

The evolving cast and behind-the-scenes changes didn't seem to affect the growing popularity of *Captain Video*. The series continued on its own unique improvisational and frugal way. Captain Video's mountaintop headquarters, as Don Hastings vividly recalls, was "literally a four-by-four card on an easel. Sometimes it fell off while we were shooting."

As was widely reported at the time, the prop budget for *Captain Video and His Video Rangers* was a paltry $25 a week. Yet out of that budget, innovative minds at DuMont devised a plethora of gadgets which were the talk of schoolyards and the dream of every covetous youngster in America.

The first two recorded instruments in the Captain's arsenal of special devices were the Opticon Scillometer (a telescope capable of peering around corners and through solid objects) and a ray gun. Charles Polachek, the original director of *Captain Video*, recalled the detailed history of those two inventions in an interview published in Jeff Kisseloff's engaging volume, *The Box: An Oral History of Television, 1920-1961.* Polachek recalled that DuMont had no prop department and only at the last minute did the need for an Opticon Scillometer and a ray gun dawn on the director. Fortunately, the DuMont Studio where *Captain Video* was produced was located in Wanamaker's Department Store in New York City. Polachek and a companion paid a quick visit to Wanamaker's toy department in search of some type of gun they could transform into the required ray gun, but to their dismay discovered that Wanamaker's toy department was pacifist—no guns of any kind. Polachek's next trip was to the auto parts department where the Opticon Scillometer hurriedly took shape out of "a spark plug, a muffler, a rear-view-mirror and an ashtray."

Other inventions on the show were equally contrived. The Cosmic Ray Vibrator, when pointed at one of Captain Video's foes, caused him to begin twitching and shaking uncontrollably. There was also Captain Video's Thermoid Ejector, a weapon capable of shooting infrared thermal currents. The Mango-Radar could be aimed at any spot on the planet and allow Captain Video to eavesdrop on any event.

When Captain Video finally lifted off into space, he and the Video Ranger traveled in style in the Captain's private ship, the Galaxy. Discerning viewers couldn't help but notice the interior of the Galaxy was constructed out of cardboard and most of the instruments on the instrument panel had been installed with a paintbrush. Larry Menkin, one of the writers for the show, has described a typical flight in the Galaxy:

Instead of having them take off in their spaceship, we had them lying down, and we'd shake the camera. Also, when they were going through clouds, we took a great big tank of water, poured cream in it and shot through that.

Dr. Pauli, too, had his infernal devices. Pauli possessed the ability to set up "a barrier of silence" which had the effect of shutting off all sound. Pauli also had at his disposal "a cloak of invisibility."

Captain Video kept a succession of writers busy for six years, their imaginations always tempered by budget considerations. Consequently, a *Captain Video* script was long on dialogue and painfully short on the kind of rapid and exciting action later generations have come to expect. Writers including M.C. Brock, Jack Vance, Damon Knight, C.M. Kornblath, Robert Sheckley and Larry Menkin are given credit for contributing stories to *Captain Video*.

For the first couple of years, writers were also required to allow time in the middle of each script for a five-minute cutaway segment of an old western movie, perhaps the strangest aspect of the entire series. Youngsters could understand the adversarial relationship between Captain Video and Dr. Pauli, they could understand the mechanics of the Opticon Scillometer, they could comprehend the "barrier of silence" and they could explain the operation of the instrument panel in the *Galaxy*—but the sudden appearance of a segment of a *Range Busters* movie sandwiched in the middle of each *Captain Video* episode confounded more than one five-year-old. Halfway into each program, Captain Video tuned in via another invention (the Remote Tele-Carrier) to see what was happening with his Video Rangers out West where other villains were on the loose. The actual explanation for the Western sequences, however, takes us right back to DuMont's tight-fisted approach. Reportedly the original concept for *Captain Video* called for the Captain and his sidekick to serve merely as hosts to a series of Western films DuMont had purchased for broadcast. A change of plans transformed Captain Video into an action hero with his own series of adventures; however, DuMont wasn't about to waste the broadcast rights to all of those old Western movies and so *Captain Video* made room for brief appearances by John Wayne, Ken Maynard, Tex Ritter and a lengthy list of other Western heroes.

Jim Caddigan, the executive in charge of programming at DuMont and the man usually credited with conceiving *Captain Video*, explained in an interview with *Time* (December 25, 1950) presumably with a straight face, the official network line concerning the baffling appearance of all those Westerns in the middle of a space opera:

> The Western is there to give us the pace and action that we can't get in a live studio production. The hero of the Western is always supposed to be an agent of Captain Video's—that sort of ties it together.

A parade of cheaply costumed villains passed in review before the DuMont cameras in those years. Aside from the recurring Dr. Pauli (a.k.a. "The Sinister Electronic Wizard"), there was Hing Foo Sung, played by Henry Norrel, who was billed as "a wily Oriental." Other figures of note included Tobor ("Robot" spelled backwards), played by Dave Ballard, and Nargola, played by Ernest Borgnine. In their tribute to early television, *The Great Television Heroes*, Donald Glut and Jim Harmon estimated that in Captain Video's career over 300 villains crossed paths with "the Guardian of the World."

When the budget was stretched to the point that the show couldn't hire enough actors for all the required parts, the program director would double up on the parts by disguising actors with false beards and other forms of camouflage. Charles Polachek recalls resorting to the use of stagehands' shadows to augment his cast.

Al Hodge as Captain Video took his responsibilities toward his young viewers seriously, as did most of the heroes of early television. They shared the sentiment that they were guests in each and every home and they felt obligated not to abuse their welcome. At the same time that Hodge was appearing weekdays as Captain Video, he was appearing Sunday mornings as a Sunday school teacher in Manhasset, Long Island, and freely tied the two roles together. In discussing his juggling of roles, Hodge told one interviewer:

> Every week, without fail, I see several new faces in class. At the end of each session, I notice that the newcomers have been taken aside and, in hushed whispers, learn that I am Captain Video himself. The identification does have a very good aspect. At least three times a week on *Captain Video*, we deliver short messages to our youthful listeners. We stress the Golden Rule, tolerance, honesty and personal integrity. I'm thankful for the opportunity for being associated with the show that helps, in a small measure, to illuminate for the young people of America, the importance of courage, character and the sense of moral values.

In the fall of 1954, a Senate subcommittee under the chairmanship of Robert Hendrickson (Republican, New Jersey) held hearings to determine the extent to which the new medium of television was contributing to the alarming rise in juvenile delinquency. A TV schedule which seemed filled to overflowing with six-guns, ray guns and Cosmic Ray Vibrators was suspected of at least some culpability. Al Hodge was called to testify and in a sense justify his own performance over the previous four years. "Of course, you have to have villains in a hero program or there's not any use for a hero," Hodge pointed out.

Hodge's testimony underscored a crucial difference that needed to be made between violence perpetrated by a clearly defined villain and the countermeasures employed by role models such as Captain Video. Television heroes of the 1950s struggled constantly with the issue. Hodge attempted to define the approach taken on his own show:

> We don't even use the word "kill." We use weapons like the stun gun which immobilize but don't pain... We don't use capital punishment. We confine our criminals to rehabilitation centers on the planet Ganymede...

Chairman Hendrickson asked Hodge if he, as Captain Video, would stamp on someone's hand—a reference to an instance of media violence previously viewed by the committee. *Newsweek* (November 1, 1954) reported his answer:

> Oh no, said Video, he would never stamp his foot on a helpless man's hand because it was in bad taste—unless, of course, it was a temporary thing done simply to hold a villain in place, and then it might be in good

taste. Video carefully added that even when he was just cruising around in the solar system in his spaceship, he always kept on the lookout for a "moral value."

Although the tangle of rationalizations may seem amusing, the answers were framed as honest answers by an actor with moral convictions, struggling to respond to a hypothetical confrontational situation.

Captain Video and His Video Rangers ceased production in April 1955 close to the time the DuMont Network finally caved in to financial weakness and dissolved. There had been spinoffs from the original series, of course. Columbia Pictures released a 15-part *Captain Video* serial starring Judd Holdren in 1951. A Saturday version titled *The Secret Files of Captain Video* and starring Hodge ran biweekly, from September 5, 1953, to May 29, 1954, and featured half-hour stories of a nonserial format. Reportedly NBC offered to purchase the rights to *Captain Video* when DuMont closed up shop but was turned down. Al Hodge continued in the role of *Captain Video* by hosting a series of cartoons over station WABD until August 16, 1957, when one of the great superheroes of the 1950s quietly walked off stage.

Technical Information

FORMAT: Live science fiction adventure serial featuring the adventures of Captain Video, self-proclaimed "Guardian of the Safety of the World."

BROADCAST HISTORY: *Network*: DuMont. *Original Airdates:* June 27, 1949, to April 1, 1955. *Total Episodes:* Unknown.

Signature

OPENING: With the Overture to Wagner's "Flying Dutchman" playing in the background, an echoing voice invoked the name of Captain Video. Fred Scott followed with a brief explanation of how Captain Video fought the forces of evil from his "mountain retreat," using "scientific secrets and scientific weapons." The echoing voice then repeated Captain Video's name.

CLOSING: Again over the background of Wagner's "Flying Dutchman" Overture, Fred Scott encouraged the audience to meet him "right here, Rangers," for (echoing voice) "Captain Videoooo and His Videoooo Rangers...."

Production Staff

Production: DuMont. *Theme Music:* Richard Wagner, Overture to the "Flying Dutchman." *Producers:* James L. Caddigan, Olga Druce and Frank Telford. *Directors:* Charles Polachek, Larry White, Pat Fay and Arnee Nocks. *Writers:* M.C. Brock, Jack Vance, Damon Knight, James Blish, Carey Wilber, C.M. Kornblath, Robert Sheckley and Larry Menkin.

Regular Cast

Captain Video
    Richard Coogan (6-27-49 to 12-12-50)
    Al Hodge (12-15-50 to 4-1-55)
The Video Ranger   Don Hastings
Dr. Pauli   Bram Nossen (6-27-50 to 6/50)
    Hal Conklin (6/50 to 1954)
    Stephen Elliott (12-16-54 to 3-11-55)
Commissioner Bell   Jack Orsen (1949 to 1950)
Commissioner Cary
    Ben Lackland (1950 to 1955)
Announcer   Fred Scott

Episode Guide

No episode guide available for this series.

Captain Z-RO

Time travel was central to the teleplays of *Captain Z-RO*, "research explorer in time and space." The concept of a temporal and spatial explorer was the brainchild of Roy Steffens, who introduced Captain Z-RO to viewers of San Francisco station KRON in 1951. The program was originally a live production broadcast in 15-minute installments five days a week. In 1955, *Captain Z-RO* appeared in a syndicated package of complete-in-themselves half-hour filmed episodes.

The series was produced on a minuscule budget, with actors frequently taking two and three roles in the same play. Steffens intended his series to be both educational and entertaining. The program seems to have taken its inspiration from both DuMont's *Captain Video* and Don Herbert's popular educational *Mr. Wizard*. While Herbert each week demonstrated principles of science to one or two awestruck youngsters, Captain Z-RO would recount an episode from history to his young assistant Jet. Owning a time machine helped the explications immeasurably.

Captain Z-RO maintained an aggressive hands-on attitude toward time travel. He was neither paralyzed by the fear of fatally altering history through his meddling nor afflicted with the fatalistic assumption that events of the past were destined to unfold in a certain way and nothing can reverse what has already taken place.

Like most stereotypical scientific geniuses of 1950s vintage, Captain Z-RO maintained and operated out of an elaborate secret laboratory laden with exotic devices like a Trillatron, Electro Chamber and a Cycle Reactor.

Invariably, when Captain Z-RO and Jet tuned in on an event from the past, the Captain would discover that events were not corresponding to the history books. That would be Z-RO's pretext to involve himself directly in the action we were witnessing unfold on the view screen. Whether it was recovering an intercepted message vital for George Washington's survival at Valley Forge or thwarting the plans of Genghis Khan to conquer all of China, Captain Z-RO seemed to spend much of his time correcting the errors of history. Nonetheless, the series imbued its young viewers with a sense of history and made the past come to life for them. Only in three filmed instances did Captain Z-RO concern himself predominantly with matters of space travel: "Roger the Robot," "Meteor" and "Adventure in Space."

Captain Z-RO shares the distinction, along with *Flash Gordon* and *Commando Cody,* of being among the last of the juvenile-oriented science fiction TV shows of the 1950s before the direction abruptly changed and the emphasis shifted to adult science fiction.

Opening signature for the filmed version of Roy Steffens' *Captain Z-RO*.

Technical Information

FORMAT: Fifteen-minute live serial; later converted to filmed half-hour series, exploring time travel and significant historical events in the development of Western civilization.

BROADCAST HISTORY: *Network:* Local KRON, San Francisco (1951), and KTTV, Los Angeles (1953); Syndication 1955–1956 (Distributed by Atlas Television Corporation). *Seasons:* 3. *Total Episodes:* 77 (51 live and 26 B/W filmed).

Signature

OPENING: Two voices introduced the show. The first, with an echo effect, described Captain Z-RO's laboratory somewhere on "the planet called Earth" and explained Z-RO's mission: "To learn from the past … to plan for the future." The second voice spoke over the sound of a telegrapher's key, urging the audience to "please stand by" for direct transmission to Z-RO's lab.

CLOSING: Voice 2 reminded the audience to "stand by" for the next transmission.

Production Staff

Production: Captain Z-RO Productions, Inc. *Producer:* Kathleen K. Rawlings. *Associate Producer:* Henry Brown. *Scripts:* Roy Steffens. *Director:* Dave Butler.

Director of Photography	Joseph P. Dieves
Assistant Director	Florence Dieves
Film Editor	Lew Smith
Recording Engineer	Stewart Macondray
Set Designer	Leslie Green
Technical Supervisor	John Corso

Filmed at W.A. Palmer Films, Inc.

Regular Cast

Captain Z-RO	Roy Steffens
Jet	Bobby Trumbull
	Jeff Silvers
	Bruce Haynes

Episode Guide

(1955-56 syndicated series)

Christopher Columbus (December 18, 1955).

Daniel Boone (December 25, 1955).
Cast:

	Billy Hicks
	Joseph Miksak
	Richard Glyer
	Leon Forbes
	Muriel Landers

Marco Polo (January 1, 1956).

Benedict Arnold (January 8, 1956).

King John (January 15, 1956).

Magellan (January 22, 1956).

Pony Express (January 29, 1956). Captain Z-RO intervenes to save the life of a Pony Express rider and to save the relay station at Fort Bridger from destruction by fire.

William Tell (February 5, 1956).
Cast:

	Sydney Walker
	Stuart Rawlings
	Richard Glyer
	Joseph Miksak
	Jack Sullivan

Roger the Robot (February 12, 1956). Captain Z-RO invents an experimental robot to explore the surface of Venus. Due do to an accident, the Robot materializes in San Francisco's Fisherman's Wharf district and proceeds to terrorize all of San Francisco.

Blackbeard the Pirate (February 19, 1956).

Attila the Hun (February 26, 1956).

Robin Hood (March 4, 1956). The Sheriff of Nottingham crafts a plan to capture the outlaw hero, Robin Hood, and only the timely intervention of Captain Z-RO prevents the plan from succeeding.

Washington and Howe (March 11, 1956). A dejected Gen. Washington faces mass desertion at Valley Forge within the next few hours and only word carried by a special messenger pledging French aid to the Continental Army can reverse the situation. Unfortunately, Gen. Howe has intercepted the message and imprisoned the messenger. Captain Z-RO fires up his time machine, retrieves the message and frees the courier just in time to save the rebellion.

Cast:	*Gen. Washington*	Joseph Miksak
	Gen. Howe	Edward Sterlingson
	Lt. Hammond	Joseph Miksak
	Lt. Preminger	F. Edward
	Lt. Merrill	F. Steeling
	Col. Butler	Edward Fisher, Jr.
	Sgt. Stevens	Jack Fleming
	Messenger	F. Edward
	British Guard	F. Jack

The Rosetta Stone (March 18, 1956).

Hernando Cortez (March 25, 1956). Captain Z-RO and Jet uncover a mutinous plot to assassinate Hernando Cortez. Captain Z-RO and Jet rush back into time to prevent Cortez's murder and to assure his victory over the Aztecs.

Cast:	*Cortez*	Mike Chamberlin
	Espinosa	Jack Cahill
	Ricardo	R. Steffensen
	Manuel	M. Chamberlin

Molly Pitcher (April 1, 1956).

Discovery of Gold (April 8, 1956).

Meteor (April 15, 1956). Captain Z-RO, Jet and Micro take the X-99 up for a shakedown mission when a meteor passes close to their ship, causing the craft to malfunction. The Captain takes a space walk in order to effect repairs.

Captain Cook and the Hawaiian Islands (April 22, 1956).

Producer and writer Roy Steffens (left) as his own title character, Captain Z-RO, and Bruce Haynes as his young assistant Jet.

Aztec Papers (April 29, 1956).

Genghis Khan (May 6, 1956). Genghis Khan plots to complete his conquest of China, but at the last moment is dissuaded by personal superstition and Captain Z-RO.
Cast: *Genghis Khan*   John Trigonis
       High Priest   Mark Sheeler
       Chung   Clifford Reynolds
       Warriors   Norman Rehm, Robert
       Warfield, Jack Sullivan, R. Steff

The Great Pyramid (May 13, 1956).

Leonardo de Vinci (May 20, 1956).

William the Conqueror (May 27, 1956).

Adventure in Space (June 3, 1956). Captain Z-RO searches for a flying saucer.

King Alfred (June 10, 1956). Captain Z-RO and Jet assist Alfred the Great in his heroic fight against the invading Danes.
Cast: *King Alfred*   Sydney Walker
       Denewulf   Roy Franklyn
       Guthram   S. Walker
       Danish Spy   Shaffer Fulton
       Hinguar   Roy Franklin

Commando Cody,
Sky Marshal of the Universe

Commando Cody, Sky Marshal of the Universe holds the distinction of being a television series that was released to theaters as a serial but devoid of the usual cliffhanger endings; all episodes were complete in themselves as in any other television series. The reason is that *Commando Cody* was made for the television market, not the theatrical market. Reportedly, the series was the first effort by Republic Pictures' television subsidiary Hollywood Television Service, Inc. Although filmed at Republic in 1953, nothing much is known about *Commando Cody* until the summer of 1955 when NBC broadcast the series on Saturday mornings. We were unable to discern the date of its theatrical release. What remains peculiar about the program, however, is that works dealing with movie serials do not include it in their studies, deferring it to works dealing with television. But television reference works remain all too brief about the series' origins and history. In effect, no one seems to want to deal with the program, but, as is often the case, many are quick to deride its limitations of budget and its absurd use of science.

The program clearly has its origins in the 1952 Republic serial *Radar Men from the Moon*, which began each episode with the title, "Introducing a New Character, Commando Cody, in..." George Wallace played Cody, a scientist working at his own Cody Laboratories. His nemesis was Retik (Roy Barcroft) the Moon Menace, who was bent on conquering the earth. Cody's greatest technological advancement was his amazing flying suit, which consisted of a leather tunic with two rocket engines attached to the back, and a bullet-shaped helmet. Cody controlled the flying suit by using three buttons on a control panel on his chest, one for activation, one for speed, and one for direction (labeled merely "on/off," "fast/slow" and "up/down," respectively). Anyone conversant with serial lore will immediately recognize that Cody's flying suit was previously worn by scientist Jeff King (Tris Coffin) in Republic's 1949 serial *King of the Rocket Men*. Cody later passed his rocket suit on to scientist Larry Martin (Judd Holdren) in the serial *Zombies of the Stratosphere* (1952), a sort of reworking of *Radar Men from the Moon*.

For *Commando Cody, Sky Marshal of the Universe*, Cody is now a government scientist working for the Interplanetary Commission, apparently a branch of the American government. He is assisted by Joan Gilbert and Ted Richards (characters from the original serial), who are helping him adapt atomic power for rocket propulsion. William Schallert portrayed a serious-minded Ted Richards in the first three episodes. Thereafter, Ted was replaced by Dick Preston, portrayed by Richard Crane (see *Rocky Jones, Space Ranger*), a less serious-minded colleague who served as comic relief at the close of each episode. The major difference between the serial and the series, however, is Cody's mask and uniform. In the original, Cody wears no mask and is dressed in a business suit; he is described as a scientist working to perfect space travel. In the television series, Cody dons mask and military style uniform and is described as an important personage with close government ties. "Everything that takes place here is strictly top secret," Commissioner Henderson tells Joan and Ted, "[and] that's why the government insists that Commando Cody wear a mask at all times. Even the people who work for him mustn't know who he is." The appellation "Commando" is never explained in the serial or the television series.

Cody's nemesis in the series is the Ruler, a mad scientist from somewhere in outer space, portrayed by Gregory Gay, who had portrayed the Martian menace Mota in Republic's *Flying Disc Man from Mars* (1951). As with earlier Republic science fiction serials, the Ruler remains in outer space but employs earthly agents, here Dr. Varney (Peter Brocco) in the first two episodes and Baylor (Lyle Talbot) in the rest.

Cost-conscious producer Franklin Adreon, who was still producing serials at the studio, designed his series around available library footage; Adreon had the entire Republic serial library at his disposal, and all the footage of Cody in flight were assembled from the previous serials. The rocket flights were also culled from previous serials, including *The Purple Monster Strikes* (1945), Republic's first effort at modern science fiction. In addition, numerous episodes involved great disasters befalling the earth; these disasters were represented by lots of stock footage culled not only from newsreels but from masterful special effects footage by the Lydecker brothers.

In sum, *Commando Cody, Sky Marshal of the Universe* was pure space fantasy of the Flash Gordon variety. Actual science was nonexistent, replaced by the colorful language of scientism. Buzzwords like "atomic" and "radiation" were dropped frequently along with such neologisms as "Thenustrium" and "Saturnium." Finding the Ruler located on planet M-27 was easy, Cody explains to Henderson, since it is in the "first planetary system west of ours." These qualities, coupled with the always impressive special effects of Howard and Theodore Lydecker, make *Commando Cody, Sky Marshal of the Universe* one of the more enjoyable diversions of the 1950s.

The information below is incomplete since we were unable to find a comprehensive credit list for each episode. In addition, the credits for the theatrical release may be different from the television release since a theatrical pressbook identified more credits and cast members than shown on the credits at the close of each television episode.

Technical Information

FORMAT: Half-hour series in which masked scientist Commando Cody uses his advanced technology to save Earth from invasion by the forces of a mad dictator named the Ruler.

BROADCAST HISTORY: *Network:* NBC; syndication through Hollywood Television Service, Inc. *Original Airdates:* July 16, 1955 to October 8, 1955. *Sponsor:* Unavailable. *Seasons:* 1. *Total Episodes:* 12 in black-and-white.

Signature

A giant spaceship streaks across the sky, and then we see Commando Cody in his flying suit leap into the air. As Cody streaks across the sky, the following title read by the announcer appears: "Commando Cody, Sky Marshal of the Universe." This is followed by a different shot of the spaceship with the title of the episode superimposed. The signature closes on a long shot of the Ruler's laboratory on Saturn.

Judd Holdren as the masked Commando Cody.

Production Staff

Production: Hollywood Television Service, Inc. (a division of Republic Pictures Corporation). *Producer:* Franklin Adreon.

Director of Photography   Bud Thackery
Film Editors   Cliff Bell and Harold Minter
Music   Stanley Wilson
Assistant Directors   Roy Wade and A.J. Vitarelli
Art Directors Frank Hotaling and Frank Arrigo
Set Decorations   John McCarthy,
             James Redd and George Milo
Sound   Earl Crain, Sr.
Makeup Supervision   Bob Mark
Special Effects Howard and Theodore Lydecker
Optical Effects   Consolidated Film Industries

Regular Cast

Commando Cody   Judd Holdren
Joan Gilbert   Aline Towne
Ted Richards (Episodes 1-3) William Schallert
Dick Preston (Episodes 4-12)   Richard Crane

Commissioner Henderson   Craig Kelly
The Ruler   Gregory Gay
The Ruler's Assistant   Gloria Pall
Officer Clancy   Dale Van Sickel

Enemies of the Universe (July 16, 1955). Commando Cody, a top secret scientist who wears a mask for security reasons, receives two new assistants, Joan Gilbert and Ted Richards, to aid him in developing and producing an atomic-powered rocketship capable of reaching the ends of the universe. Meanwhile, the Interplanetary Commission has received warnings from a mad scientist known as the Ruler, and Commissioner Henderson identifies Cody as the new sky marshal of the universe in order to combat the Ruler's threat. Cody explains to Ted and Joan that reports of flying saucers are actually reports of the Ruler's missiles attempting to land on the earth. Cody has developed a cosmic dust blanket that encircles the globe, causing any enemy craft to disintegrate before entering the earth's atmosphere. Meanwhile, the Ruler fears Cody's abilities, and he orders his agents on earth, Dr. Varney and a thug named Ross, to sabotage the rocket and learn the secret of the cosmic dust blanket. Cody is able to drive off the saboteurs and complete his rocket, adding another line of defense against the Ruler's war machine. *Director:* Fred C. Brannon. *Writer:* Ronald Davidson.

Cast: *Dr. Varney*   Peter Brocco
       Ross   Zon Murray
       Henchman   Tom Steele

Atomic Peril (July 23, 1955). Unable to penetrate the cosmic dust blanket with his warships, the Ruler sends his agent Lenato inside a small missile to Earth. Lenato carries with him a new element called Thenustrium which was developed on Planet X; he tells Dr. Varney that Thenustrium is similar to uranium but easier to control. Lenato and Varney pose as scientists who have discovered a new element, and through this treachery they are able to infiltrate Cody's laboratory. Cody understands that by combining earthly uranium with Lenato's new element he will be able to construct an atomic pile capable of reproducing itself and hence giving the rocket more power and range. With Cody away, Lenato and Varney kidnap Joan and Ted and then steal Cody's rocket. In flight, Lenato and Varney discuss their plans, but Cody overhears the conversation on a two-way radio transmitter. Cody intercepts the flight before it can leave the atmosphere and takes Lenato and Varney into custody. *Director:* Fred C. Brannon. *Writer:* Ronald Davidson.

Cast: *Lenato*   Stanley Waxman
       Dr. Varney   Peter Brocco
       Radio Voice   Roy Barcroft

Cosmic Vengeance (July 30, 1955). Commando Cody intercepts strange radio frequencies emanating from deep space. He believes these radio signals are the Ruler's messages to his unknown henchmen on earth. Using sophisticated triangulation equipment, Cody follows the radio beams to an upscale downtown business where he finds two men, Hardy and Ross, tuned in to the Ruler's frequency. A fight ensues, and Ross knocks Cody out the window. Cody uses his flying suit to return to the office, but finds it ablaze and Hardy and

Ross missing. Later, Hardy and Ross manage to steal the secret of the cosmic dust cloud and send it to the Ruler, who has made Venus his new headquarters. Cody learns of the Ruler's location, and with Ted and Joan he takes his rocket to Venus. There, Cody finds the Ruler inside an underground laboratory. The Ruler brags about his might and then orders Cody killed, but Cody escapes with one of the Ruler's powerful ray guns. The Ruler's guards give chase in a tank, but Cody uses the ray against the tank, melting the mountainside and thereby destroying the laboratory and the plans for the cosmic dust blanket. With all destroyed, the secret of the cosmic dust blanket remains safe from the Ruler. *Director:* Fred C. Brannon. *Writer:* Ronald Davidson.

Cast: *Hardy*   I. Stanford Jolley
       Ross   Zon Murray

Nightmare Typhoon (August 6, 1955). Still unable to penetrate the cosmic dust blanket with his warships, the Ruler sends a rocket filled with small missiles containing a mysterious yet potent chemical that can seed clouds. With the rocket camouflaged above the clouds, the Ruler's soldiers drop the missiles into the clouds; the missiles explode and cause torrential rains that in turn cause typhoons and floods of tremendous force, destroying entire sections of the country including New York City. Commando Cody in his flying suit pursues the rocket and manages to capture one of the missiles. He returns the missile to his laboratory where he discovers its secret. Cody then produces a counter-gas that renders the missiles harmless. Using his rocket, Cody disperses the gas into the clouds, thwarting the Ruler's latest gambit. Cody's rocket then does battle with the Ruler's ship, finally destroying it. *Director:* Harry Keller. *Writer:* Ronald Davidson.

Cast: *Baylor*   Lyle Talbot
       Mason   John Crawford
       Chris   William Fawcett
       Voice of Radar Operator Roy Barcroft

War of the Space Giants (August 13, 1955). The Ruler has discovered Saturnium, a rare element found on Saturn, that allows him to blast a hole in the cosmic dust blanket protecting earth. Through this portal, the Ruler sends a ship that begins dropping capsules filled with a deadly cosmic disease. Commando Cody uses his rocket to find the invading ship from Saturn and gives pursuit. Using a magnetic drag-line, Cody is able to tow the Saturnian ship back to Earth. Cody recognizes the element inside the ray gun as Saturnium, and so he, Dick and Joan take the rocket to Saturn. There Cody uses an aerial bomb to start a chain reaction that destroys the Saturnium. He then returns to Earth and develops the antidote for the space disease. *Director:* Franklin Adreon. *Writer:* Ronald Davidson.

Cast:
Duron	Rick Vallin
Tantor	Bill Henry
Space Soldier	Keith Richards

Destroyers of the Sun (August 20, 1955). Panic spreads across the earth when the Ruler, using another of his fantastic inventions, blocks the sun, throwing the earth into perpetual darkness. The darkness threatens the cosmic dust blanket, and Cody later learns that an accomplice at one of the dispensing stations has been slowly sabotaging the blanket. Cody believes that only the workers have the ability to sabotage the machinery, and so he lays a trap at the station. Soon he finds the saboteur, a worker named Ed Williams, who, after coming out on the losing end of a fistfight with Cody, admits he was paid by a man named Baylor. Later, Cody, Dick and Joan use Cody's rocket to take them into space where they locate the Ruler on planet M-27 of the "first planetary system west of ours." But the Ruler employs a barrier ray to keep Cody's rocket from landing. Cody uses his flying suit to penetrate the barrier and find the machinery that blocks the sun. Cody destroys the machine, and then uses the rocket to destroy the Ruler's temporary installation on planet M-27. *Director:* Harry Keller. *Writer:* Ronald Davidson.

Cast:
Baylor	Lyle Talbot
Mason	John Crawford
Foreman	Kenneth MacDonald
Bill	Marshall Reed
Ed Williams	John Day

Robot Monster of Mars (August 27, 1955). Working late at the laboratory, Cody and Dick are assaulted by a monstrous robot, controlled by Baylor, that demands the plans to the cosmic dust blanket. Cody is able to deactivate the robot, but the Ruler orders Baylor to use the powerful nerve-paralyzing ray guns against Cody. Baylor then sends two henchmen to Cody's office where Cody and Dick struggle with them. The ray gun is directed at Cody, but he sidesteps the blast, allowing the nerve paralyzer to freeze Dick. As Cody gives chase to one of the intruders, the other kidnaps Dick and takes him back to Baylor's headquarters. There, Dick is strapped to a thought-control machine, rendering Dick a puppet in Baylor's control. Dick then steals important files from Cody's laboratory, and at Baylor's insistence phones a dispensing station eight to cut the flow of energy to the dust blanket. Dick then takes the files to the Ruler, who now has his headquarters on planet L-36; Cody and Joan give chase in Cody's rocket. Meanwhile, Dick has regained control of his own mind, and, using his insignia radio transmitter, is able to guide Cody to the Ruler's headquarters. Finding one of the Ruler's robots nearby, Cody uses the Ruler's own invention to destroy the Ruler's stronghold and to free Dick. *Director:* Franklin Adreon. *Writer:* Ronald Davidson.

Cast:
Baylor	Lyle Talbot
Henchman	John Cason
Foreman	Kenneth MacDonald

Hydrogen Hurricane (September 3, 1955). The Ruler uses the hydrogen lakes beneath the dark side of the moon to turn the moon into a giant guided missile heading directly toward Earth. Because of the mass of the moon, however, the Ruler must use successive hydrogen blasts to propel it, giving Cody time to find a counteraction. But time is important since each blast causes hurricanes and storms in Earth's atmosphere that eventually threaten the cosmic dust blanket. Cody first counterstrikes by energizing the blanket by increasing the voltage at the various dispensing stations; he then takes his rocket to the moon where he is able to shut down the Ruler's apparatus before reversing the effect of the final blast. The moon drifts back into its orbit. *Director:* Harry Keller. *Writer:* Barry Shipman.

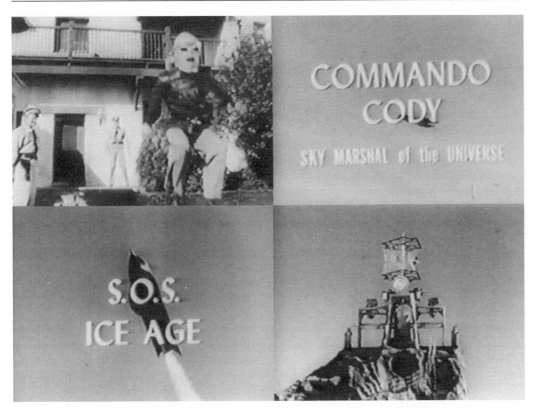

Opening for Episode 10 of *Commando Cody, Sky Marshal of the Universe.*

Cast: *Groog*   Denver Pyle
     Foreman   Kenneth MacDonald
     Bill   Marshall Reed

Solar Sky Raiders (September 10, 1955). Two of Baylor's thugs steal Joan's insignia radio, allowing the Ruler to eavesdrop on Cody's communications. As Cody prepares to change wavelengths, the Ruler takes control of Cody's communications, ordering Cody to look outside for a sign of the Ruler's cosmic power. In the sky, a second sun appears, causing the Earth's temperature to rise. Later, the Ruler orders another look outside, and Cody is alarmed to see yet a *third* sun appear. Realizing that the Ruler may have won, Commissioner Henderson is prepared to capitulate to the Ruler's demands, but Cody reasons that gravity should be increasing with the addition of each sun, but there are no indications that the earth's gravity is abnormal. Cody then realizes that the Ruler is using a cosmic mirage to reflect the sun's own energy; there are no new suns, he says, just the appearance of extra suns. Cody finds the source of the cosmic mirage and, using his rocket, destroys it. *Director:* Harry Keller. *Writer:* Barry Shipman.

Cast: *Baylor*   Lyle Talbot
     First Thug   Lane Bradford
     Second Thug   Fred Graham

S.O.S. Ice Age (September 17, 1955). On the planet Saturn, the Ruler has developed a super magnetic beam that he uses to pull the earth off its axis, causing it to freeze on one side and burn on the other. Cody uses his rocket to follow the beam to the North Pole, where his rocket crashes. Cody and Dick then use dog sleds to take them to the Ruler's outpost where they find the coupling beam. Cody and Dick disperse the alien troopers and destroy the outpost, freeing the earth from the magnetic ray. As the earth snaps back into its proper orbit and axis, violent Arctic earthquakes threaten Cody and Dick until they find refuge. *Director:* Franklin Adreon. *Writer:* Barry Shipman.

Cast: *Tantor*   Bill Henry
        Duron   Rick Vallin

Lost in Outer Space (September 24, 1955). One of the Ruler's rockets has landed on Earth, but before Commando Cody can overtake it a Mercurian named Balen flees the ship seeking sanctuary. Balen reports that the Ruler has enslaved the Mercurians, and that he seeks the help of Commando Cody and the Earth forces in overthrowing the Ruler. Cody, Dick, Joan and Balen fly to Mercury where Cody hopes to meet with the Queen of the Mercurians. But Balen, who has been planted by the Ruler, takes Dick and Joan captive while Cody is searching for the Queen. Balen and the Ruler's soldiers now take over Cody's rocket, but Cody, using his insignia radio, hears Balen's treacherous plan and takes action. Using his flying suit, Cody overtakes the rocket and apprehends Balen and the soldiers. *Director:* Harry Keller. *Writer:* Ronald Davidson.
Cast: *Balen*   Mauritz Hugo

Captives of the Zero Hour (October 8, 1955). The Ruler sends a detachment of his soldiers to lure Commando Cody to Mercury, where the Ruler hopes to steal the dispeller ray that allows Cody passage through the dust blanket. Cody captures the Ruler's soldiers and forces them to radio the Ruler that they have been successful. But before they can set their trap for the Ruler, Cody, Joan, and Dick are mistaken for enemy soldiers and taken captive by the Mercurians, allowing the Ruler and his forces to take control of Cody's ship. The Mercurian Queen recognizes Cody and orders his release, saying that only Commando Cody can free the Mercurians from the Ruler's grip. With the aid of the Mercurian forces, Cody and Dick disguise themselves as Mercurians loyal to the Ruler and gain entry into the rocket. Once inside, they assault the Ruler and his soldiers, finally overpowering the enemy. Cody then takes the Ruler back to Earth for imprisonment, thereby preventing the mad scientist from enslaving the universe. Commissioner Henderson states that peace will return to the cosmos and all planets will interact with one another in friendship. *Director:* Harry Keller. *Writer:* Ronald Davidson.
Cast: *Groog*   Denver Pyle
        Queen of the Mercurians Joanne Jordan

Flash Gordon

As science fiction took root in popular television in the 1950s, it seemed only natural that *Flash Gordon* and *Buck Rogers* be included if only for their positions in the genre. The first to make the transition to television was *Buck Rogers*, whose success in television was less than notable.

The producers of *Flash Gordon* obviously hoped for a better reception for their hero. Already the subject of three popular serials featuring Buster Crabbe, *Flash Gordon* had been only moderately successful on radio but popular in comic form (as was *Buck Rogers*). With *Buck Rogers* leaving television on January 30, 1951, *Flash Gordon* was ready to fill the void three days later.

Some television historians have demonstrated confusion relative to *Flash Gordon's* appearance on New York television station WABD, the flagship of the DuMont Network, when *Flash Gordon* commenced on Saturday evening, February 3. Contrary to some interpretations, these telecasts were not episodes of the *Flash Gordon* series with Steve Holland. Rather, WABD was broadcasting chapters of the original *Flash Gordon* serial with Buster Crabbe. After two weeks of viewing, *New York Times* television critic Jack Gould found the experience unsettling, and he embarked on a one-man crusade to put a stop to further telecasts of the serial. In a highly charged column, Gould urged DuMont executives to pull the

serial from the air, lest irreparable psychological harm be done to the many young children watching the program. Gould wrote:

> The television broadcaster must learn that there is a limit to the extent to which the emotions of children can be exploited in the pursuit of higher Hooper ratings. Under the best of circumstances the parent has his hands full in providing guidance in what his child sees on TV. When he has no way of knowing what a program will be, such as was the case of *Flash Gordon*, his guard may be down. At such times the very least that television can do is to watch its low punches.

In conciliation wholly unlike today's knee-jerk defiance, station executives acquiesced to Gould's impassioned demands, and the following week the *Flash Gordon* serial was displaced by WABD's hastily rescheduled *Frontier Theater* showcasing Sam Newfield's *Gunsmoke Trail* (1938), a Range Busters Western that had as much "violence" (albeit less fantastic) as the *Flash Gordon* serial.

In 1953, King Features, distributor of the *Flash Gordon* comic strip, was persuaded to turn its product into a weekly TV series. King Features signed with Motion Pictures for Television Inc. (MPTV), a programming syndicator founded by former Universal Pictures executive Matty Fox (who had worked on the original serials) for the syndication of 39

Opening signature of the *Flash Gordon* television series.

half-hour *Flash Gordon* episodes. The series would be produced by Intercontinental Television Films, which in turn signed with two separate European production companies, Interwest Films of West Germany and La Telediffusion of France, to actually get the job done.

The decision had been made to produce the films overseas as part of a general trend at the time. *Newsweek* commented on the foreign production trend in 1954 under the catchphrase "See Scenic Europe—Then visualize it for the video back home":

> Such a motto might be nailed up on the recruiting posters of the 20-odd American TV production outfits now making their half-hour movies in foreign parts. The main reason for their shift, artistically, is a long-suppressed craving for authenticity. The scenery overseas, it is said, is so scenic. Other reasons for the exodus from Hollywood and New York: (1) Financing is some-

times easier, (2) costs are sometimes less and (3) life as an expatriate is so delightful.

Actual foreign locales enhanced the scenic authenticity of such series as *Captain Gallant of the Foreign Legion* (1955/57), with Buster Crabbe, and *Assignment Foreign Legion* (1957); moreover, series like *Foreign Intrigue* (1951/55) and *Dangerous Assignment* (1952) were at least intellectually sound in pursuing political themes relevant to the actual locales in which they were filmed. Flash Gordon's venue, however, was outer space, not Berlin or Marseilles, which had been selected as shooting locations for the series. The decision to produce *Flash Gordon* overseas was more economic than aesthetic; here, fiscal advantages, particularly labor, were most attractive to cost-conscious producers. The use of European actors in supporting roles meant major savings since the performers were virtually unknown in the American market but possessed the much needed skills crucial to smooth low-budget filmmaking. These European actors almost never received on-screen credit.

To fill the role of Flash Gordon, the decision was made to search for someone who resembled Alex Raymond's comic strip figure. To this end, King Features and ITF took note of artists' models, and they found a young model and actor named Steve Holland. Tall, darkly handsome, with a commanding physique, Holland met their physical expectations of the part; amazingly, he had the added qualification of sounding a great deal like Buster Crabbe.

Holland had already begun to capture public attention in a most unusual fashion. For avid readers of Fawcett's *Bob Colt* comics, a nameless Holland had become a major figure by portraying Fawcett's popular cowboy hero during the run of the series, from November 1950 to May 1952. Interestingly, Fawcett built the towering figure of Bob Colt around Holland's likeness, even to the extent of issuing photo covers of Holland costumed as Colt rather than the traditional cover paintings. Accordingly, comic artist George Evans based his drawings on Holland's precise physical appearance.

Holland's ability at modeling would flourish following his Flash Gordon years, gaining him a reputation as one of the most talented models of the day. In the post–*Flash Gordon* years, Holland's career as an actor was never a stellar one even though he appeared in many small film roles and on stage at various times, notably in versions of *South Pacific* and *Mr. Roberts*. Holland was, however, in great demand by illustrators for paperback covers. He took credit for appearing on thousands of covers, portraying such luminaries as the Avenger, Mike Hammer, Conan the Barbarian, Shell Scott and Nick Carter. His best work was modeling Doc Savage for the Bantam Books editions that began in 1964; Holland's image of the famed "Man of Bronze" solidified the model and the subject. In fact, cover artists came and went at Bantam while Holland continued as Doc Savage. Reportedly, when artist Joe DeVito was hired to illustrate the *Doc Savage* paperbacks in the 1980s, the young artist interviewed several new models with the

intention of finding a newer image, but in the end DeVito admitted he was dissatisfied with what he had seen and went back to Steve Holland. "Nobody but nobody poses like Steve Holland," DeVito said in a 1992 interview. "I've never seen a model as poised and as balanced. He *is* Doc Savage."

DeVito's positive comments partly, at least, assuage the sting of negative criticism frequently leveled at Holland's performance as Flash Gordon.

After finding their Flash Gordon, the framers of the television series turned their attention to the role of Dale Arden and the pivotal role of Dr. Hans Zarkov.

A relatively unknown actress named Irene Champlin was selected to play the third film incarnation of Dale Arden (succeeding Jean Rogers and Carol Hughes). Champlin graduated from the American Academy of Dramatic Arts and had been a member of Sanford Meisner's Professional Group; she had recently appeared with Helmut Dantine in *Guerrilla Girl* (1953), a minor film about the postwar Greek Communist resistance movement. To take over the role of Dr. Zarkov, bearded Joe Nash, an actor with a deft delivery, was picked.

Initially, production responsibilities fell to German producer Wenzel Luedecke and Interwest Films for six months of filming in West Berlin. Wallace Worsley, Jr., son of the famed American silent director (*The Hunchback of Notre Dame* [1923]), was tapped to direct scripts primarily written by Earl Markham and Bruce Elliot. The memorable theme was scored by Kurt Heuser.

Flash Gordon was in constant syndication throughout most of the 1950s, and despite serious production flaws it managed to retain a fascination for young audiences. The lead players in the series were all credible and capable performers. Holland may not have been a first-rank actor but the role didn't require one. What Holland brought to the part was a talented model's intuitive understanding of movement and an artist's perception of light and shadow as it falls upon a subject. What complements his posing is the fact that he understands the artist's craft so well; in fact, Holland was a painter who shared the same appreciation—

Flash Gordon's *Skyflash* in flight.

even reverence—for light and shadow that *Flash Gordon* creator Alex Raymond brought to his own work.

To see this in action, one need only to concentrate on Holland's movements, gestures and physical reactions. What becomes quickly apparent is that he is a performer with a shrewd sense of his own space.

Irene Champlin's Dale Arden was superficially like many other secondary female characters of the era (e.g., Vena Ray in *Rocky Jones, Space Ranger*). She was ever willing to follow the men for a worthwhile purpose, such as saving the world from destruction, and she invariably fell prey to one villain after another, a situation that would require the timely intervention of a heroic male rescuer like Flash Gordon. But Champlin's Dale was far from the passive and helpless creature frequently depicted at the time; uniquely, Dale not only packed a ray gun and could hold her own in a fight, but more importantly she possessed an emotional strength that was lacking in her female counterparts (and sometimes in her two male companions as well).

The casting of Joe Nash as Dr. Zarkov was innovative; Zarkov was the least exaggerated of the series' characters. Nash's image substituted the era's typically elderly, bespectacled eccentric scientist for a youthful, athletic philosopher-scientist who, like Dale, packed a ray gun and held his own in combat.

The only other actor to appear with any frequency was American actor Henry Beckman, whose Commander Richards functioned as head of the crucial government authority the Galaxy Bureau of Investigation (or GBI). Beckman, like nearly everyone else in the cast save the principal players, did not receive screen credit. Richards was illustrative of the sense of respect for authority that was so endemic not only in Flash Gordon's galaxy but in the American 1950s as well.

Finally, accompanying Flash, Dale and Zarkov on many of their most important missions aboard the *Skyflash*—pride of the galactic fleet and obviously named in Flash's honor— was a squawking parrot named Casey whose comic relief served as the voice of doom, articulating such "encouraging" prophecies as "Gonna crash, Flash" and "Gonna fail, Dale."

Thirty-nine episodes of *Flash Gordon* were filmed in Europe. According to Steve Holland, the first six months were spent filming in West Berlin; after that, filming transferred to Marseilles for another three months before wrapping up the series. The transfer to Marseilles occasioned certain production changes of which the most notable was the transfer of production from Interwest to La Telediffusion. At this point, Luedecke was replaced by American producer Edward Gruskin, and American Wallace Worsley was replaced by Gunther von Fritsch, the German co-director of Val Lewton's *The Curse of the Cat People* (1944). Kurt Heuser's exciting theme remained, but incidental music was supplied by French composer Roger Roger. The look of the series now eschewed the expressionistic sets and chiaroscuro lighting for more mundane sets and lighting, effecting a change in mood and tone from a dark introspection so typical of classical German cinema to lighter high adventure. The costuming took on a more conservative stylishness. In fact, costuming seemed to be an especially vexing problem for the filmmakers. The German episodes featured Flash and Zarkov in one-piece, stodgy, dark uniforms that seemed cumbersome, but the French episodes featured Flash in a white polo shirt with a characteristic lightning bolt across his chest. More colorful yet indicative of the series' parsimonious budget were the costumes worn by Flash's nemeses: Tyrants appeared variously attired in what appeared to be Nazi uniforms and South American guerrilla fighters' fatigues. The subterranean hunchbacked dregs of the German episode "The Earth's Core" were dressed literally like Quasimodo, and the underwater people of "The Water World Menace" were clad in ordinary black rain slickers and swim fins. The result was an often— and perhaps unintended—visual expressionism that complemented the expressionistic narratives.

Flash Gordon premiered in the important New York market on October 1, 1954, on station WNBT. The premise of the entire series was succinctly summarized in voiceover narration at the beginning of one of the later episodes, "The Race Against Time":

> In the year of our Lord 3063, it is a galaxy of peace where not only worlds of different civilizations have learned to live together, but worlds of different life forms. And this [exterior building shot] is the Galaxy Bureau of Investigation—where the great scientific and economic minds of the planets work in democratic unity to preserve peace, prosperity and equality among all men. But powerful and evil forces throughout the galaxy are trying to gain control of those GBI secrets by which the democratic balance is maintained.

Dr. Zarkov, the leading scientific mind of the GBI, and Flash Gordon and Dale Arden, the leading investigators for the organization, formed an unbeatable triumvirate on behalf of the "democratic balance" in the universe.

Perhaps an explanation for *Flash Gordon*'s popularity with viewers can be found in the nature of the very elements adults have found most disconcerting, namely that the series' lack of adequate budgets and its reliance on exaggerated characterizations and events necessitated a child-like improvisation, something with which youngsters playing daily on school playgrounds or in their own backyards could readily identify. *Flash Gordon* remains a black-and-white sphere void of profundities for the modern rationalist, and yet this very sphere becomes its strength for those with a true imagination.

Technical Information

FORMAT: Filmed half-hour adventure series featuring the exploits of Flash Gordon, chief operative for the Galactic Bureau of Investigation.

BROADCAST HISTORY: *Network:* Syndicated. *Original Airdates:* October 1, 1954– Spring 1955. *Seasons:* 1. *Total Episodes:* 39 black-and-white.

Signature

Against a black backdrop of stars the title "Flash Gordon" appears. A momentary fade to black is followed by the episode title. Then follow three rather formal studied poses of Flash Gordon, Dale Arden and Dr. Zarkov in that order.

Production Staff

Production: Inter-Continental TV Films. *Theme Music:* Kurt Heuser. *Producers:* Wenzel Luedecke and Edward Gruskin. *Directors:* Wallace Worsley, Jr., and Gunther von Fritsch. *Head Writers:* Earl Markham and Bruce Elliot.

Assistant Director	Alain Jessua
Technical Director	Louis Grospierr
Art Director	Raymond Gabutti
Director of Photography	Jean Isnard
Dialogue Director	Sipora Van Praag
Cameramen	Arndt Rautenfeld, Herbert Koerner, Alex Dulac and Rene Guissart
Sound	Jean Bertrand and Willy Szdzui
Film Editors	Roger Pacaut and Heinz Haber
Assistant Film Editor	M.L. Barbero
Unit Managers	Rene Noel and Ernst Liepelt
Sets	Raymond Gabutti and Helmut Nentwig
Incidental Music	Roger Roger
Miniatures	F.W. Wintzer, LAX
Production Manager	Fred Surin and George Zorer
Production Consultant	Joseph Zigman

Filmed in West Berlin and Marseilles

Regular Cast

Flash Gordon	Steve Holland
Dale Arden	Irene Champlin
Dr. Hans Zarkov	Joseph Nash
Commander Richards	Henry Beckman

Episode Guide

(Alphabetical listing of titles. No clear order of play dates is available.)

Akim the Terrible. Akim the Terrible rules a planet where honesty is a crime and the First Law is "The old, the weak and the sick shall all perish by the hand of the strong." Anyone who opposes the law is subjected to a mind-altering machine which bends them to Akim's will. When a GBI investigator lands on the planet, he is captured and brainwashed with instructions to kill Flash Gordon. The assassination plot fails and Flash and Dale set out for the planet to put an end to Akim's rule of terror.

The Brain Machine. This is the second installment in the saga of Zydereen, the Mad Witch of Neptune. On Neptune, the methane converter which transforms the poisonous atmosphere of the planet to breathable oxygen has been blown up by Dr. Zarkov and Commander Richards by remote control from Earth. Richards and Zarkov have acted under the hypnotic influence of Zydereen, the Mad Witch of Neptune. Dale and Flash land on Neptune and furiously attempt to get the auxiliary converter on line before the planet's entire population is killed. When one of Zydereen's agents attempts and fails to destroy the auxiliary converter, Flash and Dale follow the agent's trail back to Zydereen. *Writer:* Edward Gruskin.
Cast: *Zydereen, the Mad Witch of Neptune*
Marie Powers

The Breath of Death. Flash's ship is hijacked and crashes on a planet with an unbreathable atmosphere.

The Claim Jumpers. Asteroid prospectors become victims of claim jumpers, and Flash must intervene.

The Dancing Death. A machine capable of forcing men to literally dance themselves to death threatens Flash's life.

Deadline at Noon. In a galaxy of dead planets, Flash, Dale and Zarkov discover one planet after another mysteriously exploding. Earth is to be the next target of a bomb of incredible destructive power. A fanatic with a hatred of Earth planted the bomb a millennium in the past and it is up to Flash, Dale and Zarkov to travel back to the 20th century and disarm the device before it explodes in their own time.

The Deadly Deception. A bomb-carrying android threatens to blow up a crucial meeting.

Death in the Negative. Cygni, "a bitter planet ruled by a bitter queen," is one of the poorest and most desolate planets in the universe. Cygni's queen demands a special meeting of the Galaxy Council. The queen assembled a scientific team which has provided her with the awesome power to drain all positive force from every living plant and creature. The queen demands that half the resources of every planet in the galaxy be shipped to Cygni or she will use her power to eliminate all life. Flash races against time to locate and destroy the scientific installation which provides the queen with her power.
Cast: *Queen of Cygini*   Tala Birell

Duel Against Darkness. An evil sorcerer keeps a planet shrouded in ignorance and fear, and it is up to Flash and his friends to deliver the planet from the magician's spell.

The Earth's Core. A mysterious series of earthquakes lead Dr. Zarkov to believe that an intelligent force exists below the earth's surface. Zarkov, Flash and Dale travel to the earth's core in a mechanical mole designed by Zarkov with the intention of discovering the truth behind the increasingly powerful earthquakes.

The Electro Man. On the planet Odin, the metallic inhabitants bow to their god, Electro Man.

Encounter with Evil. A villain calling himself "Evil" appears to threaten mankind.

Escape Into Time. Dale is kidnapped by a criminal named Bidzar who then escapes back into the Stone Age by means of a time device.

The Forbidden Experiment. Dr. Zarkov is taken prisoner by a deranged scientist.

The Frightened King. The King of Xeres is haunted by malevolent spirits and Flash must find a way to preserve the king's sanity and put an end to whatever plot is behind the sudden appearance of the spirits.

The Great Secret. Sinister forces are trying to take over Dr. Zarkov's new invention, a device capable of changing the orbits of planets.

Heat Wave. Preparing to invade the earth, aliens use a heat ray to turn up the temperature—high enough to incinerate human life but just the right temperature for the aliens.

The Hunger Invasion. Huge insects have been wreaking incredible destruction on a succession of planets. Flash and his friends must find a way of stopping the insects from inflicting further damage.

The Law of Velorum. Dale has a double, a Queen who is under a death sentence, and Dale is expected to stand in for the sovereign.

The Lure of Light. A scientist designs a device which enables a rocket ship to travel faster than light. Flash volunteers to have the *Skyflash* retro-fitted for the test. If the device works, it will have the added benefit of permitting travel through time. The vengeful Queen of Diana kidnaps Dale and demands the secret of the device which Dale helped to construct. Dale refuses to reveal the secret and is killed. Flash travels back in time to prevent Dale's death and to capture Diana's insane queen.

The Matter Duplicator. A new invention—a matter duplicator—requires precious gems in order to function, but the gems have disappeared.

The Micro-Man Menace. An evil genius invents a machine capable of shrinking everyone on the planet and threatens to do just that unless he is given supreme power.

Mission to Masca. A revolution on the planet Masca results in a planet ruled by women.

The Mystery of Phoros. Flash and Dale are on a mercy run to deliver a vaccine to the planet Ceres. The rulers of a rival planet try to thwart the mission.

The Planet of Death. An expedition to the planet Tarsit results in the death of all expedition members but one. The survivor returns to Earth to tell a fantastic story of an ancient curse. Defying the ancient warning, Flash, Dale and Zarkov travel to Tarsit. They discover that an alien race is making plans to use the planet as a staging ground for an invasion against Earth.

The Race Against Time. GBI control over the scientific secrets which have preserved peace in the galaxy is threatened by a political insurrection within the Galaxy Council. A crucial vote to decide the issue is soon to take place on Mars. Commander Richards is assigned to carry Earth's deciding vote to Mars. Traveling aboard the *Skyflash*, Richards and Flash are forced off course in a plot to prevent Earth's vote from being recorded. Flash must find a way to reach Mars in time to prevent the undermining of GBI's authority.

The Rains of Death. The Queen of Venus induces ravaging floods over the earth.

The Return of the Androids. When humanity determines that its android servants rob the human race of enterprise and initiative, the androids are mothballed and the secrets of the androids locked away for centuries. The three secrets of the androids are entrusted to representatives of the Galactic Bureau of Investigation. When would-be conquerors of the galaxy set out to discover the secrets, Flash, Dale and Zarkov must prevent the galactic coup. *Writers:* Bruce Geller and Edward Gruskin.

Saboteurs from Space. As a mechanical paralysis sweeps the earth, Flash, Dale and Zarkov are pressed into service to solve the crisis. The team encounters a strange new planet and its mad ruler who demands that Earth send him 100 top scientists in exchange for freeing the earth from his paralyzing grip.

The Shadowy Death. Flash's mission is to sign a treaty of cooperation with Saturn. The king of Saturn is amenable but his son tries to prevent the agreement.

The Skyjackers. Pirates have been seizing spaceships and Flash is assigned to put an end to their raids.

The Sound Gun. Flash and Dale's brother must contend with a terrifying new weapon which can cause destruction by sound amplification.

The Space Smugglers. Flash tracks a smuggling ring which is introducing a dangerous drug to Earth. The drug is capable of destroying people's wills and turning them into criminals.

Struggle to the End. The third and final installment in the saga of Zydereen, the Mad Witch of Neptune. From her new command post on Saturn, Zydereen begins her final push to enslave the galaxy. In possession of a destructive solar ray, the witch orders Flash and Dale to surrender themselves to her in her castle on Saturn. Flash and Dale travel to Saturn, where decoys are escorted to the castle while the real Flash and Dale plan the witch's capture. *Writer:* Edward Gruskin.

The Subworld Revenge. Flash returns to the earth's core and confronts the same ruler who once before attempted to take over upper Earth.

The Vengeance of Rabeed. After being incarcerated for 1,000 years, Rabeed is now free and plots to destroy every planet in the galaxy.

The Water World Menace. The planet Aquatania is slowly dying as a mysterious force draws off its atmosphere. The loss of oxygen is traced to an underwater race planning to flood the planet and defeat the land people. When the underwater creatures emerge in an effort to prevent Flash, Dale and Zarkov from restoring the atmosphere, they inadvertently destroy themselves.

The Weapon That Walked. GBI develops a machine capable of processing a 50-pound bar of Corillium bullion down to 50 ounces. The process solves the problem of warehousing large quantities of the precious metal but also makes stealing the metal easier. The opportunity attracts two crooks who enter GBI headquarters and make off with the Corillium with the unwitting aid of an alien woman who can turn anyone into stone merely by her gaze.

The Witch of Neptune. First installment in the saga of Zydereen, the Mad Witch of Neptune. Zydereen, a Rasputin-like influence in the royal court of Neptune, is banished. Seeking revenge, she appears at GBI headquarters and uses her powers to force Commander Richards and Zarkov to destroy by remote control the atmosphere converter on Neptune. The destruction of all life on Neptune is only averted by the quick work of Dale and Flash, who place an auxiliary converter in operation. *Writer:* Edward Gruskin.

H.G. Wells'
Invisible Man

This British series actually shared only the presence of an invisible man with H.G. Wells' novel. There was no Dr. Griffin, no insanity and no mad drive for power in the series. Rather, Dr. Peter Brady is a government researcher who accidentally makes himself invisible while experimenting with optical density and light refraction at England's Castle Hill Research Laboratories. Being invisible, however, makes him a dandy criminal investigator, and hence Brady is called upon to look into criminal activities and spy rings in the series' 26 episodes.

What is interesting about the series is that like the Lone Ranger, Brady remains a mystery throughout the series. He is never seen except as a bandaged figure, naturally, and his invisible presence is known only by his distinctive voice and by special effects, most of which are merely theatrical contrivances (objects moved about by wires) rather than optical effects. Even in the premiere episode "Secret Experiment," in which Brady loses his visibility, the actor is either obscured by laboratory apparatus or shown only from the back (although there is one shot in which we see his eyes as he peers through a portal). Adding to the mystery is that the titles credit him only as "The Invisible Man," and the actor behind

the bandages and the actor dubbing the voice are never given credit. Tim Brooks and Earle Marsh, in the sixth edition of their *The Complete Directory of Prime Time Network TV Shows* (1995), identified the voice as belonging to actor Tim Turner and wrote that the man under the bandages was one Johnny Scripps, of whom nothing is known. But there must be more than one actor dubbing the voice; in early episodes, from "Secret Experiment" through at least "Play to Kill," the Invisible Man's voice is very different from the one heard in later episodes. Further complicating the issue, Alan Morton's *The Complete Directory to Science Fiction, Fantasy and Horror Television Series* states that the voice of the Invisible Man in an hour pilot episode titled "Secrecy Experiment" belonged to actor Robert Beatty.

Essentially, the series is an espionage-crime thriller with Brady frequently dealing with agents from what the series describes as "countries from behind the Iron Curtain"; "The Prize," for instance, Brady's nemesis is an East German commissar named Gunzi, played by Anton Diffring, and in "Odds Against Death" Brady's nemesis is Johnny Caletta (Alan Tilvern), an American gangster whose henchman is dressed stereotypically in

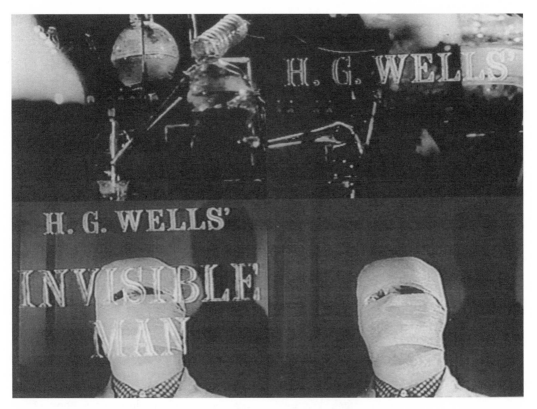

Haunting opening signature of *H.G. Wells' Invisible Man*.

black shirt and white tie. However, a few programs dealt with new and sophisticated scientific hardware, such as a new fuel dispenser in "Point of Destruction" and an anti-gravity device in "Flight into Darkness." The narrative of "The White Rabbit" follows a Nazi sympathizer's efforts at duplicating Brady's experiments in order to conquer the world. Such narratives make the series similar to programs like *Captain Midnight* and *World of Giants*.

The broadcast history of *H.G. Wells' Invisible Man* is sketchy to the point of consternation. Lacking some official log from CBS or Official Films, broadcast dates appear to be nothing more than guesses on nearly everyone's part. Some sources identify the program as a syndicated series, but Hal Erickson's *Syndicated Television: The First Forty Years 1947-1987* does not include the series; he mentions it as a CBS offering. Like most sources, Alex McNeil's *Total Television* identifies *H.G. Wells' Invisible Man* as a CBS program, but

McNeil notes that CBS broadcast only 13 of the 26 episodes. According to the television log of the *New York Times*, WCBS in New York broadcast 13 episodes of the series on Tuesday nights at eight o'clock, beginning November 4, 1958, with "Secret Experiment." The premiere date of November 4 is reiterated by Brooks and Marsh, McNeil and Lance (among others); however, Alan Morton identifies the premiere date as September 14, 1958. Most sources agree that the remainder of the 26 episodes were broadcast over WCBS in the summer of 1960 on Thursday nights at seven o'clock. Morton adds a unique claim, saying that a pilot episode titled "Secrecy Experiment" was not broadcast by CBS but was part of the American syndication package, and that this hour pilot was later broken into two episodes, the recognized pilot proper titled ("Secret Experiment") and episode 11 ("Bank Raid"). We could find no corroboration for this claim.

For reasons of simplicity, we elected to

list the dates below as they were compiled from newspaper and *TV Guide* listings for a West Coast CBS affiliate. The order of episodes may be not be in their proper sequence.

Technical Information

FORMAT: Half-hour adventure series centering on the exploits of Dr. Peter Brady, known famously as "the Invisible Man," as he fights crime and espionage in Cold War England. Brady lives with his widowed sister Diane Wilson and her young daughter Sally.

BROADCAST HISTORY: *Network* and *Airdates:* See above. *Sponsor:* Unavailable. *Seasons:* 1. *Total Episodes:* 26 in black-and-white.

Signature

A tracking shot captures a table filled with all sorts of laboratory paraphernalia; the title "H.G. Wells'" appears. As the camera comes to a stop at the end of the table, the title moves to the top of the screen. We now see a close shot of a bandaged human figure without eyes lighted in chiaroscuro effect; the full title *H.G. Wells' Invisible Man* now appears full screen, then vertically wipes down, leaving a clear shot of the figure before fading to black.

Production Staff

Production: Independent Television *Programme* (ITP) Company, Ltd. *Producer:* Ralph Smart. *Suggested for Television by* Larry White.

Production Supervisor	Aida Young
Scenario Editors	Victor Wolfson and
	Ian Stuart Black
Musical Director	Sydney John Kay
Casting Director	Harry Fine
Directors of Photography	Arthur Graham,
	Bert Mason and Brendan J. Stafford
Editors	Carmen de Ossa and
	Derek Hyde Chambers
Art Directors	Harry White and Peter Mullins
Assistant Directors	David Tomblin, Jack Drury
	and Peter Crowhurst

Sound Supervisor	Fred Turtle
Second Unit Director	Douglas Hickox
Second Unit Photography	Jack Mills

Made at National Studios, England

Regular Cast

The Invisible Man	Himself
Diane Wilson	Lisa Daniely
Sally Wilson	Deborah Watling

Episode Guide

Secret Experiment (June 13, 1959). This pilot episode begins with a pre-credits sequence narrated by Brady: "My name is Peter Brady. For some time now I've been engaged in highly secret experiments designed to bring about a great step forward in man's conquest of space and time. Here in my lab, working night and day, I've been prying into the mysteries of the future. Only a few hours ago I felt that there were secrets that would never be known to us here on Earth. And then suddenly, in the midst of routine experiments, a strange and unpredicted event took place. Whether a mistake or the natural conclusion of the experiment I cannot say. I can say that what happened is one of the most fantastic experiences in our modern day." As Brady closes his narrative, he peers intently through a portal into a radioactive chamber, as a guinea pig slowly becomes invisible. Brady urgently orders his assistant to fetch Dr. Hanning, director of Castle Hill Laboratories. As she exits, Brady labors over his notes, unaware that a radiation leak is filling the laboratory. The alarm goes off, but it is too late for Brady. As his assistant enters, Brady stands and turns to face her; she screams at his appearance and then faints. Brady has no head and no hands, just disembodied clothing, and it, too, slowly fades into invisibility. Later, government representative Sir Charles Anderson meets with Hanning, and they agree that because of Brady's unusual condition he should be held in protective custody at the laboratory. Brady, already fearing such a decision, uses his invisibility to escape to the home of his sister Diane Wilson, where he explains his unusual predicament. Brady believes that only fellow scientist John Crompton, who has also been experimenting with light refraction and optical density, can help him. Diane agrees to drive Brady to Crompton's home, but Crompton seizes the opportunity to steal Brady's secret: Crompton knocks Brady unconscious, then phones the laboratory, explaining to Hanning and Sir Charles that Brady attacked him and that Brady's invisibility has made him insane. Crompton then succeeds in stealing Brady's notes, but the Invisible Man gives chase and finally stops Crompton. Sir Charles agrees that Brady is valuable to the government, not a threat. *Writers:* Michael Connor and Michael Cramoy. *Director:* Pennington Richards.

Cast:

Dr. Hanning	Lloyd Lamble
Kemp	Bruce Seton
Sir Charles Anderson	Ernest Clark
Dr. John Crompton	Michael Goodliffe

Crisis in the Desert (June 20, 1959). As Brady seeks a return to visibility, Col. Warren of British Military Intelligence has other plans for the Invisible Man. At first Brady is reluctant to see Warren, but later relents when Brady learns that a military coup has turned a Middle Eastern country into a dictatorship. Warren convinces Brady that his invisibility will allow Brady to penetrate the newly created security measures in order to rescue a British agent named Howard. Warren tells Brady that Howard is lying unconscious in a hospital room, but adds that when he regains consciousness he will be tortured. Brady parachutes into the country where he is met by Yolande, a resistance fighter, who guides Brady to the hospital. Unknown to Brady, his parachute was seen by the secret police, and officers lie waiting for him at the hospital. But Brady's invisibility defeats the dictators, and once again British security is assured. *Writer:* Ralph Smart. *Director:* Pennington Richards.

Cast:

Yolande	Adrienne Cori
Col. Warren	Douglas Wilmer
Hassan	Eric Pohlmann
Omar	Martin Benson
Nesbib	Peter Sallis
Corporal	Derren Nesbitt
Surgeon	Derek Sydney

Behind the Mask (June 27, 1959). While on his way to Castle Hill Laboratories, Brady is flagged down by a young woman in need of assistance following a car wreck. Brady soon learns that her story about trying to miss a dog is a ruse to take Brady to the home of Raphael Constantine, a wealthy man hiding behind a mask. Constantine knows about Brady's invisibility, and says that he too wants to become invisible because he can no longer stand the sight of his own horribly disfigured face. Constantine tells Brady that he knows Brady needs a human guinea pig to restore Brady's visibility, and Constantine wants that privilege. What Brady does not know is that Constantine's desire for invisibility stems from an elaborate plan of revenge against the individuals responsible for his disfigurement. Constantine wants to become an invisible assassin who will murder a visiting diplomat from Constantine's own homeland. Brady eventually discovers Constantine's plan, and uses his invisibility to thwart the assassination. *Writers:* Stanley Mann and Leslie Arliss. *Director:* Pennington Richards.

Cast:

Raphael Constantine	Dennis Price
Max	Edwin Richfield
Maria	Barbara Chilcott
President Domecq	Arthur Gomez
Josef	David Ritch
Juan	Michael Jacques
Official	John Wynn Jones

The Locked Room (July 4, 1959). Brady learns that Tania, a female scientist from behind the Iron Curtain, who is also conducting experiments in light refraction, is visiting England. Hoping that she might help him gain his visibility, he visits her at the foreign embassy where he learns that, because of her outspoken criticism of her government, she is held in a locked room and enemy agents are preparing to return her to her country. Under the pretense of scientific diplomacy, Brady meets with Tania to work on the experiments together, but Brady manages to free Tania and arranges for passage to the United States. The enemy agents discover Brady's ruse and manage to dupe Brady into turning her over to them. The agents plan to smuggle her out of England by placing her inside a coffin, but

Brady uses his invisibility to trick the agents one final time, and Tania is a free woman. *Writers:* Lindsay Galloway and Ralph Smart. *Director:* Pennington Richards.

Cast:

Tania	Zena Marshall
Dr. Hanning	Lloyd Lamble
Dushkin	Rupert Davies
Phillips	Noel Coleman
Clerk	Emrys Leyshow
Porter	Alexander Dore

Picnic with Death (July 11, 1959). Brady's driver crashes their car into a truck that pulled out in front of him, exposing the "Invisible Man" to a number of witnesses. Brady, whose invisibility is top secret, finds himself a celebrity when Sir Charles, with little choice, announces to the world that an invisible man exists and that he is a Castle Hill scientist named Peter Brady. Brady, Diane and Sally are besieged by the public and by inquisitive reporters. Brady becomes irate at being the target of a media circus, but he soon turns his attention to Sally's friend Linda, who says that her disabled mother will be murdered by her stepfather, John Norton, a man in need of funds to pay off debts. Brady and Diane ignore Linda, believing her story to be nothing but a child's wild imagination, but Sally becomes a spy for Linda and discovers that Norton is planning a deadly picnic for Janet, Linda and Sally. *Story:* Leonard Fincham. *Teleplay:* Leslie Arliss. *Director:* Pennington Richards.

Cast:

John Norton	Derek Bond
Linda Norton	Margaret McCourt
Janet Norton	Maureen Pryor
Carol Norton	Faith Brook
Sir Charles Anderson	Ernest Clark
Stableman	Michael Ripper

Play to Kill (July 18, 1959). While driving near the coast, actress Barbara Crane is blinded by headlights from an approaching car and loses control of her own car. She misses the approaching vehicle but hits a derelict. The driver of the other car recognizes her and warns her that her career will be ruined if word got out that she was involved in a fatal accident. The driver coerces her into dumping the body over a cliff, but at the moment of committing herself she balks. The driver, however, does the deed for her, explaining that no one will ever know what truly happened that night. When Barbara's conscience gets the best of her, she begins blowing lines in rehearsals, causing tension among the cast and crew. Her troubles increase when she begins receiving calls from a man who claims he saw the whole affair on the cliff, including the dumping of the body; he agrees to remain quiet if she pays weekly for his silence. Later, Barbara is introduced to the Invisible Man by the play's director, Simon Wallace. Brady knows that she needs some kind of assistance, but Barbara refuses help. Brady then removes his clothing and becomes invisible, following her to the bank where she withdraws a large sum. Brady reasons that she is involved in a blackmail scheme, and later learns the whole story. Using his invisibility, he discovers that one of her fellow actors is behind the scheme. *Story:* Robert Westerby. *Teleplay:* Leslie Arliss. *Director:* Peter Maxwell.

Cast:

Barbara Crane	Helen Cherry
The Colonel	Colin Gordon
Tom	Hugh Latimer
Simon Wallace	Garry Thorne
Manton	Ballard Berkeley
Arthurson	Vincent Holman

Shadow on the Screen (July 25, 1959). When a ship from a country behind the Iron Curtain docks in London, seaman Stephen Vasa and his wife Sonia attempt to jump ship and seek asylum in London. Both are captured, but mysteriously Sonia is released. Later, Brady is visited by a member of a refugee organization who tries to convince Brady to help Vasa make his escape. Brady, however, rebuffs the representative, preferring to continue his experiments at Castle Hill. The refugee organization convinces Sir Charles that Vasa's credentials are in order, and Sir Charles, with the help of Sonia's desperate pleas, persuades Brady to help in liberating Vasa from the communists. Brady then meets with Sonia at her home since he is barred from the ship, and a plan is developed to free Vasa. Sonia, however, in league with members of the refugee organization, is a spy, and efforts to free Vasa are only a ruse to kidnap Brady and return him to her homeland where the communists can discover his secret of invisibility. *Story:* Ian Stuart Black. *Teleplay:* Philip Levene and Ralph Smart. *Director:* Pennington Richards.

Cast:

Sonia Vasa	Greta Gynt
Stephen Vasa	Edward Judd
Commissar	Anthony Newlands
Brataski	Redmond Phillips
Captain	André Mikehlson
Sir Charles Anderson	Ernest Clark
Woman	Irene Handl

The Mink Coat (August 1, 1959). Two thieves break into the Wilton Experimental Plant and steal microfilm copies of plans to an experimental rocket. The authorities realize that the microfilm will be smuggled out of England, and so customs agents secure every exit. Walker, the mastermind behind the burglary, has secured the microfilm inside the lining of a mink coat worn by Penny Page, a puppeteer on her way to Paris. Walker, known by the authorities, is stopped but released when a search turns up no sign of the microfilm; Walker, however, sees Penny in her coat leave for Paris. Also on board are Brady and Diane, who are embarking on a Paris holiday. Walker follows them into to Paris where he chases after Penny. Diane believes that Walker is a shady character, but Brady believes that he is only interested in the attractive girl. Walker eventually assaults Penny, but his efforts are thwarted by Penny's husband, Marcel. Brady then phones London and learns of Walker's background, and Brady foregoes his vacation to seek the microfilm. *Writers:* Lenore Coffee and Ian Stuart Black. *Director:* Pennington Richards.

Cast:

Walker	Derek Godfrey
Penny Page	Hazel Court
Marcel	Murray Kash
Bunny	Harold Berens
Customs Officer	Keith Rawlings
Madame Dupont	Joan Hickson
Photographer	John Ruddock

Blind Justice (August 8, 1959). In Egypt, pilot Arthur Holt refuses an offer by drug smugglers to carry narcotics into London, and for his refusal he is nearly gunned down. His co-pilot accepts the bribe, hides drugs inside Holt's personal belongings and then tips off the London customs officers. Holt realizes that he is now carrying the drugs, but manages to avoid the customs agents. Holt returns to his home where he calls his friend Peter Brady for help. Holt's blind wife Katherine believes a stranger at the door is Holt's friend and allows the stranger inside, where he makes another attempt on Holt's life. Brady arrives shortly after and chases the assassin, but loses him in London traffic. Brady goes to the hospital where he comforts his fatally injured friend. Brady agrees to a plan to mislead the assassin into believing that Katherine really isn't blind and that she can identify the killer. The plan succeeds, and Brady clears his friend's reputation. *Writer:* Ralph Smart. *Director:* Pennington Richards.

Cast:

Arthur Holt	Philip Friend
Katherine Holt	Honor Blackman
Sandy Mason	Jack Watling
Simmons	Julian Somers
Sparrow	Leslie Phillips
Detective-Inspector Heath	
	Robert Raglan
Detective-Sergeant	
	Desmond Llewellyn

Jailbreak (August 15, 1959). The unfaltering declarations of innocence by convict Joe Green, accompanied by his numerous attempts to break out of prison, attract the attention of Brady, who reasons that a man so committed to escape must be innocent. The prison governor refuses to grant Brady an interview with Green because overnight Green attempted one more time to break prison. Brady goes invisible and makes his way into Green's cell, where Green explains that he is innocent of murder and robbery and that he was "fingered" for some unknown reason. He tells Brady that his wallet was stolen by a mysterious woman while he was aboard a train, and that the woman can testify he was on the train while the murder was being committed. Brady and Diane visit the man who testified against Green, and after the man ejects them from his apartment Brady learns that the man and his associates plan to have Green murdered in his prison cell. Brady uses his invisibility to thwart their plan and exonerate Green. *Writer:* Ian Stuart Black. *Director:* Pennington Richards.

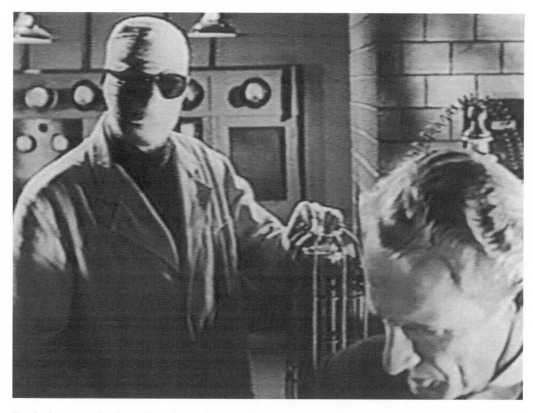

Brady discusses the fate of Professor Owens with a goverment official in the "Odds Against Death" episode of *H.G. Wells' Invisible Man.*

Cast: *Joe Green*   Dermot Walsh
         Brenner   Michael Brennan
         Sharp   Ronald Fraser
         Governor   Ralph Michael
         Doris   Denny Dayvis
         Taylor   Charles Farrell
         Robson   Maurice Kaufman

Bank Raid (August 22, 1959). With Brady's invisibility now public knowledge, thugs Crowther and Williams decide to kidnap Sally and force Brady to rob a bank for them. Their first attempt at snatching Sally is thwarted by Brady's presence, prompting Crowther to disguise himself as a doctor. He convinces the headmistress that Diane is in emergency care in the hospital, and the headmistress releases Sally into Crowther's custody. The kidnappers contact Brady and order him to meet them at an abandoned house where they will make their proposal. Diane takes Brady to the house and the kidnappers demand that Brady rob a bank and use part of the money to ransom Sally. With Sally's life in danger, Brady has no choice but to comply, but Brady's invisibility allows him to find Sally, leaving him free to apprehend the kidnappers. *Writers:* Doreen Montgomery and Ralph Smart. *Director:* Ralph Smart.

Cast: *Crowther*   Willoughby Goddard
         Williams   Brian Rawlinson
         Headmistress   Patricia Marmount

Odds Against Death (September 12, 1959). Prof. Owens is a mathematical genius whose work at Castle Hill Research Laboratories is essential to national security. When Owens sends a cable from Italy to the laboratory explaining that he is not returning to work, Brady becomes concerned since it is out of character for Owens. When Brady learns that Owens is addicted to gambling, he decides to investigate. While invisible, Brady discovers that Owens has used an elaborate mathematical system to win large sums of money at the local casino. When Brady confronts Owens about his game, Owens becomes unreasonable and harangues Brady for intruding. To break Owens' winning streak, Brady uses Diane as a front, and she begins winning huge wagers with the help of the invisible man. Owens is devastated by the loss, and only then does he reveal to Brady that two American gangsters are holding his daughter Suzy hostage while Owens makes huge sums for the thugs based on his mathematical calculations. Brady swings into action and frees Suzy and apprehends the gangsters. Later, Owens walks into the casino and wagers all his ill-gotten winnings on a single number; Brady intervenes and makes certain that Owens loses. Delighted, Owens, Suzy, Brady and Diane leave the casino for London. *Writers:* Ian Stuart Black and Stanley Mann. *Director:* Pennington Richards.

Cast: *Prof. Owens* — Walter Fitzgerald
Suzy Owens — Julia Lockwood
Johnny Caletta — Alan Tilvern
Lucia — Colette Wilde
Bruno — Peter Taylor
Croupier — Peter Elliott
Casino Manager — Olaf Pooley

Strange Partners (September 19, 1959). Brady discovers that his briefcase with five weeks of notes on his experimentation with invisibility has been stolen. He then receives a phone call from Lucian Currie, who explains that he found Brady's briefcase in his garden. Brady travels to Currie's home where he discovers the truth: Currie had the briefcase stolen in order to coerce Brady into murdering a man named Vickers, Currie's partner in a gold mine. When Brady refuses Currie's request, Currie threatens to destroy the contents of the briefcase. Brady refuses and attempts to leave, but Currie unleashes his vicious dog which can sense Brady's presence. The dog literally traps Brady, forcing Brady to acquiesce to the plan of murder. But Vickers' life is spared when Brady uses his invisibility to expose Currie's plan. *Writer:* Michael Cramoy. *Director:* Pennington Richards.

Cast: *Lucian Currie* — Griffith Jones
Inspector Quillin — Victor Platt

Collins — Jack Melford
Vickers — Patrick Troughton
Ryan — Robert Cawdon
Doctor — Reginald Hearne

Point of Destruction (September 26, 1959). Prof. Scott has developed a new jet aircraft fuel diffuser, but after four fatal experimental plane crashes, co-workers are labeling Scott a murderer. Brady investigates and learns that Scott's assistant Dr. Court is being paid by an enemy agent named Katrina to sabotage the airplanes. Brady lays a trap for Court by getting him aboard another test plane; Court gives himself away when he fears that the plane will crash. Katrina and her associate are apprehended. *Writer:* Ian Stuart Black. *Director:* Quentin Lawrence.

Cast: *Prof. Scott* — Duncan Lamont
Katrina — Patricia Jessel
Dr. Court — John Rudling
Stephan — Derren Nesbitt
Jenny — Jane Barrett
Control Officer — Barry Letts

Death Cell (October 3, 1959). Aboard a train, young Ellen Summers tells Brady she has escaped from a mental institution. She says that she is quite sane and that her pursuers are trying to kill her. Ellen also explains that she is the only witness who can clear condemned murderer George Wilson, who is also her fiancé. Shortly after Brady reluctantly agrees to investigate, Ellen disappears. Brady uses his invisibility to gain an interview with Wilson in his death cell. Wilson explains that he was with Ellen the whole day that the murder was committed, but since his arrest Ellen has disappeared. Brady next makes for the mental institution where he confronts Dr. Trevor about Ellen. Trevor says Ellen is insane and that Wilson is lying, but when Brady sees a woman who was tailing Ellen in the train, he becomes convinced that Ellen is being held captive by Trevor and his associates. Using his invisibility, Brady saves Ellen from Trevor and the nurse who were about to kill her. Brady then delivers Ellen to the authorities in time to stop the execution of Wilson. *Writer:* Michael Cramoy. *Director:* Peter Maxwell.

Cast: *Ellen Summers* — Lana Morris

Dr. Trevor	Ian Wallace
George Wilson	William Lucas
Sir Charles Anderson	Bruce Seton
Governor	Jack Lambert
Miss Beck	Bettina Dickson
Mrs. Willis	Patricia Burke

The Vanishing Evidence (October 10, 1959). Brady's friend Prof. Harper, who has been working on top secret experiments for the British government, has been found murdered and his notes missing. Fearing espionage, Britain's MI-6 secret service entreats Brady to visit Amsterdam and pursue master spy Peter Thal. Unknown to Brady, a British agent named Jenny Reyden is already on the case; MI-6 needs Brady to confirm that Harper's stolen papers are genuine. Jenny masquerades as Thal's contact, but he becomes suspicious. When he attacks her, Jenny shoots Thal. Jenny is forced to flee before she can retrieve the papers. Later, she meets Brady and explains that the papers are still in Thal's safe, and Brady agrees to use his invisibility to take the papers. But before he can act, Inspector Strang arrests Jenny. Brady finds himself not only pursuing Harper's papers but also looking for a way to free Jenny without exposing her MI-6 affiliation. *Writer:* Ian Stuart Black. *Director:* Peter Maxwell.

Cast:

Peter Thal	Charles Gray
Jenny Reyden	Sarah Lawson
Inspector Strang	Peter Illing
Prof. Harper	James Raglan
Superintendent	Ewen Solon
Porter	Michael Ripper

The Prize (October 17, 1959). Attempting to leave an Iron Curtain country to accept an international literary prize, writer Tania Roskov is denied an exit by Commissar Gunzi, who arrests her for treason since, he charges, her works censure the people of her own country. At the awards banquet, Brady, who is to receive an award for his scientific endeavors, is summoned by Prof. Kenig, head of the prize committee, who informs Brady of Tania's arrest and the cancellation of the ceremony as a protest against Tania's arrest. Brady, an admirer of Tania's democratic ideals, offers to cross the border and free the writer. Realizing that a minefield separates the two countries, Brady takes a minesweeper and succeeds in penetrating the border, much to the consternation of the border guards who see only an ambulatory minesweeper crossing the field. When Gunzi hears of the strange incident, he immediately suspects the famous invisible man and reasons that he has come to rescue Tania. Brady succeeds but not before facing harrowing gunfire and a pursuit by Gunzi. *Writer:* Ian Stuart Black. *Director:* Quentin Lawrence.

Cast:

Tania Roskov	Mai Zetterling
Commissar Gunzi	Anton Diffring
Prof. Kenig	Tony Church
General	Desmond Roberts
Captain Bera	Richard Clarke
Sentry	Clive Baxter
Agasha	Ruth Lodge

Flight into Darkness (October 24, 1959). Dr. Stephens has created an anti-gravity device, but when Brady visits to congratulate him Stephens becomes cynical, warning Brady that the device could be used against humanity. Brady reasons that Stephens is under stress and exits, but after Brady leaves Stephens destroys his papers and his laboratory. The next day, Brady is informed that Stephens has disappeared, which causes panic at Castle Hill because ministry officials are due for a demonstration of Stephens' device. Brady, however, knows the basics of Stephens' device and demonstrates it, impressing the officials. But Stephens' daughter Pat arrives along with a man named Wilson, who identifies himself as the "peace secretary" of a world peace organization. Wilson rails against the device, calling it a thing of destruction, and Pat tells Brady that her father was convinced by Wilson that the machine would lead to death and destruction. Later, Pat seeks Brady's help in finding her father, whom she believes has been kidnapped. Brady then discovers that Wilson is actually an enemy agent seeking Stephens' device, and that Wilson, too, is seeking the runaway Stephens in order to kidnap him for services behind the Iron Curtain. *Story:* William H. Altman. *Teleplay:* Ian Stuart Black. *Director:* Peter Maxwell.

Cast:

| Prof. Stephens | Geoffrey Keen |
| Wilson | Esmond Knight |

Pat Stephens	Joanna Dunham	*Arosa*	Charles Hill
Wade	John Harvey	*Milia*	Lawrence Taylor
Sewell	Colin Douglas	*Ali*	James Booth
Fisher	Alex Scott		

The Decoy (October 31, 1959). Terri Trent, half of an American singing duo, arrives in London where she finds lodgings in a seedy hotel. That night, after witnessing the murder of a man in the room across the hall, she immediately calls the desk. What she doesn't know is that the manager is in league with the murderers. Later, Brady is visiting Gen. Stockforce, commander in charge of U.S. forces in England, when Terri's twin sister Toni arrives and reports that her sister has vanished. Stockforce asks Brady to look into the affair, and Brady suggests that Toni impersonate Terri and request a room at the hotel. Toni soon learns that Terri is being held prisoner by gangsters, and that she herself is now in grave danger. *Writer:* Brenda Blackmore. *Director:* Quentin Lawrence.

Cast:	*Terri and Toni Trent*	Betta St. John
	Rubens	Robert Gallico
	Stavros	Philip Leaver
	Andraes	Wolfe Morris
	Giorgio	Barry Shawzin
	Gen. Stockforce	Lionel Murton

The Gun Runners (November 7, 1959). Hearing of the cold-blooded murder of an English engineer and his wife in front of their infant son, MI-6 agent Col. Grahame entreats Brady's help in breaking government corruption in the small Mediterranean country of Bay Akim, a haven for arms smugglers. Brady joins agent Zena Fleming in visiting the small country. Immediately upon arriving, Zena is met by a government official who resents her presence, and shortly thereafter she is confronted by an armed thug who demands that she return to England. Brady learns that the center of operations is an export company. What Brady and Zena do not know is that their every move is monitored by the gun runners. *Writer:* Ian Stuart Black. *Director:* Peter Maxwell.

Cast:	*Zena Fleming*	Louise Allbritton
	Col. Grahame	Bruce Seton
	Sardi	Paul Stassino

The White Rabbit (November 14, 1959). In France, Dr. Suzanne Dumassé follows her dog Candy to a drainage pipe where she sees a rabbit materialize. Suzanne takes the rabbit to Paris where the rabbit is placed under scientific scrutiny. Meanwhile in England, Brady receives an urgent message from Monsieur Antoine Hugo of the French government who entreats Brady to fly to Paris on urgent business. Brady is shown the rabbit and asked about his own invisibility, and Brady explains that the presence of radioactivity might explain the rabbit's invisibility. When Suzanne takes Brady to the hilltop chateau of the Rocher family, he finds the chateau surrounded by armed security guards. Rocher, a Nazi sympathizer, plans to dominate the world with an army of invisible men. When Rocher hears of Suzanne's interest in the chateau, he orders her kidnapped. Max, the security chief at the chateau, tricks Suzanne into coming to the chateau and makes her a prisoner. When Brady learns of the abduction, he penetrates the compound, prevents Suzanne from becoming an experimental subject and subdues Rocher and his fellow conspirators. *Writer:* Ian Stuart Black. *Director:* Quentin Lawrence.

Cast:	*Suzanne Dumassé*	Marla Landi
	Rocher	Paul Daneman
	Antoine Hugo	Austin Trevor
	Valois	Arnold Marle
	Prof. Blaire	Arnold Diamond
	Max	Reed De Rouen
	Louise	Myrtle Reed
	Dr. Dumassé	Keith Pyott
	Colette	Isobel Black
	Chauffeur	André Muller
	Brun	André Cherisse

Man in Disguise (November 21, 1959). While in Paris, Brady comes to the aid of a beautiful woman named Madeleine who has fainted. Brady later discovers that he has been conned, that Madeleine was only a decoy while someone stole his luggage, credentials and passport. Madeleine's partner Nick dons the bandages and passes himself off as Peter Brady, smuggling drugs into England where his partner Matt sells them. When Brady learns that someone has entered England in the guise of the Invisible Man, he heads for Scotland Yard to initiate an investigation. Brady and police woman Sgt. Winter then visit the city's nightclubs in the hope of finding Madeleine and the drug dealers. After several attempts, Brady and Winter spy a drug deal underway in a seedy night spot. Invisible, Brady switches the dope with salt, causing the buyer to claim he has been swindled. The dealer also believes that he has been conned, and vows to get even with Nick. *Writers:* Brenda Blackmore and Leslie Arliss. *Director:* Quentin Lawrence.

Cast:
Nick	Tim Turner
Madeleine	Leigh Madison
Matt	Lee Montague
Sergeant Winter	Jeanette Starke
Detective-Inspector	Robert Raglan
Sergeant Day	Howard Pays
Felton	Felix Aylmer
Club Manager	Denis Shaw

Man in Power (November 28, 1959). At a local university, Brady gives a demonstration of his experiments with invisibility to several students in the hope that they may find a cure for his condition. While Brady confers with a young Arab student named Jonetta, Jonetta is interrupted by a message that explains that a military coup has taken place in his Middle Eastern homeland. The megalomaniacal Gen. Shafari has murdered Jonetta's father and brother, leaving Jonetta heir to the throne. Shafari, however, has vowed to murder Jonetta should he attempt to occupy his rightful throne. Jonetta ignores the warning and books passage back to his homeland. In the meantime, the British government contacts Brady and asks him to aid in placing Jonetta on the throne. *Writer:* Ian Stuart Black. *Director:* Peter Maxwell.

Cast:
Gen. Shafari	André Morell
Prince Jonetta	Gary Raymond
Princess Taima	Nadja Regin
Hassan	Andrew Keir
Fayid	Derek Sydney
King Rashid	Vivian Matalon

The Rocket (December 5, 1959). Smith, the transportation supervisor at Castle Hill Laboratories, has gambled much of his savings away. In desperation he prepares to jump off a bridge, but a stranger stops him and suggests a way to pay his debts. The stranger, an enemy agent named Reitter, will pay off the debts if Smith helps him obtain confidential information about a rocket which uses a newly developed alloy for flight control. Smith reluctantly agrees, and later sells the rocket's top secret transportation routes to Reitter; in order to rendezvous with Reitter in Scotland, Smith alters the route. The change makes Brady suspicious. Brady contacts Mrs. Smith, who reveals that her husband just recently says he found a large sum of cash in the house. Brady reasons that Smith has sold out to the spies, and he alerts the authorities and saves Smith from committing treason. *Writer:* Michael Pertwee. *Director:* Quentin Lawrence.

Cast:
Smith	Glyn Own
Reitter	Russell Walters
Prof. Howard	Robert Brown
Detective-Inspector	Robert Raglan
Mrs. Smith	Jennifer Wright
Driver	Harold Goodwin
Police Sergeant	Maurice Durant
Bill	Colin Grant

Shadow Bomb (December 12, 1959). At the invitation of his friend Capt. Finch, Brady attends a demonstration of a new electronic bomb developed by the army. Gen. Martin wants Castle Hill to produce the electronic bomb sensors since he believes the new mechanism will cut down on minefield accidents. The next day, Finch prepares the demonstration in a sand pit but after setting the explosive the pit collapses, trapping Finch in the pit with the bomb. Since the sensors work on light and shadow, anyone trying to save Finch will set off the bomb. Brady then trusts that his invisibility will allow him to enter the pit and save Finch. *Writers:* Tony O'Grady [Brian Clemens] and Ian Stuart Black. *Director:* Peter Maxwell.

Cast:
Capt. Barry Finch	Conrad Phillips
Gen. Martin	Anthony Bushell
Betty	Jennifer Jayne
Lloyd	Walter Gotell
Lieutenant Daniels	Ian Hendry

The Big Plot (December 19, 1959). An airliner of foreign registry crashes in Northern England, and investigators find a canister containing uranium-235 inside an unclaimed valise. The canister is sent immediately to Sir Charles, who asks Brady to analyze it. Brady believes that it is a part to an unassembled atomic bomb, and that the other parts may be already in England. Meanwhile, customs officials have detected radioactivity emanating from the golf bag of Helen Peversham, wife of Lord Peversham, a noted pacifist. Sir Charles assigns Brady to follow both Lord and Lady Peversham in the hope that they will lead to the other parts of the bomb. Brady learns that Lord Peversham is using his wife to smuggle radioactive parts for the bomb since he is leading a group of pacifists who hope to plant an atomic bomb in every capital city of the world in order to force all nations to disarm. But Peversham's plot is thwarted by his chauffeur Hanstra and his butler Waring who, with other members of the pacifist organization, have no plans for peace at all but for extorting the west into submission. "And he thinks we will plant a bomb in Moscow," Waring jests as he and Hanstra bury an atomic bomb in Peversham's cellar. When Helen discovers their secret, she is held captive; when Lord Peversham protests, the cold-blooded Waring shoots him. Brady and Sir Charles and the Metropolitan police break into Peversham's home and apprehend Hanstra. Brady subdues Waring in the cellar and deactivates the bomb. *Story:* Tony O'Grady [Brian Clemens] and Robert Smart. *Teleplay:* Ian Stuart Black. *Director:* Peter Maxwell.

Cast:

Lady Helen Peversham	Barbara Shelley
Lord Larry Peversham	John Arnatt
Waring	William Squire
MacBane	Edward Hardwicke
Sir Charles	Ewen MacDuff
First Officer	Richard Warner
Second Officer	Derrick Sherwin
Hanstra	Terence Cooper

Johnny Jupiter

One science fiction series in particular, the marvelously eccentric and wistful *Johnny Jupiter*, enchanted both children and adults in the 1950s. The premise upon which it rested was a simple one: a television studio janitor named Ernest P. Duckweather has his heart set on becoming a TV station engineer and takes advantage of his presence in the studio to experiment with the various dials and knobs in the control room. Inadvertently—and amazingly—Duckweather makes contact with the planet Jupiter, which also has television, and is thereby introduced to Jupiterians like the mild-mannered and insightful Johnny Jupiter, his arrogant companion B-12 and a robot named Major Domo, who is required to do all of B-12's worrying. Duckweather is also introduced to Jupiterian logic which often runs counter to that employed by Earthlings. On Jupiter, for instance, Duckweather discovers that Jupiterians prize conversation over television; moreover, he learns that children sometimes have a tendency to devote too much time to reading books and playing with slide rules, and as punishment for such diversions Jupiterian children are required to watch television. Jupiterians are also puzzled by the human obsession with vacations, reasoning that if people didn't like their jobs they should find other jobs; Jupiterians, Duckweather learns, prefer "workations." In matters of the heart, Duckweather learns that when it comes to choosing between a pretty girl and a homely one, the Jupiterians select the homely one, reasoning that it is the homely one who needs the attention.

The Jupiterians (played by puppets) had the ability to scrutinize and then share truths about the human condition, the latter being cleverly represented, in the tradition of Dickens, by incarnations of human foibles. As a result, *Johnny Jupiter* appealed on two levels. First, the narratives offered entertaining object lessons about moral and ethical behavior; Johnny's commentaries about such inappropriate deportment as lying and cheating were intended to instruct children about what constitutes good conduct. Secondly, the narratives were often witty, offering similar commentary about such behavior but in a stronger and often satiric manner. *New York Times* television critic Jack Gould described it as "one long, good-natured spoofing of our own ways, customs and habits as seen through the eyes of a couple of visitors from another planet who think their civilization is pretty hot stuff, too." The scripts were obviously intended for adult audiences, but it must be emphasized that they remained in the child's voice, as it were, and never satirized the conduct under investigation by the Jupiterians; lying and cheating, for instance, received absolutely no quarter from either the child's or the adult's perspective. At the adult level, the commentary reflected the frequently

Title card for the filmed version of *Johnny Jupiter*.

corrupt nature of human behavior and mankind's shortcomings.

The origin of *Johnny Jupiter* can be found at the beginning of children's television. The faltering DuMont network originated the first successful network programming aimed at youngsters—antedating NBC's *Howdy Doody* by nine months—with a series called *The Small Fry Club*, created and produced by Bob and Kay Emery, and hosted by "Big Brother" Bob Emery.

Two years later, DuMont sought a program to appeal to both *The Small Fry Club* crowd—which was enamored of the colorful puppets—and the legions of science fiction followers who at that moment were satiated by such programs as DuMont's own *Captain Video*. Martin Stone, who had served as the executive producer of *Howdy Doody*, and writer Jerome Coopersmith then fashioned the tale of Duckweather and his association with the Jupiterians.

Jerry Coopersmith, like almost everyone else connected with the new show (like commercial television itself) was young—28 when he began writing *Johnny Jupiter*. The attention drawn to his obvious writing talent would soon win him writing assignments on such series as *Armstrong Circle Theatre*, *Alcoa-Goodyear Playhouse*, *Harry S Truman* and *Hawaii Five-O*, and lead to his creation of *The Andros Targets* for CBS in the late 1970s. He has also written a number of TV specials and the Broadway play "Baker Street."

Under the watchful eye of Theodore Bergmann, DuMont's network director, and the necessarily tight-fisted accounting department, the *Johnny Jupiter* program began to take substantive if frugal form, and the cast and crew composed what Gould, in his effusive review, called "an inspired company that is performing a half dozen wonders at once and doing it on a minuscule budget." Orchestrating these wonders was director Frank Bunetta, who assembled the various parts into a unified whole within that "minuscule budget."

Bunetta, an experienced DuMont director, succeeded admirably by also serving as director of one of DuMont's few genuine successes, *Life Is Worth Living*, a vehicle for Bishop Fulton J. Sheen.

For the Jupiterians, hand puppets were chosen over marionettes, reportedly because of the difference in cost (in terms of both construction and manipulation). Allan Stone, Martin's brother, designed and created the puppets, and their all-important personalities were placed in the hands—literally—of puppeteer Carl Harms and in the voice of longtime radio performer Gilbert Mack. Harms had previously worked with Bill and Cora Baird on their CBS series *Life with Snarky Parker* (1950) and *The Whistling Wizard* (1951-52). His work on *Johnny Jupiter*, however, was described—again by Jack Gould—as "unusually deft and life-like and a first-rate job." Gil Mack, who had appeared in a variety of character roles in such diverse radio programs as *Chick Carter, Boy Detective*; *Green Valley U.S.A.*; *Cloak and Dagger*; *Dick Tracy;* and *Everyman's Theater*, had long been noted for his adeptness at trick voices. Mack used a soft-spoken yet lively voice for Johnny in contrast to the bass monotones of the sober Major Domo.

Of these puppet characterizations, the most interesting and certainly the most colorful was that of Major Domo, the robot who had to do all the worrying for B-12. Harms's uncomplicated vertical motions—the simple up and down action of Major Domo's lower jaw and arms—complemented Mack's monotone grumbling to such a degree that Major Domo easily eclipsed the popularity of Johnny himself; Mack's voice characterization resembled in tone and timbre that of the movies' original cynic Ned Sparks, offering adult audiences a familiar persona for the Jupiterians' more skeptical observations about human behavior.

The pivotal role of Ernest P. Duckweather was assumed by veteran character actor Vaughn Taylor, who had been performing character parts on television since 1946—some 250 by his own count—when, at the age of 42, he was tapped for the Duckweather role. Simultaneous with his new role on *Johnny*

Jupiter, Taylor continued to serve as part of the repertory group performing on the prestigious live production *Robert Montgomery Presents*. But *Johnny Jupiter* provided Taylor with one of his best reviews when Jack Gould described Taylor as giving "the most beguiling performance he has ever given on TV. ... As the mild-mannered janitor, Mr. Taylor preserves the extreme delicacy and fragility of his role and endows the whole show with credibility. His is a tricky assignment well done."

Explaining his role on the series, Taylor said, "Duckweather was just a straight man for the puppets in the beginning, but that's been changed. He's simple in an intelligent way and sympathetic to everyone's problems."

Music for *Johnny Jupiter* was the purview of Ed Manson, who provided—in a typical parsimonious feint by DuMont—a simple harmonica background. Each week, however, Manson was called upon to compose one or two songs to comport with Coopersmith's often satirical lyrics.

Johnny Jupiter premiered live on Saturday evening, March 21, 1953, at 7:30. In keeping within that minuscule budget, the production format usually kept Duckweather in the studio at the control center where he conversed with Johnny and his friends. In a normal half-hour episode, a difficulty arose for Duckweather, and he in turn made contact with Johnny for insight. In a particularly interesting and certainly timely topic—even for today—writer Coopersmith once struck out at pandering television news commentators and noxious pressure groups by writing a script in which Duckweather auditions for the role of a news commentator for Jupiterian television. Duckweather commenced his audition with a story concerning two moon dwellers being apprehended by the Satellite Patrol, but an angry objection from the Moon Dwellers Association prompted the axing of the story. A second story—"A shocking exposé among underwater plant life"—brought an immediate complaint from the Underwater Vegetable League, and a third story—"a juicy tidbit" promised the audience by Duckweather—was quickly objected to by the "Juicy Tidbit Society." And so it went until Duckweather finally signed off his program with a satirical song by Coopersmith and Manson called "The Program That Doesn't Offend."

Whether the sketch was planned as a subtle rebuke to the cowed networks and quailing personalities on display during the witch-hunting heyday of Senator Joseph McCarthy is not known, but certainly Coopersmith's satirical script was highly effective and cited appreciatively by critic Val Adams in the *New York Times*. Coopersmith, quoted in Adams's review, flatly denied writing for any group, however. "I write for my own enjoyment," he said. "I assume that if the script satisfies me, it will satisfy others, too."

For all of the considerable talent which had been assembled and for all of the critical acclaim piled upon *Johnny Jupiter*, the program was, nonetheless, a product of the floundering DuMont network, and it was introduced to television audiences at a time when the fourth network was struggling to keep its financial head above water; DuMont would fold a mere two years after the premiere of *Johnny Jupiter*. DuMont canceled the series after its first trimester; despite the program's obvious merits, it had failed to attract a commercial sponsor and the network wasn't in a strong enough financial position to sustain the series until a sponsor could be signed, as DuMont had done with its enormously successful *Captain Video* series.

DuMont's decision to cancel the program, however, wasn't taken lightly by Stone. He elected to package *Johnny Jupiter* as a syndicated series through his own Kagran Corporation, which was responsible for merchandising *The Howdy Doody Show* among others. Most important was that Stone was able to secure a sponsor, something DuMont had been unable to do. Stone now filmed his series exclusively for the Hawley and Hoops company, makers of M&M's candies, which initially financed 26 episodes; the series was then "spotted" in 54 markets where high ratings and a "formidable increase"—nearly 30% according to some sources—in candy sales induced M&M and its advertising agency, Roy S. Durstine Inc. of New York, to finance an additional 13 episodes and spot an additional 31 markets, making a total of 39 episodes for 85 markets. Kagran eventually negotiated a

deal with the fledgling ABC network to air the series, and *Johnny Jupiter* returned to television in a revised edition in the fall of 1953 simultaneously as a syndicated series distributed by Associated Artists Productions and as an ABC network series.

Several subtle and not-so-subtle changes were now evident in the focus and direction of the series. Jerry Coopersmith relinquished his duties as producer to Martin Stone himself, but Coopersmith continued as story editor and principal writer. Philip London took over as puppeteer from Carl Harms.

The major change, however, was the readjusted format. The middle-aged janitor played by Vaughn Taylor was replaced by an eccentric and naive young inventor played by Wright King, who at the age of 25 was already a veteran of numerous Broadway productions including the part of the "young collector" in Elia Kazan's stage and film adaptations of Tennessee Williams's *A Streetcar Named Desire*. Ernest P. Duckweather now earned a living by working in the Frisby General Store in a town called Clayville.

The new format also required two additional human characters: the cantankerous Horatio Frisby, owner of the store, and his daughter, Katherine, Duckweather's romantic interest. Frisby was played by Cliff Hall, a veteran vaudeville straight man who had played the part of the doubting "Sharlie" to Jack Pearl's mendacious Baron Munchausen on NBC's radio comedy, *The Jack Pearl Show* (1933). Katherine was played by Patricia Peardon, who—like King—had established a career on the legitimate stage; she and Hall had appeared together in a successful production of *Junior Miss*, in which she had played the title role.

Although Gil Mack continued to supply the voices to the puppets, he had one less voice with which to contend; B-12 disappeared in order to make room for a new Jupiterian character, a mute "factory rejected" robot named Reject. On the planet Jupiter, Reject was one of Allan Stone's puppet creations manipulated by Phil London, but when he was dispatched to Earth to aid Duckweather in overcoming his many trials, Reject became a full-size costumed figure also played by London. Reject's

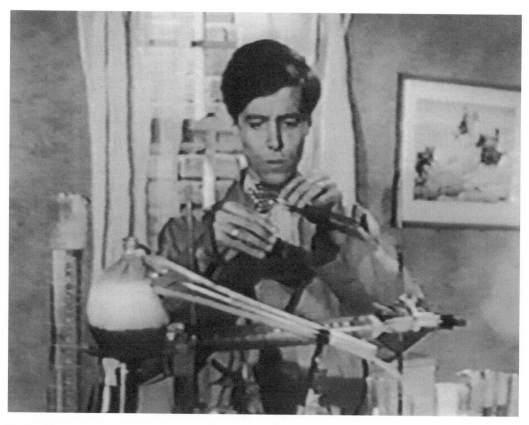

In the filmed version of *Johnny Jupiter*, Wright King played the amateur scientist and inventor Ernest P. Duckweather.

propensity for getting into trouble and his unlikely appearance (a fixed expression of surprise behind a pair of oversized eyeglasses) complemented by his gentle and delightful gestures, made Reject one of the more popular characters in the series.

In effect, Reject was Kagran's merchandising counterpart to Howdy Doody's Clarabelle the Clown. Mute and fully disguised by the robot suit, Reject could be easily played by anyone at any time in any city. Reject made his first—and as far as can be discerned his only—personal appearance on November 7, 1953, in Huntington, West Virginia, where he appeared at Evans Supermarket as well as hospitals and schools and on local programs on WSAZ-TV. The appearance was sponsored by Kagran, which spent approximately $500 on balloons, photographs and a main street parade, not so much to promote the series as much as an effort to convince M&M candies

to sponsor such appearances nationwide, something that Colgate and other sponsors of *Howdy Doody* were doing for Clarabelle. Apparently the gambit failed. Kagran pledged through announcements in trade publications that merchandising the *Johnny Jupiter* program would proceed, promising such items as balloons, puppets, coloring books and various other kinds of toys. If such merchandising actually reached fruition, the items are extremely rare today; although no one seems to know for certain, most likely the merchandising of *Johnny Jupiter* also failed.

With the format sufficiently altered for the new version, production on the series began in March 1953. Rather than being presented live from New York as it had been on DuMont, *Johnny Jupiter* was now shot on film. With Hollywood studios still defiantly opposed to television production, filmed properties at this point were the province of independent film units which were more often proficient in the "science" of film production than in the "art" of filmmaking. *Johnny Jupiter*, then, was now filmed in New York by director Howard Magwood for Sound Masters Inc., a producer of television commercials, and later by Ben Gradus for his own film production company, International Motion Picture Studios (IMPS), whose clientele consisted mainly of advertising agencies. New York cinematographer Gerald Hirschfield photographed the entire series, and scenic designs including background art of the planet Jupiter were created by Paul Heller.

Production on the series always followed the same pattern: Four scripts were blocked and rehearsed in two weeks followed by another two weeks of shooting those scripts. To conserve money, all of the puppet scenes were filmed in tandem, and most of the action was limited to master shots. Wright King recalled that an "efficiency expert" was always on the set showing ways to cut costs; at one point, King said, the efficiency expert suggested that a series of stock shots of Duckweather's reactions be filmed for insertion into episodes as needed.

The first episode of the new edition of *Johnny Jupiter* was broadcast in most markets on September 6, 1953.

Moreover, with the addition of a sponsor, the Jupiterians suddenly discovered an issue on which they could agree with Earthlings; through the lost art of the integrated commercial, the Jupiterian puppets each week were now extolling the virtues of M&M's candies:

JOHNNY: Oh, Major, it's wonderful how the Earthlings have found such a neat new way to eat fine chocolate.

MAJOR DOMO: You refer to M&M's candies, of course!

JOHNNY: Sure, the delicious milk chocolate with a thin sugar shell that melts in your mouth, not on your fingers.

MAJOR DOMO: M&M's candies ... ummmm ummmm ... the chocolate treat that's neat to eat.

While this new version of *Johnny Jupiter* remained both fun and entertaining, the exigencies of a commercially sponsored series in politically sensitive times undoubtedly peeled away some of the program's satirical edge. During the DuMont period, when the critics were hailing the show's satirical finesse and the series was without a sponsor, Coopersmith was asked if he harbored any fears that sponsors might be reluctant to touch the series because of its often derisive treatment of television. Coopersmith thought not, saying, "Anything that's done well and is entertaining has commercial possibilities. It doesn't make any difference whether it's Milton Berle or Bishop Sheen."

With commencement of the new edition of the series, Stone and Coopersmith were required to aim the program at children; such a requirement seems to have forced Coopersmith and *Johnny Jupiter* to deviate from the original intent of the series, that of appealing to both children and adults through witty and often satiric narratives. The characterizations remained outrageous and stylized, but the Dickensian function of these caricatures was for the most part avoided. The new format stressed typical sitcom narratives. For example, Duckweather's feeble attempts at maintaining his fix-it shop is exacerbated by Reject's noble but ineffectual intervention, and the predicament is eventually alleviated by Johnny's wisdom and Duckweather's good sense.

Occasional flourishes of its earlier identity did materialize; one episode scripted by Coopersmith from a story by Coopersmith and Sam Rockingham (frequently alluded to as "The Professor") featured Ross Martin as Prof. Dexter Spiegelmacher, a noted expert and lecturer on the doctrine of "money isn't everything." In this multifarious episode, Coopersmith and director Howard Magwood cleverly devised an object lesson about the evils of avarice (what Spiegelmacher professes) while exposing the folly of hypocrisy (what Spiegelmacher does). The narrative also holds up a mirror to itself, revealing in an arresting manner Coopersmith's obvious grievance about the role television has played—and continues to play—in turning creative expression into the *business of expression.*

In a guileless manner, the evils of greed are recounted by Spiegelmacher's own words. Nearly everyone in Clayville listens to Prof.

Spiegelmacher's radio program in which he espouses the Spiegelmacher System for "feeling gut mit-out loot." For Spiegelmacher, such things as being overdrawn at the bank, shaking pockets and hearing "nothing but keys rattling" and having only "the kind of lettuce that goes with sandwiches" means that a person is "lucky." However, when Spiegelmacher is approached to lecture at the local women's club, he demands substantial loot to appear.

Not all of the 39 filmed episodes of *Johnny Jupiter* made such a forceful commentary, but in their simple ways they nonetheless spoke many truths about the human condition. Johnny and his friends, through Duckweather, taught valuable lessons about growing up.

Considering the quality and success of *Johnny Jupiter*, its demise is an anomaly. Riding the crest of excellent reviews and high ratings, the filmed version of *Johnny Jupiter* survived just one season. According to Wright King, Kagran just didn't know how to best produce the series. "They got in over their heads with respect to budgets and the requirements of film production," King recalled, adding that Kagran was a company experienced with marketing and merchandising, not with film production. Money was always an issue, he said.

By March 1954, Kagran had informed the cast and crew that *Johnny Jupiter* would be coming to a conclusion after one filmed season. *Johnny Jupiter* stood out and apart from the other juvenile science fiction efforts of the early 1950s. The whimsical series challenged youngsters' imaginations while gently teaching values and imparting a little humility along the way.

Technical Information

FORMAT: Live and filmed science fiction fantasy series featuring Ernest P. Duckweather and his ongoing communication with the puppet inhabitants of the planet Jupiter.

BROADCAST HISTORY: *Network:* DuMont and syndicated. *Original Airdates:* March 21, 1953–June 13, 1953 (DuMont); September 6, 1953–May 30, 1954 (Syndicated). *Sponsor:*

M&M's Candy. *Seasons:* 2. *Total Episodes:* 52 black-and-white (13 live, 39 filmed).

Signature (Filmed Series)

The title *Johnny Jupiter* appears against a background of stars and planets. Narration begins as a sequence of scenes featuring key characters from the series shifts across the screen. The narration changes slightly from program to program, but generally recounts Ernest P. Duckweather's contact with Jupiter and his relationship with the Jupiterians. The following is representative of the series:

VOICE: This is the story of Ernest P. Duckweather, who invented the strangest television in the world. On this set he could look through endless space, 600,000,000 miles away, to far-off planet Jupiter. In a Jupiterian television station he found three friends: Johnny Jupiter, a human, more or less; Major Domo, chief of the robots; and Reject, the factory-rejected robot who was able to appear and disappear at will. Soon Duckweather found that he could turn to the Jupiterians for help whenever he was in trouble...

Production Staff

Production: Kagran Corp. *Producers:* Martin Stone and Jerry Coopersmith. *Head Writer:* Jerry Coopersmith. *Music:* Ed Manson.

Directors	Frank Bunetta, Howard Magwood and Ben Gradus
Associate Producer	Dan Klugherz
Script Editor	Jerome Coopersmith
Jupiterians Designed by	Allan Stone
Assistant to the Producer	Barry Lawrence
Production Supervisor	Walter Sachs
Director of Photography	Gerald Hirschfeld
Optical Supervision	Irving Sachs
Scenic Designer	Paul Heller
Recording Engineer	William Schwartz
Sound Effects Editor	Neil Matz
Supervising Editor	Rita Roland

Filmed in New York by Sound Masters, Inc., and International Motion Picture Studios (IMPS).

Regular Cast

Ernest P. Duckweather
             Vaughn Taylor and Wright King
Katherine Frisby   Patricia Peardon
Horatio Frisby   Cliff Hall

Puppet Voices   Gilbert Mack
Puppeteer   Carl Harms and Philip London

Episode Guide

No episode guide available for this series.

The Man
and the Challenge

As science itself became the dominant theme in the latter part of 1950s science fiction television, *The Man and the Challenge*, like *Men into Space*, favored the role of the American scientist in researching man's endurance. Presumably in preparation for space travel, the series' research centered on the contributions of Dr. Glenn Barton, an athlete, medical expert and ex–Marine modeled on real-life researcher Col. John Paul Stapp, whose fame as the rocket sled jockey made the cover of *Life* magazine and served as the inspiration for the film *On the Threshold of Space*, released by Twentieth Century–Fox in 1956. As a result, the series' emphasis was always on *the* man and not the generic man. This distinction is emphasized in the program's signature (see below) as well as the narratives.*

Producer Ivan Tors, the man behind the effective series *Science Fiction Theatre* (q.v.), explained in *Telefilm* magazine (September 1959) that "Col. Stapp's experiments on himself filled me with great admiration, and I fashioned *The Man and the Challenge* on a similar personality, a doctor and researcher, who experiments with danger and survival."

Information on this series is scant. After an exhaustive search we were able to find just one episode, "The Windowless Room," complete with commercials but lacking closing credits. Information below has been compiled by cross-referencing television listings in newspapers and other episode log sources, including *TV Guide*. Cast information has been assembled from various reference works on science fiction television.

Technical Information

FORMAT: Half-hour adventure series centering on the exploits of Dr. Glenn Barton, primary researcher for the Human Factor Institute, a government agency seeking people willing to undergo dangerous missions for the purpose of scientific observation.

BROADCAST HISTORY: *Network:* NBC; Saturday 8:30-9:00. *Original Airdates:* September 12, 1959, to September 3, 1960. *Spon-

This is a case in which network meddling may have proved beneficial to the creators. In a September 1959 newspaper interview, star George Nader mentioned that the series was originally titled Challenge. *The article added that network officials demanded a title change because they felt that the program may be mistaken for a game show, currently in disrepute because of the scandals. The title was changed and, perhaps, that made the difference in the series' approach to its theme.*

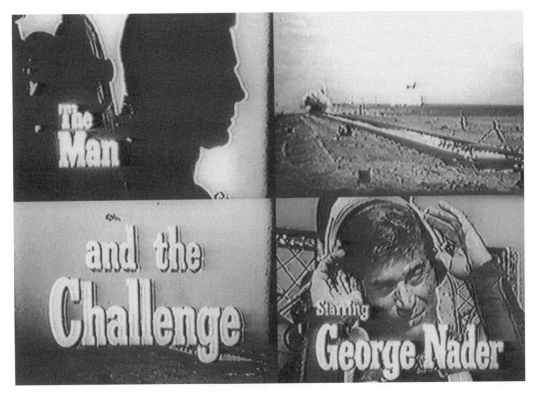

Opening signature of *The Man and the Challenge*, sponsored by the Chemstrand Corporation.

sor: Chemstrand Corporation and Winston Cigarettes. *Seasons:* 1. *Total Episodes:* 36 black-and-white.

Signature

Barton is seated in the cockpit of a rocket sled, and as he dons his crash helmet we see the title "The Man." This scene is followed by footage of the rocket sled in action over which the title "and the" zooms toward the camera. As the rocket sled slows in a gush of water, the title "Challenge" zooms toward the camera. The unidentified announcer proclaims, "The Man and the Challenge," followed by an introduction of the episode's sponsor.

Production Staff

Production: Ziv Television Programs, Inc. *Producer:* Ivan Tors. *Associate Producer:* Andrew Marton.

Regular Cast

Dr. Glenn Barton   George Nader
    Occasional Appearances: *Lynn Allen,* Joyce Meadows; *Dr. Kramer,* Raymond Bailey; *Miss Hopkins,* Doris Fesette; *Dr. Carlson,* Robert Bice

Episode Guide

The Sphere of No Return (September 12, 1959). To test human stamina at high altitudes, Barton and two other men are asked to go up in a balloon. When one of the men panics, failing the required standards, he is replaced by a woman, which draws a hostile response from the surviving pilot. *Note:* Many reviewers took umbrage over the presence of a female in the balloon, calling it the typical Hollywood gambit to garner romance. But Tors defended his story; in *TV Guide* he admitted that he took "a little license" but retorted that "nothing could have been more scientific than the presence of a woman scientist on the flight." He added that the Russians "are conducting high-altitude tests with women and are considering using women as commercial airline pilots." Tors concluded that the "tests indicate that women are calmer than men and can concentrate better."

Cast: Corey — Paul Burke
Lynn Allen — Joyce Meadows
Dr. Kramer — Raymond Bailey
Regan — Keith Vincent
Mason — Frank Kirby

Maximum Capacity (September 19, 1959). Barton sends two men into the frozen north to test their endurance in extreme levels of cold and isolation in an effort to find the best way to train men for high security jobs in the Arctic.

Cast: David Mallory — James Best
Bill Howard — Robert Conrad
Anne — Paula Raymond
Henderson — Robert Karnes
Jerry Ogden — Mike Masters

Odds Against Survival (September 26, 1959). No story information available.

Cast: Dr. Wayne Robinson — Robert Clarke
Nina Robinson — Bethel Leslie
Dr. Robert Widener — Whit Bissell

Sky Diving (October 3, 1959). To study the effects of gravity on potential astronauts, Barton travels to France to learn the art of "free fall" parachuting from renowned brother-and-sister team, Suzanne and Georges Bolet.

Cast: Suzanne Bolet — Danielle Aubrey
Georges Bolet — John Van Dreelen
Raymond — Alberto Morin

Experiments in Terror (October 10, 1959). No story information available.

Cast: David Mumford — Otto Kruger
Linda Webb — Julie Adams
Delmar Jervis — Logan Field

Invisible Force (October 17, 1959). Three Americans are being held captive in a hostile country. Barton is asked by a Washington official to form a clandestine athletic unit to free the prisoners.

Cast: Liza Dantes — Debra Paget

Jim Harrigan — William Conrad
Alice Barron — Carol Thurston
Jenks — Patrick Waltz

Escape to Nepal (October 24, 1959). In order to test the U2-21 drug, which may increase man's ability to retain oxygen at great heights, Barton puts a group of mountaineers through a rigorous test in the Rockies before sending them to the Himalayas for the ultimate test.

Cast: Dr. Morton Walker — Myron Healey
Dr. Warren Szold — John Maxwell
Marilyn Sidney — Joan Granville

Border to Border (October 31, 1959). Barton enters two antagonistic jet pilots in a Mexican auto race to prove that a team can overcome obstacles which neither can handle alone.

Cast: Tom Larson — Edward Kemmer
Danny Ryan — Don Kennedy

Trial by Fire (November 11, 1959). Barton enters an active volcano to test a new type of fire suit, and he nearly loses his life in the experiment.

Cast: Fred Conway — H.M. Wynant
Dorrie Conway — Joyce Taylor

White Out (November 14, 1959). Barton researches hypothermia in the Antarctic by reducing the body temperatures of two doctors, hoping that his experiment will lead to an understanding of how to freeze astronauts to withstand certain aspects of interplanetary flight.

Cast: Dr. Anna West — Jan Shepard
Dr. William Ryder — Phillip Terry
Lt. Joe Hale — Don Eitner

The Breaking Point (November 28, 1959). A volunteer is confined in a cell for 30 days and subjected to psychological torment in an effort to determine his breaking point.

Cast: Robert Carson — Alfred Ryder
Sam Randolph — John Marley
Lynn Allen — Joyce Meadows
Leon Ulmer — Tony Monaco

Jungle Survival (December 12, 1959). The Human Factor Institute sends Glenn Barton on a dual mission: to test survival techniques in the Amazon basin and to determine the fate of four lost fliers.

Cast: *Jim Connor*   Dean Harens
Anne Sanders   Marcia Henderson
Bill Locke   Mike Masters

I've Killed Seven Men (December 12, 1959). No story information available.

Cast: *Paul Cheever*   Lin McCarthy

Man Without Fear (December 19, 1959). Glenn Barton uses the chemical LSD-25 (which removes fear) on a firefighter, but a raging forest fire proves that fear is a necessary part of courage.

Cast: *Mike Mapes*   John Day
Ed Burke   Frank Gerstle
Helen   Tracey Roberts
Jim Phillips   Nick Nicholson

The Visitors (December 26, 1959). No story information available.

Cast: *Ken*   Bert Remsen
Burro Charlie   Fuzzy Knight
Old Gene   Robert J. Wilke

The Storm (January 1, 1960). Glenn Barton is asked to clear the reputation of a man who died under mysterious circumstances.

Cast: *Roger Blanchard*   Fred Gabourie
Patricia Halakua   Roberta Haynes
Bill Blake   Lee Johnson
Dean Curtiss   Byron Morrow

Killer River (January 9, 1960). Barton rescues a parachuted pilot from a cliff high above the Colorado River.

Cast: *Sawyer*   John Archer
Stanhope   Michael Keith

Rodeo (January 23, 1960). Barton probes the effects of a new rocket belt upon mind and body at a rodeo.

Cast: *Sally Somers*   Ann Robinson
Dr. John Quint   Myron Healey
Big Ed Casey   Neil Grant
Announcer   Chuck Parkerson

The Windowless Room (January 30, 1960). A crack test pilot crashes his aircraft, resulting in a self-induced paralysis that is slowly

destroying his career and his marriage. Using the latest techniques in hypnosis, Barton restores the pilot's confidence. *Writer:* Laszlo Gorog. *Director:* Andrew Marton.

Cast: *Dan Wright*   Jack Ging
Phyllis Wright   Sue Randall
Dr. Kramer   Raymond Bailey
Miss Hopkins   Doris Fesette
Forest Ranger   Michael Keith
Patient   Irwin Ashkenazy

Nightmare Crossing (February 6, 1960). Barton tests candidates for command positions in space.

Cast: *John Napier*   Keith Larsen
Harley   Tony Monaco
Colonel   Mike Keene
Radio Officer   Pat McCaffrey
Winters   Jack Catron

The Lure of Danger (February 13, 1960). Barton seeks the type of individuals who subconsciously want to destroy themselves, trying to learn why some men desire death.

Cast: *Cartina*   Miguel Landa
Grantina   Felipe Turich
Arejevo   Robert Mercy
Dr. Lopez   Edward Colmans

Recovery (February 20, 1960). No story information available.

Cast: *Capt. Norris*   John Archer
Madge Costain   Eloise Hardt
Ensign Fowler   Jack Catron

Buried Alive (February 27, 1960). Barton proves the potential of Yoga to avert tragedy.

Cast: *Buzz Harmon*   Robert Gothie
Dr. Carlson   Robert Bice
Doug   Don Eitner
Donaldson   Dean Harvey
Lynn Allen   Joyce Meadows

Recondo (March 3, 1960). Four escaped convicts hold the Warden's daughter hostage.

Cast: *Warden Tanner*   Jack Harris
Ruth Tanner   Marianne Hill
Charlie Burke   Arvid Nelson
Graham Landry   Jay Douglass
Darcey   Bern Bassey

Flying Lab (March 12, 1960). To prove ignorance and fear cause lack of efficiency, Barton conducts a complex experiment.

Cast: *Winters*   Keith Vincent
      Scott   Jack Hilton
      Ryder   Robert Knapp
      Davis   Page Slattery

Hurricane Mesa (March 19, 1960). Barton conducts a test on an unsuspecting flier to prove that the pilot can be switched successfully to a desk job.

Cast: *Jim Harper*   Jack Ging
      Dr. Carlson   Robert Bice

Astro Female (March 26, 1960). Barton pits four women against four men to prove that women can equal if not surpass males as astronauts.

Cast: *Gina Reed*   Maureen Leeds
      Amy Brown   Adrienne Hayers
      Joan Lee   Joan Granville
      Jean Gillespie   Ethel Jensen

The Extra Sense (April 2, 1960). Barton parachutes from a high precipice to prove that emotional stress promotes telepathy.

Cast: *Col. Bill Blake*   Frank Maxwell
      Sgt. Lowery   Paul Comi

Man in a Capsule (April 9, 1960). Barton conducts a survival test on the surface of the ocean.

Cast: *Max Edwards*   Darryl Hickman
      Steve Paley   Fred Beir
      Radio Operator   Dick Jeffries
      Maxey   Donald Gamble

The Dropper (April 23, 1960). No story information available.

Cast: *Morgan Jones*   Jack O'Brien
      Alan Wells   Arthur Heller
      Dropper   Jerry Summers
      Capt. Whitlow   Tyler McVey
      Radio Operator   Howard McLeod
      Judo Expert   Mike Masters

High Dive (April 30, 1960). No story information available.

Cast: *Sylvia Honig*   Olive Sturgess
      Ed Honig   Charles Alan Bell
      Matt Adams   Michael Keith
      Judge Banner   Vernon Rich
      Bill Andrews   Charles R. Keene

Daredevils (May 7, 1960). Convinced that the secret of survival lies in body chemical reactions, Barton puts the king of stunt car drivers through a dangerous test.

Cast: *Pete Knowland*   Don Kennedy
      Betty Knowland   Christine White
      Dr. Herter   Ted Knight
      Miss Hopkins   Doris Fesette

Shooter McLaine (May 21, 1960). Barton narrowly escapes death when a scientist ignoring his own physical limits and Barton's warnings misreads test instruments.

Cast: *McLaine*   John Milford
      Betty Fuller   Mala Powers
      John Mickelson   Dick Rich
      George Harley   Charles Tannan

Early Warning (May 28, 1960). No story information available.

Cast: *Clifford Beck*   Philip Ober
      Eleanor Beck   Bethel Leslie
      Col. Pierce   Andy Thompson
      Pentagon Chief   Marshall Kent

Breakoff (June 4, 1960). No story information available.

Cast: *Dr. Lindstrom*   Karl Swenson
      Helen Vincent   Miranda Jones

Highway to Danger (June 11, 1960). Barton subjects himself to driving conditions which have killed five truck drivers as he researches highway hypnosis.

Cast: *Kitty*   Karen Scott
      Swede   Hank Patterson
      Tamarin   Barney Biro

Men into Space

Originally titled *Moon Probe* and later simply *Space*, Ziv's *Men into Space* premiered on CBS on Wednesday night, September 30, 1959, nearly two years to the day after the launching of Sputnik I and, more dramatically, only 17 days after yet another monumental feat performed by the Soviet Union, the circling of the moon by the Russian space probe, Lunik II.

There is little doubt that the launching of Sputnik I served as impetus for the production of *Men into Space* and, considering the political climate of the times, just such a program was needed to inspire confidence in America's ability to conquer space. Sputnik had struck a serious blow to the American ego and sense of complacency.

Early in the development of the *Men into Space* series, the cooperation of the Department of Defense was secured on the condition that the Defense Department would be granted script approval. The Department of Defense and the United States Air Force seemed principally concerned with technical accuracy, i.e., the truthful depiction of the theories of space exploration, rather than any editorial control over the series' content. Considering the devastating blow to America's technology meted out by Sputnik's launch, the air force had little choice but to present an image to the American public that was concerned more with the air force's scientific capabilities to supersede the Soviet Union than with any presumed ideological superiority.

Capt. M.C. Spaulding of the USAF's Ballistic Missile Division was named technical advisor of the series. He managed a pool of advisors from various government agencies including the air force's Air Research and Development Command, the School of Aviation Medicine and the Office of the Surgeon General. Location filming would take place at the Space Medicine Center at Randolph Field, Texas; Wright-Patterson Air Force Base in Dayton, Ohio; Cape Canaveral in Florida; Edwards Air Force Base in California; and the navy's testing ground at Point Magu near Santa Barbara, California. The "moon" existed on a sound stage at the Ziv studios off Santa Monica Boulevard in Hollywood.

Brought in to produce the series was veteran producer and art director Lewis J. Rachmil. A graduate of the Yale University School of Fine Arts, Rachmil began his film career in 1930 serving as art director for the Paramount Long Island studios in New York. Moving to Hollywood in 1935, he began a long association with Harry Sherman Productions, serving first as art director and finally as associate producer. Since 1940, he was the associate producer for all of the Hopalong Cassidy features, and in 1945 became head of production for the remaining Hopalong Cassidy features released through United Artists. In 1947, Rachmil

147

became head of production at General Service Studio in Hollywood. He later moved to RKO as a producer of such program features as *Bunco Squad* (1950), *Roadblock* (1951) and director William Cameron Menzies' *The Whip Hand* (1951). In 1952 he joined Columbia Pictures and produced, among many programs, Fritz Lang's *Human Desire* (1954) and William Asher's offbeat science fiction thriller *The 27th Day* (1957).

Considering Rachmil's tenure as a producer of low-budget films and his background in art, he was a logical choice to supervise a series that would rely heavily upon art direction to depict its "other world" locations, but was budgeted at a modest $50,000 per episode. In a shrewd venture, Rachmil secured the talents of preeminent space artist Chesley Bonestell to provide the production design (or, as the credits read, "Space Concepts") of the series. Bonestell had done much the same thing for producer George Pal's features *Destination Moon* (1950), *When Worlds Collide* (1951), *The War of the Worlds* (1953) and *Conquest of Space* (1955). Bonestell also received recognition for his evocative cover illustrations for both *Colliers* and *Life* magazines; among his most important paintings was the 10 x 40 foot mural of the moon's surface painted for the Boston Museum of Science only two years before his work with *Men into Space*.

Praising Bonestell's knowledge of space, a CBS spokesman bragged that Bonestell could "tell you the exact angle of incidence of the sun's rays on Deimos," adding, "When the series enters the realm of conjecture—what the surface of the moon will look like, for instance—its ideas are not based on imagination or fancy."

Bonestell carried with him to his work on *Men into Space* essentially the same "concept" of the moon's appearance which he had used on previous occasions. Bonestell envisioned the moon as a great craggy vastness, filled with sharp, jagged and treacherous obstacles. By the mid–1960s, lunar orbiting satellites would prove that the moon had a much smoother surface, the result of being softened by eons of meteorite bombardment. Bonestell would be forced to admit his mistake.

While Bonestell designed the "look" of

the series, Rachmil buried himself in stacks of publications which dealt seriously with the exploration of space. From this research, and the advice of experts, Rachmil declared that his series would emphasize the "correctness" of technical problems men and women would encounter in space exploration and the colonization of the moon. But Rachmil found himself with a technical problem all his own. A maximum budget of $50,000 per episode didn't allow for spectacular special photographic effects so crucial to a series about space exploration. Although he had at his disposal thousands of feet of government film of rocket and missile testing, only special effects footage could depict man's venture into space. By necessity, Rachmil sought the talents of Jack Rabin, Irving Block and Louis DeWitt, a trio of special effects experts who catered mainly to budget-minded producers. Their plight was compounded by the air force's insistence on accuracy; hence, any cost-cutting gimmicks or even small deviations from the accepted designs of actual space probes and space stations were prohibited. All spacecraft and even the moon colony itself were constructed according to air force specifications. In the long run, Rabin, Block and DeWitt managed to pull it off, offering exceptional photographic effects under serious budgetary restrictions. (All three men received credit in the pilot episode, but only DeWitt received credit in the remaining episodes.)

To simulate floating sequences in the weightless and near-weightless conditions of space, Rachmil turned to Peter Foy, the theatrical rigging specialist who maneuvered Mary Martin through the air in her many performances of the play *Peter Pan*. Rachmil and the technical advisors, however, had Foy change his technique; Peter Pan had been flying, they rightfully argued, but men and women in space are helpless, and so Foy had to alter his equipment (a contraption consisting of rope, airplane cable and piano wires, some of which were half the thickness of pencil lead) so that the astronauts would, as he said, "float awkwardly." After several attempts, Foy discovered that the machinery didn't allow for rapid changes of pace, and so he operated the controls manually, a task made all the more difficult considering the weight of the actors (dressed in 75-pound spacesuits) suspended at a height of 40 feet and flown along a 100-foot soundstage. Compounding his task further was the need to "float" the electronic equipment carried by the astronauts as well as the large, bulky mockups of the space probes themselves, all in a single setting.

Finally, after two years of research and negotiations, a cast and crew were assembled to produce the pilot episode. William Lundigan, whose connection with the Ziv organization went back to 1955 when he appeared as a test pilot in the premiere episode of *Science Fiction Theatre*, was selected to play Col. Edward McCauley, a veteran air force commander chosen to lead America's efforts toward colonizing the moon. Lundigan was supported by Angie Dickinson as his wife, Mary, and Charles Herbert as the couple's son, Peter.

While Rabin, Block and DeWitt handled the photographic effects, Cy Simonson, whose previous work included the *Adventures of Superman* series, handled the stage effects, and Maxwell Smith, who supervised the electronics on *Science Fiction Theatre*, handled the instrumentation and equipment. Edward Cronjager photographed the pilot (he was replaced by William F. Whitley for the duration of the series), and Robert Kinoshita was art director. Joe Wonder, who served as production supervisor on many Ziv programs, returned for yet one more series, organizing the many facets of production.

With the pilot finished and sponsorship secured (American Tobacco Company, namely Lucky Strike cigarettes, and Gulf Coast gasoline), production on the series went into full operation. Directorial assignments were shared among several directors, including William Conrad, Herman Hoffman, Walter Doninger, Alvin Ganzer, Charles Haas, Lee Sholem and Otto Lang. Various writers, mostly freelancers, worked under the supervision of story editor Robert Warnes Leach. Joseph Silver replaced Thomas Scott as film editor. Angie Dickinson was replaced by Joyce Taylor as Mary McCauley; the only other recurring characters were Maj. Norgarth and Gen. Devon, played by Tyler McVey and Russ Conway, respectively, but their appearances were infrequent.

Each episode would begin with several scenes from the episode accompanied by the uncredited announcer whose oracle-like voice, deep and prophetic, offered what amounted to commentary on the theme of the episode. For example, in "Contraband," the theme of human nature is clearly outlined. After explaining that progress in technology will enable man to travel to distant planets, the narrator tempers the "sense of wonder" by remarking that "no matter where he travels, one thing will always be the same: man himself. Human nature will not change in the strange outposts of space. There will always be love and hate, courage and fear, and even greed. This is the story of an expedition to a distant world that was brought to the brink of disaster by one man's greed."

"Moon Probe," the premiere episode, told of an orbital flight of the moon; commander McCauley and his crew found the going much rougher than would the crew of Apollo 8, with an identical real-life mission, just nine years later. The Apollo 8 mission went perfectly; in "Moon Probe," one of the spacecraft's stages fails to separate and McCauley is required to free the trouble-prone second stage. In the process the Colonel is set helplessly adrift in space. Miraculously he is eventually taken back on board when the XMP-13 maneuvers into position for the rescue.

Owing to its government research origins, "Moon Probe" emphasized the technical triumph of putting the first men into space, but Arthur Weiss's script was not devoid of the human element, as much a requirement of the narratives as the technical hardware itself. In providing prospective writers with editorial guidelines, story editor Leach made it clear that what he wanted were "dramas with strong documentary tone which tell of man's attempt to conquer space. *Authenticity plus humanizing elements for the characters involved are of the utmost importance* [emphasis added]." "Moon Probe" centers on the scientific wherewithal necessary to launch three explorers into space and then to rescue one of them when an accident hurls him into space. Director Walter Doniger chose a documentary style: Relying heavily upon closeups, he creates suspense through the intrusive use of cross-cutting, particularly in cross-cutting four elements (McCauley adrift in space; the rescuers giving chase; ground control directing the rescuers; the anxious family and reporters awaiting McCauley's fate.)

The "humanizing element," particularly Mary and Peter waiting for developments, offered insight into the approach taken by *Men into Space*. The first hint of this approach comes after McCauley is hurled into space. The ground commander orders tracking stations in the *free world* to monitor McCauley, but immediately corrects himself: "No, make it worldwide." In the denouement, the Colonel tells McCauley that "missiles can be repaired in flight, now you've proved that beyond any doubt." But the stoic McCauley, holding a model of the missile, replies, "Something else was proved, too, let's not forget it. For one half hour the entire world made one human life more important than anything else."

CBS touted *Men into Space* as "a documentary of the future—solidly rooted in fact." As an example, in 1958 the Soviet astronomer Nikolai Kozyrev noted activity in the crater Alphonsus which he suggested might have been of volcanic origin. Considerable scientific attention was suddenly focused on the Alphonsus crater and possible explanations for the reported activity. This real-life debate soon found itself incorporated into a series script. In "Moon Cloud," broadcast in February 1960, McCauley and two brilliant scientists explore the Alphonsus crater seeking an explanation. The expedition is seriously complicated by the jealous hatred one of the scientists harbors for the other.

McCauley represented one of those quiet, heroic figures which have now gone out of style. As the series developed, he evolved into almost a perfect paradigm of the way America was then pleased to view itself. At a time when the military was held in high esteem, McCauley was proudly exhibited as the best that the military had to offer. His presence was a reassurance to the nation that its welfare was in strong capable hands. Lundigan occasionally found McCauley a little too perfect and rebelled against the image. Rachmil once reported, "Bill's only problem is that he doesn't want to appear infallible. When he asks for a script change, it's because he thinks McCauley

is being too noble. We've made McCauley more human, I think, because Bill has complained: 'I'm no hero, so take me off the hook.'"

Eight months after *Men into Space* left the air, President Kennedy stood before Congress and set forth his agenda for space: "I believe this nation should commit itself to achieving the goal, before the decade is out, of landing a man on the moon and returning him safely to Earth." To former viewers of the *Men into Space* series, much of what would follow in the coming years would seem familiar as life fulfilled art.

Technical Information

FORMAT: Filmed half-hour series projecting a Cold War vision of the colonization of the moon and the early exploration of space. BROADCAST HISTORY: *Network:* CBS. *Original Airdates:* September 30, 1959 to September 7, 1960. *Sponsors:* American Tobacco, National Carbon, Longines-Wittnauer. *Seasons:* 1. *Total Episodes:* 38 black-and-white

Signature

OPENING: The program's signature was a montage beginning with a stylized launching of an Atlas ICBM succeeded by a flight from the earth to a vast ocean of stars. Simultaneously, the narrator acknowledged "the cooperation of the Department of Defense and especially the United States Air Force in the development of the following new dramatic television program." In the network version, a package of Lucky Strike cigarettes appeared as the narrator explained that *Men into Space* was "presented tonight by Lucky Strike." The title itself literally came forward from the far shores of space, accompanied by David Rose's commanding theme which relied heavily upon brass, pounding tympani and full stops for emphasis.

Production Staff

Production: Ziv Television Programs, Inc. *Theme Music:* David Rose. *Producer:* Lewis J. Rachmil.

Associate Producer	Mel Epstein
Story Editor	Robert Warnes Leach
Space Concepts	Chesley Bonestell
Technical Advisor	Capt. M.C. Spaulding
Production Manager	Joe Wonder
Director of Photography	William F. Whitley
Film Editors	Thomas Scott and Joseph Silver
Art Direction	Robert Kinoshita
Set Decorations	Charles Thompson
Assistant Director	Dale Hutchinson
Special Effects	Cy Simonson
Photographic Effects	Louis DeWitt
Instruments and Equipment	Maxwell Smith
Audio Supervisor	Al Lincoln
Sound Editor	Sid Sutherland
Music Editor	Milton Lustig
Wardrobe	Pat Kelly
Makeup	George Gray and John Holden

Regular Cast

Col. Edward McCauley	William Lundigan
Mary McCauley	Angie Dickinson
	Joyce Taylor
Peter McCauley	Charles Herbert
Maj. Gen. Norgarth	Tyler McVey
Gen. Devon	Russ Conway

Episode Guide

Moon Probe (September 30, 1959). As his family watches from the control room, Col. Edward McCauley, commanding the first rocket into outer space, takes a desperate gamble when the second stage of the rocket fails to jettison. *Director:* Walter Doniger. *Writer:* Arthur Weiss.

Cast:

Mary McCauley	Angie Dickinson
Maj. Billy Williams	Paul Burke
Peter McCauley	Charles Herbert
Air Force Liaison Officer	Paul Richards
Joe Hale	H.M. Wynant
Ground Controller	John Vivyan
Communications Officer	
	Edward Kemmer
Technical Officer	William Phipps
Reporter	Robert Cornthwaite
Reporter	Stacy Harris

Moon Landing (October 7, 1959). After McCauley's first effort at a Moon landing fails, and his second attempt leaves one crew member seriously injured during blastoff, Senator Jim Sloane questions the necessity of the mission and its tremendous cost. *Director:* Walter Doniger. *Writer:* James Clavell.

Cast:

Maj. Patrick Donon	Joe Maross
Maj. Mason Trett	Don Oreck
Senator Jim Sloane	Karl Swenson
also Paul Lambert, Dean Harens, Ernestine Barrier, Jack Mann, Edward Paul and Andrew Glick	

Building a Space Station (October 21, 1959). While assembling the prefabricated units of a space station, the estranged son of an air force general is trapped when the sleeve of his spacesuit is caught between sections. McCauley races against time to rescue the man. *Director:* Otto Lang. *Writer:* Meyer Dolinsky.

Cast:

Lt. Smith	Don Dubbins
Capt. Forsythe	Christopher Dark
Paula Smith	Nancy Hadley
Gen. Hicks	Bartlett Robinson
Capt. Michaels	Don Kennedy
Maj. Hall	Jack Mann
also Michael Galloway and Walter Stocker	

Water Tank Rescue (October 28, 1959). When one of his crew members suffers a heart attack on the moon, McCauley faces a new kind of dilemma: if the victim fails to get medical attention he will die, but the tremendous forces of gravity built up inside a rocket ship during blastoff will also kill him. Remembering the "iron maiden" experiment at Wright Field, McCauley improvises a water gravity shield out of cargo tanks to protect the stricken man from the tremendous pressures. *Director:* Otto Lang. *Writer:* Ib Melchior.

Cast:

Lt. Rick Gordon	Jon Shepodd
Carol Gordon	Joan Taylor
Maj. Warnecke	Paul Langton
Capt. Hal Roberts	Gar Moore
also Stephen Talbot, Richard Travis, Peter Walker and Barry Brooks	

Lost Missile (November 4, 1959). An unmanned, nuclear-powered rocket goes out of control around the moon. McCauley takes off to intercept the rocket and deactivate its atomic engines before the rocket crashes into the moon and renders it radioactive for thousands of years. *Director:* Walter Doniger. *Writer:* Michael Plant.

Cast: Dr. William Thyssen   Harry Townes
    also Marcia Henderson, Ken Lynch, Gavin MacLeod and Jeremy Slate

Moonquake (November 11, 1959). A tremendous "moonquake" opens great fissures, separating McCauley from an expedition testing seismographic activity on the moon. McCauley must improvise a bridge in order to rescue the stranded scientists. *Director:* Lee Sholem. *Writer:* William Templeton.

Cast: *Capt. Tom Farrow*   Arthur Franz
    Dr. Peter Riber   Denver Pyle
    also Bek Nelson, Ross Elliott, Britt Lomond, Robert Karnes, Ann Doran, Mike Keene, Leonard Graves and Sumner Williams

Space Trap (November 18, 1959). A manned lunar spaceship, hurtling toward Earth at 24,000 mph, is in danger of incinerating in Earth's atmosphere if its speed is not reduced. When the crew does not answer and the ship fails to respond to ground control, McCauley and crew blast off to intercept the ship. *Director:* Charles Haas. *Writers:* Marianne Mesner and Francis Rosenwald.

Cast: *Dr. Charles Cooper*   Peter Hansen
    Capt. Dan Freer   Robert Gist
    Gen. Devon   Russ Conway
    Lt. Pat Warren   Dallas Mitchell
    Lt. Neil Templeton   Ronald Foster
    also Michael Chapin and Joe Haworth

Asteroid (November 25, 1959). Astrophysicist Dr. Stacy Croydon and McCauley determine that an asteroid is impractical for use as a space station. As McCauley sets charges to destroy the asteroid, Croydon raises his sun visor to examine a rock sample and is blinded. McCauley must either deactivate the demolition charge or find the missing Croydon before detonation. *Director:* Lee Sholem. *Writer:* Ted Sherdeman.

Cast: *Dr. Stacy Croydon*   Bill Williams
    Dr. Waring   Herbert Rudley
    Lynn Croydon   Joyce Meadows

Edge of Eternity (December 2, 1959). After a geologic explosion damages a ship's reserve oxygen tanks, McCauley and two crewmen blast off for the nearest space station to replenish the supply. With the oxygen running low, the three remaining members of the expedition draw lots for the oxygen, but the winner refuses to take the advantage. *Director:* Nathan Juran. *Writer:* Kalman Phillips.

Burnout (December 9, 1959). A board of inquiry determines that two astronauts panicked during a reentry experiment, causing their craft to incinerate upon entry into Earth's atmosphere. McCauley is ordered to conduct a second experiment, and his crew members encounter the same symptoms of trouble the original astronauts encountered. *Director:* Alvin Ganzer. *Writer:* Donald Duncan.

Cast: *Lt. Gen. Malcolm Terry*   John Sutton
    Capt. Bob Stark   Lance Fuller
    Maj. Gibbie Gibson   Robert Clarke
    Molly Gibson   Donna Martell
    also Barbara Bestar, Ken Drake and Tom McNamara

First Woman on the Moon (December 16, 1959). Renza Hale, wife of a scientist, is chosen for the same space mission as her husband. She begins to rebel at the restrictions placed upon her, and one day she takes a walk in space and is very surprised that anyone should fear for her safety. McCauley, sensing the growing problem, orders her to accompany her husband on his mapping missions.

Cast: *Renza Hale*   Nancy Gates
    Maj. Hale   H.M. Wynant
    Major Markey   Harry Jackson

Christmas on the Moon (December 23, 1959). When a comet is scheduled to cross the earth's orbit on Christmas Day, McCauley heads a mission to the moon to study the comet. Skeptical scientist Dr. Jim Nichols comes to terms with his own lack of faith when his friend and mentor, Dr. Farrar, suffers a life-threatening attack of appendicitis and a meteor shower prevents help from reaching the lunar outpost. McCauley risks his life to get aid while Dr. Nichols prays for the first time in his life. Just when all seems lost, the confirmation of a long-held scientific theory comes almost as a miracle as meteoric ice is used to sustain the stricken Farrar until help arrives. As the comet passes Earth as a "Christmas Star," Nichols experiences the true meaning of Christmas. *Director:* Richard Carlson. *Teleplay:* David Duncan. *Story:* Lawrence Louis Goldman.

Cast: *Jim Nichols*   Keith Larsen
Oliver Farrar   Whit Bissell
also Patricia Manning, Paul Langton, Del Russel and Sean Bartlett

Quarantine (December 30, 1959). A virus under study by a biologist forms a mutation, felling him and causing McCauley to quarantine the lunar base, cutting off all contact with Earth. As the dying biologist seeks a cure for the infection, McCauley determines that there may be a connection between the viral mutation and a second scientist's experiments in high frequency magnetics. *Director:* Walter Doniger. *Writer:* Stuart James Byrne

Cast: *Dr. Randolph*   Warren Stevens
Dr. Horton   Simon Oakland
Dr. Hamilton   John Milford
Lt. Murphy   Guy Stockwell

Tankers in Space (January 6, 1960). During the first "in-space" refueling attempt, a rocket collides with a rocket tanker, rupturing fuel tanks and releasing great quantities of highly explosive vapor. As McCauley and crew members struggle to disengage their rocket from the tanker, they learn that the tanker has become a tremendous bomb. *Director:* Alvin Ganzer. *Writer:* Arthur Weiss.

Cast: *Maj. Nick Alborg*   James Drury
Col. Stoner   Philip Terry
Lt. Col. Bill Alborg Murray Hamilton
also Robert Brubaker, Mary Newton, Helen Mowery, Jenifer Lea and Jack Emrek

Sea of Stars (January 13, 1960). A runaway satellite is on a collision course with a space station. McCauley and a novice crew succeed in destroying the satellite, but the blast damages their ship, hurling them towards the sun. *Director:* Lee Sholem. *Teleplay:* Marianne Mosner, Francis Rosenwald and Kalman

Phillips. *Story:* Marianne Mosner and Francis Rosenwald.

Cast: *Lt. Art Frey*   Fred Beir
Lt. Jerry Rutledge   Jack Ging

A Handful of Hours (January 20, 1960). A crash landing on the moon leaves McCauley and his four-man crew 50 miles away from their base. As they begin their trek across the lunar landscape, the cap on the spare oxygen tank is found frozen solid, meaning that there will not be enough oxygen for the journey. *Director:* Alvin Ganzer. *Writer:* Michael Plant.

Cast: *Dr. Orrin*   William Schallert
Dr. Prescott   Mark Dana
Lt. Bob Kelly   Peter Baldwin

Earthbound (January 27, 1960). To impress a girl, a young technician stows away on a rocket, rearranging much of the electronic guidance equipment and causing the rocket to plummet through space. *Director:* Nathan Juran. *Teleplay:* Robert Hecker and David Duncan. *Story:* Robert Hecker.

Cast: *Russell Smith*   Robert Reed
Julie Wills   Anne Benton
Glen Stillwell   Byron Morrow
Capt. Williams   John Garrett
Lt. Eden   Don Edmonds

Caves of the Moon (February 3, 1960). Dr. Rowland Kennedy, despondent over the death of his wife and son, walks away from a lunar expedition seeking signs of water, causing McCauley to play a desperate game of hide-and-seek in the caves of the moon. *Director:* Lee Sholem. *Writer:* Meyer Dolinsky.

Cast: *Dr. Rowland Kennedy* John Howard
Maj. John Arnold   Paul Comi
Capt. Doug Bowers   Donald May
Mrs. Bennett   Lillian Hamilton

Dateline: Moon (February 10, 1960). An irresponsible television reporter, anxious for the "big story," fakes "scientific proof" of life found on the moon and then, against McCauley's orders, releases the story during a live broadcast from the moon. *Director:* Alan Crosland, Jr. *Teleplay:* Robert Warnes Leach. *Story:* Mike Adams.

Cast: *Jimmy Manx*   Harry Lauter

Joyce Lynn	Lisa Gaye
Paul Carlson	Ray Montgomery

Moon Cloud (February 17, 1960). While Dr. Holcomb studies the gases of Alphonsus Crater, a rim cave-in plunges him into the crater. He refuses to be rescued until the mission's objectives are accomplished. *Director:* Otto Lang. *Teleplay:* Michael Plant. *Story:* Sidney Kalcheim.
Cast:
Perry Holcomb	Robert Vaughn
Mandy Holcomb	Allison Hayes
Harold Carter	Douglas Dick

Contraband (March 2, 1960). Greed leads to criminal activity on the moon when a government ban on the return of Luna Jade by space explorers causes the Earth value of the new gem to soar. McCauley, serving as the first lunar police officer, discovers that a scientist has become not only a trafficker in the gem but a conspirator in league with a "foreign power" as well. *Director:* Alvin Ganzer. *Teleplay:* David Duncan. *Story:* Stuart James Byrne.
Cast:
Dr. Narry	James Coburn
Dr. Rice	Robert Osterloh
Dr. Bromfield	Robert Christopher
Dr. Orr	Don Ross
	also John Close
	and Pat McCaffrie

Dark of the Sun (March 9,1960). Seeking the two best qualified astronomers for a moon mission to study a solar eclipse, officials turn to "Old Solomon," a supercomputer which selects Dr. Muriel Gallagher as mission commander but remains deadlocked between two men for second in command. The men, fearing they will be left behind, conspire to romance Muriel, each hoping to induce her into marriage and thereby guarantee his position in the expedition. Muriel, in order to discourage the two, feigns a romance with Maj. Ellis, but Ellis actually loves her. *Director:* Alvin Ganzer. *Writer:* David Duncan.
Cast:
Muriel Gallagher	Carol Ohmart
Dr. Caleb Fiske	Dennis McCarthy
Dr. Torrance Alexander	Manning Ross
Maj. Paul Ellis	William Lechner
	also John McNamara
	and Robert Darin

Verdict in Orbit (March 16, 1960). Moments after launch, McCauley receives word that his son was injured in a hit-and-run accident; later, he learns that his scientist passenger was responsible for the accident. Panicked, the scientist exits the ship to be alone with his guilt. McCauley, still struggling with his own emotions, goes after the one person he has every reason to despise. *Director:* Nathan Juran. *Teleplay:* Michael Plant. *Story:* Sidney Kalchein.
Cast:
Dr. Arnold Rawdin	Peter Adams
Lt. Col. Vern Driscoll	Tod Andrews

Is There Another Civilization? (March 23, 1960). After a strange metal is found embedded in the hull of the returning M-13 spacecraft, McCauley sets out to find a larger piece for testing. But as McCauley searches, the three men who first touched the metal all die violent deaths, causing a reporter to claim that the metal was cursed. Later, tests prove that the pieces of metal came from a spaceship which has been circling the earth for 500 years. *Director:* Nathan Juran. *Teleplay:* William Templeton and Robert Warnes Leach. *Story:* Jerome Bixby.
Cast:
Maj. Bowers	John Bryant
Capt. Swanson	Paul Carr
Carey Stoddart	Joe Flynn
	also John Compton, Mike Rayhill,
	David Bedell and Howard Vann

Shadows of the Moon (March 30, 1960). Strange occurrences including disappearing footprints, falling rocks, mysterious lights and the sighting of a "monstrous creature" plague a geophysical expedition in an unexplored region of the moon. *Director:* Alvin Ganzer. *Writer:* David Duncan.
Cast:
Dr. Bernard Bush	Gerald Mohr
Maj. Boythe	Harry Carey, Jr.
Dr. George Coldwell	Mort Mills

Flash in the Sky (April 6, 1960). Dr. Durlock's unmanned Venus–bound test rocket goes out of control, and Durlock seeks McCauley's help in intercepting the craft and recovering its instruments with their valuable information. But once on board, Durlock discovers that the rocket is heavily charged by magnetic forces which pin him against the ship. McCauley's efforts at rescuing Durlock prove futile until an "act of God" cancels the magnetic force. *Director:* Walter Doniger. *Writer:* David Duncan.

Cast: *Dr. Guthrie Durlock*   John Lupton
Lorrie Sigmund   Joan Marshall
also William Hudson, Mark Houston and Robert O'Connor

Lunar Secret (April 13, 1960). McCauley uses the wreckage of an early moon expedition to save the life of an air force photographer whose oxygen equipment has been damaged by a rock slide. *Director:* Franklin Adreon. *Writer:* Michael Plant.

Cast: *Capt. Kyle Rennish*   John Hudson
Jenny   Mimi Gibson
Dr. Alice Roe   Sally Bliss
also Kort Falkenberg and Robert Courtleigh

Voice of Infinity (April 20, 1960). McCauley believes that men and women possess untapped, indefinable reserves of physical and mental strength which will carry them through any crisis, but an electronics expert who has devised a device for measuring stability under stress disagrees. Their divergent opinions are put to the test when an accident causes the space station to spin on its axis at ever-increasing speed. *Director:* Alan Crosland, Jr. *Writer:* Ib Melchior.

Cast: *Maj. Steven Hawkes*   Myron Healey
Dr. Thomas Ward   Charles Cooper
Corp. Fred Jones   Ralph Taeger
also Charles Stewart, Rand Brooks and Barnaby Hale

From Another World (April 27, 1960). While McCauley studies the geophysical makeup of an asteroid, an accident damages his oxygen supply. He blacks out, but not before he sees a strange reptile fossil embedded in the strange rock formations on the asteroid. Gen. Devon and Dr. Luraski believe McCauley's sighting is the result of flight fatigue and order him grounded. A second mission to the asteroid, however, tells an even greater secret about outer space. *Director:* Herman Hoffman. *Writer:* Beirne Lay, Jr.

Cast: *Dr. Luraski*   Edward C. Platt
Gen. Brereton   Alan Dexter
also Rand Harper

Emergency Mission (May 4, 1960). A supply ship with the son of McCauley's friend Col. Benson aboard blasts out of control and McCauley, flying an untested "Super Spaceship," attempts a rescue. McCauley's craft loses radar control and he is unable to track the runaway ship. Just as hope is thought lost, however, the boy decides to listen to some "rock 'n' roll music" which establishes radio contact with McCauley's ship. *Director:* Alvin Ganzer. *Writer:* Kalman Phillips.

Cast: *Col. Jim Benson*   Donald Woods
Anne Benson   Anne Neyland
Maj. Hodges   John Baer
also William Leslie, Wayne Mallory and Edson Stroll

Beyond the Stars (May 11, 1960). McCauley and two companions are assigned to map the dark side of the moon with a radio telescope, and to while away the long hours Maj. Charlie Randolph records songs. A freak accident kills Randolph, leaving Randolph's close friend, Lt. Leonard, in danger of a breakdown. Later, McCauley and Leonard pick up sounds of weird music emanating from a star 2,000 light years away. To save Leonard's sanity and to honor a departed friend, McCauley beams back Randolph's songs, trusting that the music will be heard by stellar musicians 2,000 light years away. *Director:* Jack Herzberg. *Writer:* David Duncan.

Cast: *Maj. Charles Randolph*   Gene Nelson
Lt. John Leonard   James Best
Donna Talbot   Sally Fraser

Mission to Mars (May 25, 1960). Both the Americans and the Russians blast off from their respective moon bases toward Mars, but McCauley learns that 20 minutes after their launch, the Russians experienced an accident which hurled their ejected rescue capsule toward the far reaches of space. McCauley decides to scrap the mission and rescue the cosmonauts. *Director:* William Conrad. *Writer:* Lewis Jay.

Cast: *Col. Tolchek*   John Van Dreelan

Capt. Jim Nicholls	Jeremy Slate
Maj. Ingram	Jack Hogan
Maj. Ralph Devers	Don Eitner
also Ted Roter and Wil Huffman	

Moon Trap (June 1, 1960). Maj. Tom Jackson's first trip to the moon goes awry when his spacecraft develops trouble and crashes 400 miles from the American lunar base. With an insufficient oxygen supply, Jackson orders his three-man crew into a cave where they seal themselves in and attempt to survive on the liquid oxygen stored in the cave. *Director:* Otto Lang. *Writer:* Lewis Jay.

Cast:	*Maj. Tom Jackson*	Dan Barton
	Dr. Parker	Richard Emory
	Capt. Dick Jackson	Don Burnett
	Harriet	Robin Lory

Flareup (August 17, 1960). The incompetence of a Russian space commander causes a rocket crash that kills the entire crew. To cover his tracks, the commander charges McCauley's crew with sabotage. McCauley must meet treachery with treachery in order to avert World War III on Earth. *Director:* Herman Hoffman. *Teleplay:* Donald Duncan. *Story:* Sidney Kalcheim.

Cast:	*Maj. Kralenko*	Werner Klemperer
	Russian General	Edgar Barrier
	Capt. Webb	Skip Ward
	Col. Alexandrov	Eric Feldary
	Capt. Rumbough	Preston Hanson
	Maj. Gen. Mallon	Larry Thor
	Russian Captain	Jay Warren
	also Lee Raymond	

Into the Sun (August 24, 1960). Unable to forget the part he played in a serious spaceflight accident, Bob King leaves the air force. But after an atomic engine fails on a ship carrying McCauley toward the sun, officials turn to King to rescue McCauley. *Director:* Jack Herzberg. *Teleplay:* Lewis Jay. *Story:* Fred Freiberger.

Cast:	*Bob King*	Paul Picerni
	Maj. Tex Nolan	Harp McGuire
	Gen. Adams	Nelson Leigh
	also Mack Williams	

The Sun Never Sets (August 31, 1960). While in England advising the British space program, McCauley objects to the design of a second-stage rocket engine. When the British launch the spacecraft anyway, the second stage malfunctions, hurling the craft into a tumbling orbit around the earth. With the aid of a novice British astronaut, McCauley pursues the crippled ship and succeeds in rescuing the crew. *Director:* Alvin Ganzer. *Writer:* Lewis Jay.

Cast:	*Vice Marshal Terry*	John Sutton
	Neil Bedford Jones	David Frankham
	Capt. Tom Hetherford	Robin Hughes
	Lady Alice	Mavis Neal
	also Roy Dean and Sydney Smith	

Mystery Satellite (September 7, 1960). On a trip to the moon, McCauley and his crew sight a strange object and give chase, but the object eludes them. Later, another ship encounters the same object near the earth; in its zeal to capture the object, however, the crew fails to heed instrument warnings and the ship burns up in the earth's atmosphere. McCauley and his crew finally intercept the craft and discover that it has been flying in space for eons. *Director:* William Conrad. *Writer:* Lewis Jay.

Cast:	*Maj. Tim O'Leary*	Brett King
	Col. Frank Bartlett	Charles Maxwell
	Capt. Don Miller	Edward Mallory
	Maj. Vic Enright	Mike Steele
	Maj. Gen. Albright	Harry Ellerbe
	Sgt. Tucker	Mel Marshall
	Maj. Bob Williams	George Diestel

Flight to the Red Planet (1960). The first flight to Mars is cut short after McCauley discovers a cracked fuel tank fitting on Phobos, one of Mars' two moons. To complicate matters, a civilian scientist wanders off in search of rock samples, forcing McCauley to waste valuable time searching for him. This final episode of *Men into Space* was not broadcast by CBS but was included in the syndication package. *Director:* David Friedkin. *Writer:* Lewis Jay.

Cast:	*Maj. Devery*	Marshall Thompson
	also Michael Pate, Tom Middleton, Harry Ellerbe and John Zaremba	

Out There

Out There was an innovative adult science fiction series conceived by CBS as that network's antidote to ABC's adult science fiction offering *Tales of Tomorrow*, unveiled only a couple of months earlier.

CBS hurried *Out There* onto the fall 1951 schedule as a "sustainer," a program without a sponsor but presented by the network in the hope of eventually attracting a commercial backer. Sustaining series were once common occurrences on radio, and radio continued to exert a powerful influence on early television at the same time that TV was undercutting its rival at every turn.

Presented live, as most series were at the inception of television, *Out There* also wove filmed segments into its broadcasts, an unusual approach for the time. Reviewer Jack Gould, writing in *The New York Times* (November 4, 1951), predicted that *Out There* might prove to be one of the best of the many science fiction entries on television, which only underscores the fallibility of critics; after 12 broadcasts, the series was pulled from the air after failing to attract a sponsor.

CBS, however, briefly lavished time, money, talent and considerable energy on the series in an effort to turn it into a paying proposition. They reportedly spent some $10,000 a week on the series, a not inconsiderable sum for its day, much of it going into the production of special effects designed to give the adult themes a certain credence and credibility. Nor was CBS parsimonious when it came to paying for scripts. *Out There*'s story budget was $650 per episode, which compared favorably with such prestigious (and commercially sponsored) series as *Armstrong Circle Theatre* (NBC) and *Danger* (CBS) which were each slated at $750 for story budgets.

CBS story editor Arthur Heinemann sought out previously published science fiction stories which would readily adapt to the demands of live television. Such stories as Robert Heinlein's "Green Hills of Earth," Ray Bradbury's "The Man" and Theodore Sturgeon's "Mewhu's Jet" would be tapped for eventual adaptation.

For the premiere broadcast, producer John Haggott and director Byron Paul presented "The Outer Limit," a story by Graham Doar, culled from the December 24, 1949, pages of the *Saturday Evening Post*. The play focused upon the efforts of an extraterrestrial being, Commander Xegion (Wesley Addy), to convince a captured American jet pilot that the earth's infatuation with atomic weapons was viewed with alarm by other worlds, and that if Earth failed to curb its experimentation with atomic weaponry the planet would soon be destroyed.

It was probably *Out There*'s adult approach to science fiction that doomed the series to an early extinction. Television science fiction in the early fifties was virtually the exclusive province of the juvenile set, with the exception of *Tales of Tomorrow*. *Out There* simply premiered at the wrong end of the decade to achieve success.

Arthur Heinemann advised writers interested in working on the series, "In general this program deals with the more human aspects of science fiction, centering around people as they are affected by phenomena of the world of the future, interplanetary communications and beings from other worlds." Producer John Haggott explained to *Newsweek* (January 7, 1951), "Although we whang through space, we're more interested in mechanization's probable effect on human beings." The humanization concept of science fiction which *Out There* stressed would eventually find acceptance through such later series as *Science Fiction Theatre*, *Men into Space* and *The Man and the Challenge*.

Technical Information

FORMAT: Live half-hour anthology series, interspersed with filmed sequences, dramatizing the work of popular science fiction authors.
BROADCAST HISTORY: *Network:* CBS. *Original Airdates:* October 28, 1951 to January 13, 1952. *Total Episodes:* 12 black-and-white. *Seasons:* 1. *Sponsor:* Sustaining.

Production Staff

Executive Producer: Donald Davis. *Producer:* John Haggott. *Director:* Byron Paul.

Episode Guide

Outer Limit (October 28, 1951). Adapted from a story by Graham Doar.
Cast: *Commander Xegion*   Wesley Addy

Ordeal in Space (November 4, 1951). Adapted from a story by Robert Heinlein.
Cast: John Ericson
                             Robert Paige

Rod Steiger
Edward Maroney
Joe Mantell
Howard Weirum
William A. Lee

The Sense of Wonder (November 11, 1951). Adapted from a story by Milton Lesser.
Cast: Paul Anderson
                             Nancy Franklin
                             Joseph Sweeney
                             Russell Collins
                             Noel Leslie
                             Casey Allen
                             Wright King

Misfit (November 18, 1951). Adapted from a story by Robert Heinlein.
Cast: Wendell Phillips
                             Gene Saks
                             Thomas Cole
                             Eddie Hyans
                             Jerry Paris
                             Arthur Batanides
                             Ray Danton
                             John Sylvester

Susceptibility (November 25, 1951). Adapted from a story by John D. MacDonald.
Cast: Leslie Nielsen
                             Bethel Leslie
                             Fred Stewart
                             Susan Steele
                             Joe Silver
                             Jack Weston

The Green Hills of Earth (December 2, 1951). Adapted from a story by Robert Heinlein.
Cast: Mary Sinclair
                             John Raitt
                             Logan Field
                             David McKay
                             Eddie Hyans
                             Harry M. Cooke
                             Herbert Nelson
                             Jay Barney

Mewhu's Jet (December 9, 1951). Adapted from a short story by Theodore Sturgeon.
Cast: Janie Alexander

Richard McMurray
Mort Marshall
Eileen Heckart
John Boruff
Dennis Alexander

Seven Temporary Moons (December 16, 1951)
Cast: Ann Gillis
G. Albert Smith
Robert Pastene
Robert P. Lieb

The Man (December 23, 1951). Adapted from
a story by Ray Bradbury.
Cast: Henry Worth
Philip Bourneuf
Peter Hobbs
Stewart Bradley
John McGovern
Logan Field
Jennifer Bunker
Florence Anglin

The Bus to Nowhere (December 30, 1951)
Cast: Whit Bissell

Kim Stanley
Bruce Hall
Leonard Barry
Arthur Batanides
Eddie Bruce
Nancy Franklin
Julian Noa
Allan Frank
Bruce Druy

Guest in the House (January 6, 1952)
Cast: Butch Cavel
Perry Wilson
Joy Hilton
Robert Webber
Dan Morgan

The Castaway (January 13, 1952)
Cast: Ernest Graves
Robert F. Simon
Herbert Berghof
Fred Scollay
George Pleasant
Jack Carron
Casey Allen
Grant Gordon

Rocky Jones, Space Ranger

Rocky Jones, Space Ranger was yet another imitator of *Captain Video and His Video Rangers; Space Patrol; Tom Corbett, Space Cadet; and Rod Brown of the Rocket Rangers;* among myriad other space operas vying for time on television stations. Indeed, the series' likeness to the other series is made obvious by the title alone. But the essential difference between *Rocky Jones* and the others is that *Rocky Jones* was produced on motion picture film rather than broadcast live; *Rocky Jones* holds the distinction of being the first space opera television series to be produced on film. (*Adventures of Superman* was the first science fiction series on film.)

Such a distinction may seem trivial, but the use of film allowed for tighter and more controlled formal qualities than live drama would allow. Therefore, *Rocky Jones* has the look and feel of a motion picture. Technically, images are clear with good contrast and excellent gradations of gray due to excellent camerawork by veteran Hollywood cinematographers Walter Strenge, Guy Roe, and Ernest Miller. These qualities are especially striking when viewing 16mm prints of the series, and would be even more pronounced if one had access to an original 35mm print.

Beyond the mere technical quality of the series, film production allowed for larger and more varied set designs and, perhaps most importantly, for location shooting. With regard to the former, art director McClure Capps designed stylish futuristic sets filled with gadgetry designed by Loren Sackett that, like those found in the other series, looked impressive but had no basis in science. Foremost among the fanciful instruments was the omnipresent vizeograph, which, in the context of science fiction television, seemed to be an advanced design of Captain Midnight's own visaphone. But the vizeograph did more than just show an image and record a sound; it was a two-way television system that could see and hear just about anything. More important, it could destroy the observed subject at the push of a button on its console. The device is itself declared a dangerous instrument when Secretary Drake tells Vena, in "Beyond the Curtain of Space," that the vizeograph under his command had been watching her every move and, had she become a threat to security, he could have destroyed her with it. In the same episode, Rocky uses the vizeograph to apparently destroy a traitorous space ranger.

Location shooting was restricted pretty much to that 1950s icon Griffith Park Observatory and to a high voltage power station that served as the rocket launch pads. The observatory stood in for Prof. Newton's laboratory, but the surrounding porticos frequently served as platforms to buildings on other planets. The entrance to the observatory served as the entrance to Space Ranger headquarters. The power station was an impressive set; its serpentine metal structure, along with its huge transformers and insulators along with was a readymade edifice for Capps' futuristic set design when coupled with matte paintings and miniatures.

The use of film also allowed for greater flexibility in sound design through postproduction capabilities. More importantly, the use of film allowed for the creation of intricate photographic effects designed by veteran Jack R. Glass, whose work in the second season of *Adventures of Superman* is highly creative and effective.* In particular, the take-offs and landings of Rocky's ship, the XV-2, or Orbit Jet (and in later episodes the XV-3, or Silver Moon), combined miniatures with live action footage shot at the power station. When this sequence is cut with closer angles of live action also filmed at the power station, the effect is one of a seamless futuristic setting. In another impressive sequence, Rocky employs a derelict flying saucer to escape a prehistoric planet in "Blast-Off"; the cleverly effected spinning disk rivals the higher-end saucers in films like Robert Wise's *The Day the Earth Stood Still* (1951). The photographic effects (typical of low-budget films of the era) are numerous, effective and wholly relevant to the narratives. The photographic effects never draw attention to themselves, but remain unobtrusive, visually complementing the story. The photographic effects give *Rocky Jones, Space Ranger* the look of a Hollywood film.

Perhaps sending the series into theaters was at least part of the intention of Roland Reed Productions since, with three exceptions, three chapters comprise each *titled* episode of *Rocky Jones, Space Ranger*. For example, "Beyond the Curtain of Space" is parceled over three weeks with each title designated by Chapter One, Chapter Two, and Chapter Three. Rather than functioning as cliffhangers, the individual episodes serve as book chapters with one incident giving way to another until a tightly structured denouement brings everything to a close in the final chapter. Such a format allowed for the episodes to be strung together into feature-length films. One feature in particular, *Manhunt in Space*, has the feel of a theatrical movie if only for its stylized main titles at the beginning and its seamless editing among the three chapters.

But the reason for the *Rocky Jones* features remains elusive since we could find no evidence of any theatrical releases (nor any evidence of television runs). Apparently other sources also find this puzzling since everyone omits playdates. Alan Morton, in *The Complete Directory to Science Fiction, Fantasy and Horror Television Series*, writes that *some* of the episodes were made into features for both theatrical and television release, but Morton cites no dates for any releases. Allan Asherman, in an insightful summary of the making of *Rocky Jones, Space Ranger* in the March and May 1990 issues of *Filmfax* magazine, notes that the series' original distributor, Official Films Inc., edited the series into 12 features with each running 78 minutes for television release in 1956. But he gives no specific dates; and, even though our research was far from exhaustive, we found no 1956 dates for the features.

Whether the features made it to America's screens remains unclear, but certainly Reed had a precedent to go by. Monogram Pictures—and its successor Allied Artists—strung together two episodes of television's *Wild Bill Hickok* to form a series of theatrical features. Lippert Pictures followed suit by editing episodes of *Ramar of the Jungle* into features and releasing them under such titles as *The White Goddess* (1953) and *Eyes of the Jungle* (1953). Twentieth Century–Fox would do the same for *Adventures of Superman* in 1954. But these features are merely separate episodes sewn together; some of the *Rocky*

Only Glass receives screen credit, but Allan Asherman, in the March 1990 issue of Filmfax, *adds the following to the effects crew: camera operators Dave Smith and Art Semels; camera assistants Herb Bond, Charles Bohny, Gorman Wiman and Hugh Wade; and camera loader George Le Picard. Asherman writes, "Working with other artists, whose names have yet to come to light, they executed the miniature buildings, artwork for starfields, composites for the establishing shots of the Space Rangers' headquarters and rocketport, and miniature spacecraft, and assembled all the effects scenes."*

Jones features, on the other hand, blend the episodes quite well, maintaining a coherent and seamless narrative. If these features failed to make it to theaters it was a loss for science fiction movie audiences.

Like the other space operas, *Rocky Jones* extolled the moral values of a political system very much like that of the United States of America. In this case, Rocky Jones (Richard Crane) was a Space Ranger with the United Worlds of the Solar System, and his job was to police the solar system and make it safe from enemies. Rocky's superior was Drake (Charles Meredith), the Secretary General of the United Worlds and secretary of Space Affairs for the planet Earth, who functioned more like a diplomat than a military leader. Drake was always concerned with peace; apparently his goal was to unite all the planets in the solar system into one democratic ideal that, obviously, resembled America. He states in "Crash of Moons" that "each world does its share for the benefit of all," which is an obvious reference to our own "one nation … indivisible" motto.

Rocky's domain remained confined to Earth's solar system. While other series reached far and away into the universe, Rocky's limit was apparently Pluto (at least in 1954). The inhabited planets and moons he frequently visited, such as Cassa 7 and Ankapor, were explained as newly discovered worlds within our own solar system. The worlds of Negato and Posito were described as "gypsy moons" that wandered about the solar system without orbits of their own.

Rocky's primary foe was a femme fatale named Cleolanta, played by Patsy Parsons, of whom nothing is known. According to the program, Cleolanta was a "Suzerain" of Ophicius, i.e., presumably, the leader, and she commanded a guard whose uniforms looked suspiciously like those of Soviet troops. Her demeanor is well documented, being described by Secretary Drake in "Crash of Moons" as an "arrogant woman" who "won't allow her people any information about life on other moons or planets." (Rocky adds, "Even the possession of an astrophone set is punishable by death.") In the introductory episode "Beyond the Curtain of Space," her treachery is revealed only by her excessive facade of innocence. She tells Rocky that he and his friends Prof. Newton and young Bobby are "free to come and go … [and] see our country" because "we have nothing to hide." Later, she explains that "letting the rest of the universe know the truth about Ophicius is difficult [because] people who don't understand us go back with lurid tales, but those who do elect to remain and share our life with us" are happy and content. Unknown to Rocky and his fellow rangers, Cleolanta possesses a mighty tool for helping those people "elect" to stay; the vicious Darganto, her lieutenant, tells Newton that "you've been granted an extraordinary privilege: Bobby has been near you, and allowed weekly visits, and proudly I say my own son does not know my face, as Bobby will not long remember yours" before using a brainwashing device (which resembles a globe mounted on the wall) on Newton.

Cleolanta's fascism notwithstanding, the series' primary depiction of evil was treason. Next to Cleolanta, Rocky's nemesis is a "fallen ranger" named Griff (Leonard Penn), who has sworn an allegiance to Cleolanta. In "Beyond the Curtain of Space," Griff serves as Secretary Drake's lieutenant, and as such he is in a good position to relay confidential information to Cleolanta. At one point, Cleolanta's agent Darganto tells Griff that one traitor is worth more than a whole army. When Drake catches Griff, Drake muses about "a traitor in that uniform" before exclaiming that "space rangers and traitors—they don't go together!" Drake then tries to take Griff captive but finds himself a captive of Griff and his followers. Rocky learns of Griff's treason, and, interestingly, when Rocky catches up with Griff, the traitor flees in a futuristic car (described by Asherman as a "custom jag," meaning a customized Jaguar filling in for the car of the future). A stoic Rocky merely enters Drake's office and uses the vizeograph to find the fleeing Griff. When Rocky gets Griff in focus, Rocky pushes the button which presumably kills Griff since the car explodes. (Curiously, Griff reappears, alive and well, as a prisoner of the United Worlds in "Silver Needle in the Sky.")

Traitors are also found in "The Pirates of Prah" (known in feature form as *Manhunt in Space*) when it is learned that Ranger Ken

(James Griffith), a communications officer on Cassa 7, is feeding classified information to a band of space pirates headed by scoundrels Rinkman and Dr. Vanko, both defectors from Earth and the United Worlds of the Solar System. In "Inferno in Space," Dorton, a civilian worker for Earth's Space Affairs, is promised power by the mad Agar in exchange for freeing Agar from prison; together they steal a rocket ship, but as the earth is about to be destroyed by the Cirkonian force, Dorton repents and calls for Rocky for help. Dorton is rescued by Rocky, and in this instance, the traitor is redeemed.

According to Asherman, a pilot episode was produced in 1952 that featured Robert S. Carson in the role of Secretary Drake and Crystal Reeves as Vena Ray. The pilot, which apparently had no title, was directed by Abby Berlin from a script by Warren Wilson. Asherman writes that only a 26-minute segment of the pilot survives, but it contains retakes featuring the present cast and uses the score by Alexander Laszlo rather than the pilot's original score that was assembled from music libraries. Asherman also writes that the segment is incorporated into the episode "Bobby's Comet" (*Menace from Outer Space*).

Hollingsworth Morse directed all 39 episodes of the series. He and D. Ross Lederman, who directed all 39 episodes of *Captain Midnight*, make a unique team. Filmed television involved various filming setups and postproduction work, and normally at least two directors were used on a series so that one could shoot an episode and supervise its postproduction while the other prepared the next episode. What we can say here about the series directed by Morse and Lederman is that their programs sustained a continuous if not personalized quality throughout the series' run, a rarity among filmed television shows.

Morton gives a program order and playdates for the *Rocky Jones* series, but a log compiled by Andy Anderson in the May 1990 issue of *Filmfax* shows a different program order; in fact, Anderson identifies the episodes according to a continuous chapter series, showing "Beyond the Curtain of Space" as Chapters 1, 2, 3, "Bobby's Comet" as Chapters 4, 5, 6, and so on. Our investigation of various television listings revealed no particular program order; moreover, we could find no uniform playdates. Also, because we found much of the following material by viewing the features rather than the individual episodes, we have elected to give plot summaries for the whole rather than each chapter; the feature titles are in parentheses, and when the feature title is the same as the episode title we have marked it with a dagger (†). We were unable to find any of the single chapter episodes except "Vena and the Darnamo"; hence, descriptions for "Escape into Space" and "Kip's Private War" are compiled from television listings and other reference works.

According to Asherman, James Lydon replaced Scotty Beckett as Biff, Rocky's lieutenant, and Reginald Sheffield replaced Maurice Cass as Rocky's science adviser, Prof. Mayberry. At what point the change occurred eluded us since we were unable to locate any episodes noting the change in the cast, but Morton shows Lydon as a member of the cast of "The Cold Sun," which is, according to Anderson, episodes 27, 28 and 29. In the final episode, "The Trial of Rocky Jones," Sheffield is seen in a flashback to "The Cold Sun." According to Asherman, Biff (or Biffen Cardoza) was Queen Juliandra's lieutenant on Herculon, and was chosen by Juliandra as a "Space Ranger 'exchange' candidate." The reason for Newton's exit is not stated.

For the sake of clarity, and bolstered by interior evidence from the episodes themselves, we have used Anderson's order despite the chaotic episode order found in various listings. In addition, we have eliminated airdates since published listings give vastly differing dates. Finally, lacking cast sheets and scripts, we were reduced to spelling the alien names below phonetically.

Technical Information

FORMAT: Half-hour series told primarily in 15 three-part installments about the exploits of Rocky Jones, a Space Ranger with the United Worlds of the Solar System.

BROADCAST HISTORY: *Network*: Syndication originally through Official Films Inc. and later through MCA. *Original Airdates:*

Opening for "Beyond the Curtain of Space," the first episode of *Rocky Jones, Space Ranger*.

February 27, 1954, through April 17, 1954, according to McNiel; April 10, 1954, through December 4, 1954, according to Morton; and Asherman cites January 1954 as the premiere date for markets. *Sponsor:* Unavailable. *Seasons:* 1. *Total Episodes:* 39 black-and-white on film.

Signature

The series opens on a typical 1950s artistic rendering of outer space over which the title "Rocky Jones, Space Ranger" appears and is spoken by the announcer. This is followed by a second title, "Starring Richard Crane," before dissolving into the episode title and chapter number, again all spoken by the announcer.

Production Staff

Production: Roland Reed Productions, Inc. and Space Ranger Enterprises. *Director:*

Hollingsworth Morse. *Producer:* Roland Reed. *Executive Producer:* Guy V. Thayer, Jr. *Associate Producer:* Arthur Pierson. *Musical Score:* Alexander Laszlo.

Directors of Photography	Walter Strenge, Ernest Miller and Guy Roe
Supervising Editors	Roy Luby and Fred Maguire
Editors	Richard Brockway and Gene Fowler, Jr.
Film Coordinator	James Cairncross
Production Manager	Dick L'Estrange
Art Director	McClure Capps
Set Decorations	Rudy Butler
Photographic Effects	Jack R. Glass
Special Effects	Carl Friend and Ira Anderson
Assistant Director	Dick Moder
Sound	Charles Althouse, Joel Moss and Jack Goodrich
Sound Editor	Cathey Burrow
Music Editor	Robert Raff
Casting Director	Bill Tinsman
Technical Adviser	Dick Morgan
Technical Instruments	Loren Sackett
Makeup	Ernie Park

| *Script Continuity* | Hazel W. Hall |
| *Costumes* | Berman Costume Company |

Filmed at Hal Roach Studios

Regular Cast

Rocky Jones	Richard Crane
Winky	Scotty Beckett
Biffen "Biff" Cardoza (final five episodes)	
	James Lydon
Vena Ray	Sally Mansfield
Prof. Newton	Maurice Cass
Bobby	Robert Lyden
Secretary Drake	Charles Meredith
Prof. Mayberry (final five episodes)	
	Reginald Sheffield

Episode Guide

Beyond the Curtain of Space (Beyond the Moon). A young philologist named Vena Ray storms into Secretary Drake's office and informs him that Prof. Newton and his young ward Bobby have not defected to Ophicius, the planet ruled by an evil queen named Cleolanta, as the rumors say, but that they have been kidnapped by Cleolanta. Drake sends Rocky and Winky to Ophicius to find out the truth, and he orders Vena to accompany the two Space Rangers. The presence of a woman on board the Orbit Jet disturbs Rocky until she proves herself a valuable member of the crew. On Ophicius, Rocky learns that Newton and Bobby are under Cleolanta's power; he also learns that Cleolanta knows every move being made by the United Worlds of the Solar System. Rocky suspects a spy at headquarters, and during a fight with Darganto, Cleolanta's lieutenant, Rocky discovers that the spy is Drake's own lieutenant, Ranger Griff. Newton and Bobby are rescued from Ophicius, and Griff is exposed as the spy. Trying to escape, Griff is apparently killed when Rocky uses the vizeograph to locate and destroy him. *Writer:* Warren Wilson.

Cast:	*Cleolanta*	Patsy Parsons
	Griff	Leonard Penn
	Darganto	Frank Pulaski
	Ranger Clark	William Hudson

Bobby's Comet (Menace from Outer Space). Prof. Newton discovers what he believes is a new comet, and so he names the comet after Bobby. But upon further analysis Newton learns that what he thought was a comet is actually a weapon on a collision course with Earth. Rocky, Winky, Newton, Vena and Bobby take the Orbit Jet into space to repel the weapon, and then search for its source. They lose power near a distant planet called Fornax. Landing safely, the crew soon learns that the weapon was fired from Fornax. Newton recognizes Prof. Cardos among the inhabitants, and Newton explains to Rocky that Cardos was a brilliant but egotistical scientist. Rocky remembers that Cardos is wanted for murder on Earth for killing two assistants just to prove a theory. When Rocky inquires about the weapon launched toward Earth, Zoravac, the ruler of Fornax, explains that he was only protecting his people from aggression by the United Worlds. Rocky learns that Cardos has been deceiving Zoravac, claiming that the United Worlds is an evil empire out to enslave all planets in the solar system. Rocky also learns that Fornax is rich with a special element that can be alloyed into a powerful rocket fuel booster. After visiting with the Earth people, Zoravac has a change of heart, but to prove to himself that the Earth people are not tyrants he seeks an audience with Secretary Drake. Zoravac then accompanies Rocky and Winky to Earth while Newton, Bobby, and Vena remain behind as hostages; Vena and Zoravac's "vonsoom" (his wife) become good friends, and Bobby and Volaca, Zoravac's young daughter, also become good friends. Meanwhile, on Ophicius, Cleolanta learns of the secret element on Fornax and dispatches Darganto and Griff (who somehow managed to escape the explosion on Earth) to Fornax to make a deal. With Zoravac gone, Griff and Darganto find Cardos, and he agrees to overthrow Zoravac and join Cleolanta's forces. Meanwhile, on Earth, Zoravac joins the United Worlds, and he and Rocky and Winky return to Fornax to find Ophician forces there mining the element. Rocky succeeds in destroying the Ophician ship, and takes Darganto and Griff prisoner. *Writer:* Warren Wilson.

| **Cast:** | *Zoravac* | Walter Coy |

Prof. Cardos	Nestor Paiva
Volaca	Patsy Iaonne
The Vonsoom	Joanne Jordan
Cleolanta	Patsy Parsons
Griff	Leonard Penn
Darganto	Frank Pulaski
Cardos' Henchman	Charles Horvath

Rocky's Odyssey (The Gypsy Moon). The crew of the Orbit Jet discovers two moons, Negato and Posito, linked together by a violent atmosphere; Rocky describes them as "gypsy moons" since they have no permanent orbit. A ship from Posito fires upon them, and as they descend toward the planet the Orbit Jet is suddenly controlled by a magnetic ray that pulls the ship toward the Posito stronghold. A language barrier exists between the Earth people and the people of Posito, and so, with Vena's help, conversations are translated through a special machine called a "universal translator" aboard the Orbit Jet. Bovaro, the leader of Posito, is making war against the people of Negato in an effort to free the two moons; Bovaro's wife, Cotanda, is the only rational voice on Posito. Bovaro is friendly toward Rocky, but the Posito ruler will allow nothing to stand in the way of his offensive strikes against Negato, and to this end Bovaro orders Rocky and the crew to leave the Orbit Jet so that he can use the ship in an assault against Negato. But as long as Rocky and his crew remain inside the ship, Bovaro is unable to use it, and so Rocky and the crew find themselves prisoners in the rocket. Bobby is reading Homer's *Odyssey* and he suggests that they pretend to leave the ship so that Bovaro will take it inside the stronghold. The stratagem works, and Rocky takes command of Bovaro's stronghold. Rocky then makes a flight to Negato where he encounters another obstacle from the *Odyssey*: "Negato music," an irritating sound that drives enemies mad. Using their space helmets to block out the sound, the crew seeks Torvak, the ruler of Negato, but in order for Rocky to speak with Torvak, Rocky must keep his helmet open. Soon the siren music takes its toll, driving Rocky mad; he turns against the crew until Winky disconnects the audio and brings Rocky back to his senses. Rocky convinces both Torvak and Bovaro to live in peace. Meanwhile, Cleolanta has intercepted many of Rocky's communications, and with the aid of her own language machine she feigns a message using Rocky's voice to Secretary Drake demanding that he meet on Ankapor for an important conference. Drake agrees, and he and Ranger Higgins depart for Ankapor. The message, of course, is a ruse to trap Drake. Cleolanta and her new lieutenant, Atlasande, masquerade as Vena and Rocky in order to deceive La Volga, Ankapor's ruler, into believing that a goodwill visit from the United Worlds is imminent. Drake and Higgins arrive, and Drake is captured by Cleolanta. Her plan is to use Rocky's voice to rally the citizens of Ankapor, and then force Drake to plead with the citizens to join the Ophician alliance. Rocky, learning of Cleolanta's plan, takes the Orbit Jet to Ankapor, where he, Winky, Vena, Prof. Newton and Bobby disguise themselves as natives to penetrate the city in search of Drake. They eventually find Higgins, and he takes them to Drake. Rocky uses the public address system to rally the citizens on behalf of the United Worlds before rescuing Drake from Cleolanta's grip. *Writer:* Warren Wilson.

Cast: *Bovaro*	John Banner
Cotanda	Erika Nordin
Cleolanta	Patsy Parsons
Atlasande	Harry Lauter
La Volga	Dayton Lummis
Ranger Higgins	Judd Holdren
Ranger Clark	William Hudson

Escape into Space. This is a single chapter episode we were unable to locate. In it, Allan Asherman writes, "[a] racketeer made his 'Escape into Space' ... [where] he intended to buy a moon somewhere and live in luxury, but his ship was crippled by meteors, and he was saved by Rocky and his friends, who were on their way to Fornax." *Writer:* Warren Wilson.

Cast: *Zoravac*	Walter Coy
Volaca	Patsy Iaonne
	also Frank Wilcox

The Pirates of Prah (Manhunt in Space). Vena is hitching a ride on cargo ship CM-7 with Ranger Reggie in command to meet Rocky and the others on planet Cassa 7. Sud-

The palace of Yarra on the planet Medina, rendered in typical 1950s space art for the *Rocky Jones* episode "Forbidden Moon."

denly, the cargo ship is intercepted by an alien ship piloted by pirates from the moon Prah. Vena recognizes the pirate leader as Rinkman, a defector from the United Worlds. Rinkman is aided by a second defector named Dr. Vanko, and they are in league with none other than Cleolanta. Vena and Reggie make it to Cassa 7 where Vena is reunited with her brother Paul, who commands trade on Cassa 7. He explains that many cargo ships have been "skyjacked." Because the pirates seem to know the trade routes, Rocky believes that someone with inside knowledge is feeding them information. Ken, the communications officer, believes the culprit is a Martian named Haggar Nu, who is nowhere to be found. Later, Rocky finds the Martian, but Haggar Nu explains that Ken framed him and that the actual traitor is Ken, who is in league with Cleolanta and her Ophicians. Using Prof. Newton's "Cold Light," a machine that drops the temperature to such an extent that it distorts light waves (thereby leaving any object invisible), Rocky penetrates Prah where he and his crew subdue Rinkman and Vanko and their pirates. *Writer:* Arthur Hoerl.

Cast:

Cleolanta	Patsy Parsons
Rinkman	Henry Brandon
Dr. Vanko	Gabor Curtiz
Ken	James Griffith
Atlasande	Harry Lauter
Haggar Nu	Ted Hecht
Markoff	Mickey Simpson
Link	Dale Van Sickel
Reggie	Ray Montgomery
Higgins	Judd Holdren

Forbidden Moon.†* Panic breaks out on space station RV-5 as a deadly disease runs amok, causing station commander Clark to send an urgent warning to Secretary Drake. Rocky and the crew of the Orbit Jet race to RV-5 where they find the station staggering in orbit. Rocky secures the RV-5, boards it and rescues Clark.

The dagger (†) indicates that the feature title is the same as the episode title (see page 163).

Prof. Newton deduces that Clark is suffering from some kind of radioactive malady. Rocky later learns that the impish Agar, deposed ruler of Medina, is using the deadly radioactive disease to blackmail the United Worlds into submission. Agar's sister Yarra, who now rules Medina, denounces Agar's actions and swears to help the United Worlds. Agar starts a rebellion, and with a handful of supporters he tries to stop Rocky and the crew from landing on a forbidden moon where they hope to find the antidote. As the disease spreads and becomes more deadly, Agar's own supporters defect, seeking Rocky's help. *Writer:* Marianne Mosner.

Cast:

Agar	Vic Perrin
Yarra	Dian Fauntelle
Ranger Clark	William Hudson
Landor	Lane Bradford
Rotasium Guard	Fred Graham

Silver Needle in the Sky (Duel in Space). Rocky and the crew of the Orbit Jet transport several diplomats to an important interplanetary peace conference on the neutral planet of Paratane. But troops from Ophicius interrupt the conference and detain the diplomats. Cleolanta then offers to trade the diplomats for the release of Griff and Darganto. Secretary Drake agrees to the swap, and space station XO-7 is agreed upon as the location for the prisoner exchange. Aboard the station, Atlasande delivers the diplomats and Rocky delivers the two prisoners. Once the swap is made, however, Atlasande orders the diplomats to remain on the space station while preeminent scientist Dr. Hillary Tyson is taken to Ophicius. But the jealous Darganto decrees that he is now in charge and orders the Rangers and the diplomats executed. Atlasande reminds Darganto that he is still in command; his orders, Atlasande reminds Darganto, are to bring Dr. Tyson back to Ophicius. Rocky wishes to fight for Dr. Tyson, but Tyson stops Rocky, regretfully agreeing to depart with the Ophicians. Tyson secretly takes a pill that will make him appear dead for several minutes, thereby confusing the Ophicians. Later, Darganto and Griff sneak off to the power unit where they sabotage the oxygen system, guaranteeing in Darganto's eyes the deaths of his

enemies. On route to the Ophician ship, Dr. Tyson collapses and is taken for dead. Atlasande orders the troops to take Tyson's body to the ship so he can demonstrate to Cleolanta that he did not fail the mission, but Darganto has convinced the troops that he is in charge and they refuse Atlasande's order. Meanwhile, Rocky and the other captives are beginning to feel the lack of oxygen. Rocky locates the air duct, and space engineer Gen. Ortho explains that the power unit is no more than 15 feet away, but the duct is too small for a man. Bobby is then called into service, and he makes his way to the power unit where he escapes. Rocky and Winky are freed, and Winky fixes the oxygen unit, but on their way back to the others they find the body of Dr. Tyson, who soon awakens from his deep coma. The diplomats are rescued and station XO-7 is secured. Meanwhile, Cleolanta is chastising Atlasande for his failure when she learns that Tyson is alive; Darganto exclaims that Tyson could not possibly be alive since he and Griff sabotaged the space station. His admission vindicates Atlasande, and both Griff and Darganto await Cleolanta's punishment for disobeying her orders. *Writer:* Fritz Blocki.

Cast:

Cleolanta	Patsy Parsons
Dr. Hillary Tyson	Dayton Lummis
Atlasande	Harry Lauter
Griff	Leonard Penn
Darganto	Dean Cromer
Ranger Andrews	Rand Brooks
Dr. Loran	Rudolph Anders
Gen. Ortho	Kenneth MacDonald
Duveen	Lane Bradford
Magni	Mickey Simpson
Marshall	Cliff Ferre

Kip's Private War. This is the second single chapter episode. Kip, the son of a criminal, becomes a ward of the Space Rangers. Since Kip resents the Rangers' moral dedication to the United Worlds, he plays pranks to see their reactions. One of his pranks goes awry, allowing the vicious criminal Pinto Vortando to gain advantage over the Rangers. Seeing the error of his ways, Kip uses one of his practical jokes to help the Rangers capture Pinto. *Writer:* Warren Wilson.

Cast:

Pinto	Ted Hecht

E.G. Norman		*Trinka*	Nan Leslie
Robin Morse		*Bovaro*	John Banner
Robert Foulk		*Cotanda*	Maria Palmer
		Ranger Andrews	Rand Brooks
		Lassbaun	Lane Bradford

Crash of Moons.† Prof. Newton discovers that Posito, one the gypsy moons, is on a direct collision course with Ophicius. Rocky's job is to evacuate the people of Posito and to convince Cleolanta that her planet is in grave danger. Bovaro and Cotanda agree to lead their people to safety. Rocky then explains the circumstances to Torvak, ruler of Negato, who is willing to accept the refugees from Posito. Cleolanta won't allow foreign transmissions into her world, so the populace of Ophicius are not aware of the impending doom. Rocky knows that there is an underground at work in Ophicius, and he continues transmitting, hoping that the underground will intercept his message and spread it to the populace. On Ophicius, the leader of the underground is none other than Trinka, wife of Cleolanta's lieutenant, Atlasande. She hears Rocky's urgent message and relays it to her husband, but when a second broadcast is heard by Atlasande he arrests his own wife for treason. Hearing no response from Ophicius, Rocky decides to penetrate the security zone in the hope that he can save Cleolanta not only from the crash of the moon but from herself as well. Rocky and his crew are immediately arrested and taken to Cleolanta; Rocky tells her of the approaching moon, but Cleolanta believes that it is deceit from the United Worlds and orders Rocky and the crew imprisoned. Trinka, however, manages to convince her husband of the peril, and he holds Cleolanta at bay while the United Worlds sets up a massive evacuation effort by employing hundreds of rocket ships to carry the Ophicians to safe territory. Aboard the Orbit Jet, Cleolanta watches as Posito destroys Ophicius. She realizes that the United Worlds forces were dedicated to the survival of her people; Secretary Drake says, "It isn't the land that makes the country, it's the people." Cleolanta changes her ways and extends the hand of friendship to Rocky and to the United Worlds of the Solar System. *Writer:* Warren Wilson.

Cast: *Cleolanta*   Patsy Parsons
         Atlasande   Harry Lauter

Blast-Off.† The Orbit Jet (with Rocky and Bobby aboard) makes a crash-landing on a planetoid inhabited by two primitive peoples, the Valley People and the Hill People. Toro, the leader of the Valley People, and his daughter Moanna believe Rocky is a god, the "All-High," who landed centuries before and taught the people a peaceful philosophy. Zakar, the ruler of the Hill People and Moanna's suitor, believes that there is no All-High and that Rocky is merely an intruder bent on enslaving the peoples. Rocky and Bobby begin repairs on their ship, but since the planetoid is primitive they must return to ancient practices; Rocky designs a makeshift forge and teaches the people how to use it. Fearing Zakar, Toro assigns Bobby a bodyguard named Poli, a giant who Bobby teaches to play the flute. Meanwhile, Secretary Drake assigns Ranger Sandy to take Vena and Prof. Newton on a search for Rocky. Back on the planetoid, Zakar and his tribe cause a massive rock slide that destroys the Orbit Jet. Moanna, running to the site, accidentally touches a deadly flower that fills her system with poison. Rocky races her back to Toro's cave where the Shaman begins a ritual to cure her. Zakar tells Toro that nothing but trouble has occurred since Rocky appeared, and the Shaman agrees. The tension grows when Sandy lands in order to rescue Rocky and Bobby. Prof. Newton uses modern medicine to revive Moanna, but not before Zakar leaves for the hills to cause a second landslide. When Moanna realizes what Zakar is doing, she runs to stop him but she is too late; the rocks have destroyed the second spaceship. Zakar, running to save Moanna from another avalanche, is knocked to the valley floor and seriously injured. He is taken back to Toro's cave where Prof. Newton's medical skill saves another life. With both rockets destroyed, however, there is little chance of the Rangers leaving the planetoid. Moanna tells them about the All-High's vehicle, which is a flying saucer. Sandy and Prof. Newton manage to get the saucer in operating condition. Rocky reasons that the saucer was left by someone from a far distant world. The Rangers board the flying saucer and leave the planetoid for Earth. In their wake, the Valley People and the Hill People join hands in peace. *Teleplay:* Arthur Hoerl. *Story:* Marianne Mosner.

Cast:

Toro	Walter Coy
Moanna	Donna Martell
Poli	Don Megowan
Zakar	Paul Marion
Orak	Peter Ortiz
Shaman	Charles Stevens
Marshall	Cliff Ferre

The Cold Sun.† A strange crust is enveloping the sun, cooling and endangering the planets of the solar system. Prof. Mayberry and Dr. Reno devise a tortanic missile that, fired from a moon of Mercury, could reignite the sun. Rocky and his crew take flight for Herculon where they encounter peaceful Queen Juliandra and her evil twin Noviandra. In addition, Dr. Reno joins with his protégé, the athletic Rudy DiMarco, in an attempt to take control of Herculon. *Writer:* Warren Wilson.

Cast:

Queen Juliandra	Ann Robinson
Dr. Reno	Tom Browne Henry
Rudy DiMarco	Richard Avonde

Inferno from Space (The Magnetic Moon). A "nuclear storm" threatens the earth; its source is a Cirko, described by Prof. Mayberry as a "planetary nebula," or a moon shrouded in the vapor from continuous nuclear explosions. The explosions are so powerful that the vapor is hurtling toward the earth where, for some mysterious reason, it ignites only wood. Meanwhile, the impish Agar has escaped from prison with the aid of Dorton, a civilian worker at Space Affairs. Agar and Dorton manage to steal a rocket ship and head into space. As the Cirkonian force grows more intense, Dorton repents and calls Rocky for assistance. Agar then jettisons Dorton overboard, but Rocky manages to rescue him. Meanwhile, Prof. Mayberry devises a plan to repel the Cirkonian force. He suggests that the Silver Moon cover the surface of Cirko with giant magnetic elements that will pull the force back toward itself; on Earth, he adds, a battery of giant

mirrors should be constructed to reflect the power back to Cirko. The plan is accepted, and Secretary Drake contacts Juliandra of Herculon for permission to use Herculon as a base. Agar arrives on Herculon masquerading as a doctor from Venus who wishes to observe the Cirkonian force. The treacherous Shima, Juliandra's counsel, recognizes Agar, and together they form an alliance; Agar will help Shima usurp the throne of Herculon, and in return Shima will help Agar return to Medina. At the right moment, Shima, with the assistance of her giant henchman Naboro, takes Juliandra captive. Later, Rocky and Biff approach Cirko when they receive a distress signal from Juliandra's ship. They detour to aid her, but find themselves captives of Shima and Agar. Agar destroys the controls of the Silver Moon before departing, leaving the ship with Rocky, Biff and Juliandra on a collision course with Cirko. Rocky orders the magnetic elements dropped on Cirko and then attempts a valiant maneuver; he straps an atomic missile to the side of the Silver Moon, using it to alter their course. On Agar's ship, however, Agar betrays Shima, telling her that he is heading back to Medina, at which point she orders Naboro to assault him. Naboro goes mad and destroys the ship's instruments, causing the ship to glide into the path of the reflected Cirkonian force. The ship explodes, the earth is saved and Juliandra is returned to power on Herculon. *Writers:* Marianne Mosner and Francis Rosenwald.

Cast:

Juliandra	Ann Robinson
Shima	Pamela Duncan
Agar	Charles Davis
Dorton	John Alvin
Marshall	Cliff Ferre
Naboro	Tor Johnson

Vena and the Darnamo. This is the third and final single chapter episode. Rocky and the crew of the Silver Moon stop to refuel at space station OW-9, where Ranger Clark asks for their destination. Rocky sheepishly answers Mandora and shows him an umbrella he received from a trader with a shady cargo (this appears to be a reference to Pinto Vortando); the trader claimed he got it from Mandora. Rocky and the crew then depart for Mandora, and upon landing discover that the planet is primitive, thick with jungle. While exploring the jungle, Vena finds an injured wild dog and removes a sliver from its paw. Bobby equates the event with the story of Androcles and the lion. Just then they are attacked by natives. The crew flees to the Silver Moon where they discover the umbrella is missing and that someone is aboard. The someone turns out to be a little old lady named Mrs. Pilkington, who thanks Rocky for returning her umbrella and invites them all to her jungle home. There, she tells them about her ancestors, and Rocky recognizes the names of Quentin J. O'Brien and especially Cyrus Pilkington, who was known as "Prof. Crackpot and his Sky-Wagon"; he explains that both men were early scientists interested in space travel. Mrs. Pilkington reveals that they were influenced by Jules Verne, and how her ancestors said that if Verne can write them, they can make them. Mrs. Pilkington also explains that the animal Vena saved was a Darnamo, a descendent of Earth dogs. At this point, the natives assault the house because they believe that the crew has brought evil, and that a sacrifice must be made to the Darnamo god. Later, Vena is kidnapped by the natives and taken to a sacrificial stake where they prepare to burn her alive. Rocky gives chase, but he is knocked unconscious by the natives. As the natives begin their sacrificial ritual, the Darnamo appears and chases the natives off. Rocky regains his senses, extinguishes the fire and then frees Vena. Rocky then christens Vena "Miss Andy," and Bobby catches on that her rescue was just like that in the story of Androcles and the lion. Mrs. Pilkington opts to stay behind because she is considered a "montoro dusperando" ("beautiful white goddess") to the natives. On Mandora, she says, she is a beautiful woman, but back on Earth she would be just another old lady. *Writer:* Warren Wilson.

Cast: *Mrs. Pilkington*   Ida Moore
      Ranger Clark   William Hudson
      First Mandoran   Charles Horvath

Out of the World (The Robot of Regalio). The planetoid Hermes is being pulled out of its orbit by a powerful magnetic ray emanating from the planet Regalio. Rocky and his crew are dispatched in the Silver Moon to

Regalio where they join forces with Juliandra to thwart the evil plans of Nizam, the ruler of Regalio. *Writer:* Arthur Hoerl.

Cast: *Juliandra*   Ann Robinson
      Nizam   Ian Keith
      Rykon   Ed Penny

The Trial of Rocky Jones (Renegade Satellite). Rocky lands the Silver Moon on the planet Ankapor, which is a haven for criminals because La Volga, the ruler, refuses to sign any extradition treaties. Meanwhile, La Volga has been befriended by Griff (who now masquerades as a trader), Dr. Reno and the sly Rudy DiMarco, who passes himself off as an Olympic champion. While relaxing in a café, Rocky, Biff, Vena, and Bobby are greeted by their old friend Pinto Vortando, who has given up his life of crime to become a respectable citizen, even though he prefers begging to working. Concerned about Rocky's presence, Griff, Reno and DiMarco form an alliance, and Reno comes up with a plan to put Rocky Jones out of commission forever. DiMarco charms Pinto with food and drink, and leads him down a dark alley where they await Rocky. Once Rocky is seen, Rudy assaults Pinto, causing Rocky to come to Pinto's aid. Dr. Reno calls for help while Griff takes Pinto captive. La Volga and his aide stop the fight, and DiMarco accuses Rocky of assault and attempted robbery. Rocky is placed under arrest, and Biff, Vena and Bobby are confined to the Silver Moon. Later, Griff's henchman, Commander Zandorf, masquerading as Pinto's friend, breaks Rocky out of jail. The escape alarm is sounded, and Rocky is taken captive by Griff, who drugs Rocky and then places him aboard his own cargo ship. Griff and Zandorf set the automatic pilot and the ship takes off with Rocky aboard. Griff then reports that Rocky has escaped jail and is attempting to flee in Griff's own rocket. La Volga gives pursuit and returns Rocky to Ankapor. Rocky is then placed on trial, with Dr. Reno serving as prosecutor and Biff serving as Rocky's defense counsel. Through legal maneuvering, Biff is able to bring forth character witnesses who explain—via flashbacks from previous episodes—Rocky's stalwart character. Meanwhile, on space station OW-9 Ranger Clark finds Pinto a captive aboard

Zandorf's ship. Zandorf and his crew are apprehended and Pinto is returned to Ankapor. Pinto testifies about the incident, but Reno claims that Pinto's story is all lies. La Volga is about to pass judgment on Rocky when a tremendous earthquake shakes Ankapor. Rocky leads an injured La Volga and his young daughter Jonica to safety before capturing Griff, Dr. Reno and Rudy DiMarco. La Volga realizes that he has been duped and that Rocky is not guilty. La Volga allows for the extradition of the criminals and vows that Ankapor shall no longer be a haven for space criminals. *Writer:* Warren Wilson.

Cast: *La Volga*   Dayton Lummis
Jonica   Melinda Plowman
Griff   Leonard Penn
Dr. Reno   Tom Browne Henry
Rudy DiMarco   Richard Avonde
Pinto Vortando   Ted Hecht
Commander Zandorf   Robert Bray
First Native   James Griffith
Ranger Clark   William Hudson

Rod Brown of the Rocket Rangers

The space wars of the 1950s heated up with the arrival of *Rod Brown of the Rocket Rangers* on CBS in the spring of 1953. *Captain Video* (DuMont) and *Space Patrol* (ABC) were pulling in substantial advertising dollars plus an equally attractive amount in commercial licensing fees for the rights for toy, clothing and comic book tie-ins. CBS intended to have a share of the market.

CBS, which originally presented *Tom Corbett, Space Cadet* to television audiences late in 1950, apparently lacked faith in the series and permitted it to emigrate over to ABC after only three months. This was a tactical mistake. The *Tom Corbett* series (along with *Captain Video* and *Space Patrol*) dominated the science fiction adventure field and CBS was frozen out of the competition.

To remedy the situation, CBS officials developed a carbon copy of *Tom Corbett* and called their series *Rod Brown of the Rocket Rangers*. To further draw on the Corbett inspiration, the network hired George Gould (who had directed *Tom Corbett*) and veteran *Corbett* writers Jack Weinstock and Willie Gilbert. In its eagerness to make *Rod Brown* a rousing success, CBS reportedly tried to lure Tom Corbett himself (Frankie Thomas) over to the new project. Considerable similarities also existed

between the opening signatures of the rival shows.

Talent raids among networks was nothing new; CBS had raised the practice to a high art in the late 1940s when network head Bill Paley snagged a number of top comedians from NBC, including Jack Benny. However, the network's blatant appropriation of the *Tom Corbett* format (right down to the space terminology used on the program) provoked Rockhill Productions to file suit against CBS. In its defense, CBS argued that since it had originally presented *Tom Corbett*, the network retained certain rights and privileges which it was exercising in the production of *Rod Brown*.

The lawsuit was eventually settled out of court and the terms of the settlement were not divulged. CBS, however, continued with *Rod Brown*. The three young rangers who formed the nucleus of the show were Rod Brown, played by 27-year-old Cliff Robertson, and his comrades Fred Boyle (Bruce Hall) and Wilbur "Wormsey" Wormser. "Wormsey" was portrayed by Jack Weston and functioned primarily as comedic relief for the series. The team operated out of Omega Base in the 22nd century, took their orders from Commander Swift (John Boruff) and manned the spaceship Beta.

The only modest departure *Rod Brown*

made from *Tom Corbett*, *Captain Video* and *Space Patrol* was in discarding the traditional serial format. Each *Rod Brown* episode was a self-contained adventure that began and ended within a 30-minute time span. (The other series had also begun to drift away from the strict serial format.)

Rockhill wasn't the only critic to go on record against *Rod Brown*. About the time Congress began delving into the possibility of a link between television violence and the increase in juvenile delinquency, *TV Guide* found *Rod Brown* suspect for the types of messages it was sending young viewers. *TV Guide* faulted the show for straying too "closely to the line of violence" and for demonstrating "little or no attempt to be educational, informative or even entertaining." As *TV Guide* implied, television programs in the 1950s were expected to at least make an honest effort at delivering worthwhile and instructive messages, and failure to do so deserved public condemnation. *Rod Brown*'s only purpose appears to have been CBS's desire to milk profits from the juvenile science fiction fad.

Rod Brown ran for 58 episodes and then disappeared from the air after fighting the usual assortment of killer robots, gigantic apes, space pirates and dinosaurs. What the show could not fight was the general perception that it had nothing new to offer its viewers.

Technical Information

FORMAT: Live half-hour adventure series featuring Rod Brown and the Rocket Rangers as they enforce peace among the disparate civilizations throughout the galaxy in the 22nd century.

BROADCAST HISTORY: *Network:* CBS. *Original Airdates:* April 18, 1953 to May 29, 1954. *Seasons:* 2. *Total Episodes:* 58 black-and-white.

Signature

Without having seen any episodes of the series, we must reconstruct the opening based upon written descriptions. Apparently, much

like *Tom Corbett*, *Space Cadet*, *Rod Brown* opened with an announcer's voice-over narration coupled with filmed sequences of rocket ships soaring upward and out of sight.

Production Staff

Production: CBS Television. *Producer:* William Dozier. *Director:* George Gould. *Writers:* Jack Weinstock and Willie Gilbert.

Regular Cast

Ranger Rod Brown   Cliff Robertson
Ranger Wilbur "Wormsey" Wormser
                                          Jack Weston
Ranger Frank Boyle   Bruce Hall
Commander Swift   John Boruff

Episode Guide

SEASON 1

Operation Decoy (April 18, 1953)

The Case of the Invisible Saboteurs (April 25, 1953)

The Planet of Ice (May 2, 1953)

Whispers of the Mind (May 9, 1953)

The Crater of Peril (May 16, 1963)

The Globe Men of Oma (May 23, 1953)

The Adventures of the Venusian Sea (May 30, 1953)

The Little Men of Mercury (June 6, 1953)

World of the Doomed (June 13, 1953)

The Strangler Tree of Triton (June 20, 1953)

Stranger from Outer Space (June 27, 1953)

The Phantom Birds of Bolero (July 4, 1953)

The Black Cloud of Callisto (July 11, 1953)

The Suits of Peril (July 18, 1953)

Apples of Eden (July 25, 1953)

Space Bugs (August 1, 1953)

The Martian Queen (August 8, 1953)

The Fire Daemons of Deimos (August 15, 1953)

The Big Hammer (August 22, 1953)

The Volcanos of Venus (August 29, 1953)

The Death Ball (September 5, 1953)

The Unseen Planet (September 12, 1953)

SEASON 2

The Madness from Space (September 19, 1953)

The Looters of Leeron (September 26, 1953)

The Octopus of Venus (October 3, 1953)

Colossus of Centauri (October 10, 1953)

The Lights from Luna (October 17, 1953)

The Twin Planet (October 24, 1953)

The Treasure of Tesore (October 31, 1953)

The Robot Robber of Deimos (November 7, 1953)

The Magic Man of Mars (November 14, 1953)

The Stickmen of Neptune (November 21, 1953)

The Money Makers of Juno (November 28, 1953)

The Deep Sleep (December 5, 1953)

The Cyclops of Themis (December 12, 1953)

The Electric Men (December 19, 1953)

The Copernicus Diamond (December 26, 1953)

The Stone Men of Venus (January 2, 1953)

Energy Eaters from Luna (January 16, 1953)

Operation Dinosaur (January 23, 1953)

Escape by Magic (January 30, 1953)

The Invisible Force (February 6, 1953)

Return of the Stickmen (February 13, 1953)

The Fishman of the Venusian Sea (February 20, 1953)

The Strong Man of Mayron (February 27, 1953)

The Eel of Iapetos (March 6, 1953)

The Strange Men of Leefri (March 13, 1953)

The Monkey That Couldn't Stop Growing (March 20, 1953)

The Plan of Planet H (March 27, 1953)

Invasion from Dimension X (April 3, 1953)

The Matter Transfer Machine (April 10, 1953)

Terror in the Space Lighthouse (April 17, 1953)

Assignment Danger (April 24, 1953)

Bird Girl of Venus (May 1, 1954)

The Exploding Man (May 8, 1954)

The Metal Eaters (May 15, 1954)

The Man Who Was Radioactive (May 22, 1954)

The Cobalt Bomb (May 29, 1954)

Science Fiction Theatre

Science fiction in the early years of television was almost exclusively dominated by "space opera"—tales of outer space adventure similar in theme and expression to Westerns. Between the years 1949 and 1955, television was busy offering such pulp escapism as *Captain Video and His Video Rangers*; *Rocky Jones, Space Ranger*; *Space Patrol*; *Captain Z-RO*; *Atom Squad*; and *Rod Brown of the Rocket Rangers*, series whose narratives generally eschewed any adherence to scientific accuracy for the sheer joy of "make believe." But in the spring of 1955, Ziv Television premiered an anthology series which based its narratives on scientific speculation, a series whose base was not one of fantasy but one of extrapolation; the stories projected current scientific knowledge into its next logical step. The series, titled simply and appropriately *Science Fiction Theatre*, sublimated the immediate emotional heart-pounding gratification offered by tales of bug-eyed Martians and assorted other hideous apparitions, concentrating instead on extrapolations of existing scientific thought, offering entertaining and remote possibilities.

Viewed in the context of its times, *Science Fiction Theatre* is easily understandable both in terms of the decision to place it on the air and the semi-documentary approach chosen as its format. The 1950s was a decade of radical advances in science and technology, and the decade's popular artistic expression reflected these radical changes in our way of life. Films, especially, recounted dramas whose milieu had a distinct air of scientific advancement about them. Films like Irving Pichel's *Destination Moon* (1950) and Byron Haskin's *Conquest of Space* (1955) depicted rockets and missiles and described man's efforts to reach the stars.

Emerging from this throng of science fiction, however, were three films produced by Ivan Tors which stand out not so much for their science fiction—although they are science fiction in the strictest sense—but for their "science fact." Curt Siodmak's *The Magnetic Monster* (1953), Richard Carlson's *Riders to the Stars* (1954) and Herbert L. Strock's *Gog* (1954) were dramas rooted heavily in extrapolation. *The Magnetic Monster* depicts the search for a dangerously unstable new element called "serranium." The film uses the then-new knowledge of isotopes to speculate on what the next scientific revolution may be (the development of a new element, for example) and the problems that may arise from such a leap in scientific experimentation.

Gene Plotnik, in the April 16, 1955, issue of *Billboard*, an amusement industry trade publication, reported that Ziv executives, aware of all the spectacular scientific advances in the news, "began talking about a science fiction series that would be firmly based in actual research." Ziv conceived of a new approach, however, favoring adult themes woven about

Opening signature of *Science Fiction Theatre*, ending with host Truman Bradley preparing to show the audience "something interesting."

current preoccupations of scientific thought. The approach would be semi-documentary in nature, shooting in actual locations or detailed replications of locations.

It was only natural for film producer Ivan Tors, committed to dramas based in realism, and the executives of the Ziv organization to pool their talents and deliver *Science Fiction Theatre* to 1950s audiences. (Tors had wanted to get into television production as early as 1952 when he, actor Richard Carlson and writer-director Curt Siodmak formed A-Men TV Productions. *The Magnetic Monster* was so successful that Tors tried to launch a series about the fictional government agency the Office of Scientific Investigation featured in the film. For one reason or another the series never made it beyond speculation.)

For *Science Fiction Theatre*, Tors was given a budget of $1.5 million, which included provisions for location shooting at Air Force bases, universities and private laboratories. Tors then assembled a staff composed mainly of his film crew. Tors' art director, George Van Marter, wrote several of the episodes; Charles Van Enger, who photographed *The Magnetic Monster*, supervised the first season cinematography; Herbert L. Strock, director of Tors' *Gog* and *Battle Taxi*, directed several episodes and served as supervising editor; and science fiction filmmaker Jack Arnold also directed several episodes, including "No Food for Thought," whose "science" served as rationale for Arnold's story of a giant spider in the feature *Tarantula* (1955). Maxwell Smith, who served as Tors' scientific advisor for the films, was credited as "Scientific Advisor on Electronics and Radiation," and was in charge of a six-man special research department with a budget of $75,000, charged with the responsibility of checking with universities and government agencies for assurance of scientific accuracy. Among the cooperating agencies were UCLA, USC, the California Institute of Technology, Johns

Hopkins University, the Smithsonian Institution, the Los Angeles County Museum, the U.S. Defense Department and the Douglas, Lockheed and North American Aircraft organization.

Finally a format was conceived. Ray Llewellyn's theme music, a broad, stately fanfare dominated by brass instruments, would play as the camera moved slowly and purposefully around a room filled with scientific instruments. But the room was not the scientific laboratory so prevalent in film history or in the juvenile TV entries which had dominated the first half of the 1950s. Gone now were the glass tubes and flasks of steaming liquids. In their stead was a room filled with some of the most recent technologically advanced devices, some of which were indeed esoteric yet convincing all the same. But more important, this laboratory setting was not the refuge of the mad scientist; it was the study of a gentleman scientist, and after several seconds the camera discovers the scientist, the host and narrator of the series, veteran radio announcer Truman Bradley.

Bradley was the only recurring figure on the program, lending stability to the anthology format chosen. More importantly, his appearance and demeanor lent credibility to the seriousness with which the audience was encouraged to view the program. Trained primarily on radio as an announcer on such programs as *Lady Esther Screen Guild Players*, *The Prudential Family Hour*, *Suspense*, *The Red Skelton Show* and *The Burns and Allen Show*, Bradley conveyed sincerity and conviction. Always neatly attired in conservative suit and tie, graying hair neatly brushed into place, Bradley presented the ideal picture of the cultured avuncular host to whom the most serious consideration should be given.

Bradley opened each program by introducing himself and then proposing to show us "something interesting." We would then watch as Bradley demonstrated some scientific principle which formed the basis of the story we were about to see. In this sense Bradley was imitating the role of Don Herbert, host of the popular children's educational scientific program *Mr. Wizard*, and Lynn Poole, host of the low-budget but critically acclaimed series for adults, *Johns Hopkins Science Review*.

After the demonstration, Bradley would introduce that week's story. At some point in the introduction or in his wrap-up of the program, Bradley would usually take pains to assure us that the story was just that, a story, that it did not actually happen. But the possibility, he assured us, was there, and that was precisely what *Science Fiction Theatre* represented—a study in possibilities. Bradley would end each episode by telling us that he'd be back "one week from today with another story from the world of fiction and science." In this sense, he disassociated his series from the traditional television space operas by emphasizing that even though his series was called *Science Fiction Theatre*, the dramas presented were actually rooted in issues of science. The difference is crucial but sometimes misunderstood. Tors' approach to science fiction has sometimes been called timid by those who seem to prefer a more flamboyant approach to the genre. Tors, however, had a different motivation—to advance a general public awareness of the inherent drama in science. To Tors' way of thinking, the way to achieve this was to place the heaviest emphasis on the "science" half of the science fiction equation.

Ivan Tors could scarcely have joined with a better partner than Ziv for the development and promotion of a documentary approach to science fiction. In its 12-year history of television production, Ziv's "headline consciousness" (as one observer called the organization's tendency to dramatize topical interest stories) was invariably coupled with a missionary zeal to sell the company product. Bud Rifkin, one-time executive vice-president at Ziv in charge of sales, quoted in Jeff Kisseloff's *The Box: An Oral History of Television, 1920-1961*, described the Ziv sales force:

> We built the best sales organization in the country. We had covered the country with offices in Atlanta, Dallas, Los Angeles, Chicago, New York and so on. Every salesperson would be taught how to sell each of our shows. He had marvelous brochures and flip charts…. If he was sent to a city, he couldn't leave that city until the show was sold.

When it came to selling *Science Fiction Theatre* to local sponsors, *Broadcasting-Telecasting* magazine (May 9, 1955) laid out in detail what each salesman carried with him into the field:

1. A 12-page (16 to 21 inches) flip-over brochure.
2. Sales talk file, with fact-sheets and other exhibits.
3. Promotion kit containing a three-color poster, a two-color streamer, a *Science Fiction Theatre* ticket, a two-color newspaper-styled tabloid, letters to dealers signed by Truman Bradley and mailed from Hollywood, on-the-air promotion material, newspaper ads and mats, publicity stories and pictures and a publicity hand-book explaining how to use contests, special events and civic activities in promoting the program.
4. "Enthuse" kit containing plant posters, letters from the "boss" to his employees' wives, payroll stuffers on "your company's new plan to increase business and to help brighten your job future," plans for using the public address system and the switchboard to publicize the program, even a design for a postage meter promotion.
5. Mounted poster
6. Science and science fiction reprints from *Colliers*, *Saturday Evening Post* and *Life*.
7. Audition print of a *Science Fiction Theatre* program.
8. Film trailers.
9. Projector and screen.
10. Ziv-TV instructional book, showing that Ziv Television Programs is a good firm to do business with.

Ziv sales personnel lined up an impressive list of sponsors, including Olympia Brewing Company, PictSweet Frozen Foods, Arizona Public Service, Tobin Packing Company, Conoco, Continental Oil, Emerson Drug and Serutan.

On April 5, 1955, Ziv premiered *Science Fiction Theatre* in 125 markets—including all of the top 60 television stations in the nation—with its pilot episode "Beyond," featuring William Lundigan. (Lundigan appeared a year earlier in Tors' film *Riders to the Stars*, and would appear four years later in yet another Ziv "science fact" series, *Men into Space*.) After

only eight weeks on the air, *Billboard* called *Science Fiction Theatre* "No. 1 among new series," and ranked it as the number one best dramatic series. *Billboard* reported that the series fell no lower than second place during its entire 78 episode run. Frederick W. Ziv, the chairman and president of the company bearing his name, was enthusiastic about the series. In an interview in the May 9, 1955, issue of *Broadcasting-Telecasting*, he said he thought he had "achieved a truly adult series in a field that could have been completely juvenile. This achievement has not been easy; it's entailed a laborious load of meticulous research. But it's paid off."

The pilot episode, "Beyond," shot in color as were all of the 39 first season episodes (presumably for reissue value), is the story of a test pilot, Fred Gunderman, and his strange encounter with a flying saucer. Gunderman bails out of his experimental plane claiming that a flying saucer was about to crash into his craft. Back safely on the ground, Gunderman encounters disbelief of his explanation. Radar had failed to pick up any nearby craft. Eventually, the theory is formulated that Gunderman had been flying high enough and fast enough to have entered a state of weightlessness and that the flying saucer he thought he saw had been nothing more than a fountain pen floating in the weightlessness of the cockpit. A final twist is presented when new computations prove that weightlessness had not taken place; the discovery of a magnetized piece of wreckage from Gunderman's plane leaves the viewer wondering (a popular theory of the time maintained that flying saucers were powered by magnetic energy).

A generally favorable review of *Science Fiction Theatre* and its opening episode appeared in the April 2, 1955, *Billboard*; the anonymous reviewer opined that the "camerawork, pacing and editing are excellent. Indeed, Ziv's general production quality seems to become more polished with each new release." A review in the April 13, 1955, *Variety* was lukewarm to the production values and story development of "Beyond," but praised the Ziv organization for its "documentary style" and the series' uniqueness.

Science Fiction Theatre presented its share

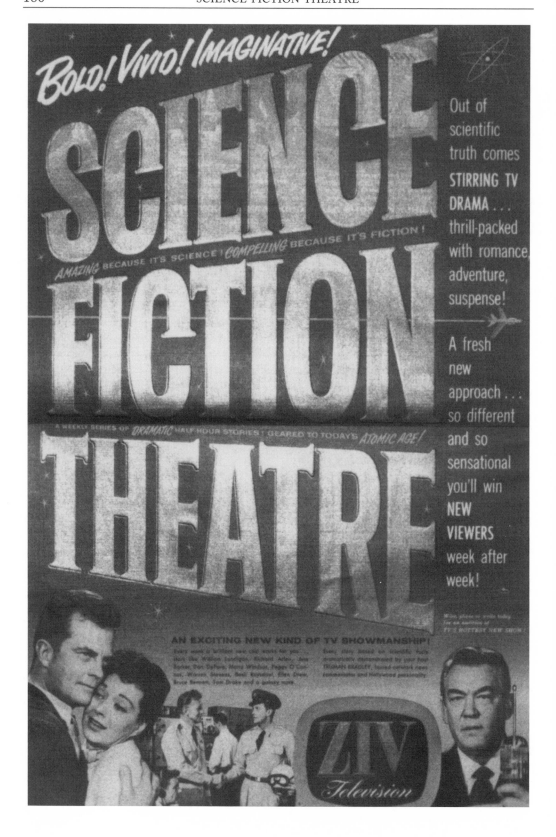

of speculation concerning unidentified flying objects, but it never attempted to offer a definitive answer to that or any *other* question about any alien life forms. Mysterious and alien forces were often left unseen and just suggested. In the 1955 episode "The Hastings Secret," investigators in the jungles of Peru attempt to learn the whereabouts of a missing scientist. They eventually arrive at the grisly truth that he has been consumed by man-eating termites. We never see the termites feeding on the remains of their victim; such detail is left to the imagination of the viewer. And even when such unusual life forms were shown, they took on a deceptively ordinary and nonthreatening appearance. In "Living Lights," the story of a young scientist who replicates life as it must exist on the planet Venus, the creatures were nothing more than small circles of light comparable in appearance to spots of sunlight; they looked as threatening as the focus of any flashlight beam.

In an episode first broadcast to some markets on May 6, 1955, *Science Fiction Theatre* forcefully demonstrated the ability of the unseen to weave a spell over an audience willing to play along in a game of imagination. "Y.O.R.D." began in typical fashion with Truman Bradley demonstrating with charts and equipment the underpinning theme of that week's program. After a discussion of the human brain and a demonstration of the latest techniques for measuring brain activity, Bradley outlined the nature of that week's inquiry:

> And now comes the question: Is the electrical activity of our brains confined within our own nervous systems, within our own bodies? Is it possible that one day we shall master this secret of broadcasting directly from one mind to another? This is the theme of our story, a tale of fiction from the borderlands of science. Fiction today but how about tomorrow?

At a remote experimental weather station situated at the magnetic North Pole, U.S. military personnel had begun to manifest startling psychic abilities: They were able to read each other's thoughts. Investigation leads to the conclusion that an extraterrestrial spacecraft is caught in the magnetic pull of the earth, sending out frantic telepathic pleas for help which are being picked up by the station crew. An intense effort is then launched to communicate with and provide assistance to the alien craft, but apparently to no avail as the spacecraft crashes and all telepathic contact is ended. "Y.O.R.D." concludes with the scientist speculating that perhaps there will be another encounter. Truman Bradley then comes back on the screen to ask us:

> What do you think? Do you think there will be a next time? Or should I say, do you think there will be a *first* time? After all, the story you have just seen is fiction; it did not happen. But can it happen? Will it happen? Do you want it to happen?

The last original episode of *Science Fiction Theatre* aired in most markets on February 8, 1957. The Russians launched Sputnik I into Earth orbit just eight months later, thereby inaugurating what has been called the "space race." By then, however, it was too late to put *Science Fiction Theatre* back into production to capitalize on the country's suddenly rekindled interest in things scientific and technological. But the Ziv organization, still as headline-conscious as ever, hurried two series into production, *The Man and the Challenge* (also produced by Ivan Tors) and *Men into Space*, both designed to benefit from the new public preoccupation with America's summons into space.

Technical Information

FORMAT: Half-hour filmed anthology series depicting extrapolations of present scientific theory and suggesting future possibilities.

BROADCAST HISTORY: *Network:* Syndicated. *Airdates:* April 5, 1955 to February 8, 1955. *Sponsor:* Multiple sponsors. *Seasons:* 2. *Total Episodes:* 78 (39 color, 39 black-and-white).

Signature

OPENING: Each episode opens with the camera prowling about a large scientific study

Opposite: **Trade advertisement for the release of *Science Fiction Theatre*.**

filled with impressive electronic instruments. Ray Llewellyn's theme music, a broad, stately fanfare dominated by brass instruments, plays majestically. Eventually the camera discovers an absorbed Truman Bradley.

BRADLEY: How do you do, ladies and gentlemen; I'm your host, Truman Bradley. Let me show you something interesting.

CLOSING: Bradley: I'll be back one week from today with another story from the world of fiction and science.

Production Staff

Production: Ziv Television Programs. *Producer:* Ivan Tors.

Directors of Photography	Robert Hoffman and Curt Fetters
Camera Operator	Dick Rawlings
Production Supervisor	Barry Cohn
Assistant Directors	Ed Stein and Jay Sandrich
Production Coordinator	Joe Wonder
Sound Mixer	Garry Harris
Video Supervisor	Donald Tait
Film Editors	Thomas Scott and James Dyer
Audio Supervisor	Quinn Martin
Sound Editor	Monroe Martin
Music Editors	Milton Lustig and Haynes Pagel
Special Scientific Effects	Harry Redmond, Jr.
Scientific Advisor on Electronics and Radiation	Maxwell Smith
Set Decorator	Clarence Steenson
Set Designer	Robert Kinoshita
Property Master	Max Pittman
Wardrobe	Alfred Berke
Script Supervisors	Larry Lund and Noreen Cantrell

Regular Cast

Host	Truman Bradley

Episode Guide

SEASON 1

Beyond (April 5, 1955). Jet ace Fred Gunderman, flying at three times the speed of sound, bails out of his experimental craft when it looks like he's going to collide with a flying saucer. Skeptical authorities back on the ground refuse to believe Gunderman's story until an important piece of wreckage suggests the pilot may have been correct. *Director:* Herbert L. Strock. *Writers:* Robert Smith and George Van Marter. *Story:* Ivan L. Tors.

Cast:	*Fred Gunderman*	William Lundigan
	Helen Gunderman	Ellen Drew
	Gen. Troy	Bruce Bennett
	Dr. Everett	Tom Drake
	Col. Barton	Douglas Kennedy
	Dr. Carson	Basil Ruysdael
	also Michael Fox, Robert Carson and Mark Lowell	

Time Is Just a Place (April 15, 1955). The Browns welcome a strange new family into the neighborhood, the Hellers. The Hellers possess a "sonic broom," an "x-ray flashlight" and other gadgets of advanced design. When confronted for an explanation, the Hellers tell of a bleak future they have tried to escape by means of illegal time travel. In the midst of an electrical storm, when all power has been lost, the Hellers disappear mysteriously. *Director:* Jack Arnold. *Writer:* Lee Berg. *Story:* Jack Finney.

Cast:	*Al Brown*	Don DeFore
	Nell Brown	Marie Windsor
	Ted Heller	Warren Stevens
	Ann Heller	Peggy O'Connor

No Food for Thought (April 22, 1955). A biologist and his staff make themselves human guinea pigs for experiments with synthetic foods. When one of the staff dies as a result of the experiment, an outside doctor must find a cure for the plague overtaking the research team. *Director:* Jack Arnold. *Writer:* Robert M. Fresco.

Cast:	*Prof. Emanuel Hall*	Otto Kruger
	Dr. Paul Novak	John Howard
	Jan Corey	Vera Miles
	Dr. Lee Suyin	Clarence Lung
	Sheriff Simpson	Stanley Andrews
	also Hal K. Dawson and Hank Patterson	

Out of Nowhere (April 29, 1955). The Continental Defense Command is alerted when bats collide with a skyscraper. If the "radar" that protects bats from collision has been interfered with, the nation's defense screens must also be affected. *Director:* Herbert L. Strock. *Writer:* Donn Mullally.

Cast: *Dr. Osborne*   Richard Arlen
        Dr. Jeffries   Jess Barker
        Gen. Kenyon   Carlyle Mitchell
        Superintendent   Irving Mitchell
        Dr. Milton   Jonathan Hale
        Fleming   Hal Forrest
        Robb   Craig Duncan
        also Elsie Barker
       and Robert Templeton

Y.O.R.D. (May 6, 1955). Weather station personnel at the magnetic pole receive strange telepathic signals which turn out to be from an alien spacecraft in distress. When the scientists understand the nature of the problem, they try to contact the crew of the spaceship telepathically with landing instructions. *Director:* Leon Benson. *Writers:* Leon Benson and George Van Marter. *Story:* Ivan Tors and George Van Marter.

Cast: *Dr. Lawton*   Walter Kingsford
        Edna Miner   Judith Ames
        Col. Van Dyke   Louis Jean Heydt
        Capt. Hall   DeForest Kelley
        Lt. Dunne   Ken Tobey
        also John Bryant and Clark Howat

Stranger in the Desert (May 13, 1955). A radioactive eagle that has miraculously recovered leads Gil Collins and Bud Porter on an exciting hunt for uranium. The uranium proves to be a mirage but a strange old man searching for plant life intrigues Collins. When the old man disappears from the desert, it appears that he may have literally disappeared off the face of the planet. *Director:* Henry S. Kesler. *Writers:* Curtis Kenyon and Robert M. Fresco. *Story:* Ivan Tors.

Cast: *Gil Collins*   Marshall Thompson
        Bud Porter   Gene Evans
        Ballard   Lowell Gilmore
        also John Mitchum and Ray Bennett

The Sound of Murder (May 20, 1955). Dr. Tom Mathews uses his scientific knowledge to battle the false charge that he murdered a co-worker and stole secret papers. The case against Mathews seems irrefutable; several people clearly identified Mathews' voice during compromising situations. *Director:* Jack Arnold. *Writer:* Stuart Jerome. *Story:* Ivan Tors.

Cast: *Dr. Tom Mathews*   Howard Duff
        Dr. Van Kamp   Wheaton Chambers
        also Russ Conway, Christine Larson,
       Whit Bissell, Edward Earle,
       Ruth Perrott, Charles Maxwell,
       Olan Soulé, Julie Jordan,
   Charlotte Lawrence and Paul Peters

The Brain of John Emerson (May 27, 1955). A police sergeant, miraculously escaping death after a bullet in the brain, discovers that he has undergone a complete change in personality, interests and technical knowledge. The officer learns that the brain surgeon who saved his life has died of a heart condition. However, knowing that he was soon to die, the surgeon transferred his vast scientific knowledge to the brain of the police sergeant. *Director:* Leslie Goodwins. *Writer:* Rik Vollaerts.

Cast: *John Emerson*   John Howard
        Mrs. Turner   Ellen Drew
        Joan   Joyce Holden
        Capt. Damon   Robert Simon
        Dr. Franklin   Michael Fox
        Nurse   Jackie Blanchard
        also Charles Maxwell

Spider, Inc. (June 3, 1955). An assistant geologist discovers a rare specimen, a transparent rock which encases a giant spider, which convinces him that it contains nature's secret process for making petroleum. Mounting debts and his wife's pregnancy almost prevent the scientist from exploring his theory. *Director:* Jack Arnold. *Writer:* Jerry Sackheim.

Cast: *Joe Ferguson*   Gene Barry
        Ellie Ferguson   Audrey Totter
        also Ludwig Stossel, Robert Clarke,
       Herbert Rudley, Frank Hanley,
       Phil Arnold and George Meader

Deadline at 2 A.M. (June 10, 1955). Samuel Avery, a brilliant biochemist, has a young assistant who is being blackmailed. Avery's attachment to his co-worker leads the scientist to take a dangerous gamble. Avery uses the formula he has been developing to increase human strength to provide him the physical prowess to make certain the blackmailer never disturbs Avery's assistant again. *Director:* Henry S. Kesler. *Writer:* Ellis Marcus. *Story:* Ivan Tors.

Cast: Bill Reynolds   Skip Homeier
    Dr. Samuel Avery   John Qualen
        also Ted De Corsia, Virginia Hunter
            and Douglas Henderson

Conversation with an Ape (June 17, 1955). A young bride has an unexpected shock when her new husband, a scientist working with animals, takes her home to meet his pet chimpanzee. The chimpanzee is key to the scientist's efforts to develop a form of communication between man and animals. The bride's antipathy to the chimp increases to the point that she prepares to leave. She is only prevented from leaving by the sudden appearance of an escaped prisoner who holds the household captive until the chimp comprehends the situation and reacts to the scientist's communicated instructions. *Director:* Herbert L. Strock. *Writer:* Rik Vollaerts.

Cast: Nancy Stanton   Barbara Hale
    Dr. Guy Stanton   Hugh Beaumont
    Pete Lane   Paul Birch

Marked Danger (June 24, 1955). White mice sent into the ionosphere by rocket undergo a strange transformation and Darwinian evolution is taken a step further. When the capsule containing the mice falls back to Earth it is discovered by a prospector and his wife. While the prospector makes arrangements to report their find and collect a reward, his wife tampers with the canister containing the mice and subjects herself to a deadly gas. *Director:* Leigh Jason. *Writers:* Jerry Sackheim and Stuart Jerome. *Story:* John Bennett

Cast: Dr. Engstrom   Otto Kruger
    Fred Strand   Arthur Franz
    Lois Strand   Nancy Gates
        also Steve Pendleton, John Pickard,
            John Alvin and Phyllis Cole

Hour of Nightmare (July 1, 1955). Two freelance photographers travel to Mt. Yapachi in Mexico to photograph mysterious flying objects. A vanishing guide, strange lights in the sky and the corpse of a creature from another planet make their trip a memorable one. The freelancers feel sure they have made the find of the century when they take pictures to prove their story. However, when the film is developed the negatives are blank. *Director:* Henry S. Kesler. *Writer:* Lou Huston.

Cast: Mel Wingate   William Bishop
    Verda Wingate   Lynn Bari
    Ed Tratnor   Charles Evans
    Commandante   Tony Barrett
    Ramon Sanchez   Christopher Dark

The Strange Dr. Lorenz (July 15, 1955). An examination of a small boy miraculously cured of third degree burns leads a young doctor to the apiary of Dr. Lorenz, who delivers honey and amazing healing power to the sick. *Director:* Leigh Jason. *Writer:* Norman Jolley.

Cast: Dr. Lorenz   Edmund Gwenn
    Dr. Fred Garner   Donald Curtis
    Helen   Kristine Miller
        also Charles Wagenheim,
            Hank Patterson
            and Madge Cleveland

100 Years Young (July 22, 1955). A retired man confides in a research chemist that he is over two centuries old and that he remains alive through ingestion of small doses of a deadly poison. *Director:* Herbert L. Strock. *Writer:* Jerry Sackheim. *Story:* Arthur Fitz-Richard

Cast: Bernice Knight   Ruth Hussey
    John Bowers   John Abbott
    Mike Redding   John Archer
        also Charles Meredith
            and Larry Hudson

The Frozen Sound (July 29, 1955). A poison that doesn't kill ants and a paperweight that reproduces voices 2000 years old are clues in a case involving top secret information being mysteriously obtained from a sealed room. *Director:* Leigh Jason. *Writer:* Norman Jolley. *Story:* Norman Jolley and Ivan Tors.

Cast: Dr. David Masters
                        Marshall Thompson
    Linda Otis   Marilyn Erskine
    Dr. Milton Otis   Ray Collins

| *Hannah* | Elizabeth Patterson |
| *Dr. Gordine* | Michael Fox |

The Stones Began to Move (August 12, 1955). A pair of stones from an Egyptian pyramid, a stone that defies gravity and a slain anthropologist are woven into a drama based on a scientific theory about the building of the great pyramids. Victor Berenson is called in to examine the amazing properties of two ancient Egyptian gems which seem to have mystical powers of levitation. *Director:* Lew Landers. *Writer:* Doris Gilbert. *Story:* Ivan Tors and Doris Gilbert.

Cast:	*Victor Berenson*	Basil Rathbone
	Virginia Kincaid	Jean Willes
	Morton Archer	Jonathan Hale
	Ahmed Abdullah	Richard Flato
	also Robin Short, Carol Thurston, Russ Conway and Helen Van Camp	

The Lost Heartbeat (August 19, 1955). Research scientist Dr. Richard Marshall tries to build a mechanical heart powered by solar energy. The urgency of the project is underscored by the fact that the mechanical heart is the only possible means of extending the life of a critically ill colleague. *Director:* Henry S. Kesler. *Writer:* Stuart Jerome. *Story:* R. Dewitt Miller and Anna Hunger.

Cast:	*Dr. Richard Marshall*	Zachary Scott
	Dr. John Crane	Walter Kingsford
	Joan Crane	Jan Shepard
	also Thomas McKee, John Mitchum, Ted Thorpe, Gordon Wynn and Pierce Lyden	

The World Below (August 26, 1955). An experimental submarine smashes into a reef deeper in the ocean than man has gone before. Several crewmen escape in a pressure capsule with photographs of a modern, glowing city beneath the sea. At first they are regarded as heroes for their spectacular discovery until the city under the sea is proven a hoax and they must scientifically explain what they actually saw. *Director:* Herbert L. Strock. *Writer:* Lee Hewitt.

Cast:	*Capt. Forester*	Gene Barry
	Jean Forester	Marguerite Chapman
	Prof. Weaver	Tol Avery
	also George Eldredge, Paul Dubov, William Stout, James Waters,	

John Phillips and George Mather

Barrier of Silence (September 9, 1955). A U.S. scientist working on top-secret atomic projects mysteriously disappears from a German city. When he reappears two weeks later, he can remember nothing of what has happened to him. He is unable to communicate with those around him and appears to be in some type of trance. *Director:* Leon Benson. *Writer:* Lou Huston.

Cast:	*Dr. Elliott Harcourt*	Adolphe Menjou
	Prof. Sheldon	Warren Stevens
	Karen Sheldon	Phyllis Coates
	Thornton	Charles Maxwell
	Neilson	John Doucette

The Negative Man (September 16, 1955). When Vic Murphy is blasted by electricity from a computer, his intelligence soars beyond genius and enables him to hear and see things no man has ever experienced. *Director:* Henry S. Kesler. *Writer:* Thelma Schnee. *Story:* Ivan Tors.

Cast:	*Vic Murphy*	Dane Clark
	Sally Torens	Beverly Garland
	Pete	Carl Switzer
	also Robert Simon, Joe Forte, Pat Miller, David Alpert, Tom Daly and Peter Davis	

Dead Reckoning (September 29, 1955). On an emergency flight to the Arctic, a pilot runs into a strange magnetic storm. An attempt at an emergency landing is further complicated when heavy sunspot activity causes instruments to fail. *Director:* Herbert L. Strock. *Writer:* Gene Levitt.

Cast:	*Capt. John Berry*	James Craig
	Lt. David Kramer	Steve Brodie
	Evelyn Raleigh	Arleen Whelan
	Lt. Bookman	Adam Williams
	Sgt. Cooper	Art Lewis
	also Everett Glass, Frank Gerstle and Tom Anthony	

A Visit From Dr. Pliny (September 30, 1955). Dr. Pliny, a visitor from another planet, announces he has a source of power greater than atomic energy in his pocket comb. He has come to share his wealth of knowledge with the world, free of personal reward. Dr. Pliny is regarded as an eccentric crackpot and is forced to flee ahead of the medical authorities who want to hospitalize the old gentleman. Only after Dr. Pliny's departure does the device he left behind prove he may indeed have been telling the truth. *Director:* Henry S. Kesler. *Writer:* Sloan Nibley.

Cast:

Dr. Pliny	Edmund Gwenn
Mr. Thomas	William Schallert
Dr. Brewster	John Stephenson
George Halsey	Morris Ankrum
also Juney Ellis, Marilyn Saris, Howard Wright and Victoria Fox	

Dead Storage (October 7, 1955). A baby woolly mammoth is brought to life after being frozen in the Arctic for half a million years. The next step is to find a means of sustaining the creature's life. For a time the animal seems to thrive but eventually seems to lose its will to live and in the end science is unable to sustain the creature. *Director:* Jack Hertzberg. *Writer:* Stuart Jerome. *Story:* Ivan Tors.

Cast:

Dr. Myra Griffin	Virginia Bruce
Warren Keith	Walter Coy
Dr. Avery	Douglas Henderson
Dr. McLeod	Booth Colman
Dr. Robinson	Robert H. Harris

The Strange People at Pecos (October 14, 1955). Radar expert Jeff Jamison believes his next door neighbors are spies from outer space. Jamison is more convinced than ever when he learns that the neighbors' little girl is apparently unable to feel pain. When the message "Martians Go Home" is scrawled on a sidewalk, the little girl feels pain of a different kind. *Director:* Eddie Davis. *Writer:* Doris Gilbert.

Cast:

Jeff Jamison	Arthur Franz
Celia Jamison	Doris Dowling
Junior Jamison	Barry Froner
Terry Jamison	Andrew Glick
Arthur Kern	Dabbs Greer
Amy Kern	Judith Ames
Laurie	Beverly Washburn
also James Westerfield, Paul Birch and Hank Patterson	

The Human Equation (October 21, 1955). Biochemist Dr. Lee Seward sees the men working around him resort to violent behavior, and a cleaning lady is killed by one of the staff members for no discernable reason. A thorough test of all possibilities finally lays the blame on toxic fumes generated as part of their research. *Director:* Henry S. Kesler. *Writer:* Norman Jolley.

Cast:

Dr. Lee Seward	MacDonald Carey
Nan Guild	Jean Byron
Dr. Clements	Peter Adams
Governor	Herbert Heyes
Dr. Upton	Tom McKee
also Michael Winkelman, George Meader, Elizabeth Whitney and Marjorie Bennett	

Target Hurricane (October 28, 1955). Meteorologist James Tyler must cope with a mysterious hurricane moving toward Miami, just when he learns that his son is camping directly in the storm's path. *Director:* Leigh Jason. *Writers:* Robert Schaefer and Eric Freiwald. *Story:* Ivan Tors.

Cast:

James Tyler	Marshall Thompson
Hugh Fredericks	Ray Collins
Judy Tyler	Margaret Field
Bobby Tyler	Gary Marshall
Walter Bronson	Robert Griffin
also John Doucette, John Bryant and Will. J. White	

The Water Maker (November 4, 1955). A scientist is summoned to the desert laboratory of a deceased scientist to evaluate the late scientist's plans for creating water in the arid areas of the earth. *Director:* Herbert L. Strock. *Writer:* Stuart Jerome. *Story:* Jerry Sackheim

Cast:

Norman Conway	William Talman
Sheila Dunlap	Virginia Grey
David Brooks	Craig Stevens
also Elmore Vincent and John Mitchum	

The Unexplored (November 11, 1955). Prof. Alex Bondar loses his seminar in psychic research because the new dean of the college believes his work is nonsense. When clairvoyance leads searchers to an auto wreck and a missing colleague, Prof. Bondar's theories appear to be validated. *Director:* Eddie Davis. *Writer:* Arthur Weiss

Cast:

Prof. Alex Bondar	Kent Smith
Julie Bondar	Osa Massen

| Henry Stark | Harvey Stephens |
| *Mrs. Canby* | Madge Kennedy |

also George Eldredge, Paul Hahn,
Ruta Lee and George Crise

The Hastings Secret (November 18, 1955).
The daughter of a scientist missing in the
jungles of Peru organizes an expedition to
search for her father. When the expedition
reaches the scientist's camp, all of his research
has been left behind but the man has vanished
without a trace. An expert on termites, the
scientist appears to have made a spectacular
discovery, a new type of termite capable of
digesting many things—including human
beings. *Director:* Jack Herzberg. *Writer:* Lee
Hewitt.

Cast: *Bill Twinning*	Bill Williams
Pat Hastings	Barbara Hale
Dr. Clausen	Morris Ankrum

Postcard from Barcelona (November 25,
1955). Strange postcards from Barcelona complicate the efforts of an investigative team to
decipher the life and work of one of the great
scientists of the century. The scientist's daughter, bitter over the years of exclusion from her
father's life, hinders the research at first and
only gradually comes to appreciate the loneli-
ness her father had endured as he hid from the
world his ongoing scientific communication
with representatives from another galaxy.
Director: Alvin Ganzer. *Writer:* Sloan Nibley.
Story: Tom Gries and Ivan Tors.

Cast: *Dr. Burton*	Keefe Brasselle
Dr. Cole	Walter Kingsford
Nina Keller	Christine Larson

also Cyril Delevanti and Charles Cane

Friend of a Raven (December 2, 1955). A state
welfare worker tries to help a 10-year-old boy
who has the amazing power to communicate
with animals and anticipate impending dangers. The boy's phenomenal power developed
after he lost his ability to speak or hear as a
result of an accident. But in helping him regain
his lost senses, is the welfare worker really
helping the boy? *Director:* Tom Gries. *Writer:*
Richard Joseph Tuber.

| **Cast:** *Jean Gordon* | Virginia Bruce |
| *Tim Daniels* | Richard Eyer |

Walter Daniels	William Ching
Dr. Hoster	Bernard Phillips
Frank Jenkins	Charles Cane

also Isa Ashdown

Beyond Return (December 9, 1955). Dr.
Erwin Bach saves a dying girl with a miracle
serum, and finds she has become a human
chameleon. This plain, timid girl can now
change—at will—to a beautiful, charming and
immoral menace. *Director:* Eddie Davis.
Writer: Doris Gilbert. *Story:* John Jessel.

Cast: *Dr. Edwin Bach*	Zachary Scott
Kyra Zelas	Joan Vohs
Dr. Dan Scott	Peter Hanson

also Tom de Graffenried,
Alan Reynolds, Dennis Moore,
Lizz Slifer, James Seay,
Kay Faylen and Toni Carroll

Before the Beginning (December 16, 1955).
Biophysicist Dr. Ken Donaldson develops a
revolutionary electronic photon gun—a device
to create life—then must use the untested invention to cure his dying wife. *Director:* Alvin
Ganzer. *Writer:* Arthur Weiss. *Story:* Arthur
Weiss and Ivan Tors.

Cast: *Dr. Ken Donaldson*	Dane Clark
Kate Donaldson	Judith Ames
Dr. Norman Heller	Phillip Pine

also Ted De Corsia
and Emerson Treacy

The Long Day (December 23, 1955). Sam
Gilmore decides to lead a mob against a neighbor as soon as night falls. However, a scientific
experiment goes wrong and darkness does not
come. The experiment gone awry forces the
would-be vigilantes to search their own con-
sciences and wonder if their hatred and fear
isn't the reason that night refuses to fall. *Director:* Paul Guilfoyle. *Writers:* George and Ger-
trude Fass.

Cast: *Sam Gilmore*	George Brent
Robert Barton	Steve Brodie
Laura Gilmore	Jean Byron

also Raymond Bailey,
Bradford Jackson,
Michael Winkelman, Michael Garth,
Addison Richards, DeForest Kelley
and Carol Thurston

Project 44 (January 6, 1956). The discovery of a revolutionary new rocket fuel moves up the timetable for a Mars landing by ten years. A volunteer crew is assembled, but as testing begins, it looks as if man is incapable of surviving the physical and emotional demands of such a journey. *Director:* Tom Gries. *Writer:* Lou Huston.

Cast: *Dr. Arnold Bryson* Bill Williams
Janice Morgan Doris Dowling
Ed Garrett Biff Elliot
also Mack Williams, Mary Munday, Toni Carroll, Patricia Parsons, Amanda Webb, Vickie Bakken, Tom Bernard, Kenneth Drake and Bob Nelson

Are We Invaded? (January 20, 1956). Dr. Walter Arnold, an astronomer with a strong aversion to reports of flying saucers, encounters a believer—his daughter's journalist-boyfriend. The journalist collects an impressive amount of evidence and testimony supporting the existence of flying saucers but the astronomer scientifically disproves the case until confronted with a photograph that could only have been taken from a distant point in the universe. *Director:* Leon Benson. *Writer:* Norman Jolley.

Cast: *Dr. Walter Arnold* Pat O'Brien
Seth Turner Richard Erdman
Barbara Arnold Leslie Gaye
Mr. Galleon Anthony Eustrel
also Paul Hahn

Operation Flypaper (February 3, 1956). Dr. Phillip Redmond must somehow catch a thief who is removing critical scientific secrets out of occupied rooms without being seen or heard. Not only is the thief stealing sensitive scientific secrets, he is also literally making off with time itself. *Director:* Eddie Davis. *Writer:* Doris Gilbert.

Cast: *Dr. Phillip Redmond* Vincent Price
David Vollard George Eldredge
John Vollard John Eldredge
Alma Ford Kristine Miller
MacNamara Dabbs Greer
also Mauritz Hugo and William Vaughn

The Other Side of the Moon (February 17, 1956). Astronomer Larry Kerston invents a revolutionary telescope-camera which photographs other worlds in action. The camera leads scientists to the conclusion that the far side of Earth's moon is being used as a dumping ground for another world's nuclear wastes. *Director:* Eddie Davis. *Writers:* Robert M. Fresco and Richard Joseph Tuber.

Cast: *Larry Kerston* Skip Homeier
Prof. Carl Schneider Philip Ober
Kathy Kerston Beverly Garland
also Bill Henry, Mack Williams, Paul Guilfoyle, Paul Hahn, Peter Davis and Peter Dunne

SEASON 2

Signals from the Heart (April 6, 1956). Prof. Tubor and Dr. Stark are called upon to save a policeman's life by remote control when the heart they are monitoring begins to give out. The officer suffers a heart attack while chasing a hoodlum and it is up to the scientists to alert authorities to the officer's plight. *Director:* Herbert L. Strock. *Writer:* Stuart Jerome. *Story:* Ivan Tors.

Cast: *Dr. Warren Stark* Peter Hanson
Prof. Tubor Walter Kingsford
Alma Stark Joyce Holden
Tom Horton Gene Roth
also Riza Royce, Greg Moffett, Gordon Barnes, Larry Kerr and Michael Garth

The Long Sleep (April 13, 1956). Research scientist Sam Willard is forced to perform a strange experiment to save his wife and child from a madman. When a distraught father carries his dying son into Dr. Willard's office after reading of Willard's pioneering research, the doctor is given an ultimatum. The doctor must either perform a miracle and save the dying boy or lose his own wife and son. *Director:* Paul Guilfoyle. *Writer:* Arthur Weiss. *Story:* Ivan Tors.

Cast: *Dr. Samuel Willard* Dick Foran
John Barton John Doucette
Ruth Taney Nancy Hale
also Helen Mowery, Barry Froner, William Erwin and Eddie Gallagher

Who Is This Man? (April 20, 1956). While hypnotizing a shy young man in an effort to help the boy overcome his inhibitions, Dr. Hugh Bentley discovers that the young man has regressed to another lifetime. In that life, the man was a 19th-century gunman who was hanged. A comparison between the man's handwriting while under hypnosis and a sample of the gunman's handwriting on file with the state historical society seems to confirm the startling story. *Director:* William Castle. *Writer:* Charles B. Smith.

Cast: *Dr. Hugh Bentley*   Bruce Bennett
      Dr. Karl Krause   Harlow Wilcox
      Tommy Cooper   Charles Smith
      also David Alpert, Tom Pittman,
            Lisa Davis, Tom Bernard,
                  Maureen Cassidy,
            Don Eitner and Sam Scar

The Green Bomb (April 27, 1956). A red alert and a green bomb touch off a breathtaking search for stolen atomic materials that could destroy an entire city. *Writer/Director:* Tom Gries. *Story:* Ivan Tors.

Cast: *Frank Davis*   Kenneth Tobey
      Maxwell Carnaven   Whit Bissell
      Ralph Scott   Robert Griffin
      also Melville Ruick, Charles Maxwell,
            Robert Sherman, Eve McVeagh,
            Leo Needham and George Huerta

When a Camera Fails (May 4, 1956). A brilliant scientist invents a microscope which serves as a camera capable of reproducing images of the distant past. Unfortunately, he is the only person who can see the pictures. The inventor's obsession eventually lands him in a sanitarium. Only when his assistant makes a startling discovery is the scientist vindicated. *Director:* Herbert L. Strock. *Writer:* Norman Jolley. *Story:* Ivan Tors.

Cast: *Dr. Hewitt*   Gene Lockhart
      Dr. Johnson   Mack Williams
      Dr. Herbert   Than Wyenn
      also Byron Kane, Opal Euard
            and Lewis Auerbach

Bullet Proof (May 11, 1956). Scientist Jim Connors is approached by a criminal with something of value to sell—a piece of metal apparently from a flying saucer. The metal has extraordinary properties and appears to be impervious to bullets. *Director:* Paul Guilfoyle. *Writer:* Lee Hewitt.

Cast: *Jim Connors*   Marshall Thompson
      Jean Rudman   Jacqueline Holt
      Prof. Rudman   John Eldredge
      Ralph Parr   Christopher Dark
      also Gene Roth and John Mitchum

The Flicker (May 18, 1956). Mysterious brain waves complicate Police Lt. Kiel's complex investigation of a killer without motive. Although positively identified by several eyewitnesses as the man responsible for committing a murder, a young man seems to have no knowledge of what he has done and no motive for the crime. *Director:* Herbert L. Strock. *Writer:* Lou Huston. *Story:* Robert E. Smith.

Cast: *Lt. Kiel*   Victor Jory
      Dr. Kincaid   Michael Fox
      Steve Morris   Bradford Jackson
      also Judith Ames and Irene Bolton

The Unguided Missile (May 25, 1955). A magazine editor suffers from strange recurring dreams in which America's most closely guarded secrets are revealed to her. The authorities are determined to discover how the editor is coming into possession of such sensitive secrets and their investigation leads them to explore a theory of inadvertent thought transference. *Director:* Herbert L. Strock. *Writer:* Arthur Weiss.

Cast: *Jan O'Hara*   Ruth Hussey
      Henry Maxon   Peter Hanson
      Prof. Bernini   Francis McDonald
      also Morris Ankrum,
            Tom Browne Henry and Lizz Slifer

End of Tomorrow (June 1, 1956). A mysterious cure-all drug seems like a blessing to the earth, until a diabolical side effect threatens to end man's existence by putting an end to human fertility. *Director:* Herbert L. Strock. *Writer:* Peter R. Brooke.

Cast: *Keith Brandon*   Christopher Dark
      Jane Brandon`   Diana Douglas
      Rudyard Parker   Walter Kingsford
      Prof. Reimers   Dabbs Greer
      also Arthur Marshall and Michael Garth

The Mind Machine (June 8, 1956). An elderly scientist becomes almost totally paralyzed and reveals the strange secret of his mind machine to young Dr. Alan Cathcart by means of the only muscle he has control over, his index finger. The scientist indicates that upon his death his still-living brain will transmit a message into the scientist's brain machine, which will allow for the decoding of brain impulses. *Director:* Paul Guilfoyle. *Writer:* Ellis Marcus.

Cast: *Dr. Lewis Milton*   Cyril Delevanti
Dr. Alan Cathcart   Bill Williams
Dr. Mark Cook   Brad Trumball
also Sydney Mason,
Lonie Blackman, Fred Coby,
Jim Sheldon and Helen Jay

The Missing Waveband (June 15, 1956). Dr. Milhurst receives (via radio) advanced data on building satellites and other important scientific subjects. He believes his informant is a fellow scientist from behind the Iron Curtain. Milhurst and his colleagues eagerly await each new transmission. At the same time they become concerned about the safety of their informant and seek to pinpoint his location via application of some of the very technology he has provided them. To their amazement, their informant appears to be sending his scientific knowledge to them from another world. *Director:* Jack Herzberg. *Writer:* Lou Huston. *Story:* Ivan Tors.

Cast: *Dr. Milhurst*   Dick Foran
Prof. Van Boorne   Stafford Repp
Dr. Lawrence   Gene Roth
Dr. Maxwell   Michael Fox

The Human Experiment (June 22, 1956). A woman scientist intent on helping the mentally ill develops a powerful new serum and begins testing it at her isolated home in the country. Her new serum transforms the patients into superhuman beings who hold the woman a prisoner. *Director:* Paul Guilfoyle. *Writer:* Doris Gilbert. *Story:* Ivan Tors.

Cast: *Dr. Tom MacDougal*
Marshall Thompson
Dr. Ballard   Virginia Christine
Claudia Barrett   Jean Richardson
also Julie Van Zandt,
George D. Barrows,
Gloria Clark and Alan Paige

The Man Who Didn't Know (June 29, 1956). An atomic-jet pilot crashes. When he recovers in the hospital six months later he has no knowledge of past happenings, although remarkable surgery has saved his life. *Director:* Herbert L. Strock. *Writer:* Rik Vollaerts.

Cast: *Mark Kendler*   Arthur Franz
Peggy Kendler   Susan Cummings
Al Mitchell   Bruce Wendell
also Voltaire Perkins, Guy Rennie,
Granville Dixon, Joe Hamilton,
Bill Erwin and Paul Lukather

The Phantom Car (July 20, 1956). Geologist Arthur Greis and his wife Peggy encounter a mysterious driverless car roaming the desert. The car critically injures Peggy and continues on its way. Greis and the local sheriff attempt to stop the car and learn its secret before it can injure someone else. The car's next victim is an elderly inventor who reveals that he developed the car to prevent accidents, but his experiment has gone horribly wrong. *Director:* Herbert L. Strock. *Writer:* Lee Hewitt.

Cast: *Arthur Greis*   John Archer
Peggy Greis   Judith Ames
Barney Cole   Tyler McVey
also Herbert C. Lytton,
William Fawcett, Joe Colbert,
Pat Donahue and Troy Melton

Born of Fire (July 27, 1956). Steve Conway is called in to solve the deaths of two prominent scientists who were killed by a mysterious fireball, possibly of extraterrestrial origin. *Director:* Herbert L. Strock. *Writer:* Stewart Jerome. *Story:* Ivan Tors

Cast: *Steve Conway*   Wayne Morris
Dr. Davis   Frank Gerstle
Dr. Lindstrom   Harlan Warde
also Leonard Mudie, John Dennis,
William Vaughan, Paul Harber,
Bruce Payne and George Pembroke

Legend of Crater Lake (August 3, 1956). A rural schoolteacher is confronted by three hostile pupils with the power of telekinesis. Despite her efforts to understand and befriend the children, their pranks and hostility grow to dangerous proportions. *Director:* Paul Guilfoyle. *Writers:* Lue Hall and Bill Buchanan.

Cast: Marion Brown — Marilyn Erskine
Dr. Tom Harris — Bradford Jackson
Rosellen Avitor — Jo Ann Lilliquist
Billy Avitor — Freddy Ridgeway
Susan Avitor — Nadene Ashdown
also Paul Guilfoyle

Living Lights (August 10, 1956). A biochemist creates the atmosphere of Venus in a bell jar to prove that mosses and lichens can survive in an alien atmosphere. But he doesn't expect the strange creatures of floating light that appear in, then escape from, the jar. *Director:* Herbert L. Strock. *Writer:* Ellis Marcus. *Story:* Ellis Marcus and Ivan Tors.

Cast: Bob Laurie — Skip Homeier
Grace Laurie — Joan Sinclair
Charles Irwin — Michael Garth
also Darlene Albert, Jason Johnson and Robert Weston

Jupitron (August 17, 1956). A scientist and his wife fall asleep on the beach while taking their vacation. They supposedly awaken on the planet Jupiter and encounter a scientist who reveals extraordinary secrets to them. When they re-awaken back on Earth they are unsure if what they both dreamed was real or imaginary. *Director:* Paul Guilfoyle. *Writer:* Arthur Weiss.

Cast: Dr. John Barlow — Bill Williams
Nina Barlow — Toni Gerry
August Wyckoff — Lowell Gilmore
Dr. Norstad — Michael Fox
also Arthur Marshall and Paul Guilfoyle

The Throwback (August 24, 1956). A scientist exploring the effect of family genes upon the present tries to warn a playboy auto-racer of his impending death, but the theory seems too fantastic to be taken seriously. *Director:* Paul Guilfoyle. *Writer:* Thelma Schnee.

Cast: Norman Hughes — Peter Hanson
Joe Castle — Edward Kemmer
Anna Adler — Virginia Christine
also Tris Coffin, Jan Shepard and Bill Welsh

The Miracle of Dr. Dove (August 31, 1956). A security officer attempts to locate three missing scientists. His inquiry leads him to the office of Dr. Dove, who claims to be much older than he looks. Dr. Dove has apparently arranged for a new life for the missing scientists by providing them with his rejuvenation formula. Dove's story seems beyond belief until he proves his account by growing incredibly old overnight. *Director:* Herbert L. Strock. *Writer:* George Arness. *Story:* George Arness and Ivan Tors.

Cast: Dr. Dove — Gene Lockhart
Jeff Spencer — Robin Short
Ed Gorman — Charles Wagenheim
Alice Kinder — Kay Faylen
Sean Daly — Rhodes Reason
also Cyril Delevanti and Virginia Pohlman

One Thousand Eyes (September 7, 1956). Police scientist Gary Williams must solve the murder of a famous scientist by unraveling the mystery of the inventor's secret new device. Williams' investigation is complicated by the murdered man's wife, a long-ago love. And the process is even more bizarre as Williams seems to encounter the inventor's ghost hovering at the scene of the murder. *Director:* Paul Guilfoyle. *Writer:* Stuart Jerome.

Cast: Gary Williams — Vincent Price
Ada March — Jean Byron
Lt. Moss — Bruce Wendell
also David Hughes and Tom Dillon

Brain Unlimited (September 14, 1956). Dr. Jeff Conover is working on a new anti-blackout serum. What Conover doesn't anticipate is the side effect of greatly accelerated mental activity. *Director:* Tom Gries. *Writer:* Sloan Nibley. *Story:* Sloan Nibley and Ivan Tors.

Cast: Dr. Jeff Conover — Arthur Franz
Elaine Conover — Diana Douglas
also George Becwar, Doug Wilson, Bob Wehling, Melinda Plowman and Burt Mustin

Death at My Fingertips (September 21, 1956). Dr. Donald Stewart finds himself in deep trouble when a murderer strikes and leaves Stewart's fingerprints on the weapon. Stewart insists he wasn't even in town when the murder took place, but the fingerprints insist otherwise and Stewart's only hope is to prove that finger-prints can be duplicated by means of synthetic skin. *Director:* Tom Gries. *Writer:* Joel Malcolm Rapp.

Cast: *Dr. Donald Stewart*   Dick Foran
      Eve Patrick   June Lockhart
      Mark Davis   John Stephenson
      also Michael Granger, David Alpert,
      William Vaughan, Lonie Blackman
                    and Charles Postal

Sound That Kills (September 28, 1956). Atomic physicist Richard Weissman has invented a sonic vibrator which someone has used to commit murder. The evidence clearly points to Weissman and he must use all of his scientific ingenuity to clear himself. *Director:* Herbert L. Strock. *Writer:* Meyer Dolinsky.

Cast: *Dr. Richard Weissman* Ludwig Stossel
      Dr. Sinclair   Ray Collins
      Ed Martin   Charles Victor

Survival in Box Canyon (October 12, 1956). A plane carrying a scientist has crashed somewhere in the desert. A nuclear test is schedules for the area. Civil Air Patrol Major Sorenson gambles his life on an electronic computer's suggestion where the search should be concentrated. *Director:* Herbert L. Strock. *Writer:* Lou Huston.

Cast: *Dr. Sorenson*   Bruce Bennett
      Ellen Barton   Susan Cummings
      Dr. Milo Barton   DeForest Kelley

The Voice (October 26, 1956). Flying in his private plane with evidence which will clear a young man sitting on death row, a trial attorney crashes. Paralyzed and unable to speak, the man discovers that he is able to summon help and attention through the power of his mind alone. *Director:* Paul Guilfoyle. *Writer:* Doris Gilbert.

Cast: *Roger Brown*   Donald Curtis
      Anna Brown   Kristine Miller
      Dr. Mendoza   Anthony Eustrel
      also Bill Phipps, Morris Ankrum,
      Billy Griffith, Julian Burton,
      Anna Navarro, Hal Hoover,
      Roland Varno, Beverly Barnes
                    and Bruce Payne

Three Minute Mile (November 9, 1956). A biology professor experiments with a way to speed up bodily processes electronically, thereby creating supermen. The professor's eager young assistant, a star athlete who has turned his back on athletics, attracts considerable attention and speculation. When the assistant's girlfriend is injured in an accident, the professor's electronic device saves her life but critically injures the inventor. *Director:* Eddie Davis. *Writer:* George Arness.

Cast: *Nat Kendall*   Marshall Thompson
      Brit   Martin Milner
      Jill   Gloria Marshall
      also Robert Bice, Bill Henry
                    and John Eldredge

The Last Barrier (November 16, 1956). The U.S. secretly tests a new rocket by launching it around the moon. To offset the inevitable sightings of the rocket, the government plants false stories that the rocket is actually a flying saucer. But when reports come in of flying saucers being seen in areas that couldn't possibly have observed the rocket, officials are stumped. Then mysterious radar blips appear to follow the returning rocket and contribute to the rocket's crash landing back on Earth. *Director:* Paul Guilfoyle. *Writer:* Rik Vollaerts.

Cast: *Robert Porter*   William Ching
      Dan Blake   Bruce Wendell
      Wayne Masters   Tom McKee
      also Sydney Mason, Lee Millar,
      Jason Johnson, Jim Sheldon
                    and George Barrows

Signals from the Moon (November 23, 1956). An important Asian diplomat is shot and critically injured while on a diplomatic mission to the United States. The only surgeon who has a chance of successfully removing the bullet lodged in the diplomat's brain is in mid–Pacific, 5,000 miles away. The only possibility is to hook up a signal relay between the hospital in Washington, D.C., the surface of the moon and the ship carrying the surgeon. *Director:* Paul Guilfoyle. *Writer:* Tom Gries.

Cast: *Gen. Frank Terrance*   Bruce Bennett
      Dr. Edwards   Michael Fox
      Dr. Werth   Rob Shield

also Don Brodie, Alfred Linder, Steven Ritch and Bhupsen CH. Guha

Dr. Robot (November 30, 1956). When a digital computing machine designed to translate human languages appears to have been tampered with, an investigator is brought in to evaluate the staff working on the project. What appears to be a case of international espionage takes a different turn when it is learned that a staff member has been secretly using the computer to evaluate medical alternatives for his critically ill wife. *Director:* Eddie Davis. *Writer:* Ellis Marcus.

Cast: *Dr. Edgar Barnes*   Peter Hanson
        Fred Lopert   Whit Bissell
        Douglas Hinkle   Doug Wilson
        also John Stephenson, Robert Weston, Elizabeth Flournoy and Esther Furst

The Human Circuit (December 7, 1956). A dancer in a nightclub collapses screaming in pain during a routine rehearsal. The dancer claims to have seen an atomic explosion that in real life just occurred secretly on a small island. The authorities are suspicious until the dancer's clairvoyant powers are demonstrated beyond question. When the dancer "sees" an airplane exploding in midair and a crewman parachuting to safety, the clairvoyant not only saves a life but finds romance as well. *Director:* Eddie Davis. *Writer:* Joel Malcolm Rapp.

Cast: *Dr. Albert Neville*   Marshall Thompson
        Dr. George Stoneham   William Ching
        Nina LaSalle   Joyce Jameson
        also Phil Arnold, Gretchen Thomas, Thomas Anthony, James Waters, Renee Patryn and Leo Needham

Sun Gold (December 14, 1956). When evidence of a 2,000 year old nuclear explosion is uncovered high in the Peruvian Andes, a scientist and an archaeologist set out to learn what took place. They find the skeleton of a "visitor from the sky" who provided the ancient Incas with incredible secrets, including the ability to harness sunlight. *Director:* Eddie Davis. *Writer:* Peter R. Brooke.

Cast: *Susan Calvin*   Marilyn Erskine
        Howard Evans   Ross Elliott

Tawa   Paul Fierro
also Julian Rivero

Facsimile (December 21, 1956). When three members of a scientific research team are stricken within hours of each other with unrelated medical problems, an investigation is launched. The lab they work in has been picking up and amplifying pain impulses from a hospital across town. Each stricken scientist had received the pain impulses of a patient at the hospital. *Director:* Eddie Davis. *Writers:* John Bushnell and Stuart Jerome. *Story:* John Bushnell.

Cast: *George Bascomb*   Arthur Franz
        Barbara Davis   Aline Towne
        Hugh Warner   Donald Curtis
        also Fred Coby, Thomas B. Henry, Than Wyenn and Lynn Cartwright

The Miracle Hour (December 28, 1956). A boy, blinded in an automobile accident, is taken from doctor to doctor and receives the same grim prognosis: he will never see again. One doctor offers a small ray of hope when he begins experimenting to determine if the boy can be made to respond to colored lights. *Director:* Paul Guilfoyle. *Writer:* Stanley H. Silverman

Cast: *Jim Wells*   Dick Foran
        Cathy Parker   Jean Byron
        Tommy Parker   Charles Herbert
        also Donald Curtis, Riza Royce and Ken Christy

Killer Tree (January 4, 1957). Scientist Paul Cameron and his wife Barbara encounter a tree that has an ancient reputation for breathing death. They discover that the area immediately around the tree releases a colorless, odorless and deadly gas. *Director:* Eddie Davis. *Writer:* Lou Huston. *Story:* Robert E. Smith.

Cast: *Paul Cameron*   Bill Williams
        Barbara Cameron   Bonita Granville
        Clyde Bishop   Keith Richards
        Skinner   Hank Patterson
        Deputy   Terry Frost

Gravity Zero (January 11, 1957). Two scientists, about to lose their university jobs, astound the scientific world with a process of neutralizing gravity. *Director:* Paul Guilfoyle. *Writer:* Donald Cory.

Cast: *Dr. John Hustead*   Percy Helton
     Elizabeth Wickes   Lisa Gaye
     Ken Waring   William Hudson
       also Walter Kingsford and Lizz Slifer

The Magic Suitcase (January 25, 1957). An old man and his grandson pick up a stranger on a mountain road and offer him a ride. The next morning the stranger has gone but left his suitcase behind. The suitcase appears to be a power plant capable of putting out an unlimited amount of energy. *Director:* Paul Guilfoyle. *Writer:* Lou Huston. *Story:* William R. Epperson.

Cast: *Grandpa Scott*   Charles Winninger
     John Scott   William Vaughan
     Eileen Scott   Judith Ames
       also James Seay, Freddy Ridgeway, George Douglas, Theodore Lehmann and Arthur Marshall

Bolt of Lightning (February 1, 1957). A famous scientist is killed when his laboratory mysteriously incinerates under temperatures twice that of the sun. An eyewitness claims the destruction was the work of a spaceship. As rumors and speculation grow, the scientist's daughter destroys her father's notes and impedes the investigation. *Director:* Eddie Davis. *Writer:* Meyer Dolinsky.

Cast: *Dr. Sheldon Thorpe*   Bruce Bennett
     Cynthia Blake   Kristine Miller
     President Franklin   Sydney Smith
       also Lyle Talbot, Bruce Payne, Steve Mitchell and Connie Buck

The Strange Lodger (February 8, 1957). Research engineers probe the mystery of a TV set tuned to a nonexistent channel 84. A mild little man appears to be using the mystery channel to transmit the encyclopedia back to his home world in order to inform his race about the earth. After he has finished his work, the alien provides a spectacular show to those monitoring channel 84 by beaming himself off the earth. *Director:* Eddie Davis. *Writer:* Arthur Weiss.

Cast: *Dr. Jim Wallaby*   Peter Hanson
     Maggie Dawes   Jan Shepard
     Bill North   Charles Maxwell
       also Daniel White, Frances Pasco, Cyril Delevanti, John Zaremba, George Gilbreath, Hugh Lawrence and Troy Melton

Space Patrol

Space Patrol combined with *Captain Video* and *Tom Corbett, Space Cadet* to exert a remarkable and enduring influence on television audiences in the early– to mid–1950s. The young found the appeal almost irresistible, although evidence showed a healthy number of adults were peeking at some of the same programs as their children. *Space Patrol* seemed to be a particular favorite of adults, even though many grownups claimed to look in only for the "high camp" value of the series.

Space Patrol was set in the 30th century, much later in time than *Captain Video* and *Tom Corbett*, products of the 22nd century and 24th centuries, respectively. *Space Patrol* had almost an "anything goes" attitude closer in execution to *Captain Video* than *Tom Corbett*. Whereas *Tom Corbett* operated within the scientific guidelines laid down by its technical consultant Willy Ley, *Space Patrol* was less bound by the science of 20th century Earth. A millennium into the future, who was to seriously argue with the new science of *Space Patrol*?

If any one science fiction series had to be pulled out of the 1950s ether and offered as representative of the outer space phenomenon that overtook early television, it would probably be *Space Patrol*. *Space Patrol* successfully built upon so many cultural, political and social impulses of its day that it is a difficult series to ignore.

Space Patrol, if its own publicity is to be believed, was conceived in the cockpit of a navy plane somewhere above the South Pacific during World War II. In this case, the publicity has a ring of authenticity, considering that the creative force behind *Space Patrol*, William "Mike" Moser, once studied philosophy at Gonzaga University and was likely to ponder subjects like time and space and future worlds. "It started me wondering and thinking about the universe," Moser claimed in 1952, speaking of those long hours of contemplation when he apparently recalled his own childhood influences in those lonely hours above the Pacific.

Today it has become axiomatic to think of much of our science fiction literature as having been derived from cowboy culture; it is said that science fiction tales are merely updated versions of a Ken Maynard, Tom Mix or Roy Rogers morality play. Perhaps, but TV science fiction, in the 1950s particularly, was at least as much influenced by the police procedural. Popular series such as *Dragnet* and *The Lineup* provided fully as much inspiration, if not more.

When Mike Moser persuaded Los Angeles station KECA to try his *Space Patrol* idea as a local 15-minute-a-day serial, the station was buying a police procedural set a thousand years in the future. Buzz Corry would become Joe Friday, bringing criminals to justice on behalf of the law he was sworn to uphold.

Space Patrol epitomizes science fiction

Opening signature of *Space Patrol*, recorded on film for the otherwise live program.

television in the 1950s through a trend toward galactic law and order. One thing none of the TV science fiction series foresaw changing was human nature. Law and order, effected through duly sworn governmental agencies, arises time and again as a theme in *Space Patrol* as well as in *Tom Corbett, Atom Squad, Rod Brown of the Rocket Rangers* and *Rocky Jones, Space Ranger*. Like its Western series counterparts, *Space Patrol* was something of a disguised morality play. But unlike the typical Western, wherein justice was often dispensed by private parties, *Space Patrol* and the other science fiction shows insisted on justice being carried out by legally deputized officers of the law.

The format of *Space Patrol* was typical of the TV genre. The United Planets (like Tom Corbett's Solar Alliance and Captain Kirk's Federation), peaceful in nature, understood that individuals and rogue states would from time to time challenge the social and political order. The United Planets authorized its Space

Patrol to police the galaxy. The Space Patrol force operated out of Terra, described as a manmade planet placed in orbit between Earth and Mars. The flagship of the Space Patrol fleet was the Terra. Over the years, new and improved models of the Terra were unveiled on the program. The final version was the Terra V.

Space Patrol took up its duties, according to most sources, on March 13, 1950, over KECA, Los Angeles. Initially, the commander-in-chief of the Space Patrol was actor Glenn Denning, who played the role of Kit Corry. Denning survived in the role for only a short time, perhaps 25 or 30 episodes. The reasons for Denning's departure are obscure. Some sources suggest the actor left the role as the result of a dispute with program officials. Other sources maintain Denning was ousted from his commander-in-chief assignment because he simply could not withstand the pressures of live television. These accounts suggest Denning too often appeared on the set unfamiliar with his lines. Nina Bara, who played Tonga, also recalled that Denning sometimes actually fell asleep in the middle of a live broadcast. Denning's replacement was a young actor just out of the Pasadena Playhouse, Ed Kemmer. Assigned to play Kit's Brother Buzz, Kemmer remained at the helm of *Space Patrol* for the duration of the series.

Other key cast members included Lyn Osborn as Cadet Happy, Virginia Hewitt as Carol Carlisle, Ken Mayer as Major "Robbie" Robertson and Norman Jolley as Secretary General Carlisle. Cadet Happy was Corry's eager young apprentice; naive in an amiable sort of way, afflicted with an irrepressible sense of humor and a willingness to follow his commander into any situation, Happy was critical to the success of *Space Patrol*. Tonga began as a villainess but was eventually reformed by means of the "brainograph," a device with the capability of erasing antisocial behavior right out of a person's brain. Carol was Corry's love interest and the only one permitted to refer to the commander by his first name. Robbie was Corry's dependable, stalwart right-hand man and chief of security. Secretary General Carlisle was head of the United Planets and Carol's father.

Live television in the 1950s, particularly live local television, was not a particularly high-paying endeavor. Reportedly, Kemmer, Osborn and the other key performers on the show earned eight dollars per appearance in the first months of the series. Live television burned the energies of everyone involved. *Space Patrol*, which was so uniquely representative of the live process, was no exception.

When *Space Patrol* premiered on KECA in March 1950, it was as a 15-minute daily serial broadcast live five days a week. By the end of 1950, *Space Patrol* was picked up by ABC for national distribution. Starting on December 30, 1950, *Space Patrol*, in addition to continuing on with its local daily run, appeared as a half hour series aired on Saturdays. ABC also elected to run *Space Patrol* as a radio series, utilizing the same cast. Not only was such a schedule taxing for the players but for the production staff as well. As *Space Patrol* expanded, Mike Moser found himself required to turn out 82,000 words a week in order to keep the series afloat. Eventually, Moser began delegating most of the scripting to other writers—most notably Norman Jolley.

Space Patrol was an unrelenting series. Most of the time there were no seasonal breaks; the series simply remained on the air. Any performer needing time off was simply written out of the scripts for a time.

As the series took off, finding a receptive audience (estimated at seven million in 1952) and eager sponsors, the salaries of the cast began to reflect the show's growing success. From eight dollars an episode in 1950, Lyn Osborn was reporting an annual *Space Patrol* salary of $45,000 just four years later.

The growing success of *Space Patrol* meant more money to channel back into production. In 1952, *Life* (September 1, 1952) placed the weekly production costs for *Space Patrol* at $25,000, a significant sum by early TV standards. *Life* counted among the beefed-up production crew seven prop men, five electricians, nine carpenters, one video- and three audiomen, three graphic artists, two directors and four technicians.

Live television had a great deal in common with radio in terms of program content, competition for talent and subservience to sponsor demands. When *Space Patrol* was picked up by ABC and suddenly acquired a sponsor (Ralston-Purina), the program underwent something of a metamorphosis. Sponsors wanted their products to be endorsed live—on camera—by the stars of the program. Therefore, every *Space Patrol* performance had to include Buzz or Happy, or both, consuming a bowl of Rice Chex or Wheat Chex and smiling into the camera while assuring seven million viewers of the product's wholesomeness. Ed Kemmer once recalled the problems involved with doing live commercials on *Space Patrol*:

> Hap and I would finish a fight scene way up on the catwalks, out of breath, dirty. You could be a little bloody—real blood, a scratch here and there, and sweaty as hell. You're wiping yourself with a towel, trying to look at the script.

Selling cereal under such circumstances required considerable acting skills.

Guest players on *Space Patrol* occasionally would succumb to the intense pressure associated with facing a live camera; it was one of the hazards of live television. Kemmer explained to one interviewer:

> You could see that curtain—it's actually like a curtain—come down in front of them. I'd look at their faces and know they couldn't tell me their own names. I mean, they didn't know what to say next if their lives depended on it. The whole scene had to be finished by Hap and me because they were "gone," totally gone.

One actor playing a villain went blank for an entire broadcast. The other actors, thinking on their feet, transformed the villain into a telepath and interpreted his lines for the audience. Such panic would set in even though cue cards were reportedly affixed to the walls to help actors deal with just such exigencies.

Integral to the telling of *Space Patrol* and the other science fiction programs, then and now, are the special effects. In the 1950s the special effects were intended to assist in moving the story forward, unlike today when special effects are often out of control and actually become the story. Special effects on *Space Patrol* were often the result of simple camera tricks and the use of clever miniatures. They were admittedly a far cry from today's deified special effects which are frequently dazzling but are nonetheless merely soulless computerized contrivances.

The annoying habit of contemporary critics to disparage live television for its "cheap cardboard" sets and "laughable" special effects underscores an essentially unimaginative personality. In 1953, Arthur Rankin, Jr., writing in *Theatre Arts* (January, 1953), addressed the difference between Hollywood special effects and the live television variety:

> Illusion in television is created more by the amateur magician than the professional technician. Hollywood has film, endless retakes and stop motion. TV must create its illusions on the spot, before your eyes. It takes Hollywood a year and a large fortune to make *King Kong* a monster worthy of the name. TV has only dimes and days...

Space Patrol, nonetheless, employed three of the best special effects experts in the business: Franz, Oscar and Paul Dallons. The Dallons brothers had lent their special expertise to such films as *The Devil Commands* (1941) and *Donovan's Brain* (1953). The trio was also brought in by the producers of TV's *Captain Midnight* to help set up the impressive Secret Squadron laboratory.

Required to perform their special effects wizardry live on *Space Patrol*, the Dallons dangled realistic miniatures on invisible wires, providing the illusion of flight through space. Thanks to the Dallons, most of the special effects worked on *Space Patrol*—though not always. Kemmer recalls the time he was captured by a tribe of Amazons and the action called for an arrow to be fired at him by one of the female warriors. The Dallons assured Kemmer that the arrow was safely secured to a rubber band which would prevent the arrow from doing any damage. Unfortunately, something went wrong and the arrow struck, as Kemmer vividly recalls, "about three feet below" the Commander's head.

Mike Moser insisted that *Space Patrol* reinforce and not undermine the basic tenets of a strong family value system. *Space Patrol* dealt with simple lessons of good and evil; evil was always defeated in the end. Villains such as Prince Baccarratti, Mr. Proteus and Agent X were never rewarded for their efforts. Moser told an interviewer in 1952, "If we cause a single nightmare we've failed in our purpose." Young viewers were never to fear; their heroes would always prevail on *Space Patrol*.

Bela Kovacs had proven incredibly popular as the villainous Prince Baccarratti. His marvelously played villain was constantly after power or revenge against Buzz Corry and the Space Patrol for spoiling his plans. Moser reprised Baccarratti in episode after episode to the delight of youngsters addicted to the show. Finally, however, Moser reluctantly came to the conclusion that he was going to have to remove Baccarratti as a continuing threat. "I can't keep you in. Corry looks like a fool," Moser reportedly told Kovacs. Moser understood that the upright Corry had to prevail or the lesson to young viewers would be a negative one, no matter how much prosperity Baccarratti was bringing to the series. In fact, after a time, whenever Baccarratti was featured, Ed

Commander Corry's *Terra V* in flight over a futuristic city in *Space Patrol*.

Kemmer reportedly received numerous letters from concerned youngsters warning Commander Corry of Baccarratti's plans and offering helpful suggestions as to how Corry could defeat the prince.

Moser handed Kovacs production assignments when it was time to temporarily put Prince Baccarratti out of action. However, Baccarratti continued to emerge from time to time as a threat to the galaxy.

The sudden death of Mike Moser in an automobile accident in 1954 did not mean an immediate end to *Space Patrol*, though it did mean a shifting in personnel. Helen Moser, Mike Moser's wife, assumed the title of executive producer and Bela Kovacs moved into the spot of associate producer.

Moser's premature death, however, may explain the failure of another Moser idea to reach television. *Life* (September 1, 1952) parenthetically mentioned Moser's resolve to produce a program to be called *Report to Earth*, geared toward an adult audience. No further record of the proposed series seems to exist. However, we are left to speculate that if Moser had been able to bring *Report to Earth* to fruition, he might conceivably have bridged the coming transition from a juvenile to an adult-oriented approach to science and fiction.

Television historian Alan Morton writes that after Sputnik recaptured the public's interest in space exploration, *Space Patrol* was hurriedly put on the syndication market under the title *Satellite Police*. New titles and credits were spliced onto the old kinescopes. By then, however, time had passed *Space Patrol* by, even if the series *was* set in the 30th century.

Technical Information

FORMAT: Live 15- and 30-minute adventure series, frequently in serialized form, detailing the heroic adventures of Buzz Corry, Commander-in-Chief of the Space Patrol.

BROADCAST HISTORY: *Network:* ABC. *Original Airdates:* December 30, 1950 to February 26, 1955. (These are the network airdates. However, *Space Patrol* actually began as a local show out of KECA TV, Los Angeles, on March 13, 1950.) *Sponsors:* Ralston/Purina and Nestles. *Seasons:* 5. *Total Episodes:* 210 black-and-white. (This total reflects the half-hour network version. In addition, an estimated 900 local 15-minute episodes were aired.)

Signature

The signature of *Space Patrol* was so distinctive that it remained untouched over the course of the series, except for some minor tinkering required after the first Commander Corry was written out of the series. During his tenure as announcer, Jack Narz would excitedly provide the voice-over narration as a montage of massive winged spaceships climbed toward the sky. This was followed by the appearance of Space Patrol Headquarters with its overpowering presence composed of utilitarian angles and a gleaming but faintly antiseptic facade. The words *Space Patrol* would suddenly appear, dominating the screen. After a commercial break, the episode title would appear against a background of shifting clouds.

Production Staff

Production: Mike Moser Enterprises. *Producers:* Mike Moser and Dik Darley. *Executive Producers:* Helen Moser and Mike Devery. *Associate Producer:* Bela Kovacs. *Director:* Dick (Dik)Darley. *Writers:* Mike Moser, Lou Huston and Norman Jolley.

Technical Directors	
	Irwin Stanton and Bob Trachinger
Production Managers	
	Darrell Ross and E. Carlton Winckler
Audio Engineers	Charles M. Lewis,
	Jim Banks and Tom Ashton

Lighting	Truck Krone
Art Directors	Carl Macauley and Seymour Klate
Special Effects	Oscar Dallons,
	Paul Dallons and Franz Dallons
Engineering Effects	
	Cameron Pierce and Al Teany
Cameramen	Alex Quiroga, Johnny DeMoss
	and Bob Trachinger
Video Engineer	Gene Lukowski
Musical Director	Lew Spence
Stage Manager	Jim Johnson

Episode Guide

The final two seasons of the series are reflected below. The stories ran once a week in a 30-minute serialized format.

SEASON 4

The Black Gauntlet (August 23, 1953). Prince Baccarratti plots to make himself supreme dictator of the United Planets.
Cast: *Prince Baccarratti*   Bela Kovacs

The Mystery of Planet X (August 30, 1953). Buzz Corry travels to Planet X, Baccarratti's home world.

The Trap of Planet X (September 5, 1953). Dinosaurs impede travel in the jungles on Planet X for Tonga and Robbie.

The Primitive Men of Planet X (September 12, 1953). Hiding in a huge cave to escape from the threat of dinosaurs, Buzz encounters a race of half-human creatures.

The Hate Machine of Planet X (September 19, 1953). Baccarratti has developed a "hate machine," which when pointed at Terra causes its people to hate each other.

Black Falcon's Escape from Planet X (September 26, 1953). Baccarratti has imprisoned both Buzz and Robbie. With his enemies out of the way, Baccarratti continues laying his plans to take over the United Planets.

Destruction from Planet X (October 3, 1953). Baccarratti softens up Terra for his takeover by unleashing a series of man-made earthquakes.

Ice Demon of Planet X (October 10, 1953). Baccarratti prepares to unleash the Ice Demons against the Space Patrolers who have evaded his earlier death traps.

The Slaves of Planet X (October 17, 1953). Hidden below Baccarratti's stronghold is a secret mine where the prince has a number of imprisoned scientists slaving on his behalf.

The Giant of Planet X (October 24, 1953). Prince Baccarratti bests Buzz and Happy by subjecting them to a powerful ray capable of greatly diminishing anyone in size.

The Metal Eaters of Planet X (October 31, 1953). A worm of incredible size consumes the ship that Buzz and Happy were hoping to use to escape Planet X.

The Falcon's Web of Planet X (November 7, 1953). Still plotting to rid himself of Buzz and Happy, Prince Baccarratti intends to use a force barrier against his two enemies.

Castle's Destruction on Planet X (November 14, 1953). Fleeing his fortress, Baccarratti leaves behind a trap for Corry and Happy.

Valley of Illusion on Planet X (November 21, 1953). Prince Baccarratti attempts to elude Buzz and Happy by escaping into the Valley of Illusion. The valley is a nightmarish dream world where it takes a strong mind to survive.

Doom of Planet X (November 28, 1953). Prince Baccarratti finally falls into the hands of the Space Patrol.

The Alien and the Robot (December 5, 1953). The Space Patrol encounters a robot and its alien mistress, Letha, who has hatched an extortion scheme against the United Planets.

The Robot's Escape (December 12, 1953). Letha and the robot are on the loose and threatening to use a powerful "retardo-ray" against

Letha's enemies. The ray is capable of turning people into statues. Buzz is in close pursuit.

The City of Living Statues (December 19, 1953). Buzz is too late to save the inhabitants of Canal City, where Letha has aimed her ray.

The Mystery of the Missing Asteroids (December 26, 1953). Buzz is called upon to capture a couple of futuristic claim jumpers who have infringed on another miner's asteroid.

The Phantom Space Pirate (January 2, 1954). Capt. Dagger, a space pirate, makes plans to rob the treasury of the United Planets.

The Space Vault Robbery (January 9, 1954). Capt. Dagger's ambitious plan is thwarted and he is captured by the Space Patrol.

The Pirate's Escape (January 16, 1954). Capt. Dagger makes his getaway, poorer for the experience.

The Amazons of Cydonia (January 23, 1954). Buzz Corry has traveled to the jungles of Venus to search for a couple of missing scientists. Before he can complete his mission, however, he is captured by a tribe of Amazons.
Cast: *Amazon Queen*   Dorothy Ford

The Monsoon Trap of Cydonia (January 30, 1954). Complicating Buzz and Happy's search for the missing scientists is an Amazon queen intent on enslaving the Space Patrolers. A killer monsoon threatens to bring destruction to anyone caught in its wake.
Cast: *Johnson*   Ben Welden
          Amazon Queen   Dorothy Ford

The Men-Slaves of Cydonia (February 6, 1954). When Happy is injured, the only way that Corry can save his friend is to indenture himself to the Amazon queen.

The Deadly Radiation Chamber (February 13). Buzz and Happy are trying to find an explanation for the sudden closing of three atomic energy facilities when they find themselves trapped inside a radiation chamber.
Cast: *Mr. Proteus*   Marvin Miller

The Plot in the Atomic Plant (February 20, 1954). Mr. Proteus is revealed as a criminal trying to take charge of all atomic power belonging to the United Planets.

The Blazing Sun of Mercury (February 27, 1954). Proteus tries to incinerate Buzz, Happy and Robbie on Mercury.

The Big Proteus Swindle (March 6, 1954). Proteus begins buying up atomic power on the black market and bilks the Security Council out of a fortune at the same time.

The Escape of Mr. Proteus (March 13, 1954). The Space Patrol follows Proteus to Venus, where he has gone with the proceeds from his swindle.

Mr. Proteus and the Poison Gas (March 20, 1954). Proteus loses the money he had stolen but manages to escape Buzz and Happy's grasp.

The Revenge of Mr. Proteus (March 27, 1954). Tired of being relentlessly chased by Buzz and Happy, Proteus devises a plan to stop his pursuers permanently.

The Capture of Mr. Proteus (April 3, 1954). Buzz and Happy track Proteus down on Venus and take him prisoner.

Baccarratti's "Z" Ray (April 10, 1954). Baccarratti appears with his twin brother, Zarra.

Marooned in the Past (April 17, 1954). The Space Patrolers are confined in Hollywood in the 20th century after failing to capture Baccarratti's twin.

Evil Spirits of the Great Thunderbird (April 24, 1954). Buzz and Happy are able to make their way back to the 30th century in time to discover Zarra has unleashed a withering attack against the United Planets.

The Fall of the Kingdom of Zarra (May 1, 1954). Zarra has designs on the throne of Venus and plans to stake his claim by kidnapping his own brother, Prince Baccarratti. Zarra

also kidnaps Robbie and Cadet Happy, planning to coerce the United Planets into recognizing his claim to Venus.

The Prisoner of the Giant Comet (May 8, 1954). A gigantic comet manages to capture Carol in its wake and it is up to Buzz, Happy and Robbie to free her.

The Demon Planet (May 15, 1954). The trio of Space Patrolers succeed in snatching Carol out of the comet's path but find the Terra V drifting toward a mysterious planet of "living rocks."

Lost in Galactic Space (May 22, 1954). The Space Patrolers manage to lift off from the Demon Planet with its deadly rocks. However, once in space they become hopelessly lost and their life support system begins to fail.

The Hidden Treasure of Mars (May 29, 1954). Buzz, Happy and their friend Dr. Lambert are tricked into believing that a group of thieves are the descendants of an ancient Martian race, the Carnacans. The phony Carnacans are in search of a treasure hidden in a recently discovered underground city, once home to the Carnacan race. When the Space Patrolers and Dr. Lambert question the story they have been told, they are taken prisoner. Dr. Lambert faces torture unless he agrees to use his knowledge of the Carnacans in an effort to locate the treasure.

Cast: *Dr. Lambert*   I. Stanford Jolley
        Sollum   Ben Welden
        Axel   Ron Sha'an

The Martian Totem Head (June 5, 1954). Buzz and Happy return to the ancient city to capture the phony Carnacans who imprisoned them. Along the way, Corry solves the riddle which had obscured the secret of the Carnacans. Pursued by the thieves, Happy and Buzz hide inside an ancient pyramid, but are captured. Happy is locked inside a cell; the walls move inward, threatening to crush the young cadet. Corry agrees to solve the riddle in exchange for sparing Happy's life. The thieves are finally done in by their own greed when they trigger a booby trap laid by the ancient Carnacans to protect the treasure.

Trapped in the Pyramid (June 12, 1954). Sollum, his henchmen, Buzz and Happy are trapped inside the Carnacan's Great Pyramid when the city is destroyed. After finding a secret exit, Sollum pulls a gun and escapes, leaving the rest of the prisoners still trapped inside the pyramid. When Corry and Happy are able to extricate themselves, they set out after Sollum and finally capture the elusive criminal.

The Underwater Spaceship Graveyard (June 19, 1954). When Major Robertson and Carol encounter "Agent X" on Venus, they follow him in their spaceship out over the ocean. Their pursuit takes them underwater to a spaceship graveyard. Once underwater they encounter a lumbering mechanical monster.
Cast: *Agent X*   Norman Jolley

The Giant Marine Clam (June 26, 1954). Buzz comes face to face with Agent X in the latter's underwater hideout. Agent X extorts Corry's help by threatening Happy and Carol.

Marooned on the Ocean Floor (July 3, 1954). Buzz captures Agent X, but the criminal soon escapes again and plots to draw unsuspecting spaceships down into the Venusian Ocean.

Season 5

Mystery of the Disappearing Space Patrolmen (September 4, 1954). Major Robertson and two young cadets are kidnapped by an unseen entity calling itself Manza.

The Space Patrol Periscope (September 11, 1954). Buzz and Happy are captured by the invisible being that snatched Major Robertson and the cadets.

The Space War (September 18, 1954). Icarian spaceships prepare to battle Manza, and the Space Patrolers appear caught in the middle.

The Defeat of Manza (September 25, 1954). Manza is finally defeated and his prisoners set free after the Icarians and Commander Corry stage a successful military operation.

The Giants of Pluto III (October 2, 1954). Operating out of a laboratory on Pluto, Dr. Kurt has been turning humans into robots. The latest to fall victim to Kurt's process is Major Robertson.

The Fiery Pit of Pluto III (October 9, 1954). Buzz and Happy are captured by Dr. Kurt and are soon to be turned into obedient robots.

The Manhunt on Pluto III (October 16, 1954). Buzz and Happy try to turn Dr. Kurt's human robots against their creator.

Theft of the Rocket Cockpit (October 23, 1954). Carol and Happy are abducted by hoodlums who have taken possession of an experimental spaceship. The hoodlums then set course back in time to the 20th century.

The Atom Bomb (October 30, 1954). In the 20th century the hoodlums pretend to be military police. During an atomic test they are exposed to a heavy dose of radiation.

Danger: Radiation (November 6, 1954). After being exposed to radiation, the hoodlums seek medical help in the form of a rural doctor.

The Exploding Stars (November 13, 1954). The discovery of a series of exploding suns aligned in a straight path toward the United Planets alarms Corry and the Space Patrol. When Corry and his crew set out to investigate, they learn of a danger that threatens the destruction of the entire galaxy. Contraterine (antimatter) appears to be responsible for igniting the star systems. While observing the next sun slated to go nova, the crew of the Terra V discover an elaborate machine responsible for igniting the stars. Corry oversees the decommissioning of the mysterious machine.
Cast: *Dr. Van Meter*   Rudolph Anders

The Dwellers of the Prime Galaxy (November 20, 1954). To prevent the collision of their galaxy with that of the United Planets, an alien race has been igniting stars.

Terra, the Doomed Planet (November 27, 1954). Ahyo, a representative of the race of aliens out to preserve their galaxy by destroying ours, captures Buzz and Happy and prepares to eliminate Terra. Held in place by a force field, Corry seems helpless to prevent Ahyo's plan from succeeding.

Revenge of the Black Falcon (December 4, 1954). Prince Baccarratti plans his revenge against Corry and Happy, the pair responsible for his previous capture. Buzz and Happy are kidnapped and taken to Earth in the year 1692 to be burned at the stake as sorcerers.
Cast: *Prince Baccarratti*   Bela Kovacs
      also Bill Baldwin, Oliver Blake,
             Jack Brown and Gail Bonney

The Sorcerers of Outer Space (December 11, 1954). Buzz and Happy stand trial and are sentenced to die for practicing witchcraft.

The Defeat of Baccarratti (December 18, 1954). Buzz and Happy, escaping execution thanks to an enlightened woman colonist, set out to defeat Baccarratti one more time.

A Christmas Party for Happy (December 25, 1954). Christmas on Terra is a dismal affair for Happy until a surprise visit by a pair of old friends turns it into a joyous occasion.

Lair of the Space Spider (January 1, 1955). A search for vanished spaceships leads Corry into the clutches of the Space Spider, the merciless ruler of a doughnut-shaped planet, Arachna.

Web of Arachna (January 8, 1955). The three Space Patrolers try to defeat the giant spider with help from one of the spider's former victims.

Collapse of the Spider's Web (January 15, 1955). Buzz, Happy and Robbie finally defeat the Space Spider and destroy the spider's deadly web.

The Androids of Algol (January 22, 1955). Two aliens have developed the wherewithal to create a race of androids. The aliens capture Corry and plan to create an android double for him, thereby gaining control of Space Patrol and ultimately the United Planets.
Cast: *Secretary General*   Paul Cavanagh
      Yula   Valerie Bales
      Raymo   Larry Dobkin

Double Trouble (January 29, 1955). Back on Terra, the plot to take over the Security Council with android doubles is unfolding. Corry and Major Robinson return home to thwart the plan.

The Android Invasion (February 5, 1955). Buzz and Robbie decommission the android doubles in time to prevent the takeover of the Security Council.

The Wild Men of Procyon (February 12, 1955). The Terra V follows a trail of radiation to determine its source and cause. The cause turns out to be a planet devastated by atomic war. When a space station is discovered in orbit around the dead planet, Corry and his crew investigate and are caught in an explosion which forces the Terra V to land on Procyon IV. On the planet's surface, crazed survivors of the atomic holocaust steal the crew's meager supply of water.
Cast: *The General*   Bert Holland
      The Corporal   Charles Horvath

Marooned on Procyon IV (February 19, 1955). The survivors of the atomic holocaust plot to steal the Terra V and escape Procyon IV. Corry and his crew offer to rescue the two survivors, but the men in their demented state refuse to believe Corry's offer and kidnap Robbie and Carol to use as bargaining chips.

The Atomic Vault (February 26, 1955). As the crew of the Terra V prepares to blast off from Procyon IV, Cadet Happy is attacked and rendered unconscious. When Carol goes in search of Happy, she is kidnapped by two mysterious figures responsible for the sneak atomic attack which destroyed the planet. The kidnappers are searching for a secret formula capable of making a spaceship impervious to destruction. Buzz and Robbie are taken prisoner next. When the kidnappers set in motion plans to activate an atomic pile and blow up Procyon IV, Buzz manages to free his colleagues and they escape the planet at the last possible moment.

Cast: *High Commissioner Menzo*   Bela Kovacs
           Lt. Rayzo   Robert Boon

Tales of Tomorrow

Tales of Tomorrow and the ill-fated *Out There* stood virtually alone at the beginning of the 1950s as ongoing attempts at presenting a mature level of science fiction for television. *Tales of Tomorrow* was produced in cooperation with the Science Fiction League of America and exhibited a level of sophistication not approached until Rod Serling and *The Twilight Zone* captured the public imagination. Reportedly, George Foley's production company obtained virtually all of its story material, the TV rights to some 2,000 stories, through an arrangement with the Science Fiction League. Adaptation assignments were parceled out to a variety of regular writers. Prospective writers for the series were advised that "the important factor here is the reaction of science-fiction theme on the characters." Owing to the limitations of early television, the casts were generally restricted to one starring role and no more than four principal roles.

Then as now, TV science fiction generated an almost fanatical band of followers, prescient of the *Star Trek* devotees of the current day. In an interview with the *New York Times* (September 23, 1951), Foley commented on the vehement reactions many of the viewers demonstrated when confronted by futuristic concepts with which they disagreed. "It's amazing," he said, "the different opinions people have on things of the future which may be centuries away."

In order to avoid such controversy, *Tales of Tomorrow* often sidestepped long range extrapolations. Writers for the series were instructed to keep the action contemporary (even though extraordinary). They were cautioned also to avoid "comedy, bug-eyed monsters, futuristic sets and costumes." The result was, nonetheless, a series of imaginative stories tailored to work within the framework of a live stage play rather than a filmed motion picture presentation. Critics and historians who voice positive reactions to a series like *Tales of Tomorrow* frequently do so in the context of surprise and admiration that the series was able to transcend its lack of high quality special effects.

In its two years on the air *Tales of Tomorrow* was not without controversy, prompted in part, we would suggest, by the program's efforts to present a more adult view of the science fiction genre. At least twice, the noted and influential TV critic for the *New York Times*, Jack Gould, attacked the series for dramatic deficiencies in rather sharp and caustic terms. In a February 4, 1952, column, Gould wrote negatively of one of *Tales of Tomorrow*'s most ambitious efforts, a two-part live adaptation of Jules Verne's *Twenty Thousand Leagues Under the Sea*. The adaptation by Max Ehrlich occasioned an outburst from Gould, who attacked the entire production as "nothing so much as a soap opera staged in an aquarium." Gould,

For *Tales of Tomorrow*, the opening signature was recorded on film, but the episode title and credits were broadcast live.

however, saved his heartiest criticism for "Another Chance." Three days after the play aired, Gould unleashed a broadside against it *and* the ABC Network. The teleplay, in Gould's words

> ...was an item of indescribable trash and totally bereft of any dramatic worth. For its climax there was shown the gruesome choking to death of a girl. Then her lifeless feet and legs were dragged around the room as the camera came in for a sustained close-up. The scene was thoroughly unpleasant.

The incensed critic culminated his fulminations with a veiled call upon the network to exercise "a little housecleaning." Gould's attack may not have had much to do with *Tales of Tomorrow* folding production some four months later; nonetheless, critics such as Gould did wield considerable influence over the infant television industry in the 1950s. For instance, Gould's attack on station WABD for airing the *Flash Gordon* serial prompted station executives to pull the serial from their schedule immediately rather than incur the writer's further wrath.

Tales of Tomorrow demonstrated both a commercial and critical viability. Its willingness to try classic presentations such as Mary Shelley's *Frankenstein*, Oscar Wilde's *The Picture of Dorian Gray* and H.G. Wells' *The Crystal Egg*, along with a generous mix of original stories, infused the series with a sense of purpose and direction. Interestingly enough, the several episodes of *Tales of Tomorrow* we were able to evaluate for the compilation of this present work did not substantiate Gould's criticism, although the two episodes which offended his sensibilities were not among the shows we saw. Our viewing of *Tales of Tomorrow* suggested a series which operated succinctly and convincingly within the scope of early live television. The violence and horror were suggested to the audience rather than presented literally before the camera's eye. In that quaint age when suggestion, innuendo and intimation were quite sufficient to create a sense of dread and even terror, the wanton, gratuitous and unceasing assault upon our senses as practiced by film and television today had no place in the popular culture.

Tales of Tomorrow ran for two full years—84 episodes—under less than ideal circumstances. Its adult approach was almost heretical at a time when juvenile science fiction was the common denominator. As an anthology series bereft of a continuing framework or weekly host, the series faced severe obstacles in its effort to build an audience. Later anthology series running in the same vein, such as *Science Fiction Theatre* and *The Twilight Zone*, recognized the inestimable contribution a host serving as anchor could make. Nonetheless, *Tales of Tomorrow* clearly demonstrated that science fiction and fantasy, if presented in the proper framework, held a viable appeal for mom and dad as well as for the junior members of the family. The series was sufficiently well received to convince ABC to try *Tales of Tomorrow* as a radio series starting on January 1, 1953, but the effort lasted only two months. CBS picked up the radio version but retained the series for only six weeks.

Technical Information

FORMAT: Live half-hour anthology series featuring original and classic tales of science fiction and fantasy.

BROADCAST HISTORY: *Network:* ABC. *Original Airdates:* August 3, 1951 to June 12, 1953. *Sponsors:* Kreisler Watch Bands and C.H. Masland & Son. *Seasons:* 2. *Total Episodes:* 84.

Signature

OPENING: A gloved hand pushes up a lever and immediately the audience's attention is drawn to a hissing electric arc. A voice of doom introduces the show and its sponsor.

Production Staff

Production: George F. Foley, Inc. *Music:* Robert Christian. *Producer:* Mort Abrahams.

Lighting	Ralph Hebel
Audio	George Whitaker
Set Designer	James Trittipo
Director of Graphic Art	Arthur Rankin, Jr.

Produced in cooperation with the Science Fiction League of America and Richard H. Gordon.

Episode Guide

SEASON 1

Verdict from Space (August 3, 1951).

A Child Is Crying (August 17, 1951). A young girl displays extraordinary mental abilities, exceeding those of the greatest scientists of the day. The government attempts to use her as a weapon in the Cold War. The girl is removed from her parents' control and placed in a scientific environment. An ability to control people with her mind and to foretell the future are included among her extraordinary gifts. *Director:* Don Medford. *Writer:* Alvin Sapinsley. *Story:* John D. MacDonald.

The Woman at Land's End (August 24, 1951).

The Last Man on Earth (August 31, 1951).

Errand Boy (September 7, 1951).

The Monsters (September 14, 1951)

The Dark Angel (September 28, 1951).

The Crystal Egg (October 12, 1951). The proprietor of a London West End curiosity shop delivers a mysterious crystal egg to a university professor for the scientist's opinion on its worth and properties. The "egg" proves to be a window to Mars. When the professor loses possession of the egg, he frantically tries to convince skeptics that he is not insane. *Director:* Charles S. Dubin. *Writer:* Mel Goldberg. *Story:* H.G. Wells.

Cast: *Prof. Vaneck*   Thomas Mitchell
       Mr. Cave   Edgar Stehli

Mrs. Cave	Josephine Brown
Georgette	Sally Gracie
Walker	Gage Clarke

Test Flight (October 26, 1951).

The Search for the Flying Saucer (November 9, 1951).

Enemy Unknown (November 23, 1951).

Sneak Attack (December 7, 1951).

The Invaders (December 21, 1951).

The Dune Roller (January 4, 1952). On a small island, a mysterious form of rock grows and moves. Two scientists examining the phenomenon develop the theory that an ancient meteor that once plowed into the island is attempting to reassemble itself. *Writer:* Charles O'Neil. *Story:* Julian C. May.

Cast:	*Sam Thomas*	Bruce Cabot
	Jean Burgess	Nancy Coleman
	Dr. Carl Burgess	Nelson Olmstead
	Sally	Lee Graham
	Cap Zanse	Truman Smith

Frankenstein (January 18, 1952). Mary Shelley's chilling story of a monster brought to life by an obsessed scientist. The seeming indestructibility of the lumbering creature adds an extra measure of horror as Dr. Frankenstein and his companions try desperately to undo the doctor's affront to God. *Writer:* Henry Myers. *Story:* Mary Shelley.

Cast:	*Victor Frankenstein*	John Newland
	The Monster	Lon Chaney, Jr.

also Mary Alice Moore, Farrell Pelly, Peggy Allenby, Raymond Bramley and Michael Mann

20,000 Leagues Under the Sea, Part 1 (January 25, 1952).

20,000 Leagues Under the Sea, Part 2 (February 1, 1952).

What You Need (February 8, 1952).

Age of Peril (February 15, 1952).

Memento (February 22, 1952)

The Children's Room (February 29, 1952). A secret "Children's Room" at a local university attracts the attention of intellectually advanced youngsters including Walt, the young son of a professor at the school. The professor uncovers the startling truth that his son and the other children are "mutants" being groomed to assist an alien race in a distant part of the galaxy. *Director:* Don Medford. *Writer:* Mel Goldberg. *Story:* Raymond F. Jones.

Cast:	*Rose*	Claire Luce
	Edythe	Una O'Connor
	Bill	John Boruff
	Walt	Tarry Green
	Miss Perkins	Lisa Ayers
	Man in Cloakroom	Charles Kenney
	First Child	Grant Roberts
	Second Child	Mark Henderson
	Third Child	Nancy Ann Kramer

Bound Together (March 7, 1952). The story of what happens to the wife of a rocket pilot when his ship is reported lost in space.

The Diamond Lens (March 14, 1952).

Fountain of Youth (March 21, 1952).

Flight Overdue (March 28, 1952).

And a Little Child (April 4, 1952).

Sleep No More (April 11, 1952).

Time to Go (April 18, 1952).

Plague from Space (April 25, 1952).

Red Dust (May 2, 1952).

The Golden Ingot (May 9, 1952).

Black Planet (May 16, 1952).

World Of Water (May 23, 1952).

Little Black Bag (May 30, 1952).

The Exile (June 6, 1952).

All the Time in the World (June 13, 1952)

The Miraculous Serum (June 20, 1952).

Appointment on Mars (June 27, 1952). A three-man expedition to Mars successfully reaches the Red Planet, but the euphoria of their success soon gives way to disappointment and fear as the desolation and alien nature of the planet take hold. One of the explorers becomes convinced that the expedition is being observed. In the end, all three men lie dead on the planet's surface and unseen Martians gloat over their victory. *Director:* Don Medford. *Writer:* S.A. Lombino.

Cast: *First Astronaut*   Leslie Nielsen
     Second Astronaut   William Redfield
     Third Astronaut   Brian Keith

The Duplicates (July 4, 1952).

Ahead of His Time (July 18, 1952).

Sudden Darkness (August 1, 1952).

Ice From Space (August 8, 1952).

SEASON 2

A Bird in Hand (August 22, 1952).

Thanks (August 29, 1952).

The Seeing Eye Surgeon (September 5, 1952).

The Cocoon (September 12, 1952).

The Chase (September 19, 1952).

Youth on Tap (September 26, 1952).

Substance X (October 3, 1952). A young woman returns to her small rural hometown at the behest of a food conglomerate. Her assignment is to discover what the people of the community are using for food after their only food outlet closes. She discovers a scientist who has developed a food substitute called "Substance X." Unfortunately, anyone who diets on Substance X is unable to eat normal food from that time forward. *Writer:* Frank DeFelitta.

Cast: *Selena*   Vicki Cummings
     Carmichael   James Maloney
     Paula   Charlotte Knight
     Samuel   Will Kuluva

The Horn (October 10, 1952).

Double Trouble (October 17, 1952).

Many Happy Returns (October 24, 1952).

The Tomb of King Tarus (October 31, 1952). An archaeological expedition discovers the tomb of the Egyptian king Tarus and the curse that accompanies the mummy. When the sarcophagus is opened, the mummy is still breathing. A hysterical member of the team shoots and kills the mummy. The expedition searches the tomb in an effort to discover the secret of the mummy's protracted lifetime. When the elixir of life is discovered the members fight over the it. Two of the three lose their lives and the third is doomed to eternal life trapped inside the tomb. *Writer:* Mann Rubin.

Cast: Walter Able
     Charles Nolte
     Richard Purdy

The Window (November 7, 1952).

The Camera (November 14, 1952).

The Quiet Lady (November 21, 1952).

The Invigorating Air (November 28, 1952).

The Glacier Giant (December 5, 1952).

The Fatal Flower (December 12, 1952).

The Machine (December 19, 1952).

The Bitter Storm (December 26, 1952)

The Mask of Medusa (January 2, 1953).

Conqueror's Isle (January 9, 1953).

Discovered Heart (January 16, 1953). A scout for a hostile invading force from outer space arrives at a lonely lighthouse with the intention of using the lighthouse as a signaling station. A precocious little girl wins the alien's heart and moves the extraterrestrial to surrender his life to prevent the invasion. *Writer:* David Durston.

Cast: *Josie*   Susan Hallaran
      Stranger   Jim Boles
      Rose   Alfreda Wallace
      Frank   Frank Milan
      Phil   Robert Patten
      Capt. Hayes   William Lee

The Picture of Dorian Gray (January 23, 1953).

Two Faced (January 30, 1953).

The Build Box (February 6, 1953).

Another Chance (February 13, 1953).

The Great Silence (February 20, 1953).

Lonesome Village (February 27, 1953).

The Fury of the Cocoon (March 6, 1953). An expedition into the tropics is plagued by dissension, desertions and an invisible bloodsucking leech of gigantic proportions which has arrived from outer space. The dwindling expedition is able to make its escape by means of a simple insecticide. *Writer:* Frank DeFelitta.

Cast: *Susan*   Nancy Coleman
      Brenegan   Peter Capell
      Borden   Cameron Prud'Homme

The Squeeze Play (March 13, 1953).

Read to Me Herr Doktor (March 20, 1953). An elderly professor with failing eyesight builds a robot (Herr Doktor) to read aloud to him the novels the professor had never had time to read in his younger days. The relationship between the professor and Herr Doktor becomes a very personal and intimate one. The literature imbues the robot with the desire to be a complete man. Their roles are soon reversed: The robot becomes a malevolent force, demanding that the professor read aloud to the robot. When Herr Doktor falls in love with the professor's daughter, the robot learns that the books he has been reading were wrong and Herr Doktor dies of a broken heart. *Director:* Don Medford. *Writer:* Alvin Sapinsley.

Cast: *Patricia*   Mercedes McCambridge
      Prof. Kimworth   Everett Sloane
      The Voice   Ernest Graves
      Sidney   William Kemp

Ghost Writer (March 27, 1953).

Past Tense (April 3, 1953).

Homecoming (April 10, 1953).

The Rivals (April 17, 1953).

Please Omit Flowers (April 24, 1953).

The Evil Within (May 1, 1953).

The Vault (May 8, 1953).

Ink (May 15, 1953).

The Spider's Web (May 22, 1953).

Lazarus Walks (May 29, 1953).

What Dreams May Come (June 12, 1953).

Tom Corbett, Space Cadet

Tom Corbett, Space Cadet became one of the most successful of all the science fiction series of early television. Along with *Captain Video* and *Space Patrol*, *Tom Corbett* literally created the "space opera kick," as it was referred to in the 1950s. Based (more or less) on the novel *Space Cadet* by Robert Heinlein, *Tom Corbett* was easily the most scientifically accurate of the entries. It was also, unquestionably, the program with the most complicated broadcast history.

It premiered on CBS on October 2, 1950; some sources indicate that the series was called *Chris Colby, Space Cadet* and then *Tom Corbett, Space Cadet* starting with the second broadcast. The "premiere" episode we viewed, however, does not substantiate this; the "Tom Corbett" name appears to have been in place from the outset. Nonetheless, one immediate change which is documented was a switch in one of the show's lead actors. Michael Harvey had been hired to play the part of Capt. Steve Strong; however, reportedly on the first broadcast, Harvey froze, the terror of every actor performing before a live audience. Harvey was replaced by Edward Bryce, who retained the part throughout the series. After three months, *Tom Corbett, Space Cadet* departed CBS for ABC, where it ran from January 1, 1951, to

September 26, 1952. During both of these runs, *Tom Corbett* was presented in a traditional three-times-a-week serial format with plot lines sometime taking weeks to run their course before switching to a new story.

In the summer of 1951, NBC elected to air *Tom Corbett, Space Cadet* as a replacement for *The Victor Borge Show*, which had gone on summer hiatus. Half-hour episodes were created from kinescopes of the ABC serials and new connective scenes were shot of Tom Corbett (Frankie Thomas) tying up loose ends of each story. NBC's summer version of *Tom Corbett* ran from July 7, 1951, to September 8, 1951. Meanwhile ABC continued to run its version of *Tom Corbett*, giving the series the distinction of airing simultaneously on two networks. ABC also generated a radio version of *Tom Corbett* on its radio network. The radio series aired from January 1, 1952, to June 26, 1952, included the TV cast and was sponsored by Kellogg's Pep. The familiar voice of Jackson Beck was heard in the announcer's role. The radio version ran in half-hour segments on Tuesdays and Thursdays. *Tom Corbett, Space Cadet* was one of the few television shows to make the reverse trip to radio. Coincidentally, one of the handful of other shows to make a similar journey was *Tom Corbett*'s chief rival *Space Patrol*, as well as a short-lived version of the adult science fiction series *Tales of Tomorrow*.

Tom Corbett next turned up on television as a DuMont program, airing every other Saturday from August 29, 1953, to May 22, 1954. During its DuMont stint, *Tom Corbett* alternated with *The Secret Files of Captain Video*. The series relied on a 30-minute, self-contained format.

In its final season, *Tom Corbett, Space Cadet* found itself back on NBC; this time the show was sponsored by Kraft Foods and utilized a 30-minute format. NBC reportedly ran a radio simulcast of the show. This final version ran from December 11, 1954, to June 25, 1955.

The internal format of *Tom Corbett* remained essentially the same throughout the run of the series, even with the various changes in length, network and sponsor affiliation and the inevitable cast and crew changes. Script editor Albert Aley once described to an interviewer the basic structure of the show:

> Put Frank Merriwell in a spacesuit and throw in *The Three Musketeers*, and you'd be getting at the general idea. Merriwell and his sidekicks operated out of Yale. Corbett and his sidekicks operate out of Spaceport, at Space Academy in the year 2352. Space Academy is the West Point of the Universe. The Universe is at peace in 2352. Space Academy is the instrument of the Solar Guard, the peace-enforcement unit of the Solar Alliance. Earth people have colonized Mars, Venus and Titan, a satellite of Saturn. Tom Corbett, along with two other Space Cadets and an officer of the Solar Guard, takes off in his rocket-powered spaceship, the *Polaris*, to maintain peace on the colonized planets and to explore the possibility of colonizing others.

This working vision of the series, as outlined in an extensive *New Yorker* piece (March 1, 1952), remained constant throughout the various television and radio incarnations. *Tom Corbett* deliberately eschewed spectacular and romanticized nonsense and opted instead to create stories fabricated on legitimate scientific possibilities as they might conceivably exist 400 years in the future. Allen Ducovny, who produced *Tom Corbett*, touted his show's plausibility:

The basic appeal of *Tom Corbett* is its realism. Our stories are not in the realm of fantasy. The action is within the limits of physical possibility. It has believability. No disintegrator rays. No mad scientists. No lobster men from Neptune. It is our policy to show the process of interplanetary travel, and the conditions on the planets we travel to, as accurately as science can today.

In a sense, the *Polaris* was a legitimate forerunner of the U.S.S. *Enterprise*. Not only did the program rely on fundamental science, but the writers were consumed with a healthy interest in creating identifiable characters. Four hundred years in the future, humankind was still grappling with a schizophrenic nature: greed, envy, revenge and the nobler instincts of courage, self-sacrifice and commitment to a moral ideal.

The crew of the *Polaris* was led by Tom Corbett, played by Frankie Thomas. Corbett was the ideal against which young viewers could measure themselves. Tom was bright, always prepared to take a chance in a just cause, courageous, willing to face up to mistakes and try to rectify them whenever he could. Corbett also believed in something beyond his own existence. In an age when television was expected to provide healthy role models, Corbett was close to perfect. When Corbett's senior commanders Capt. Strong and Cmdr. Arkwright put in an appearance, it seemed clear that Corbett was destined to go up the ranks just as these veteran officers had done—with distinction and honor. And if, from time to time, Corbett seemed a little too much of a good thing—a little too humorless and a little too by-the-book—his teammates were on hand to provide a humanizing relief.

Cadet Roger Manning (Jan Merlin) was arguably the most complex of all the cadets to spend time aboard the *Polaris*. Superficially at least, Manning appeared to be a big mouth, an opportunist, something of a troublemaker, and prone to cut corners and disobey orders wheever it would serve his purposes. Inevitably, Manning's negative attributes would lead the wayward cadet into trouble and his companions would have to help extricate him. Most viewers knew someone like Manning, though as the series progressed

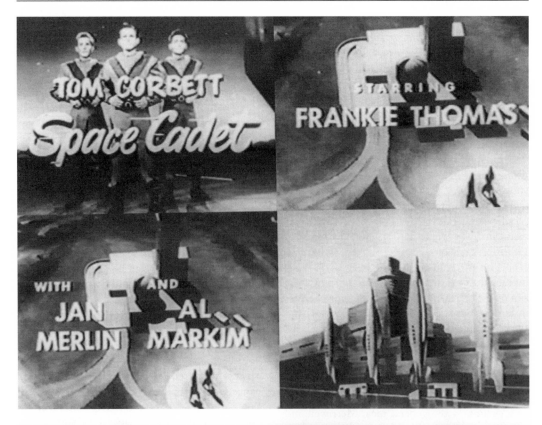

Roger's positive qualities slowly manifested themselves in spite of his efforts to appear the cynical, rough-edged character he wanted the world to see. Manning's courage was never in question, nor was his ability to perform his duties. Whenever one of his companions was in trouble, Roger would use his skill and courage to help solve the problem, while maintaining an outward cynicism to divert attention from his actions. Roger was even known to offer a gruff apology on occasion. Uncomfortable displaying the sorts of qualities inherent in Corbett's makeup, Manning preferred to deny that he possessed those same selfless qualities.

Illustrative of Manning's character is an exchange between Roger and Astro taken from "Operation Starlight." On a planet 100,000,000 years behind earth on the evolutionary scale, the *Polaris* team meets up with a herd of dinosaurs heading in the boys' direction. Astro has severely sprained his ankle and appears to be doomed:

ASTRO: I'm afraid I'm just so much dead weight.
ROGER: When were you any different, you Venusian ape? But don't worry. Just hang on to Uncle Roger and I'll get you outta this.

The third original *Polaris* team member was the Venusian, Astro. Astro's desire to serve in the Solar Guard was almost as strong as Corbett's. Astro was the most withdrawn and introspective member of the *Polaris* unit. Portrayed by Al Markim, Astro was much more an enigma than either Tom or Roger. While Tom and Roger seemed oblivious, if not immune, to self-doubt, Astro seemed plagued with introspective questions about his own worth as a cadet. Like his two compatriots, Astro had courage as well as initiative and resourcefulness. However, whenever a script called for one of the *Polaris* crew to undergo psychological trauma, it was usually Astro who drew the assignment and then had to fight his way back to self-confidence.

Murray Robinson, writing of *Tom Corbett* in *Collier's* magazine (January 5, 1952), succinctly defined the appeal of the three cadets:

The charm of the Space Cadet show... is the fact that the boys, products of the wonderful twenty-fourth century, still act like American youngsters circa 1951. They squabble, brag, show jealousy and generally behave like typical teenagers.

Other cadets filled in from time to time on board the *Polaris*, but none had the appeal of the original trio. When Jan Merlin left the series at the end of the 1952 season, he was replaced by Jack Grimes in the role of T.J. Thistle. Thistle was as self-conscious in his way as the withdrawn Venusian. Thistle's small physical stature often haunted the cadet, making him question whether he was up to duty in the Solar Guard. Nonetheless, Thistle's doubts didn't keep him from carrying out his responsibilities as a member of the *Polaris* crew.

The *Tom Corbett* writers took the time to nurture the characterizations of the young cadets, a decision which strengthened the series immeasurably and, combined with plots born of careful scientific consideration, produced an entertaining and highly regarded program. When television later turned its back on juvenile science fiction in favor of adult reality-based science fiction, it wasn't far-fetched to imagine Tom Corbett having grown up to serve along side Col. McCauley or Dr. Glenn Barton. The same couldn't be said for the Video Ranger, Cadet Happy or Captain Z-RO's protégé, Jet.

To insure the "science" aspect of the science fiction in *Tom Corbett*, the series employed Willy Ley, the noted rocket expert, as a consultant. Ley took his responsibilities seriously, scrutinizing each script, frequently requiring revisions whenever writers Jack Weinstock and Willie Gilbert got overzealous and tried to move the series too deep into the quagmire of unsupportable fiction. Ley's behind-the-scenes influence was crucial to the

Opposite: Two opening signatures for *Tom Corbett, Space Cadet*. The signature at top (four frames) was shot entirely on film and used for the first several seasons. The signature at bottom (four frames) featured titles superimposed over film of a V-2 rocket launch, followed by a star background. This signature was used for the last season, which was sponsored by Kraft.

Frankie Thomas as Tom Corbett.

series, providing the same kind of legitimacy that Truman Bradley's presence afforded *Science Fiction Theatre.*

For example, when Weinstock and Gilbert were developing their dinosaur story, they intended to set the *Polaris* down in a sea of lush green grass. Ley nixed the idea, arguing that a planet 100,000,000 years behind Earth's development would not have green grass. "Green growth came much later in Earth's history," Ley argued.

Another example of Ley's influence on the show was his more or less ongoing argument with the writers over collisions in space. According to Ley at the time:

> The writers are always wanting their ship to hit something out in space. Thank God I've got them to stop hitting asteroids for a while. The possibilities of a spaceship's encountering an asteroid in its path, you know, are so slight as to be negligible. The writers were overdoing it. They wanted to hit an asteroid practically every week. "Please, boys," I told them. "Only once or twice a year."

During the ABC run of the series, the typical *Tom Corbett* script began with the outline of an idea between writers Weinstock and Gilbert, who would then submit their concept to producer Allen Ducovny and script editor Albert Aley. Ley then entered the picture to evaluate the scientific merits of the plot and to offer any changes he thought were needed. Weinstock and Gilbert would take a week to turn out their script and it would then be handed over to George Gould, the director of the series. A week later the play would go out live over the ABC hookup.

Tom Corbett ran until the juvenile science fiction "kick" played itself out. As late as 1957 the series was reportedly being considered for revival. The program's influence on the popular culture of the early and mid–1950s was enormous. Not only had *Tom Corbett* been a TV and radio series, but also a newspaper comic strip syndicated in 84 newspapers nationwide as well as a series of hardback adventure novels published by Grosset and Dunlap. Additionally, the program sponsored dozens of commercial items including lunch boxes, records, space helmets, View-Master sets, electronic walkie-talkies, suspenders, comic books and watches (not to mention the many premium giveaways crafted by the program sponsors).

Expressions popularized on the show became integral parts of adolescent speech. Phrases such as "spaceman's luck," "go blow your jets" and "great rings of Saturn" may have confounded segments of the population, but the appeal of *Tom Corbett* was always to that portion of the public open to possibilities.

Technical Information

FORMAT: Live action adventure series featuring the exploits of Space Cadet Tom Corbett and the crew of the spaceship *Polaris* as they train for commissions in the Solar Guard.

BROADCAST HISTORY: *Networks:* CBS (October 2, 1950—December 29, 1950); ABC (January 1, 1951—September 26, 1952); NBC (July 7, 1951—September 8, 1951); DuMont (August 29, 1953—May 22, 1954) and NBC (December 11, 1954—June 25, 1955). *Sponsors:* Kellogg's Cereals, Red Goose Shoes, John C. Roberts Shoes and Kraft Foods. *Seasons:* Five. *Total Episodes:* Unknown (15-minute, black-and-white), 57 (30-minute, black-and-white).

Signature

The opening signature of *Tom Corbett, Space Cadet* was rewritten when the format and sponsor changed. The most compelling signature came during the initial stage of the series when Kellogg's Pep ("the build-up wheat cereal") sponsored the show and it ran as a 15-minute, three-times-a-week serial. The switch to a 30-minute, self-contained once-a-week format occasioned a more prosaic opening signature.

The 15-minute format featured filmed sequences of rockets lifting off from launching pads. On behalf of Kellogg's Pep, the voice of Jackson Beck invited the audience "to rocket into the future" with Corbett. Frankie Thomas's voice was then heard counting down to blast off. Beck then repeated his sonorous introduction of the name "TOM CORBETT...SPACE CADET!"

The 30-minute format featured an announcer placing the series "in the year 2354 A.D." Like the 15-minute format opener, this signature referred to Corbett's time as "the age of the conquest of space."

Production Staff

Production: Rockhill Productions. *Producers:* Allen Ducovny and Albert Aley. *Directors:* George Gould and Ralph Ward. *Writers:* Jack Weinstock, Willie Gilbert, Albert Aley, Frankie Thomas, Ray Morse, Stu Byrnes, George Lowther, Palmer Thompson, Art Wallace and Richard Jessup.

Assistant Producers	
	Muriel Maron and Phillip Tantillo
Technical Advisor	Willy Ley
Technical Directors	
	Noel Warwick and Fidelis Blunk
Production Assistants	Muriel Maron,
	Phillip Tantillo and Hal Bowden
Senior Technicians	
	Burch Hayden and Phillip Tantillo
Audio Engineer	William Woglom,
	John Goordano and Neal Smith
Video	Al Sielski
Costumes	Eddie Taliaferro
Lighting	Carl Gaiti and Dick Schmidt
Music	Hank Silberg
Scenic Designer	Tom Jewett
Sound Effects	Agnew Horine
Visual Effects	NBC Special Effects

Regular Cast

Tom Corbett	Frankie Thomas, Jr.
Astro	Al Markim
Roger Manning	Jan Merlin
Capt. Steve Strong	Michael Harvey
	Edward Bryce
Cmdr. Arkwright	Carter Blake
T.J. Thistle	Jack Grimes
Eric Rattison	Frank Sutton
Alfie Higgins	John Fiedler
Announcer	Jackson Beck

Occasional Appearances: Dr. Joan Dale, Margaret Garland; *Roy Cowan,* Ralph Camargo

Episode Guide

This episode guide reflects only the half-hour presentations which commenced in the summer of 1951. As explained previously, the 1951 summer episodes were edited versions of the 15-minute serials. The kinescopes were edited and tied together with new explanatory material featuring Frankie Thomas.

NBC: SUMMER 1951

Space Week (July 7, 1951). Space Week consumes the cadets of Space Academy. The competition is particularly fierce between the *Polaris* and *Vulcan* units led by Tom Corbett and Eric Rattison, respectively. The competition takes an unhealthy turn when an exam paper is stolen. *Director:* George Gould. *Writers:* Jack Weinstock and Willie Gilbert.

The Martian Revolt (July 14, 1951). Cmdr. Arkwright senses treachery when he is informed from Mars that Space Academy is going to be broken into three units. Arkwright determines to discover the true motives behind the effort to dismantle his command. The commander's concern is justified when the *Polaris* unit encounters a secret society on Mars apparently dedicated to armed insurrection. *Director:* George Gould. *Writers:* Marc Siegel and Anne Siegel. **Cast:** *Cmdr. Elblas*   Joe DeSantis   *Captain Bex*   Ralph Camargo

Trial in Space (July 21, 1951). Astro is temporarily sidelined when it is suspected that he might have "space fever," which would prevent him from ever again traveling in space. When Astro proves himself a hero after a passenger ship is struck by a meteor, Astro eventually is cleared for flight. *Director:* George Gould. *Writers:* Jack Weinstock and Willie Gilbert. **Cast:** Cadet Harvey   John Weaver

Graveyard of the Rockets (July 28, 1951). The *Polaris* unit is on a mission to track down a missing scientist. Their search takes them to a rocket graveyard in space where they face several dangers, including an impenetrable fog. *Director:* George Gould. *Writer:* George Lowther.

The Asteroid of Death (August 5, 1951). The asteroid of death is composed of antimatter and threatens anyone and anything with which it comes in contact. Compounding efforts to neutralize the asteroid is a young stowaway. *Director:* George Gould. *Writers:* Jack Weinstock and Willie Gilbert.
Cast: *Jodie Morton*   Clifford Sales

The Mystery of Alkar (August 11, 1951). Alkar is a mysterious dark planet orbiting out beyond Neptune. The hostility of the planet is manifested in a threat against the entire Solar Alliance. *Director:* George Gould. *Writers:* Frankie Thomas and Ray Morse.
Cast: *Elblas*   Joe DeSantis
            Luxor   Ralph Rigs

The Lost Colony of Venus (August 18, 1951). Supposedly the jungles of Venus hide a "lost colony" established hundreds of years before by Earth settlers. In the company of a soldier of fortune named "Ace of Space" Bradley, the Cadets set out to solve the riddle of the lost colony. *Director:* George Gould. *Writer:* George Lowther.
Cast: *"Ace of Space" Bradley* Chester Stratton

Summer Maneuvers, Part 1 (August 25, 1951). A serious malfunction forces the *Polaris,* manned by Roger, Astro and Eric, to make an emergency landing on Jupiter where they must effect repairs. The hostility of the environment endangers the cadets' lives. In the meantime, Tom and Capt. Strong hurry to the rescue. *Director:* George Gould. *Writers:* Jack Weinstock and Willie Gilbert.

Summer Maneuvers, Part 2 (September 1, 1951)

DuMont (1953–1954 Season)

The Million Dollar Control (August 29, 1953). In an economy move, Space Academy is slated for closure. However, when the cadets save the lives of some very important passengers aboard a stricken passenger ship in deep space, the orders are rescinded.

The Trojan Planets (September 12, 1953). The *Polaris* unit is exposed to danger when they come in contact with the deserted "trojan" planets orbiting Jupiter.

The Outpost of Danger (September 26, 1953). The crew of the *Polaris* receives an anguished appeal for help when a deadly disease threatens an isolated space outpost.

Target Danger (October 10, 1953). A mock invasion, planned as a Space Academy exercise, turns into a life and death matter for the crew of the *Polaris.* The "invasion" results in the destruction of one ship and atomic torpedoes aimed in the direction of cadets Manning and Rattison. *Director:* Ralph Ward. *Writer:* Albert Aley.

The Mountains of Fire (October 24, 1953). An agricultural station is being threatened by fire and it is up to the *Polaris* crew to find a way to preserve the station.

The Ghost Ship (November 7, 1953). A mysterious "ghost ship" is responsible for destroying numerous spacecraft.

The Beacon of Danger (November 21, 1953). The beacon warning ships of the presence of a space junkyard has been sabotaged in order to lure an unsuspecting spaceship to its doom.

Spaceship of Death (December 5, 1953). A spaceship suffers an explosion and the nearest landing area is threatened.

The Raiders of the Asteroids (December 19, 1953). Uranium hunters in the asteroid belt are being victimized by thieves. The space cadets go undercover as prospectors in an effort to catch the criminals.

The Planet of Doom (January 2, 1954). Two novice female cadets crash on Neptune and a rescue party must be quickly dispatched.

Cargo of Death (January 16, 1954). A negligent captain causes the death of his crew and later induces Manning to serve aboard his replacement ship. Tom and Astro set out to rescue their crewmate before history repeats itself. *Director:* Ralph Ward. *Writer:* Albert Aley.

Cast: | *Capt. Brad Farley* | Humphrey Davis |
| *Dickson* | Harry Bellaver |

The Iron Major (January 30, 1954). The *Polaris* crew is restricted to the ship by an over-bearing commanding officer.

The Space Projectile (February 13, 1954). Corbett and his shipmates are assigned to retrieve a projectile which has gathered information which will help the Solar Alliance choose the location for a new base.

Rescue in Space (February 27, 1954). The *Polaris* just misses being struck by a meteor but is badly damaged by the encounter.

The Earth Digger (March 13, 1954). An Earth digger, a machine used for heavy duty burrowing, causes a cave-in on the moon.

Space Station of Danger (March 27, 1954). Sabotage becomes a life-and-death matter on a space station. First, a poisonous liquid is released on the station and then a nuclear device is set to explode.

Treachery in Space (April 10, 1954). Corbett goes undercover to catch a turncoat. In order to add credibility to his story, Tom is publicly accused of treason and expelled from Space Academy.

Comet of Death (April 24, 1954). A comet severely cripples the *Polaris*.

Death Trap (May 8, 1954). A fake distress call draws Tom Corbett off of his flight plan to Mars.

The Runaway Rocket (May 22, 1954). Once more Roger Manning and Eric Rattison are in close competition, this time over the honor of joining Cmdr. Arkwright and Capt. Strong in testing the speed capabilities of a new rocket scout. To Manning's annoyance, Rattison draws the choice assignment while the *Polaris* must tag along as an escort. When the rocket scout begins pulling away from the *Polaris* as scheduled, everything seems normal. Then the rocket scout goes out of control and careens wildly in the direction of the sun. The *Polaris* crew must somehow catch up with the rocket scout, divert it from its course and rescue Arkwright, Strong and Rattison. *Director:* Ralph Ward. *Writer:* Albert Aley.

NBC (1954–1955 SEASON)

The Atomic Curtain (December 11, 1954). An atomic curtain imprisons two cadets.

Astro's Trial. (December 18, 1954). Astro must face trial when he is accused of negligently causing the crash of a spacecraft. Corbett conducts an inquiry of his own to clear Astro.

The Runaway Asteroid (January 1, 1955). The *Polaris* crew assists Capt. Strong and Cmdr. Arkwright in a complicated plan to alter the course of an asteroid orbiting in the vicinity of Jupiter and convert it into a space station. *Director:* Ralph Ward. *Writer:* Albert Aley.

Suit Up for Death (January 8, 1955). When spacesuits begin to fail, an inquiry is launched. The report which follows pinpoints the problem as a defective valve. However, Major Bemus, the quartermaster, refuses to believe the report and his abstinence could mean death for members of the Solar Guard.

Mystery of the Mothball Fleet (January 15, 1955). When a member of the Solar Guard dies under suspicious circumstances, the *Polaris* crew must investigate.

The Life Ray (January 22, 1955). "The Life Ray" is the only thing which maintains life support for a great city. When the ray stops working, the city is on the edge of obliteration. The *Polaris* crewmen attempt to correct the malfunction.

A Mighty Mite (January 29, 1955). T.J. Thistle is despondent over his small size and the fear that his physical stature may preclude him from succeeding as a cadet. An emergency occurs that only someone of T.J.'s size can deal with, and the cadet learns to respect himself again.

Ace of the Space Lanes (February 5, 1955). Capt. Roy Cowan is obsessed with setting a round-trip speed record to Titan. Cowan destroys his own ship in the futile attempt and then manages to get control of the *Polaris* in another effort to reach his goal. When Cowan puts the *Polaris* in danger, he abandons ship. *Director:* Ralph Ward. *Writer:* Albert Aley.
Cast: *Capt. Roy Cowan*   Ralph Camargo

The Asteroid Station (February 12, 1955). An investigative journalist with a bias arrives to do a story on the new asteroid station built and manned by the Solar Guard; the writer's newspaper had taken a stand against the station's construction.

The Grapes of Ganymede (February 19, 1955). Grapes contaminated with radiation are poisoning inhabitants throughout the solar system. Corbett and the *Polaris* unit must find the source of contamination.

Assignment: Mercury (February 26, 1955). The *Polaris* crew operates under the command of a hard-as-nails Major "Blastoff" Connel, who is particularly rough on T.J. The tension of the situation leads T.J. to make a near fatal error which almost causes death on Mercury. *Director:* Ralph Ward. *Writer:* Richard Jessup.
Cast: *Major "Blastoff" Connel*   Ben Stone

Smugglers of Death (March 5, 1955). Smugglers are shipping a valuable crystal called hyperionite to Earth and the *Polaris* crew draws the assignment of putting a stop to the racket.

The Mystery of the Missing Mail Ship (March 12, 1955). While handling a routine mail run, Captain Strong is decoyed by a cashiered Solar Guard officer. Strong's ship is stolen and used in a series of daring attacks on Solar Guard vessels. *Director:* Ralph Ward. *Writer:* Albert Aley.
Cast: *Roy Cowan*   Ralph Camargo

The Gremlin of Space (March 19, 1955). Assigned to a month of cargo duty for a series of mistakes, the *Polaris* crew is unexpectedly saddled with a mischievous chimpanzee. The chimp wrecks havoc with the operation of the ship and gets the *Polaris* crew in even more trouble with Capt. Strong. *Director:* Ralph Ward. *Writer:* Palmer Thompson.
Cast: *Muggs, 67th*   J. Fred Muggs I

Terror in Space (March 26, 1955). While effecting repairs on the *Polaris*'s damaged hull, Astro is set adrift in space. Although rescued by Tom and T.J., the experience leaves Astro psychologically shaken to the point that it is questionable whether he can continue to serve as a cadet. Another accident eventually answers the question. *Director:* Willie Gilbert. *Writers:* Jack Weinstock and Willie Gilbert.

Spaceship of Danger (April 2, 1955). Tom Corbett and his companions have been on vacation and are preparing to return to Space Academy to resume their assignments. Aboard a commercial passenger ship they encounter a captain making plans to scuttle his ship in a plot to collect the insurance.

The Magnetic Asteroid (April 9, 1955). The crews of the *Polaris* and *Sirius* are at odds with one another—or at least T.J. Thistle is at odds with the *Sirius*. The feud hinders the ships during an important assignment to track down a magnetic asteroid. *Director:* Ralph Ward. *Writers:* Jack Weinstock and Willie Gilbert.
Cast: *Jim Myers*   Bob Hastings

Danger in the Asteroid Belt (April 16, 1955). A training ship becomes a prison for the *Polaris* crew and a deadly one at that, as the ship is soon slated to enter an asteroid belt.

False Report (April 23, 1955). Corbett and his friends receive a fake distress signal which sends them into danger.

The Pursuit of the Deep Space Projectile (April 30, 1955). A routine mission to recover data from a deep space projectile is complicated when the projectile disappears from its projected course. The cowardice of a temporary member of the *Polaris* team results in a life-and-death situation for Captain Strong and T.J. *Director:* Ralph Ward. *Writer:* Richard Jessup.

Cast: *Alex Monroe*   Bill Lipton

Outpost of Terror (May 7, 1955). Stopping at the Triton outpost, the *Polaris* crew finds the outpost deserted with the exception of a corpse of a man who apparently succumbed to radiation sickness. *Director:* Ralph Ward. *Writer:* Albert Aley.

Cast: *Barker*   Robert Dryden

Exercise for Death (May 14, 1955). Time and again the *Polaris* unit botches efforts to impress Secretary Masters, head of the Solar Guard. Then Corbett and his friends are assigned to destroy a robot rocket circling Mars. Their efforts result in a serious danger to Martian shipping and they are left with only one chance to remove the hazard and redeem themselves. *Director:* Ralph Ward. *Writer:* Albert Aley.

Cast: *Secretary Masters*   William Johnstone

Ambush in Space (May 21, 1955). Roy Cowan escapes from prison with vengeance in mind. Stealing a freighter, Cowan and another escapee rig the freighter to explode when the *Polaris* crew comes within range. *Director:* Ralph Ward. *Writers:* Jack Weinstock and Willie Gilbert.

Cast: *Roy Cowan*   Ralph Camargo
       Brock   Bill Zuckert
       Caretaker   Geoffrey Bryant

The Stowaway (May 28, 1955). The *Polaris* has been assigned to head for Titan to participate in an important test. The daughter of a defense official hides aboard and greatly complicates the trip.

A Fight for Survival (June 4, 1955). The *Polaris* unit crash-lands an old spaceship in the hostile Venusian jungle. Corbett and his friends are called upon to use all of their survival skills. *Director:* Ralph Ward. *Writer:* Albert Aley.

Space Blindness (June 11, 1955). Cmdr. Arkwright and Prof. Hinkel are on a scientific mission to photograph an exploding star when they are blinded by the phenomenon. The *Polaris* crew must come to the rescue of their commander and the professor. *Director:* Ralph Ward. *Writer:* Art Wallace.

Cast: *Professor Hinkel*   Leon Janney

Comet of Danger (June 18, 1955). Eager for a spectacular photograph, a photographer induces the *Polaris* crew into piloting their craft through a comet's tail. The detour, however, is very nearly fatal.

The Final Test (June 25, 1955). It is graduation time at Space Academy. Corbett and his companions must successfully complete a dangerous mission to Mars in order to pass their final exam. *Director:* Ralph Ward. *Writer:* Albert Aley.

World of Giants

Ziv Television's *World of Giants* is less about science fiction than espionage; the series is a self-proclaimed espionage thriller, albeit with an interesting gimmick similar to the one used in *H.G. Wells' Invisible Man*: An accident causes the miniaturization of the program's protagonist, American secret agent Mel Hunter (Marshall Thompson). But unlike *Invisible Man*, there is no scientific experimentation that goes awry; Hunter's diminutive state is due to exposure to an experimental fuel released by an exploding rocket while Hunter was on a secret assignment in an Eastern European country. There is no scientific effort to return him to his normal state despite his opening remark that "the scientists were still hoping, still working on my case." Hunter accepts his six-inch stature, stating that "in the six months since my accident I have learned to get up in the morning as if nothing had actually changed." Later, he observes that he is a "*special* special agent," thwarting efforts by spies to infiltrate the United States.

Information on *World of Giants* is scant. We were able to find just two episodes out of a total of 13 for review (one episode is the pilot). The Ziv series was made in Hollywood, produced at first by Otto Lang who, after a few episodes, was replaced by veteran sci-fi film producer William Alland. Many science fiction sources also maintain that the series was inspired by Jack Arnold's *The Incredible*

Shrinking Man (1957), and that leftover props from that film were used.

Another interesting anomaly is the opening title "WOG." The series opens with the initials WOG prominently displayed and spoken majestically by an announcer. This is followed by an animated sequence forming "World of Giants" out of the letters WOG, which is again spoken by the announcer. In addition, following the commercial break, the title "WOG" appears at the beginning of the second act (a frequent device used by Ziv). The significance of WOG remains unclear.

Alan Morton's *The Complete Directory to Science Fiction, Fantasy and Horror Television Series* features the most extensive summary of the series despite identifying Hunter's superior as Commissioner Hogg; the pilot episode, which Morton claims is also known by the title "Secret Agent," clearly identifies the commissioner as H.E. Hall. Judging from the pilot episode, the series relies less on dialogue than on action; Hunter faces one peril after another in his hostile environment (he says he must be "careful 3600 seconds of every hour"). According to Morton, such highly skilled craftsmen as Byron Haskin, Eugene Lourié, Nathan Juran and Jack Arnold guided Hunter through his adventures. The story of the pilot, like *The Incredible Shrinking Man*, is presented from Mel's point of view. This is realized by lengthy narrations by Mel which at times are told via

223

Main titles for *World of Giants*, with its unfortunate "WOG" appellation.

stream-of-consciousness. These "thoughts" are then complemented by the use of cameras with wide angle lenses, shot from very low perspectives, that result in giving the viewer the exaggerated image of giants. Combined, these narrations and camera angles shape Mel's predicament to such a degree that we, too, find ourselves adrift in his world of giants.

What is also significant here is that such formal qualities are not limited to the action sequences; in "Look Up to a Giant," a simple introduction between Mel and his old friend and fellow agent Larry Gregson becomes a threatening exchange. The diminutive Mel stands near his mode of transportation, a specially constructed attaché case, chatting with Gregson, who is obviously perplexed by Mel's six-inch stature. Gregson reaches down to shake Mel's hand, and as he does director Lang's wide angle exaggerates not only Gregson's outstretched hand but his face as well. Since Gregson expresses frustration at what he sees, he looms over us as some giant oppres-

sive menace. But the effect is not one of demonstrating Gregson's power over us as much as it demonstrates our own vulnerability to his presence. The sequence is disconcerting to say the least, but our discomfort is eventually tempered by Mel, who graciously shakes Gregson's finger and takes the whole thing in stride.

Unfortunately, such a narrative structure does not appear in the second episode we reviewed, "Off Beat." In this episode, it is television-business-as-usual, as it were; no stream-of-consciousness narration and no obtrusive visual style, just a typical mundane delineation of story. On the other hand, the episode features some clever optical shots created by veteran David S. Horsley, who receives credit as director of photography for the episode. (Horsley, along with Clifford Stine, served as Universal's special effects expert in the 1950s, creating the stunning special effects in Joseph Newman's *This Island Earth* [1955].) Horsley seamlessly integrated Mel's tiny "doll house" home with Winters' normal-sized room; in addition, Mel's investigation of a piano is highlighted by an assault of piano keys that methodically threaten Mel, who hovers in a corner of the piano. Such effects are a distinct contrast to the effects of the pilot episode, which featured oversized props and a few rear-projection shots to depict Mel's world of giants.

Much of the following information has been culled from various reference sources, but the credits listed are taken primarily from Morton's book since he seems to be the most complete. Story material and casts have been cross-referenced between newspaper logs and *TV Guide* for accuracy, but no clear broadcast dates are available since the series was apparently syndicated on a station-by-station basis rather than by region (the usual practice for Ziv). Also, for purposes of continuity, the sequence of episodes is that of Morton's since our research showed vast disparities of broadcast order in the numerous logs examined. In addition, we have used titles as they appeared in TV listings since Morton identifies three titles that are different from the listings: "Secret Agent" for "Look Up to a Monster," "Time Bomb" for "The Bomb" and "The Chemical Story" for "Ice Chamber."

As far as can be determined, only 13 episodes were produced.

Technical Information

FORMAT: Half-hour series following the adventures of two American secret agents, Bill Winters and his friend Mel Hunter, who is six inches tall.

BROADCAST HISTORY: *Network:* Syndication. *Original Airdates:* 1959-1960. *Sponsor:* Unavailable. *Seasons:* 1. *Total Episodes:* 13 black-and-white.

Signature

The title "WOG," seen before a sky background, is spoken by an announcer. This is followed by the announcer intoning, "World … of … Giants." The scene then shifts to a very

low angle subjective shot, where we first see a car pass over, a pair of scissors fall, a footstep hit, and a teapot crash. Under this we hear Mel Hunter announcing that "one of the most closely guarded secrets" and some of the most incredible events in spy history are about to be revealed to us, in our "world of giants." The credits for Thompson, Franz and Henderson are then played.

Production Staff

Production: Ziv Television Programs. *Producers:* Otto Lang and William Alland.

Directors of Photography
    Monroe Askins and David S. Horsley
Film Editors
    Charles Craft and George Luckenbacher
Production Manager   Joe Wonder
Audio Supervisor   Al Lincoln
Set Design   Robert Kinoshita and Jack Collis
Set Decorations Lou Hafley, Bruce MacDonald
                and Charles Thompson
Costume Supervisor   Tommy Thompson
Makeup Supervisor   George Gray
Assistant Directors
    Joel Freeman and Richard Evans

Regular Cast

Mel Hunter   Marshall Thompson
Bill Winters   Arthur Franz
Miss Brown ("Brownie")   Marcia Henderson
Commissioner H.E. Hall   John Gallaudet

Episode Guide

Look Up to a Monster. The story of Mel Hunter is relayed to us through a long narration by Hunter himself. He explains, "Down through history, man's survival has been dependent upon his adaptability. You learn fast when your life is at stake. No one knows this better than I. My own life is in jeopardy 24 hours a day. Still, in the six months since my accident, I have learned to get up in the morning as if nothing had actually changed. (Pause). Bill Winters. Good old Bill.

As in Jack Arnold's *The Incredible Shrinking Man*, Mel (Marshall Thompson) finds himself at the mercy of a household cat in "Look Up to a Monster," the pilot episode of *World of Giants*.

Without him I didn't want to think what life would be like without Bill. Even *with* Bill, I'd never be safe no matter where I am. Things most people wouldn't notice could mean death to me." At this point, Bill places a pencil on a desk, and it rolls off, nearly striking Hunter. Hunter continues, "It was up to me to be careful 3600 seconds of every hour. I couldn't expect the rest of the world to live my way. To the rest of the world, my problems are not a matter of life and death. The bureau guards many fantastic secrets. But none quite so fantastic as Mel Hunter—me. Following my escape from a nightmare behind the Iron Curtain six months ago, I watched along with 14 doctors and 17 scientists and saw myself shrink to the size of a six-inch ruler. The shrinking had stopped. The scientists were still hoping, still working on my case, and I was still a special agent, a kind of *special* special agent. Agent Bill Winters and I had received word the night before to report to the commissioner's office next morning. As usual, I traveled strapped in

my chair in a specially constructed attaché case chained to Winters' wrist. In this world of giants surrounding me, it was the safest mode of travel. The half year of constant peril had taught me the hard way how dangerous even a great gust of wind can be to a man six inches tall. I had to be on guard every moment. The risks encountered as an agent for the bureau were nothing compared to the things that could happen to me in the daily job of just ordinary living." Commissioner Hall, a second official, and agent Larry Gregson then discuss Mel's condition after the commissioner explains that the latest report indicates a "medical stalemate." Winters and Mel enter where Mel is re-introduced to his old friend Larry, who remains perplexed by Mel's condition. Bill and Mel are then given their assignment: infiltrate a warehouse that is the center of an espionage ring. Because of Mel's size, he can hide inside the main office and watch as the night watchman makes his rounds, hoping the watchman will lead them to the hidden records. Winters with Mel in tow enters the office; there, Mel hides near a desk where he says he will act as a "human camera with a perfect vantage point." He confides that he has just 20 minutes to get the job done. As the watchman makes his rounds, Mel creates a distraction, and the watchman enters to find some papers on the floor. Before exiting, however, he checks the fuse box. Winters enters, and Mel tells him that the papers must be inside the box. Winters finds a wall safe behind the fuse box, but the watchman catches Winters. Mel creates a second distraction and a gunfight ensues. Winters is wounded and knocked unconscious, and the watchman is shot dead. Mel's only recourse is to get to the telephone and dial 342, the bureau's emergency number. Before he can do anything, he finds himself stalked by a cat. Mel finds refuge inside an overturned waste basket. His only hope is to cross to the overturned fire extinguisher. He cautiously makes his way, and with a sudden motion sends the CO^2 into the cat's face. The cat flees, and Mel makes his way to the telephone cord. He climbs to the desk where he manages to dial the phone and make the call to the bureau. Winters survives, but with his arm in a sling he can't do much until things are "back to normal." Mel replies with a pensive, "Normal, what a strange word." *Teleplay:* Donald Duncan and Jack Laird. *Story:* Donald Duncan. *Director:* Otto Lang.

Cast: *Commissioner Hall*   John Gallaudet
Larry Gregson   Tom McKee
Official   James Seay
Night Watchman   Craig Duncan

The Bomb. A suspicious ticking package has arrived in the mail, and Mel braves the garage in order to warn Bill of the danger. *Writer:* Charles Lawson. *Director:* Otto Lang.

Cast: *Deputy*   Tom Brown
       also Don C. Harvey and Don Eitner

Teeth of the Watchdog. Bill and Mel are sent to interview a famous actress who is suspected of being a courier for a spy ring. When the truth is revealed, Bill finds himself locked in a closet while Mel faces a Doberman pinscher. *Writers:* Joe Stone and Paul King. *Director:* Unknown; Morton credits cinematographer Monroe Askins.

Cast: Carol Kelly
                            Charles Maxwell
                            Richard Emory

Death Trap. Bill is involved in an automobile accident that flings the attaché case with Mel inside to a nearby flower garden. *Writer:* Donald Duncan. *Director:* Byron Haskin.
Cast: Tom Brown
                            Tom McKee
                            Keith Richards

The Gambling Story. Bill and Mel follow an enemy agent to a casino where they believe the casino's owner is paying off spies with a crooked roulette wheel. Bill and Mel decide to fix the odds. *Writer:* Richard Carr. *Director:* Nathan Juran.
Cast: *Duggan*   Berry Kroeger
       also Ivan Triesault, Michael Garth,
       Frank Scannell and Tom Wilde

Ice Chamber. A foreign agent leaves a chemical plant with a stolen compound in his briefcase. When Mel is sent to retrieve the vials of the secret formula, he finds himself trapped in a refrigerator. *Writers:* Meyer Dolinsky and Robert C. Dennis. *Director:* Eugene Lourié.
Cast: Peggie Castle
                            Gavin MacLeod
                            John Van Dreelen

Feathered Foes. A spy ring operating in the wilderness is using carrier pigeons to transport stolen microfilm. "Hunter's mission is strictly for the birds: to ground them" (description from *TV Guide*). *Writers:* Dan Lundberg and Hugh Lacey. *Director:* Nathan Juran.
Cast: Douglas Dick
                            Nestor Paiva
                            Gregg Palmer
                            Brett Halsey.

The Pool. While investigating a lavish, well-protected estate, Bill is shot and wounded, leaving Mel on his own to retrieve an enemy code book, copy its contents and replace it in the swimming pool. *Writer:* Lawrence Mascott. *Director:* Nathan Juran.
Cast: Allison Hayes
                            Robert Fuller

Rainbow of Fire. After a missile crashes in Mexico, Bill and Mel are dispatched to retrieve its electronic recording device. They discover that the payload is in the possession of an obstinate young boy. *Writers:* Sanford Wolf and Irwin Winehouse. *Director:* Harry Horner.

Cast:	
	Eduardo Noriego
	Eugene Martin
	Alex Montoya

The Smugglers. Bill and Mel are sent to Hong Kong to sabotage a spy ring that smuggles Chinese nationals off the mainland, but things go awry and Bill finds himself a captive of the smugglers. Mel then slips out of his attaché case and heads for the ship's radio room to summon help. *Writer:* Fred Freiberger. *Director:* Nathan Juran.

Cast:	
	Ziva Rodann
	Walter Reed
	Harry Landers

Off Beat. Several Egyptian art treasures have been stolen, and wealthy society matron Madame Corel is linked to the thefts. Bill and Mel are assigned to find the treasures, and they follow Madame Corell to the Jazz Beat club. Bill and Mel learn that at the same time the treasures were stolen, jazz pianist Chick Crescent suddenly abandoned his European tour, claiming to have been disfigured in an accident. Bill, Mel and Miss Brown attend Chick's show, but Mel, himself a jazz drummer, believes that an imposter is playing Chick. To prove it, the three of them visit Mel's old friend Daddy Dean, and Daddy agrees to visit the Jazz Beat and determine if Chick is really playing the ivories. At the club, Daddy says he believes an imposter is at the piano. Daddy determines that the piano player is an imposter by removing the man's sunglasses; for his bravado, Daddy is escorted out of the club and the bouncer orders the club vacated and closed. Mel orders Brownie to take him to the piano, and Brownie is taken captive by the mobsters while Mel escapes inside the piano. While the imposter plays, Mel is threatened not only by the beating keys but by the amplified sounds. He is saved when Madame Corel orders silence. Mel then discovers that hidden inside the piano are the Egyptian treasures. Bill enters the club, and when Mel distracts the mobsters by hitting the keys, Bill opens fire and subdues the gang of thieves. *Writers:* Kay Lenard and Jess Carneol. *Director:* Harry Horner.

Cast:	*Madame Corel*	Narda Onyx
	Chick Crescent	Johnny Silver
	Daddy Dean	Bill Walker
	Bouncer	Steve Drexel
	Man at Bar	Robert Swan
	Henchman	Frank Krieg

Unexpected Murder. Bill discovers that an ex-con has charmed the wife of a aging pharmacist into helping him smuggle counterfeit bills. *Writer:* Meyer Dolinsky. *Director:* Jack Arnold.

Cast:	
	Pamela Duncan
	Mark Roberts
	Harry Lauter.

Panic in 3-B. Enemy agents trick Bill and Brownie into leaving the apartment so they can kidnap Mel and learn the cause of his miniaturization. *Writers:* Sanford Wolf and Irwin Winehouse. *Director:* Jack Arnold.

Cast:	
	Edgar Barrier
	Marla Palmer

Bibliography

Books

Ames, Dale L. *The Captain Midnight Book*. Worcester MA: Galaxy Patrol, n.d.

Barnouw, Erik. *Tube of Plenty: The Evolution of American Television*. New York: Oxford University Press, 1975.

Bifulco, Michael. *Superman on Television: A Comprehensive Viewer's Guide to the Daring Exploits of Superman as Presented in the TV Series*. Canoga Park CA: Bifulco, 1988.

Brooks, Tim, and Earle Marsh. *The Complete Directory to Prime Time Network TV Shows: 1946–Present*. New York: Ballantine, 1995.

Burlingame, Jon. *TV's Biggest Hits: The Story of Television Themes from "Dragnet" to "Friends."* New York: Schirmer, 1996.

Chester, Giraud, Garnet R. Garrison, and Edgar E. Willis. *Television and Radio*, 3d ed. New York: Appleton-Century-Crofts, 1963.

Dintrone, Charles V. *Television Program Master Index: Access to Critical and Historical Information on 1002 Shows in 341 Books*. Jefferson NC: McFarland, 1996.

Dunning, John. *Tune In Yesterday: The Ultimate Encyclopedia of Old-Time Radio, 1925–1976*. Englewood Cliffs NJ: Prentice Hall, 1976.

Erickson, Hal. *Syndicated Television: The First Forty Years, 1947–1987*. Jefferson NC: McFarland, 1989.

Fischer, Stuart. *Kids' TV: The First 25 Years*. New York: Facts on File, 1983.

Gerani, Gary, with Paul H. Schulman. *Fantastic Television*. New York: Harmony, 1977.

Glut, Donald F., and Jim Harmon. *The Great Television Heroes*. Garden City NY: Doubleday, 1975.

Grossman, Gary H. *Saturday Morning TV*. New York: Dell, 1981.

_____. *Superman: Serial to Cereal*. New York: Popular Library, 1976.

Gunn, James, ed. *The New Encyclopedia of Science Fiction*. New York: Viking, 1988.

Halberstam, David. *The Fifties*. New York: Villard, 1993.

Heldenfels, R.D. *Television's Greatest Year: 1954*. New York: Continuum, 1994.

Kisseloff, Jeff. *The Box: An Oral History of Television, 1920–1961*. New York: Viking, 1995.

Lance, Steven. *Written Out of Television: A TV Lover's Guide to Cast Changes, 1945–1994*. Lanham MD: Madison, 1996.

Leinster, Murray. *Men into Space*. New York: Berkley Medallion, 1960.

Lentz, Harris, M. III. *Science Fiction, Horror & Fantasy Film and Television Credits*. Volume 2. Jefferson NC: McFarland, 1983.

MacDonald, J. Fred. *Television and the Red Menace*. New York: Praeger, 1985.

McNeil, Alex. *Total Television: A Comprehensive Guide to Programming from 1948 to the Present*. New York: Penguin, 1996.

Marling, Karal Ann. *As Seen on TV: The Visual Culture of Everyday Life in the 1950s*. Cambridge MA: Harvard University Press, 1994.

Morton, Alan. *The Complete Directory to Science Fiction, Fantasy and Horror Television Series: A Comprehensive Guide to the First 50 Years, 1946 to 1996*. Peoria IL: Other Worlds, 1997.

Naha, Ed. *The Science Fictionary: An A–Z Guide to the World of SF Authors, Films & TV Shows*. New York: Seaview, 1980.

Perry, Jeb H. *Screen Gems: A History of Columbia Pictures Television from Cohn to Coke, 1948–1983*. Metuchen NJ: Scarecrow, 1991.

Rovin, Jeff. *The Great Television Series*. Cranbury NJ: Barnes, 1977.

Sander, Gordon F. *Serling: The Rise and Twilight of Television's Last Angry Man*. New York: Plume, 1994.

Terrace, Vincent. *Encyclopedia of Television Series, Pilots and Specials, 1937–1973*. New York: Zoetrope, 1986.

_____. *Encyclopedia of Television Series, Pilots and Specials: The Index: Who's Who in Television, 1937–1984*. New York: Zoetrope, 1986.

Vidal, Gore, ed. *Best Television Plays*. New York: Ballantine, 1956.

Wicking, Christopher, and Tise Vahimagi. *The American Vein: Directing and Directions in Television*. New York: Dutton, 1979.

Woolery, George W. *Children's Television: The First Thirty-Five Years, 1946–1981. Part II: Live, Film and Tape Series*. Metuchen NJ: Scarecrow, 1985.

Zicree, Marc Scott. *The Twilight Zone Companion*. New York: Bantam, 1982.

Magazines and Newspapers

Adams, Val. "'Captain Video.'" *New York Times,* November 20, 1949.

_____. "'Space Opera' Hero." *New York Times*, March 26, 1950.

_____. "TV Network on Film." *New York Times*, May 27, 1951.

_____. "The World of the Future Comes to Television." *New York Times*, September 23, 1951.

"Adult Wonder Worlds." *Newsweek*, January 7, 1952.

Anderson, Andy. "'Rocky Jones' Chapter Log and Filmography: A Collector's Guide to the Universe of the United Planets." *Filmfax* no. 20, May 1990.

Asherman, Alan. "'Rocky Jones, Space Ranger,' Part One." *Filmfax* no. 19, March 1990.

_____. "'Rocky Jones, Space Ranger,' Part Two." *Filmfax* no. 20, May 1990.

Bassior, Jean-Noel. "'Space Patrol': Missions of Daring in the Name of Early Television, Part One." *Filmfax* no. 1, January/February 1986.

_____. "'Space Patrol': Missions of Daring in the Name of Early Television, Part Two." *Filmfax* no. 2, April 1986.

Berger, Meyer. "'Space Fever' Hits the Small-Fry." *New York Times Magazine*, March 16, 1952.

Coville, Gary, and Patrick Lucanio. "Flash Gordon: Cruising the Cathode Ray." *Filmfax* no. 45, March/April 1995.

_____, and _____. "Men into Space." *Filmfax* no. 21, July 1990.

_____, and _____. "Science Fiction Theatre: In Historical Perspective." *Filmfax* no. 17, November 1989.

Delson, James. "Science Fiction on Television, Part 1: 1949–1953." *Fantastic Films*, December 1978.

_____. "Science Fiction on Television, Part 2: 1953–1959." *Fantastic Films*, February 1979.

"European Bases." *Newsweek*, September 20, 1954.

Gould, Jack. "ABC Presents Verne's '20,000 Leagues Under the Sea' on TV as 'Boy-Meets-Girl' Story." *New York Times*, February 4, 1952.

_____. "'Johnny Jupiter,' a Satire on Our Ways and Customs..." *New York Times*, March 25, 1953.

_____. "Out There." *New York Times*, November 4, 1951.

_____. "Serialized Adventures of 'Flash Gordon,' Hero of the Comics, Portrayed on DuMont Network." *New York Times*, February 19, 1951.

_____. "Two Programs of Violence, One Directed to Youth on Sunday Morning, Held Danger to Industry." *New York Times*, February 16, 1953.

"Hi-yo, Tom Corbett." *Newsweek*, April 2, 1951.

"In Person—Doc Savage." *Comic Buyer's Guide*, January 10, 1992.

"Juvenile Delinquency: Captain to the Rescue." *Newsweek*, November 1, 1954.

"Kid Shows." *Who's Who in TV & Radio* 1, no. 3, 1953.

Lucanio, Patrick. "A Man and His Challenge: The Life and Films of Ivan Tors." *Filmfax* no. 29, October/November 1991.

_____, and Gary Coville. "The Johnny Jupiter Show." *Filmfax* no. 34, August/September 1992.

"The Man and the Challenge." *Broadcasting*, September 28, 1959.

Plotnik, Gene. "Ziv's 'Fiction' No Fairy Tale, But Just Science and Work." *Billboard*, April 16, 1955.

Rankin, Arthur, Jr. "The Low Cost of Fright." *Theatre Arts*, January 1953.

Robinson, Murray. "Planet Parenthood." *Colliers*, January 5, 1952.

Sarno, Joe. "Tom Corbett Television Log." *Joe Sarno's Space Academy Newsletter* no. 7, 1979.

_____. "Tom Corbett Television Log." *Joe Sarno's Space Academy Newsletter* no. 8, 1979.

"Science Fiction Theatre." *Variety*, April 13, 1955.

"'Science Fiction Theatre' Prefers Fact to Fancy in Story of a Hurricane." *New York Times*, October 29, 1955.

"7 M.P.S.; Zero 3." *Time*, December 25, 1950.

"'Space Patrol' Conquers Kids." *Life*, September 1, 1952.

Van Horne, Harriet. "Space Rocket Kick." *Theatre Arts*, December 1951.

Whiteside, Thomas. "No Lobster Men from Neptune." *The New Yorker*, March 1, 1952.

"Ziv Enlists Colleges to Research 'Science Fiction Theatre' Series." *Variety*, April 13, 1955.

"Ziv Gets a Show On the Road." *Broadcasting Telecasting*, May 9, 1955.

"Ziv-TV Starts Sales on 'Science Fiction' Films." *Billboard*, February 19, 1955.

"Ziv-TV Unveils Unique 'Science Fiction' Series." *Billboard*, April 2, 1955.

Video

The hundreds of programs viewed in preparation for this work were culled from many sources, mostly from private collections. The videotapes available on the commercial market, which account for only a small fraction of the total involved in our research, are noted below:

Adventures of Superman. "Stamp Day for Superman." Kids Klassics, 1985.

Captain Midnight. "Deadly Diamonds" and "The Frozen Man." Parade Video, n.d.

Captain Video. Two episodes, untitled. Video Yesteryear, [1992].

Flash Gordon. "Return of the Androids." Kids Klassics, 1985.

Rocky Jones, Space Ranger. "Beyond the Curtain of Space." Front Row Entertainment, 1994.

Science Fiction Television. Simitar Entertainment, 1994.

Space Patrol. "Revenge of the Black Falcon," "The Androids of Algol" and "The Android Invasion." Vol. 3. Rhino Home Video, 1990.

Space Patrol. "The Exploding Stars" and "The Atomic Vault." Vol. 3. Rhino Home Video, 1990.

Tales of Tomorrow. "Frankenstein," "Dune Roller," "Appointment on Mars" and "The Crystal Egg." Vol. 1. Nostalgia Merchant, 1982.

Tales of Tomorrow. "Past Tense," "A Child Is Crying," "Ice from Space" and "The Windows." Vol. 2. Nostalgia Merchant, 1982.

Tom Corbett, Space Cadet. Final six 15-minute episodes of "Space Pirates of Ganymede." Vol. 1. Nostalgia Merchant, 1982.

Tom Corbett, Space Cadet. "The Runaway Rocket," "Mystery of the Missing Mail Ship," "Gremlin of Space," and "Deep Space Projectile." Vol. 2. Nostalgia Merchant, 1982.

TV's Best Adventures of Superman. "Superman on Earth" and "All That Glitters." Vol. 1. Warner Home Video, 1987.

TV's Best Adventures of Superman. "Crime Wave" and "The Perils of Superman." Vol. 2. Warner Home Video, 1987.

TV's Best Adventures of Superman. "Panic in the Sky" and "The Big Freeze." Vol. 3. Warner Home Video, 1988.

TV's Best Adventures of Superman. "The Face and the Voice" and "Jimmy the Kid." Vol. 4. Warner Home Video, 1988.

Index of Episode Titles

Each episode is matched with its series according to the following: *Adventures of Superman* (AOS), *Atom Squad* (AS), *Buck Rogers* (BR), *Captain Midnight* (CM), *Captain Video* (CV), *Captain Z-RO* (CZ), *Commando Cody* (CC), *Flash Gordon* (FG), *H.G. Wells' Invisible Man* (IM), *Johnny Jupiter* (JJ), *The Man and the Challenge* (MAC), *Men into Space* (MIS), *Out There* (OT), *Rocky Jones, Space Ranger* (RJSR), *Rod Brown of the Rocket Rangers* (RBRR), *Science Fiction Theatre* (SFT), *Space Patrol* (SP), *Tales of Tomorrow* (TT), *Tom Corbett, Space Cadet* (TCSC), *World of Giants* (WOG).

General Index